HIGH COURT CASE SUMMARIES™

TORTS

Keyed to Dobbs, Hayden, and Bublick's Casebook on Torts Law, 7th Edition

WEST ACADEMIC PUBLISHING

Mat #41686218

444 Cedar Street, Suite 700
St. Paul, MN 55101
1-877-888-1330

Printed in the United States of America

ISBN: 978-1-62810-548-3

Table of Contents

Alphabetical Table of Cases

CHAPTER ONE

Tort Law: Aims, Approaches, and Processes

Van Camp v. McAfoos

Instant Facts: A three-year-old on a trike ran into the plaintiff and her Achilles tendon was injured, requiring surgery; she alleged the child was liable but the court granted his motion to dismiss.

Black Letter Rule: A child cannot be held liable in tort without some allegation of negligence or wrongful conduct on his or her part.

Dillon v. Frazer

Instant Facts: Dillon (P) presented evidence of over $500,000 in damages from an automobile accident but the jury awarded him only $6,000; although the trial judge increased that amount to $21,000, he refused to grant a new trial on the issue of damages.

Black Letter Rule: A trial court must grant a new trial on the issue of damages if the amount of the verdict is so grossly inadequate or excessive as to shock the conscience of the court and clearly indicates that the figure reached was the result of passion, caprice, prejudice, partiality, corruption, or some other improper motive.

Van Camp v. McAfoos

(Injured Party) v. (Child on Tricycle)

156 N.W.2d 878 (Iowa 1968)

LIABILITY WITHOUT FAULT WILL NOT BE APPLIED TO CHILDREN

■ **INSTANT FACTS** A three-year-old on a trike ran into the plaintiff and her Achilles tendon was injured, requiring surgery; she alleged the child was liable but the court granted his motion to dismiss.

■ **BLACK LETTER RULE** A child cannot be held liable in tort without some allegation of negligence or wrongful conduct on his or her part.

■ PROCEDURAL BASIS

State Supreme Court review of the trial court's sustaining of the defendant's motion to dismiss.

■ FACTS

Van Camp (P) alleged that three-year-old McAfoos (D) was driving a tricycle on a sidewalk when he ran into her Achilles tendon and injured her. She failed, however, to allege that the child was negligent or that his action was willful or wrongful in any way, so the trial court held there was no basis on which she could recover. The plaintiff appealed.

■ ISSUE

Was the plaintiff correct that the invasion of her person was in itself a wrong and that she need plead no more?

■ DECISION AND RATIONALE

(Becker, J.) No. A child cannot be held liable in tort without some allegation of negligence or wrongful conduct on his or her part. Where an essential element of a cause of action is not pled, the claim cannot go forward. The plaintiff here would have us impose liability without fault, but this we refuse to do, particularly with regard to a child. Fault must be discernible in the pleading and in the proof. Here, intentionally wrongful or negligently wrongful use of the tricycle is neither pled nor can it be made out from the allegation that the defendant operated a tricycle on a public sidewalk and drove the tricycle into the rear of the plaintiff without warning. Although cases from other jurisdictions have held a child of tender years liable in tort, all of those causes involved fault. This case does not fall within the scope of the others. Affirmed.

Analysis:

A motion to dismiss for failure to state a claim is based strictly on the allegations in the pleadings. The court may not look outside the complaint to find support for a plaintiff's claim; if it does, the motion is converted to one for summary judgment, in which case both sides must be afforded the opportunity to present affidavits and evidence gathered through the discovery process in support of their claims. Here, the plaintiff failed to plead an essential element of her case, so the complaint was dismissed. A dismissal may be with or without prejudice, meaning, in the latter case, the plaintiff will have the opportunity to correct the flaws in his or her pleading and try again.

■ CASE VOCABULARY

MOTION: A request by a party to the court, made orally or in writing, for a favorable order, rule, or remedy, concerning a question within the judge's discretion (*e.g.*, motion to dismiss the action, motion for retrial).

Dillon v. Frazer

(Injured Passenger) v. (Driver)

678 S.E.2d 251 (S.C. 2009)

DAMAGES AWARDS MUST ACCORD WITH UNDISPUTED EVIDENCE

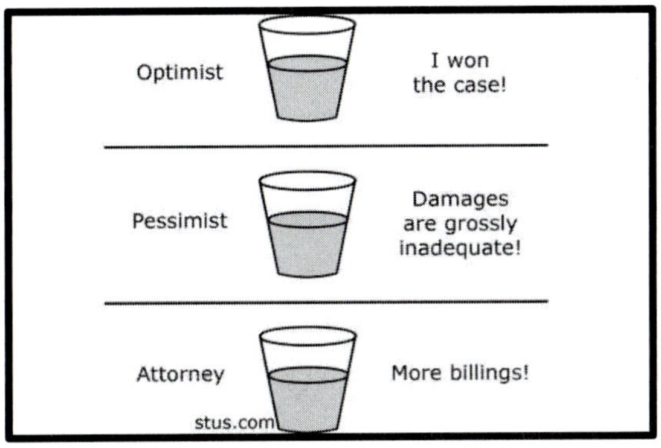

■ **INSTANT FACTS** Dillon (P) presented evidence of over $500,000 in damages from an automobile accident but the jury awarded him only $6,000; although the trial judge increased that amount to $21,000, he refused to grant a new trial on the issue of damages.

■ **BLACK LETTER RULE** A trial court must grant a new trial on the issue of damages if the amount of the verdict is so grossly inadequate or excessive as to shock the conscience of the court and clearly indicates that the figure reached was the result of passion, caprice, prejudice, partiality, corruption, or some other improper motive.

■ PROCEDURAL BASIS

State Supreme Court review of a trial court judgment increasing the amount of damages but denying a request for a new trial on the issue of damages.

■ FACTS

Dillon (P), a Canadian resident, was a passenger in his co-worker Frazer's (D) car when Frazer (D) ran a stop sign and they got into an accident. Dillon (P) suffered multiple fractures and a punctured lung. He was admitted to the hospital in South Carolina, where the accident had occurred. Due to his punctured lung, Dillon (P) was not medically able to fly back to Canada until several days after his release from the hospital. Once in Canada, he received extensive physical therapy, the cost of which was covered by the Canadian Health System. Dillon (P) was not able to return to work for ten weeks, and even once he returned he worked far less overtime than he did before the accident. Dillon (P) sued Frazer (D), claiming extensive medical expenses and lost wages. Frazer (D) admitted liability, but the amount of damages was in question. During deliberations, the jury sent questions to the judge about whether Dillon (P) had received compensation from any third parties, and the judge told them to disregard any possibility that Dillon (P) may have received third-party payments. The jury awarded Dillon (P) only $6,000 in damages, and he moved for a new trial on the issue of damages. The judge granted the motion for additur and increased the damages award to $21,000. Dillon (P) appealed, arguing that he should have been granted a new trial on the issue of damages.

■ ISSUE

Was Dillon (P) entitled to a new trial on the issue of damages?

■ DECISION AND RATIONALE

(Pleicones, J.) Yes. A trial court must grant a new trial on the issue of damages if the amount of the verdict is so grossly inadequate or excessive as to shock the conscience of the court and clearly indicates that the figure reached was the result of passion, caprice, prejudice, partiality, corruption, or some other improper motive. The failure of the trial judge to grant a new trial on the issue of damage in this case amounts to an abuse of discretion. Dillon (P) presented evidence of over $500,000 in damages. Although Frazer (D) disputed much of that amount, there was no dispute whatsoever about over $30,000 in damages, so a jury verdict of $6,000 is irreconcilably inconsistent with the unchallenged evidence. This disparity goes beyond being a mere conservative award and suggests that the jurors were motivated by improper considerations. We remand for a new trial on the issue of damages.

Analysis:

It is likely that the reviewing court was concerned that the jury minimized the damages in this case based on their belief that Dillon's (P) actual out-of-pocket losses were less than his claimed damages because of third-party payments, despite the judge's admonition that such payments were not to be considered. Generally speaking, the "collateral source rule" bars the admission at trial of evidence that the plaintiff's damages have been or will be paid by another source other than the defendant, such as the plaintiff's health or auto insurance, or workers' compensation.

■ CASE VOCABULARY

ADDITUR: [Latin, "it is increased."] The power of the court to increase the amount of damages awarded to a plaintiff by a jury as a condition for denying a new trial to a plaintiff if the defendant agrees to pay the plaintiff extra money. *Compare* remittitur.

REMITTITUR: The power of the judge to order the plaintiff to remit, or accept a reduction in the amount of the damages awarded in the jury's verdict, when the judge believes the verdict is excessively high as a matter of law. The judge may order a retrial if the plaintiff does not accept the reduction.

CHAPTER THREE

Establishing a Claim for Intentional Tort to Person or Property

Snyder v. Turk

Instant Facts: A nurse sued a doctor for battery when he grabbed her during an operation and yelled about her incompetence.

Black Letter Rule: A person is subject to liability for battery when he acts intending to cause a harmful or offensive contact, and when a harmful or offensive contact results.

Cohen v. Smith

Instant Facts: A woman sued her nurse and the hospital when, against her wishes, the nurse saw her unclothed and touched her naked body.

Black Letter Rule: An actor commits a battery if he acts with an intent to cause harmful or offensive contact to another and such a contact results.

Garratt v. Dailey

Instant Facts: A woman brought suit against a young boy when she was injured in a fall that resulted from his pulling a chair out from underneath her.

Black Letter Rule: When a person has knowledge to a substantial certainty that harmful or offensive contact will result from a certain action, a battery occurs if that action is taken, even if there is no intent to cause harm to another.

White v. Muniz

Instant Facts: A supervisor at a care facility for the elderly sued a resident when she was slapped for trying to change the resident's diaper.

Black Letter Rule: In order to find a mentally deficient person liable for an intentional tort, a jury must find that the actor subjectively intended offensive or harmful consequences.

Cullison v. Medley

Instant Facts: Cullison (P) sued the Medleys (D) for assault after they intimidated him while Mr. Medley was armed.

Black Letter Rule: Assault occurs when one acts intending to cause a harmful or offensive contact with the person of the other or an imminent apprehension of such contact.

McCann v. Wal-Mart Stores, Inc.

Instant Facts: Three store patrons sued Wal-Mart for false imprisonment when two store employees backed them into a corner and held them there for over an hour while waiting for a store security guard to arrive.

Black Letter Rule: The tort of false imprisonment occurs when conduct by one party serves to confine another within certain boundaries fixed by the actor and the victim is conscious of the confinement or harmed by it.

Snyder v. Turk

(Scrub Nurse) v. (Surgeon)

90 Ohio App.3d 18, 627 N.E.2d 1053 (1993)

A BATTERY IS AN INTENTIONAL, UNCONSENTED-TO CONTACT WITH ANOTHER

■ **INSTANT FACTS** A nurse sued a doctor for battery when he grabbed her during an operation and yelled about her incompetence.

■ **BLACK LETTER RULE** A person is subject to liability for battery when he acts intending to cause a harmful or offensive contact, and when a harmful or offensive contact results.

■ PROCEDURAL BASIS

Certification to the Court of Appeals of Ohio of an appeal of a directed verdict entered in favor of the defendant in a civil battery action.

■ FACTS

Dr. Turk (D) was performing a gall-bladder operation with the assistance of Snyder (P), a nurse. The operation was not going smoothly and Dr. Turk (D) was frustrated. Feeling that Snyder's (P) mistakes were a major reason that the operation was not going as he would like, Dr. Turk (D) grabbed her at one point, forced her head down toward the surgical opening, and said "Can't you see where I'm working? I'm working in a hole. I need long instruments." Snyder (P) sued for battery.

■ ISSUE

Can grabbing someone in a way offensive to personal dignity constitute a battery under tort law?

■ DECISION AND RATIONALE

(Wilson, J.) Yes. Dr. Turk (D) contends that there is no liability on his part for the commission of a battery against Snyder (P) absent proof of an intent to inflict personal injury upon her. He further argues that the directed verdict entered in his favor was proper because there was no evidence of his intent to inflict personal injury on Snyder (P). A person is subject to liability for battery when he acts intending to cause a harmful or offensive contact, and when a harmful or offensive contact results. Offensive contact is any contact which is offensive to a reasonable sense of personal dignity. In this case, the issue is the propriety of the directed verdict. A motion for a directed verdict assumes the truth of the evidence supporting the facts essential to the claim after giving the non-moving party the benefit of all reasonable inferences from the evidence, and refers the application of a reasonable-minds test to such evidence. Here, we believe that reasonable minds could conclude that Dr. Turk (D) intended to commit an offensive contact. Reversed.

Analysis:

Snyder demonstrates the two different ways in which a battery can take place. Certainly, as Dr. Turk (D) argued, a battery occurs when one person intentionally inflicts personal injury upon another, such as when one person punches another. A second way in which battery can occur, as this court points out, is by the offensive touching of another person, or the intentional touching of another person in a way that a reasonable person would find offensive to personal dignity. It is important to note that the views of the one committing the battery and the victim are not dispositive, but it is the view of the reasonable person that controls. Thus, if Snyder (P) were simply a hypersensitive person, and no reasonable person would find pushing her face toward the table to be offensive, there would be no battery—the fact that she was personally offended would not matter. Nor did it matter that Dr. Turk (D) did not find his own actions to be offensive to anyone.

■ CASE VOCABULARY

BATTERY: An intentional, unconsented, and offensive touching of another person.

Cohen v. Smith

(Pregnant Woman) v. (Male Nurse)

269 Ill.App.3d 1087, 207 Ill.Dec. 873, 648 N.E.2d 329 (1995)

PROTECTING PERSONAL INTEGRITY HAS LONG BEEN VIEWED AS AN IMPORTANT BASIS FOR THE LAW OF BATTERY

■ **INSTANT FACTS** A woman sued her nurse and the hospital when, against her wishes, the nurse saw her unclothed and touched her naked body.

■ **BLACK LETTER RULE** An actor commits a battery if he acts with an intent to cause harmful or offensive contact to another and such a contact results.

■ PROCEDURAL BASIS

Certification to the Appellate Court of Illinois of a trial court decision to grant a motion to dismiss in favor of the defendant in a civil battery case.

■ FACTS

Patricia Cohen (P) was admitted to St. Joseph Memorial Hospital to deliver her baby. After she was told that she would need a cesarean section, Cohen (P) allegedly informed her doctor, who informed the hospital staff, that her religious beliefs prohibited her from being seen unclothed by a male. The doctor assured her that the beliefs would be respected. During the procedure, Roger Smith (D), a male nurse, allegedly observed and touched Cohen's (P) naked body. Cohen (P) sued Smith (D) and the hospital. The trial court granted Smith's (D) motion to dismiss, and Cohen (P) appealed.

■ ISSUE

Can contact that does not cause injury but does cause offense provide grounds for a tort action in battery?

■ DECISION AND RATIONALE

(Chapman, J.) Yes. A trial court may dismiss a cause of action for failing to state a claim only if it is apparent that no set of alleged facts can be proven which will entitle a plaintiff to recovery. The Restatement (Second) of Torts provides that an actor commits a battery if: "(a) he acts intending to cause a harmful or offensive contact with the person of the other or a third person, or an imminent apprehension of such a contact, and (b) a harmful [or offensive] contact with the person of the other directly or indirectly results." Restatement (Second) of Torts, § 18 (1965). Liability for battery emphasizes the plaintiff's lack of consent to the touching. Offensive contact is said to occur when contact offends a reasonable sense of personal dignity. As such, a defendant is not only liable for contacts which do actual physical harm, but also for any contacts which, however trivial, are offensive or insulting. This application of battery to remedy offensive and insulting conduct is deeply ingrained in our legal history. Although most people in modern society have come to accept the necessity of being seen unclothed and being touched by members of the opposite sex during medical treatment, the Cohens (P) had not accepted these procedures and, according to their complaint, informed Smith (D) and the hospital of their convictions. Although others may not share these convictions, the courts have consistently recognized individuals' rights to refuse medical treatment or, in this case, determine the scope of medical treatment. Accepting as true the Cohens' (P) allegations that they informed Smith (D) and the hospital of their beliefs and that Cohen (P) was still treated as a patient without those beliefs, we conclude that the trial court erred in dismissing the battery claim. Reversed.

Analysis:

Cohen presents the Restatement (Second) view of battery, which is a view much the same as that found in *Snyder* and other cases. Indeed, the Restatement (Second) supports the idea that an offensive touching, though not physically harmful, can result in a battery. One slight difference between the two cases, however, can be found in the way in which it is determined whether there has been offensive conduct. *Snyder* clearly states that conduct is only offensive when a reasonable person would find it to be offensive. *Cohen* is slightly different, however, in that it finds offensive conduct even where a reasonable person might not, so long as it is reasonable that a person would take offense. The difference is that under the first approach, the court looks to whether a reasonable person would be offended, while under the second it looks to see whether it was reasonable for the offended person to get offended. In *Cohen,* the court clearly states that most people have accepted the fact that one must be seen unclothed and be touched during medical procedures. Thus, a majority of people would not likely find the touching that took place in *Cohen* offensive. Even though this is true, the court still accepted the actions as offensive because the Cohens found them offensive. Thus, the test for offensiveness used here is not that of the reasonable person, but of the subjective view of the one touched.

■ CASE VOCABULARY

OFFENSIVE CONTACT: Contact that offends a reasonable sense of personal dignity, or contact that a reasonable person would find offensive to personal dignity.

Garratt v. Dailey

(Young Boy) v. (Older Woman)

46 Wn.2d 197, 279 P.2d 1091 (1955)

WHEN A MINOR COMMITS A TORT WITH FORCE HE IS LIABLE AS ANY OTHER PERSON WOULD BE

■ **INSTANT FACTS** A woman brought suit against a young boy when she was injured in a fall that resulted from his pulling a chair out from underneath her.

■ **BLACK LETTER RULE** When a person has knowledge to a substantial certainty that harmful or offensive contact will result from a certain action, a battery occurs if that action is taken, even if there is no intent to cause harm to another.

■ PROCEDURAL BASIS

Certification to the Supreme Court of Washington of a trial court finding that there was no battery in a suit brought by an adult woman against a young boy.

■ FACTS

Ruth Garratt (P) suffered a fractured hip and other serious and painful injuries when, on July 16, 1951, she fell to the ground while trying to sit down in a lawn chair. How she came to fall was the subject of dispute. Garratt's (P) sister, who was present during the fall, testified that Brian Dailey (D), a five year-old boy, deliberately pulled the chair out from under Garratt (P) as she was about to sit in it. Dailey (D) testified that he had moved the chair and was about to sit in it when he saw Garratt (P) sitting down (with nothing underneath her). At that time, he jumped up and tried to move the chair to a position underneath her so as to prevent injury. Garratt (P) brought suit against Dailey (D) for the injuries. The trial court found in favor of Dailey (D), stressing that he did not have any intent to injure Garratt (P) when he moved the chair, and therefore did not commit a battery. Garratt (P) appealed.

■ ISSUE

Can a battery occur if there is no intent to injure another but there is a knowledge that a certain action will result in harmful contact and that action is taken?

■ DECISION AND RATIONALE

(Hill, J.) Yes. Brian (D), whether 5 or 55, must have committed a wrongful act before he can be held liable for Garratt's (P) injuries. Garratt (P) argues that the act of moving the chair constituted a battery, which is defined as the intentional infliction of a harmful bodily contact upon another. The rule used in determining liability for battery is found in 29 Restatement (First) of Torts § 13, which states: "An act which, directly or indirectly, is the legal cause of a harmful contact with another's person makes the actor liable to the other, if (a) the act is done with the intention of bringing about a harmful or offensive contact." The comments to this section further state that in order for an act to be done "with the intention of bringing about a harmful or offensive contact . . . [it] must be done for the purpose of causing the contact . . . or with knowledge on the part of the actor that such contact . . . is substantially certain to be produced." Had Garratt (P) proved to the satisfaction of the trial court that Brian (D) moved the chair while she was in the act of sitting down, his action would have been with the intent of causing her injury, and she would be entitled to a judgment against him. The trial court did not so find, but accepted Brian's (D) version of the facts. It then considered whether a battery was established under the facts as it found them. In this connection, we quote another section of the comments to the Restatement: "It is not enough that the act itself is intentionally done and this, even though the actor realizes or should realize that it contains a . . . risk of bringing about the contact or apprehension. Such realization may make the actor's conduct negligent or even reckless but unless he realizes that to a substantial certainty, the contact or apprehension will result, the actor has not that intention which is necessary to make him liable under the rule stated in this section." Thus, a battery would be established if, in addition to Garratt's (P) fall, it was proved that, when Brian (D) moved the chair, he knew with substantial certainty that she would attempt to sit down where the chair had been. The mere absence of any intent to injure Garratt (P) or to play a prank on her or to embarrass her, or to commit an assault and battery on her would not absolve him from liability if in fact he had such knowledge. Without such a knowledge, however, there would be no wrongful act and thus no liability. We believe that before Garratt's (P) case can be dismissed, there should be no question but that the trial court addresses this issue; hence, the case should be remanded for clarifications of the findings to specifically cover the question of Brian's (D) knowledge, because intent could be inferred therefrom. If the court finds that he had such knowledge the necessary intent will be established and Garratt (P) will be entitled to recover, even though there was no purpose to injure or embarrass her. The only circumstance where Brian's (D) age is of any consequence is in determining what he knew, and there his experience, capacity, and understanding are material. Remanded.

Analysis:

A battery can occur even when there is no intentional and offensive touching, which is the normal definition of battery. Under *Garratt,* a battery will occur when a person has knowledge to a substantial certainty that harmful or offensive contact will result from a certain action. Thus, in this case, it was found that Brian (D) might have committed a battery even though he never touched Garratt (P); the fact that he knew pulling the chair away might cause her harm was enough for the court. Some jurisdictions accept the Washington view of battery laid out in *Garratt,* but many others still require an actual touching. On remand, the trial court later found that Garratt (P) was actually in the act of seating herself when the chair was moved, and that Brian (D) knew what she was doing. On that ground, the trial court ruled in favor of Garratt (P).

White v. Muniz

(Representative of Insane Person) v. (Care Facility Supervisor)

999 P.2d 814 (Colo.2000)

INSANITY IS NOT A DEFENSE TO AN INTENTIONAL TORT, BUT IT IS A CHARACTERISTIC THAT MAY MAKE IT MORE DIFFICULT TO PROVE THE INTENT ELEMENT OF BATTERY

■ **INSTANT FACTS** A supervisor at a care facility for the elderly sued a resident when she was slapped for trying to change the resident's diaper.

■ **BLACK LETTER RULE** In order to find a mentally deficient person liable for an intentional tort, a jury must find that the actor subjectively intended offensive or harmful consequences.

■ PROCEDURAL BASIS

Certification to the Colorado Supreme Court of a state appellate court reversal of a jury verdict based on its belief that the jury was provided with an erroneous instruction.

■ FACTS

In October of 1993, Barbara White (D) placed her grandmother, Helen Everly, in an assisted living facility. While there, Everly exhibited erratic behavior, becoming easily agitated and aggressive towards others. A doctor diagnosed her with having progressive dementia, loss of memory, impulse control, and judgment; and a degenerative dementia of the Alzheimer type. On November 21, 1993, the care-giver in charge of Everly's wing asked Sherry Lynn Muniz (P), a shift supervisor, to change Everly's diaper, an effort in which Everly was not cooperating. Everly refused to allow Muniz (P) to change the diaper, and when Muniz (P) reached for the diaper, Everly struck her on the jaw and ordered her out of the room. Muniz (P) sued Everly and White (D), Everly's representative, for assault and battery. Following the presentation of evidence at trial, the judge instructed the jury that a person may suffer from dementia and still act intentionally, a person can be held to have intended an act even though her reasons and motives were entirely irrational, and that, in order to be liable for battery, a person "must have appreciated the offensiveness of her conduct." Muniz (P) objected to the last part of the instruction, the jury found for Everly, and Muniz (P) appealed. The appellate court overturned the jury verdict because it felt that the instruction was erroneous. White (D) appealed to the state supreme court.

■ ISSUE

Must a person appreciate the offensiveness of his or her conduct in order to be held liable for battery?

■ DECISION AND RATIONALE

(Kourlis, J.) Yes. It is generally agreed that an intentional tort requires some proof that the tortfeasor intended harm or offense. According to the Restatement (Second) of Torts § 13, "An actor is subject to liability to another for battery if (a) he acts intending to cause a harmful or offensive contact with the person of the other . . . and (b) offensive [or harmful] contact . . . directly or indirectly results." Traditionally, the actor had to understand that his contact would be harmful or offensive. The actor need not have intended, however, the harm that actually resulted from his action. Thus, if a slight punch to the victim resulted in traumatic injuries, the actor would be liable for all damages even if he only intended to knock the wind out of the victim. More recently, some courts around the nation have abandoned this dual intent requirement in an intentional tort setting, that being an intent to contact and an intent that the contact be harmful or offensive, and have required only that the tortfeasor intend a contact with another that results in a harmful or offensive touching. Under this view, a victim need only prove that a voluntary movement by the tortfeasor resulted in a contact which a reasonable person would find offensive or to which the victim did not consent. Colorado requires a dual intent, so we reject Muniz's (P) argument and find that the trial court delivered an adequate instruction to the jury. Operating in accordance with the instructions, the jury had to find that Everly appreciated the offensiveness of her conduct in order to be liable for the intentional tort of battery. We presume that the jury looked into the mind of Everly, and reasoned that she did not possess the necessary intent to commit an assault or a battery. A jury can, of course, find a mentally deficient person liable for an intentional tort, but in order to do so, the jury must find that the actor intended offensive or harmful consequences. As a result, insanity is not a defense to an intentional tort according to the ordinary use of that term, but is a characteristic, like infancy, that may make it more difficult to prove the intent element of battery. Reversed.

Analysis:

While mentally deficient persons can be held liable for torts, they must be able to comprehend the offensiveness of their actions before liability can attach. Because Helen Everly could not comprehend that her actions were offensive, Muniz (P) had no claim for damages. *White* also addresses "dual intent." The Colorado Supreme Court disapproves of abandonment of the dual intent requirement: "These [abandoning] courts would find intent in contact to the back of a friend that results in a severe, unexpected injury even though the actor did not intend the contact to be harmful or offensive. The actor thus could be held liable for battery because a reasonable person would find an injury offensive or harmful, irrespective of the intent of the actor to harm or offend." In the opinion of the Colorado Supreme Court, then, the dual intent requirement is necessary so that a simple slap on the back of a friend will not be considered a battery.

■ CASE VOCABULARY

DUAL-INTENT REQUIREMENT: A requirement that, in order for a battery to be established, there must be both intent to contact and an intent to cause harmful or offensive results.

INTENTIONAL TORT: A tort that can only be committed when there exists intent, general or specific, to act. Examples of intentional torts include assault, battery, trespass, and false imprisonment.

Cullison v. Medley

(Assault Victim) v. (Father)

570 N.E.2d 27 (Ind.1991)

THE JURY DETERMINES WHETHER THE APPREHENSION OF HARMFUL CONDUCT WAS REASONABLE

■ **INSTANT FACTS** Cullison (P) sued the Medleys (D) for assault after they intimidated him while Mr. Medley was armed.

■ **BLACK LETTER RULE** Assault occurs when one acts intending to cause a harmful or offensive contact with the person of the other or an imminent apprehension of such contact.

■ PROCEDURAL BASIS

On appeal to review a decision of the Indiana Court of Appeals affirming summary judgment for the defendants.

■ FACTS

Cullison (P) met Sandy Medley (D) in a grocery store parking lot. After exchanging pleasantries, Cullison (P) invited Sandy to come back to his home to talk. Cullison (P) returned home alone and was later awakened by a knock at the door. After getting dressed, Cullison (P) found Medley's (D) father, mother, and other family members standing in his living room with Medley (D). Medley's (D) father had a pistol strapped to his thigh, while her mother kept her hand in her pocket as she spoke to him, convincing Cullison (P) that she, too, was carrying a gun. The presence of the others intimidated Cullison (P). While Medley's (D) father never withdrew the gun from its holster, he grabbed at it several times while making threatening remarks. Cullison (P) was never touched, but feared he would be shot. After the Medleys (D) left his house, Cullison (P) experienced chest pains and had a heart attack. Shortly thereafter, Cullison (P) learned that Medley's (D) father had shot a man in the past. Several months later, Medley's (D) father, again armed with a pistol, glared at Cullison (P) in a restaurant while standing with the pistol one foot from Cullison's (P) face. As a result of these experiences, Cullison (P) sought psychiatric help. Cullison (P) sued the Medleys (D) for assault. The trial court granted the defendants' motion for summary judgment and the Indiana Court of Appeals affirmed. Cullison (P) appealed to the state supreme court.

■ ISSUE

Did the court err in granting summary judgment to the defendants on the plaintiff's assault claim?

■ DECISION AND RATIONALE

(Krahulik, J.) Yes. "[A]ssault, unlike battery, is effectuated when one acts intending to cause a harmful or offensive contact with the person of the other or an imminent apprehension of such contact." No physical contact is required to establish assault, so long as a reasonable person would fear that harmful or offensive contact is imminent. Here, the court of appeals determined that because the father never removed the gun from its holster, his threats were conditional and did not express an intent to harm Cullison (P). Further, having alleged only emotional distress,

Cullison (P) failed to establish the necessary damages to sustain an assault claim. Because assault is an injury to the mind rather than the body, however, mental anguish and emotional distress are recoverable damages. Similarly, Cullison (P) has presented sufficient facts to allow a reasonable juror to find that, by surrounding him in his home while armed and grabbing at the pistol, the Medleys (D) intended to frighten Cullison (P). It is for the jury to decide whether Cullison (P) had a reasonable apprehension of harmful or offensive contact. Reversed and remanded.

Analysis:

The court's conclusion creates an interesting situation. If an action for assault can be sustained by establishing emotional damages, it would be difficult to imagine an assault claim without a companion claim for intentional infliction of emotional distress. But not all intentional infliction of emotional distress claims will constitute assault, since emotional distress may arise without an apprehension of harmful contact.

■ CASE VOCABULARY

APPREHENSION: Fear; anxiety.

ASSAULT: The threat or use of force on another that causes that person to have a reasonable apprehension of imminent harmful or offensive contact; the act of putting another in reasonable fear or apprehension of an immediate battery by means of an act amounting to an attempt or threat to commit a battery.

EMOTIONAL DISTRESS: A highly unpleasant mental reaction (such as anguish, grief, fright, humiliation, or fury) that results from another person's conduct; emotional pain and suffering.

McCann v. Wal-Mart Stores, Inc.

(Store Patron) v. (Store Owner)

210 F.3d 51 (1st Cir.2000)

FALSE IMPRISONMENT CAN OCCUR DESPITE AN ABSENCE OF PHYSICAL BARRIERS OR PHYSICAL FORCE

■ **INSTANT FACTS** Three store patrons sued Wal-Mart for false imprisonment when two store employees backed them into a corner and held them there for over an hour while waiting for a store security guard to arrive.

■ **BLACK LETTER RULE** The tort of false imprisonment occurs when conduct by one party serves to confine another within certain boundaries fixed by the actor and the victim is conscious of the confinement or harmed by it.

■ PROCEDURAL BASIS

Certification to the United States Court of Appeals for the First Circuit of an appeal of a jury verdict granting $20,000 in damages to a victim of false imprisonment.

■ FACTS

On December 11, 1996, Debra McCann (P) and two of her children went shopping at the Bangor, Maine, Wal-Mart (D). The McCanns (P) paid for their purchases at 10:10 p.m. As they were leaving the store, two Wal-Mart (D) employees stepped in front of their cart, blocking their exit from the store. They then told McCann (P) that her children were not allowed in the store because they had been caught stealing on a prior occasion. The two employees were mistaken. Despite McCann's (P) protestations, one employee told McCann (P) that they had the records to prove their allegations, that the police were being called, and that the McCanns (P) "had to go with her." The employees never called the police, but instead contacted a store security officer who would be able to identify the earlier shoplifter. Eventually the officer arrived at the store and informed the two employees that the McCanns (P) were not the family whose son had been caught shoplifting. The McCanns (P) left the store at 11:15 p.m. They brought suit and the jury awarded them $20,000 on their claim of false imprisonment. Wal-Mart (D) appealed.

■ ISSUE

Can false imprisonment be found when there is no actual physical force exerted against the person confined?

■ DECISION AND RATIONALE

(Authoring Judge Not Stated) Yes. The gist of the common law tort of false imprisonment is conduct by the actor which is intended to, and does in fact, confine another within boundaries fixed by the actor and, in addition, the victim is either conscious of the confinement or is harmed by it. While confinement can be imposed by physical barriers or physical force, much less will do. It is generally settled that mere threats of physical force can suffice, and it is also settled that the threats may be implicit as well as explicit, and that confinement can also be based on a false assertion of legal authority to confine. In this case, the direction to the McCann's (P) to follow the employee, the reference to the police, and the continued presence of the employees were enough to induce reasonable people to believe either that they would be restrained physically if they sought to leave, or that the store was claiming lawful authority to confine them until the police arrived, or both. Wal-Mart (D) asserts that under Maine law, the jury had to find "actual, physical restraint," a phrase taken from *Knowlton v. Ross,* 95 A. 281 (1915). This is a good example of taking language out of context. In *Knowlton,* the wife of a man who owed a hotel for past bills entered a hotel office and was told that she would go to jail if the bills were not paid. The hotel did not ask her into the room, did not touch her, and did not tell her that she could not leave. The threat of jail was also just "evidence of an intention to imprison at some future time." In context, the reference to the necessity of "actual, physical restraint" is best understood as a reminder that a plaintiff must actually be confined, which Ms. Knowlton was not. Taking too literally the phrase "actual, physical restraint" would put Maine law broadly at odds with both the Restatement and a practically uniform body of common law in other states that accepts the mere threat of physical force, or a claim of lawful authority to restrain, as enough to satisfy the confinement requirement for false imprisonment. Affirmed.

Analysis:

False imprisonment occurs when a person confines another intentionally without lawful privilege and against his consent within a limited area for any appreciable time, however short. Further, as *McCann* points out, the victim must "either [be] conscious of the confinement or . . . harmed by it." Evil motive is not a necessary element of a false imprisonment claim. In this case, false imprisonment was found because the McCanns were confined without their consent and were aware of the confinement. It did not matter that the confinement lasted merely one hour—that was enough time to constitute false imprisonment. Nor did it matter that the McCanns were not harmed in any way, as false imprisonment is a trespassory tort and therefore no harm needs to be shown to collect damages (so long as the plaintiff is aware of the confinement). In most cases, exclusion from a place, as opposed to confinement to a place, will not be grounds for a suit for false imprisonment. Thus, a refusal to allow a person to enter a certain premises will not be the grounds for an action for false imprisonment.

■ CASE VOCABULARY

FALSE IMPRISONMENT: An intentional tort involving the confinement of a person to a physically limited area without lawful justification or consent.

CHAPTER FOUR

Defenses to Intentional Torts—Privileges

Touchet v. Hampton

Instant Facts: Hampton (D) claimed that his attack on Touchet (P) was justifiable self-defense, given Touchet's (P) threatening phone calls and voicemail messages.

Black Letter Rule: Mere words, even though designed to excite or irritate, cannot excuse a battery.

Katko v. Briney

Instant Facts: The Brineys (D) set up a spring gun in their unoccupied farm house. The spring gun went off and injured Katko (P) when he broke into the house.

Black Letter Rule: A landowner may not use a spring gun to defend an unoccupied farm house.

Brown v. Martinez

Instant Facts: Martinez (D) shot and injured Brown (P) when Brown (P) and some other boys trespassed on Martinez's (D) land to steal watermelons.

Black Letter Rule: A landowner may not use force calculated to cause death or serious bodily injury to prevent a trespass or an unlawful act not amounting to a felony.

Gortarez v. Smitty's Super Valu, Inc.

Instant Facts: A store clerk wrongly suspected Gortarez (P) of stealing a fifty-nine-cent car freshening vaporizer and alerted store security personnel, who forcibly detained Gortarez (P) after he left the store by putting him in a choke hold; Gortarez (P) was injured and sued the store and security guard.

Black Letter Rule: A merchant, or his agent or employee, with reasonable cause may detain on the premises in a reasonable manner and for a reasonable time any person suspected of shoplifting for questioning or summoning a law enforcement officer.

Surocco v. Geary

Instant Facts: Geary (D), the mayor of San Francisco, authorized Surocco's (P) house to be blown up in order to stop the progress of a raging fire.

Black Letter Rule: A person is not liable for destroying another's property if it is necessary to prevent an imminent public disaster.

Vincent v. Lake Erie Transportation Co.

Instant Facts: During a fierce storm, a steamship was repeatedly thrown against a dock, causing damage to the dock.

Black Letter Rule: Damage caused to another's property due to necessity requires compensation for the actual harm caused.

Touchet v. Hampton

(Former Sales Manager) v. (Dealership Owner)

950 So. 2d 895 (La. Ct. App. 2007)

VERBAL THREATS DO NOT JUSTIFY A BATTERY AGAINST THE SPEAKER

■ **INSTANT FACTS** Hampton (D) claimed that his attack on Touchet (P) was justifiable self-defense, given Touchet's (P) threatening phone calls and voicemail messages.

■ **BLACK LETTER RULE** Mere words, even though designed to excite or irritate, cannot excuse a battery.

■ PROCEDURAL BASIS

State appellate court review of the trial court's decision granting the defendant's motion to dismiss on the ground of self-defense.

■ FACTS

Touchet (P) was a sales manager at a Mitsubishi dealership owned by Hampton (D). Touchet's (P) employment was terminated during the summer of 2002 in an apparently amicable fashion. Shortly thereafter, however, Touchet (P) started calling Hampton (D) at the dealership and making fun of the business, cursing at Hampton (D), threatening him, and ominously telling Hampton (D) he knew where he lived. After these calls continued for awhile, Hampton (D) went to Touchet's (P) new place of employment, an RV dealership, allegedly to talk about their situation. When he entered Touchet's (P) office, Touchet (P) abruptly turned around in his chair and cursed at Hampton (D). Hampton (D) allegedly thought Touchet (P) was going to hit him, so he got in the first punch; in fact, he continued to hit Touchet (P) for about twenty seconds until Touchet's (P) co-worker pulled Hampton (D) off of Touchet (P). Touchet (P) sued Hampton (D) for battery. After a bench trial, Hampton (D) moved to dismiss, claiming that the evidence showed he acted in self-defense. The trial court granted the motion and Touchet (P) appealed.

■ ISSUE

Did the evidence support a finding that Hampton (D) was acting in self-defense?

■ DECISION AND RATIONALE

(Amy, J.) No. Mere words, even though designed to excite or irritate, cannot excuse a battery. Words, written or spoken, sometime prior do not justify a physical attack on the one by whom they were written or spoken. Neither the messages that Touchet (P) left on Hampton's (D) voicemail nor the epithet yelled just before the assault justify Hampton's physical attack on Touchet (P).

A defendant's actions can be justified as self-defense only if there was an actual or reasonably apparent threat to his safety and the force employed was not excessive in degree or kind. The privilege of self-defense is based on the prevention of harm to the actor, not on the desire for retaliation or revenge. Hampton (D) testified that he felt threatened by the voicemail messages Touchet (P) had left on his answering machine, and that he went to the RV Center to tell Touchet (P) to stop harassing him. When Touchet (P) quickly turned around in his chair and yelled an obscenity at Hampton (D), then started to rise from his chair, Hampton (D) allegedly was scared that Touchet (P) would carry out his threats, so he struck him. Witnesses testified, however, that Touchet (P) made no threatening moves toward Hampton (D). Touchet (P) himself testified that Hampton (D) burst into his office saying, "I'm going to kill you." Under these circumstances, the record does not support a finding that there was an actual or reasonably apparent threat to Hampton's (D) safety.

Even if Touchet (P) had made a threatening move, Hampton (D) could have left the premises. Instead, he repeatedly struck Touchet (P) and had to be pulled off of him. If a defendant uses excessive force in repelling an actual or apparent threat to his safety, his self-defense claim cannot stand. Hampton (D) struck Touchet (P) while Touchet (P) was still sitting at his desk, and Touchet (P) never struck Hampton (D) back but instead tried to protect himself by covering his face. For these reasons, the granting of a motion to dismiss on the issue of self-defense was manifestly erroneous. On remand, however, Hampton (D) will have the opportunity to present additional evidence. Reversed and remanded.

Analysis:

A battery is a harmful or offensive contact with a person resulting from an act intended to cause the plaintiff to suffer such a contact. The appellate court noted in this case that the trial court did not address whether the essential elements of battery were satisfied, but instead only addressed the issue of self-defense. Thus, the appellate review was limited to that issue as well. To escape liability for damages resulting from a battery, the defendant may prove that his actions were privileged or justified, such as by self-defense, but the record did not support the conclusion that Hampton's (D) actions were so justified in this case.

■ CASE VOCABULARY

BENCH TRIAL: Trial held before a judge, without a jury, during which the judge acts as the factfinder.

Katko v. Briney

(Intruder) v. (Landowner)

183 N.W.2d 657 (Iowa 1971)

OWNER MAY NOT USE A SPRING GUN TO DEFEND UNOCCUPIED FARM HOUSE

■ **INSTANT FACTS** The Brineys (D) set up a spring gun in their unoccupied farm house. The spring gun went off and injured Katko (P) when he broke into the house.

■ **BLACK LETTER RULE** A landowner may not use a spring gun to defend an unoccupied farm house.

■ PROCEDURAL BASIS

Appeal of a tort action for damages.

■ FACTS

After suffering years of break-ins, the Brineys (D) set up a spring gun in an unoccupied farm house they owned. The spring gun was rigged with a wire from the bedroom doorknob to the gun's trigger and was aimed to hit an intruder's legs. There was no sign warning intruders about the gun. Katko (P) and a friend broke into the house to steal bottles and fruit jars. When Katko (P) entered the bedroom, the shotgun went off and blew away much of his right leg. Katko (P) was fined and sentenced to jail for larceny. The jury awarded Katko (P) actual and punitive damages. The Brineys (P) appealed, claiming that the law permits using a spring gun to prevent unlawful entry into a dwelling.

■ ISSUE

May a landowner use a spring gun to defend an unoccupied farm house?

■ DECISION AND RATIONALE

(Moore, C.J.) No. The value of human life and health outweighs a landowner's interest in protecting property. Therefore, a landowner may not use force intended or likely to cause death or serious harm to defend property against an intruder, unless the intruder threatens the property's occupants with death or serious harm. Here, the farm house was unoccupied, and Katko (P) did not threaten anyone with death or serious harm. The Brineys (P) could not use more force when they were not present than they could have used if they were present. Accordingly, the Brineys (D) were not justified in using a spring gun to protect their property. Affirmed.

■ CONCURRENCE

Someone who possesses land is privileged to use reasonable force to defend the possession against intrusion or harm. However, the possessor must limit the force to meet the apparent need for it. Reasonable force is usually the least force that is reasonably likely to be effective to defend the property. Deadly force or force likely to cause grave bodily harm may not be used against a peaceable intruder. Deadly force may be used only if the intruder appears to threaten a person with deadly force. Special rules apply to spring guns, as the Brineys (D) used here. Indeed, this is the most famous American case dealing with spring guns. Under the Restatement, a spring gun is allowed, but only when the homeowner could have used such force in person. This rule is often difficult to apply, but courts have generally held that homeowners may protect a dwelling place by spring guns against intruders who are entering or attempting to enter in the course of a felony or attempted felony. A homeowner has no privilege to use spring guns against mere trespassers or those committing minor crimes outside the home.

Analysis:

Katko (P) broke into the farm house to steal bottles and jars. Although he entered the house with the intent to commit a crime, he was allowed to recover. The court based its decision on the Restatement's view that human life and limb are more important than property interests. This holding seems also influenced by the fact that the Brineys (D) did not live in the farm house and were not present at the time Katko (P) broke in. A home, unlike a warehouse or an office building, is meant to satisfy the fundamental needs for human safety and refuge. Had the Brineys (D) lived there, the court's holding may have been different. Case law is split regarding whether a sign warning intruders that they risk deadly force if they enter a dwelling protects the landowner from liability. In that case, the intruder may be held to have assumed the risk of entering the dwelling. Some courts have barred recovery by someone who is injured in the course of his "own wrong." These courts have held that someone who commits a crime "forfeits" his civil rights. However, it is unlikely this rule would apply if a homeowner intentionally and unnecessarily shoots the criminal. Similar rules would likely apply to other deadly traps, such as electrified wire and vicious dogs.

Brown v. Martinez

(Trespasser) v. (Landowner)

68 N.M. 271, 361 P.2d 152 (1961)

LANDOWNER MAY NOT USE FORCE CALCULATED TO CAUSE DEATH OR SERIOUS BODILY INJURY TO PROTECT PROPERTY

■ **INSTANT FACTS** Martinez (D) shot and injured Brown (P) when Brown (P) and some other boys trespassed on Martinez's (D) land to steal watermelons.

■ **BLACK LETTER RULE** A landowner may not use force calculated to cause death or serious bodily injury to prevent a trespass or an unlawful act not amounting to a felony.

■ PROCEDURAL BASIS

Appeal of dismissal of tort action for damages.

■ FACTS

Two boys entered Martinez' (D) land to steal watermelons. Brown (P) was standing outside the property when Martinez (D) came out of his house and fired a rifle away from the boys to scare them away. The bullet hit Brown (P), severely injuring him. The trial court dismissed Brown's (P) claim against Martinez (D).

■ ISSUE

May a landowner use force calculated to cause death or serious bodily injury to prevent a trespass or an unlawful act not amounting to a felony on property?

■ DECISION AND RATIONALE

(Moise, J.) No. Force used to defend property must be appropriate. The law places a higher value on human safety than on property rights. Here, there is no evidence that Martinez (D) believed that Brown (P) threatened his own safety. Accordingly, he was not privileged to use any force calculated to cause death or serious bodily injury where only his property was threatened. Reversed.

Analysis:

A homeowner may use reasonable force to defend his land or chattels against intrusion or taking, but the homeowner must limit the force to meet the apparent need for it. Reasonable force is the least force that would be effective in defending the property. Deadly force and force likely to cause grave bodily harm may not be used against a peaceable intruder. Here, Martinez (D) shot his gun in the opposite direction from the boys stealing his watermelons, intending only to frighten them. That constitutes an assault. Unfortunately, a bullet hit Brown (P), whom Martinez (D) may not have known was present. Even just a threat of deadly harm seems out of proportion to the risk of lost watermelons.

Gortarez v. Smitty's Super Valu, Inc.

(Customer) v. (Store)

680 P.2d 807 (Ariz. 1984)

UNREASONABLE FORCE MAY NOT BE USED AGAINST SHOPLIFTING SUSPECTS

■ **INSTANT FACTS** A store clerk wrongly suspected Gortarez (P) of stealing a fifty-nine-cent car freshening vaporizer and alerted store security personnel, who forcibly detained Gortarez (P) after he left the store by putting him in a choke hold; Gortarez (P) was injured and sued the store and security guard.

■ **BLACK LETTER RULE** A merchant, or his agent or employee, with reasonable cause may detain on the premises in a reasonable manner and for a reasonable time any person suspected of shoplifting for questioning or summoning a law enforcement officer.

■ PROCEDURAL BASIS

A merchant, or his agent or employee, with reasonable cause may detain on the premises in a reasonable manner and for a reasonable time any person suspected of shoplifting for questioning or summoning a law enforcement officer.

■ FACTS

Sixteen-year-old Gortarez (P) and his cousin were shopping at Smitty's (D). The cousin was paying for an item in the automotive department when Gortarez (P) picked up a fifty-nine-cent car freshening vaporizer and asked the clerk if he could pay for it at the front of the store, when he finished the rest of his shopping. The clerk told him yes, but was suspicious that Gortarez (P) was going to steal the item. The clerk kept an eye on the boys and never saw them dispose of or pay for the car freshener, so when they left the store he alerted security, telling them that the boys had just "ripped them off." Several store employees ran out of the store and confronted Gortarez (P) and his cousin, who denied all wrongdoing. Nonetheless, the store employees started to search the cousin, and Gortarez (P) told them to leave his cousin alone. A security guard then put Gortarez (P) in a choke hold. The cousins were not released until a check-out boy told the men apprehending the cousins that the supposedly "stolen" item was actually found in a catch-all basket at an unattended check-out lane in the store. Gortarez (P) required medical treatment for the injuries he sustained during the choke hold. He and his parents sued Smitty's (D) and the security guard for false arrest, false imprisonment, assault, and battery. After a jury trial, the court directed a verdict for the defendants on the false arrest and imprisonment count. The court of appeals affirmed, and Gortarez (P) appealed to the state supreme court.

■ ISSUE

Did the trial court correctly direct a verdict in the defendants' favor?

■ DECISION AND RATIONALE

(Feldman, J.) No. A merchant, or his agent or employee, with reasonable cause may detain on the premises in a reasonable manner and for a reasonable time any person suspected of shoplifting for questioning or summoning a law enforcement officer. This is Arizona's version of the "shopkeeper's privilege" set out in the Restatement of Torts. According to the shopkeeper's privilege, one who reasonably believes that another has tortiously taken a chattel upon his premises, or has failed to make payment for goods or services purchased there, is privileged, without arresting the other, to detain him on the premises for the time necessary to make a reasonable investigation of the facts. To invoke the privilege, "reasonable cause" is the threshold requirement. If reasonable cause to detain a shoplifting suspect is established, the next two questions are: (1) was the purpose of the shopkeeper's action proper (i.e., to detain for questioning or summoning a law enforcement officer); and (2) was the detention carried out in a reasonable manner and for a reasonable length of time? If the answer to any of these questions is no, the privilege is lost.

Reasonable cause and probable cause are the same for purposes of this privilege. Reasonable cause does not require a *correct* belief, as long as it was reasonable. The trial court was in the best position here to determine whether reasonable cause existed, and we defer to that court's finding. The *purpose* of the detention in this case, however, is at best a question for the jury, such that the court should not have directed a verdict. And even assuming there was a proper purpose, the privilege still may not attach if the merchant does not detain in a reasonable manner and for a reasonable time. Reasonable force may be used, but the use of force intended or likely to cause serious bodily harm is never privileged for the sole purpose of detention to investigate, and it becomes privileged only when the detainee's resistance makes it necessary for the actor to use such force in self-defense. Applying these restrictions, there is a question in this case as to whether the use of force in the restraint of Gortarez (P) was reasonable. The possible theft of a fifty-nine-cent item hardly warrants an apprehension that the two cousins were armed or dangerous. Indeed, the evidence may have supported a finding that the manner of detention in this case was *un*reasonable as a matter of law; it surely did not support the court's presumptive finding as a matter of law that the detention was performed reasonably. Reversed and remanded for a new trial.

Analysis:

Under Arizona statutory law, a private person may make an arrest for a misdemeanor when the person to be arrested has committed a misdemeanor amounting to a breach of the peace in the presence of the person making the arrest. Thus, under this statute, the privilege to arrest for misdemeanors without a warrant is limited to those misdemeanors that constitute a breach of the peace. Shoplifting is not a breach of the peace. There is also a common law privilege to use reasonable force to recapture a chattel while in fresh pursuit, but the property owner must be correct that the person has stolen the chattel. This privilege would not apply in the present case, either, because the belief that the item was stolen was incorrect. Accordingly, the defense's best bet was the shopkeeper's privilege, which is also a matter of statutory law in Arizona.

■ CASE VOCABULARY

DIRECTED VERDICT: A jury verdict ordered by the court. In civil cases, a party may receive a directed verdict if the opposite side does not present a prima facie case or a necessary defense. *See* Federal Rule of Civil Procedure 50(a). In criminal cases, a directed verdict may only be for acquittal. *See* Federal Rule of Criminal Procedure 29.

Surocco v. Geary

(Homeowner) v. (Mayor)

3 Cal. 69 (1853)

PERSON IS NOT LIABLE FOR DESTROYING ANOTHER'S PROPERTY IF NECESSARY TO PREVENT IMMINENT HARM TO THE PUBLIC

■ **INSTANT FACTS** Geary (D), the mayor of San Francisco, authorized Surocco's (P) house to be blown up in order to stop the progress of a raging fire.

■ **BLACK LETTER RULE** A person is not liable for destroying another's property if it is necessary to prevent an imminent public disaster.

■ PROCEDURAL BASIS

Appeal of tort action for damages.

■ FACTS

Surocco (P) was in the process of removing goods from his home while a fire raged nearby. Geary (D), the mayor of San Francisco, authorized Surocco's (P) house to be blown up to stop the progress of the fire and save adjacent buildings. Surocco (P) sued Geary (D), claiming that he could have recovered more of his goods if the house was not blown up. The trial court held for Surocco (P).

■ ISSUE

Is a person liable for destroying another's property if it is necessary to prevent an imminent public disaster?

■ DECISION AND RATIONALE

(Murray, C.J.) Yes. This right of necessity is considered a "natural right," independent of society or government. An individual's property rights must give way to the higher law of impending necessity. A house on fire or about to catch fire is a nuisance which is lawful to abate. Otherwise, one stubborn person could ruin an entire city. If property is destroyed without apparent or actual necessity, the destroying person would be liable for trespass. Here, blowing up Surocco's (P) house was necessary to stop the fire. Any delay in blowing up the house to allow Surocco (P) to remove more of his goods would have made blowing up the house too late. Reversed.

Analysis:

A defendant who damages or destroys another's property in the reasonable belief that by doing so he can avoid or minimize an imminent public disaster is protected against all liability. This "public necessity" is in contrast to "private necessity" cases, where the defendant is relieved of liability for trespass, but is still liable for any actual harm caused. In a public necessity case, the defendant must show that public rather than private interests were at stake, that he reasonably believed action was necessary, and that the action he took was indeed reasonable. The individual is immune from liability to induce him to act to protect the public. However, what about the property owner? Why should he be required to bear the cost of protecting the public? In the present case, making Surocco (P) bear the loss may be justified. Surocco's (P) house was about to burn down anyway. The argument could be made that Geary (D) merely hastened a loss that was inevitable. On the other hand, one could argue that because destroying Surocco's (P) house benefitted the public, the public should bear the cost.

■ CASE VOCABULARY

NECESSITAS INDUCIT PRIVILEGIUM QUOD JURA PRIVATA: Necessity gives a preference with regard to private rights.

Vincent v. Lake Erie Transportation Co.

(Dock Owner) v. (Ship Owner)

109 Minn. 456, 124 N.W. 221 (1910)

DAMAGE TO ANOTHER'S PROPERTY DUE TO NECESSITY REQUIRES COMPENSATION

■ INSTANT FACTS During a fierce storm, a steamship was repeatedly thrown against a dock, causing damage to the dock.

■ BLACK LETTER RULE Damage caused to another's property due to necessity requires compensation for the actual harm caused.

■ PROCEDURAL BASIS

Appeal of tort action for damages.

■ FACTS

The steamship Reynolds, owned by the Lake Erie Transportation Co. ("Lake Erie") (D), was moored to Vincent's (P) dock to unload its cargo. A violent storm developed. During the storm, the Reynolds was unable to safely leave the dock. Lake Erie (D) kept the ship tied tightly to the dock and replaced the ropes used to attach it as they became worn. The fierce wind and waves caused the Reynolds to be thrown against the dock, causing damage to it.

■ ISSUE

Does damage to another's property due to a private necessity require compensation?

■ DECISION AND RATIONALE

(O'Brien, J.) Yes. Necessity may require one to take or damage another's property, but compensation is still required. If the Reynolds had entered the harbor during the storm and then been thrown against Vincent's (P) dock, Vincent (P) could not have recovered. However, here, Lake Erie (D) deliberately kept the Reynolds in a position that would damage the dock. Although this was the prudent thing to do, Lake Erie (D) is liable for the damage. Affirmed.

■ DISSENT

(Lewis, J.) One who constructs a dock and contracts with ship owners for docking assumes the risk of damage caused by storms. Therefore, Vincent (P) assumed the risk of damage and Lake Erie (D) is not liable to him.

Analysis:

To invoke the private necessity privilege, a defendant must have been actually threatened or must have reasonably believed that he was threatened with serious and imminent harm. The private necessity privilege differs from the public necessity privilege in that, under the private necessity privilege, the defendant is still liable for any actual harm caused. The *Vincent* case provokes a lot of discussion because the result may be based on different grounds. For example, the opinion suggests that Lake Erie (D) is liable for restitution, rather than for tort damages, because the captain saved the Reynolds at the expense of Vincent's (P) dock.

However, this theory is based on the assumption that the Reynolds was certain to sink or be destroyed if it were cast off into the lake. But because the chance of actual destruction was quite small, the captain protected against only the slight risk of destruction, and, thus, restitution would not be appropriate. The theory that Lake Erie (D) is liable because the captain saved the ship at the expense of the dock also suggests the unlikely result that Lake Erie (D) would not have been liable if, after damaging Vincent's (P) dock, the Reynolds was destroyed anyway.

CHAPTER FIVE

Duty

Stewart v. Motts

Instant Facts: Stewart (P) suffered burns from an explosion which occurred when he poured gasoline into a car's carburetor and Motts (D) turned the key.

Black Letter Rule: There is one standard of care for negligence actions, the standard of reasonable care under the circumstances, which requires a person to exercise care in proportion to the danger of his activity.

Posas v. Horton

Instant Facts: Posas (P) was rear-ended by Horton (D) after Posas (P) stopped in the middle of traffic to avoid hitting a pedestrian who unexpectedly walked into the street pushing a stroller; at Posas's (P) personal injury trial, the judge gave the jury a sudden-emergency instruction, and the jury found in Horton's (D) favor.

Black Letter Rule: In order to be entitled to a sudden-emergency instruction, the proponent of the instruction must show that there is sufficient evidence to support a finding that he or she was suddenly placed in a position of peril through no negligence of his or her own, and in meeting the emergency acted as a reasonably prudent person would in similar circumstances.

Creasy v. Rusk

Instant Facts: Rusk (D), an Alzheimer's patient, kicked Creasy (P), his nurse, while she was trying to put him to bed, injuring her knee and lower back.

Black Letter Rule: In general, the standard of care for adults with mental disabilities is the same standard of reasonable care that governs adults without mental disabilities, with no allowance for their capacity to control or understand the consequences of their actions.

Robinson v. Lindsay

Instant Facts: Anderson, age thirteen, had an accident while driving a snowmobile which caused Robinson (P) to lose the full use of her thumb.

Black Letter Rule: When a child engages in an inherently dangerous activity, or an activity which is normally one for adults only, courts will hold the child to an adult standard of care.

Chaffin v. Brame

Instant Facts: Blinded by undimmed oncoming headlights, Chaffin (P) collided with an unlighted truck left blocking the entire right lane.

Black Letter Rule: A driver's ultimate duty is to exercise reasonable care under the circumstances, which may not always include a duty to be able to stop his vehicle within the range of its lights.

O'Guin v. Bingham County

Instant Facts: Children were crushed by the collapsing wall of a landfill pit and their parents sued the county under the theory of negligence per se.

Black Letter Rule: In order to replace a common law duty of care with a duty of care from a statute or regulation, the statute or regulation must clearly define the required standard of conduct, the statute or regulation must have been intended to prevent the type of harm the defendant's act or omission caused, the plaintiff must be a member of the class of persons the statute or regulation was designed to protect, and the violation must have been the proximate cause of the injury.

Impson v. Structural Metals, Inc.

Instant Facts: A truck driver attempted to pass a car within 100 feet of an intersection in violation of a statute, but hit the car when the car turned left.

Black Letter Rule: When there is evidence that a party has violated a statutory standard of care, the court has no duty to submit the issue of negligence to the jury where there is no evidence of a legally acceptable excuse or justification.

Stewart v. Motts

(Mechanic-Helper) v. (Repair Shop Owner)

539 Pa. 596, 654 A.2d 535 (1995)

THE STANDARD OF CARE FOR NEGLIGENCE ACTIONS IS ALWAYS REASONABLE CARE, BUT THE AMOUNT OF CARE WHICH IS REASONABLE VARIES

■ **INSTANT FACTS** Stewart (P) suffered burns from an explosion which occurred when he poured gasoline into a car's carburetor and Motts (D) turned the key.

■ **BLACK LETTER RULE** There is one standard of care for negligence actions, the standard of reasonable care under the circumstances, which requires a person to exercise care in proportion to the danger of his activity.

■ PROCEDURAL BASIS

Appeal after jury trial of personal injury action for damages.

■ FACTS

Stewart (P) stopped at Motts' (D) auto repair shop and offered to help Motts (D) repair a car's fuel tank. In order to start and move the car with the gas tank unattached, Stewart (P) suggested that he pour gasoline into the carburetor and that Motts (D) turn the ignition key at a given moment. When they did so, the car backfired and caused an explosion which caused Stewart (P) to suffer severe burns. At trial, Stewart (P) asked the judge to instruct the jury that a person must exercise a high degree of care around gasoline because it is a dangerous substance. The judge refused this request, and the jury returned a verdict for Motts (D).

■ ISSUE

Does a heightened standard of "extraordinary care" apply to negligence cases that involve dangerous instrumentalities rather than the standard of reasonable care?

■ DECISION AND RATIONALE

(Montemuro) No. We reaffirm the principle that there is only one standard of care for negligence actions that involve dangerous instrumentalities. This is the standard of reasonable care. As stated in Comment b to the *Restatement (Second) of Torts § 298* [defines reasonable care], "[t]he care required is always reasonable care. The standard never varies, but the care which it is reasonable to require of the actor varies with the danger involved in his act and is proportionate to it. The greater the danger, the greater the care which must be exercised." Our cases have stated that a reasonably prudent person must exercise a higher degree of care when their activity involves a dangerous substance such as gasoline. However, taken in context, these cases only reaffirm the principle that a reasonable man must use an amount of care which is proportionate to the danger of his activity. When we referred to a "higher degree of care," we were not creating a second tier of "extraordinary care." Rather, this language merely stated the common sense conclusion that the use of a dangerous agency requires a reasonably prudent person to exercise more care. Thus, we recognize only one standard of care in negligence actions involving dangerous instrumentalities, the standard of reasonable care under the circumstances. A reasonable man must exercise care in proportion to the danger involved in his act. The trial judge properly instructed the jury that the proper standard of care was reasonable or ordinary care under the circumstances, and that the amount of care this standard requires varies with the circumstances and must be proportionate to the level of danger involved. Affirmed.

Analysis:

A person must establish five elements in a negligence action: (1) a legal duty of care; (2) breach of that duty; (3) actual damages; (4) actual causation; and (5) proximate causation. The standard of care defines the scope of the duty of care. This case discusses the general standard of care for negligence cases, the standard of reasonable care, which is the care that a reasonably prudent person would exercise under the circumstances. In *Stewart* the court adopts the orthodox view that the standard of reasonable care applies to all negligence actions and never varies, although the amount of care which is reasonable does vary with the danger involved and is proportionate to it. As § 298, Comment b of the Restatement explains, the greater the danger, the greater the care that a person must exercise to avoid being negligent. In *Stewart* the court finds that while the standard of care remains that of reasonable care even in cases involving dangerous instrumentalities such as gasoline, the dangerousness of the gasoline requires a reasonably prudent person to exercise more care. When a case involves a dangerous instrumentality, extraordinary care *is* reasonable care.

■ CASE VOCABULARY

CARE: Attention, caution and prudence to perceive and avoid harm to oneself and others.

NEGLIGENCE: Failure to exercise the amount of care that a reasonably prudent person would exercise under the circumstances.

REASONABLE CARE: The care which a reasonably prudent person with similar information and competence would exercise under the circumstances, sometimes referred to as ordinary care or due care.

REASONABLY PRUDENT PERSON: A fictitious person who exercises those qualities of attention, knowledge, intelligence, and judgment which society requires for the protection of his own interests and the interests of others.

Posas v. Horton

(Driver) v. (Rear-ender)

228 P.3d 457 (Nev. 2010)

THE DEFENDANT CANNOT CLAIM A SUDDEN EMERGENCY DEFENSE IF SHE ACTED UNREASONABLY BEFORE THE EMERGENCY AROSE

■ **INSTANT FACTS** Posas (P) was rear-ended by Horton (D) after Posas (P) stopped in the middle of traffic to avoid hitting a pedestrian who unexpectedly walked into the street pushing a stroller; at Posas's (P) personal injury trial, the judge gave the jury a sudden-emergency instruction, and the jury found in Horton's (D) favor.

■ **BLACK LETTER RULE** In order to be entitled to a sudden-emergency instruction, the proponent of the instruction must show that there is sufficient evidence to support a finding that he or she was suddenly placed in a position of peril through no negligence of his or her own, and in meeting the emergency acted as a reasonably prudent person would in similar circumstances.

■ PROCEDURAL BASIS

State appellate court review of the trial court's denial of the plaintiff's motion for a new trial.

■ FACTS

Posas (P) was driving in her car when another woman, who was pushing a stroller, began to cross the street in the middle of traffic. Posas (P) stopped suddenly to avoid hitting the woman. Horton (D) was driving right behind Posas (P) and ran into the rear of her car. Horton (D) did not see the pedestrian crossing the street. She admitted that she was following too close and made a mistake. Posas (P) sued Horton (D) for injuries she sustained in the collision. Despite Posas's (P) objection, the trial court instructed the jury on the sudden-emergency doctrine: A person confronted with a sudden emergency that he does not create, and who acts according to his best judgment or, because of insufficient time to form a judgment, fails to act in the most judicious manner is not guilty of negligence if he exercises the care of a reasonably prudent person in like circumstances. The jury returned a verdict in favor of Horton (D). Posas (P) moved for a new trial, which the district court denied. Posas (P) appealed.

■ ISSUE

Did the trial court err in giving the sudden-emergency instruction to the jury?

■ DECISION AND RATIONALE

(Douglas, J.) Yes. In order to be entitled to a sudden-emergency instruction, the proponent of the instruction must show that there is sufficient evidence to support a finding that he or she was suddenly placed in a position of peril through no negligence of his or her own, and in meeting the emergency acted as a reasonably prudent person would in similar circumstances.

The fact that the actor is not negligent after the emergency arises does not preclude his liability for tortious conduct that produced the emergency. Here, a sudden emergency may have been created by the pedestrian, but Horton (D) herself admitted she was following too close. Horton cannot therefore claim she was confronted by a sudden emergency. She placed herself in a position of peril through her own negligence. Some emergencies should be anticipated, and the actor must be prepared to meet them when she engages in activity in which they are likely to arise. Any driver of an automobile must be prepared for the sudden appearance of obstacles and persons in the highway, and of other vehicles at intersections. The instruction in this case tended to mislead or confuse the jury, so the error was prejudicial. Accordingly, we reverse the district court and remand for a new trial.

Analysis:

The types of emergencies that courts have found to warrant a sudden-emergency instruction include dust clouds, a sudden blocking of the road, the sudden swerving of another vehicle, blinding lights, a dense patch of fog, unexpected brake failure, and a stopped vehicle with no emergency flashers activated at night. In the present case the court was not so much saying that a pedestrian's sudden appearance in the middle of heavy traffic did not create a sudden emergency, although there is a suggestion to that effect; the more salient point here was the defendant's admission that she was following too close and that she made a mistake. It was her conduct before the ostensibly sudden emergency that subjected her to liability, not how she conducted herself once the situation—sudden emergency or not—arose.

■ CASE VOCABULARY

PREJUDICIAL ERROR: Error by a court that detrimentally affects the legal rights of a party and that, if uncorrected, would result in a miscarriage of justice. This may be grounds for a new trial or for a reversal of a decision of a lower court. Same as "reversible error."

Creasy v. Rusk

(Nurse) v. (Alzheimer's Patient)

730 N.E.2d 659 (Ind.2000)

THE LAW GENERALLY HOLDS INSANE PEOPLE TO THE STANDARD OF A REASONABLE PERSON

■ INSTANT FACTS Rusk (D), an Alzheimer's patient, kicked Creasy (P), his nurse, while she was trying to put him to bed, injuring her knee and lower back.

■ BLACK LETTER RULE In general, the standard of care for adults with mental disabilities is the same standard of reasonable care that governs adults without mental disabilities, with no allowance for their capacity to control or understand the consequences of their actions.

■ PROCEDURAL BASIS

Appeal after Court of Appeals reversed summary judgment granted in a negligence action for damages.

■ FACTS

Rusk (D) was an Alzheimer's patient at a healthcare center for three years, during which time he experienced periods of anxiousness, confusion, and agitation. Rusk (D) was often combative and aggressive and would hit staff members when they tried to care for him. On one occasion when Creasy (P) and another nurse tried to put Rusk (D) to bed, he was very agitated and combative, and was hitting and kicking wildly. Creasy (P) alleged that Rusk (D) kicked her several times and injured her knee and lower back. Rusk (D) moved for summary judgment, and the trial court granted the motion. Creasy (P) appealed and the Court of Appeals reversed, holding that a person's mental capacity must be factored into the determination of whether a legal duty exists.

■ ISSUE

Does the general duty of care for adults with mental disabilities take those mental disabilities into account?

■ DECISION AND RATIONALE

(Sullivan) No. The generally accepted rule, set forth in the *Restatement (Second) of Torts § 283B* [standard of care for the mentally disabled], is that a mental disability does not excuse a person from liability for conduct which does not conform to the standard of reasonable care under the circumstances. Courts commonly hold the mentally disabled liable for their intentional and negligent torts, with no allowance for their level of intelligence, excitability, proneness to accident, or other mental or emotional disabilities. Legal scholars recognize that it is impossible to ascribe any level of fault to a person who is unable to control his or her own actions through any exercise of reason. However, they nonetheless hold the mentally disabled to the general standard of care for several policy reasons: (1) to allocate losses between two innocent parties to the party who caused the loss; (2) to encourage those responsible for the mentally disabled to prevent harm; (3) to discourage faking a mental disability to avoid liability; (4) to avoid difficulties in assessing the significance of a person's mental disability; and (5) to force the mentally disabled to pay for any damage they cause if they "are to live in the world" rather than in an institution. While the Restatement rule may be based on a policy of institutionalizing the mentally disabled, modern policy now favors community treatment and integration into the least restrictive environment, and reflects a determination to treat the mentally disabled the same way as non-disabled persons. However, both of these policies yield to the same common law rule that holds adults with mental disabilities to the same duty of care that the law requires of those without mental disabilities. Thus, the law generally holds a person with mental disabilities to the standard of a reasonable person under the circumstances, regardless of the person's capacity to control or understand the consequences of his or her actions. Notwithstanding this general rule, an Alzheimer's patient owes no duty of care to a person who is employed to care for him and who knows of the combativeness his disease causes. Rusk (D), therefore, is not liable in this case. The Court of Appeals opinion is vacated and the trial court's order granting summary judgment is affirmed.

Analysis:

In this case the court adopts the prevailing rule, expressed in § 283B of the Restatement, that the general duty of care for adults with mental deficiencies is the same as that for adults without mental deficiencies. In addition to describing the general rule, *Creasy* also provides an example of an exception to that rule: a person who is institutionalized with a mental disability and who does not have the capacity to control or appreciate his actions cannot be liable in negligence for injuries to caretakers employed by that institution. As the dissent in the appellate court concluded, "no duty to refrain from violent conduct arises on the part of a person who has no capacity to control it to one who is specifically employed to do just that." Thus, although Rusk (D), as a mentally disabled person, had a general duty to conform to the standard of reasonable care, he did not owe a duty of care to Creasy (P), an employee of the institution that he entered precisely because of his incapacity to control himself.

Robinson v. Lindsay

(Accident Victim) v. (Not Stated)

92 Wn.2d 410, 598 P.2d 392 (1979)

THE REASONABLE CARE STANDARD TAKES ACCOUNT OF A CHILD'S ABILITIES EXCEPT WHEN THE CHILD ENGAGES IN ADULT ACTIVITIES

■ **INSTANT FACTS** Anderson, age thirteen, had an accident while driving a snowmobile which caused Robinson (P) to lose the full use of her thumb.

■ **BLACK LETTER RULE** When a child engages in an inherently dangerous activity, or an activity which is normally one for adults only, courts will hold the child to an adult standard of care.

■ PROCEDURAL BASIS

Appeal of order granting new trial in personal injury action for damages.

■ FACTS

Anderson, thirteen years old, had an accident while driving a snowmobile which caused Robinson (P), eleven years old, to lose the full use of her thumb. The trial court instructed the jury that a child's duty is to exercise the same care that a reasonably careful child of the same age, intelligence, maturity, training and experience would exercise under the circumstances. Robinson (P) objected to the court's instructing the jury on this standard rather than the adult standard of care. After a jury verdict in favor of Anderson, the trial court ordered a new trial because it believed it should have instructed the jury as to the adult standard of care.

■ ISSUE

Must a child who participates in an inherently dangerous activity conform to the adult standard of care?

■ DECISION AND RATIONALE

(Utter) Yes. The jury instruction the trial court used fairly reflects current state law. In the past we have always compared a child's conduct to that expected of a reasonably careful child of the same age, intelligence, maturity, training and experience. Here we consider for the first time a child's liability for injuries that result from his or her operation of a motor vehicle or participation in an inherently dangerous activity. Because of the apparent injustice that would occur if a child engaged in such activity could escape liability by arguing that other similarly situated children would not have been more careful, courts in other jurisdictions have created an exception to the special child standard of care. Some courts have couched this exception in terms of children engaging in activities which are normally only for adults. We believe the better rationale is to hold a child to an adult standard of care whenever the child engages in inherently dangerous activity, such as operating a powerful mechanical vehicle. This rule allows children to be children, but discourages immature individuals from engaging in inherently dangerous activities. [Are "immature people" generally concerned about potential legal liability?] Children would not be held to an adult standard of care for traditional childhood activities, which generally do not cause grave danger to the child or others when a child exercises less than the amount of care expected of an adult. Other courts have emphasized the hazard to the public without this exception, particularly with respect to the operation of motor vehicles. Courts have applied the adult standard in cases in which children operated motor vehicles including motor boats, tractors, motorcycles, minibikes and automobiles. Operating a snowmobile likewise requires adult care and competence. Studies show that snowmobile accidents claim hundreds of casualties each year, and that these accidents occur more frequently among inexperienced operators. Because Anderson was operating a powerful motor vehicle, we hold him to the adult standard of care. Affirmed.

Analysis:

The standard of care for children, set forth in the Restatement (Second) of Torts § 283A, is that of a reasonable person of like age, intelligence, and experience under like circumstances. The law recognizes that the immaturity of children, particularly very young children, may make them incapable of exercising the judgment, intelligence, knowledge, experience, and prudence that the reasonable care standard requires of adults, and thus holds them to a standard of care proportionate to their capacity. Very young children may be utterly incapable of exercising any of the qualities necessary for avoiding a particular danger, while older children may be just as capable as adults. This accommodation for children reflects society's interest in their welfare and protection. Childhood is a circumstance that plainly makes certain precautions impossible, and there is little need for concern about faking childhood to avoid tort liability.

■ CASE VOCABULARY

EXCEPT: To make a formal objection during trial to a judge's ruling to show a higher court on appeal that the lawyer disagreed with it.

Chaffin v. Brame

(Night Driver) v. (Truck Owner)

233 N.C. 377, 64 S.E.2d 276 (1951)

COURT DECLINES TO USE THE "RANGE OF LIGHTS" RULE TO FIND NEGLIGENCE AS A MATTER OF LAW

■ **INSTANT FACTS** Blinded by undimmed oncoming headlights, Chaffin (P) collided with an unlighted truck left blocking the entire right lane.

■ **BLACK LETTER RULE** A driver's ultimate duty is to exercise reasonable care under the circumstances, which may not always include a duty to be able to stop his vehicle within the range of its lights.

■ PROCEDURAL BASIS

Appeal after jury trial of negligence action for damages.

■ FACTS

Chaffin (P) was driving along a highway at night when another car approached without dimming his headlights. Blinded by the lights, Chaffin (P) ran into Brame's (D) truck, which was unlighted and blocking the entire right lane. Brame (D) argued that Chaffin (P) was guilty of contributory negligence as a matter of law, but the trial court let the case go to the jury, and the jury returned a verdict for Chaffin (P). Citing *Marshall v. Southern Railway Co.* [driver must keep his vehicle under such control at night as to be able to stop within the range of its lights], Brame (D) argues that it is negligence as a matter of law to drive an automobile on a public highway in the dark at such a speed that the driver cannot stop the automobile within the distance that objects are visible ahead of it.

■ ISSUE

Does a driver have a duty to always keep his vehicle under such control at night as to be able to stop within the range of its lights?

■ DECISION AND RATIONALE

(Ervin) No. The application of *Marshall's* rule to particular cases is one of the most difficult tasks of trial law. Enhancing this difficulty, judges and attorneys tend to regard this rule as a rule of thumb, and not as a formula for applying to a recurring factual situation the principle. The purpose of this rule was to enforce the concept that courts should not permit an injured person to shift his loss to another when his loss results in part from his own failure to see the obvious. However, the rule does not require night drivers to be infallible, and it does not prevent them from recovering compensation for injuries caused by collisions with unlighted obstructions in the highway. Courts must decide each case on its own facts because the true and ultimate test is what a reasonably prudent person would do in those circumstances. The *Marshall* line of cases simply enforces the legal duty every person has to exercise ordinary care for his own safety. Viewing the evidence in the light most favorable to Chaffin (P), we may reasonably infer that Chaffin (P) was keeping a proper lookout and driving at a reasonable speed. We may also infer that when he was partially and temporarily blinded by oncoming headlights, Chaffin (P) exercised due care in reducing his speed and proceeding with extreme caution rather than stopping his car because he reasonably assumed that the oncoming driver would obey the law and dim his lights, and thus restore his normal vision. Chaffin (P) had no reason to expect a truck to be standing on the highway with no warning lights, and did all he could to avoid the truck once it became visible. Therefore, we cannot hold Chaffin (P) guilty of contributory negligence as a matter of law. No error.

Analysis:

In *Chaffin* the court refused to apply *Marshall's* "range of lights" rule as a rule of law, which would have required a directed verdict. Instead, the court construed it as a rule of thumb to guide application of the reasonable care standard in similar factual situations. In *Marshall,* a driver who was blinded by oncoming high beams ran into a railroad trestle, and the court held him negligent as a matter of law. The court stated that it was a general rule of law that a driver must exercise ordinary care, and that this duty includes a duty to keep his vehicle under such control at night as to be able to stop within the range of its lights. Similarly, Chaffin (P), also facing blinding oncoming lights, ran into Brame's (D) unlighted truck, which he left parked on the highway. The jury returned a verdict for Chaffin (P). Relying on *Marshall's* "range of lights" rule, Brame (D) argued that the case should not have gone to the jury because Chaffin (P) was contributorily negligent as a matter of law. The court explained that the "range of lights" rule only enforces a driver's duty of reasonable care, and that ultimately each case must be decided on its own facts. Because the court found that on the facts of this case it was reasonable to infer that Chaffin (P) exercised due care, reasonable jurors might find that he was not negligent, and the court thus could not hold him contributorily negligent as a matter of law.

■ CASE VOCABULARY

CONTRIBUTORY NEGLIGENCE: The now largely abolished doctrine that if a person's negligence was a partial cause of his injury, it bars his recovery of damages from another whose negligence also was a partial cause of his injury, regardless of the relative fault of the parties.

NEGLIGENCE AS A MATTER OF LAW: A judge's determination of negligence based on evidence of conduct that is so clearly below the level of care a reasonable person would exercise that a jury could not reasonably find otherwise.

SHIBBOLETH: A saying which those who hold a particular belief use, but which others usually regard as empty of real meaning.

O'Guin v. Bingham County

(Parents of Injured Children) v. (Operator of Landfill)

142 Idaho 49, 122 P.3d 308 (2005)

VIOLATION OF A STATUTE MAY BE NEGLIGENCE PER SE

■ **INSTANT FACTS** Children were crushed by the collapsing wall of a landfill pit and their parents sued the county under the theory of negligence per se.

■ **BLACK LETTER RULE** In order to replace a common law duty of care with a duty of care from a statute or regulation, the statute or regulation must clearly define the required standard of conduct, the statute or regulation must have been intended to prevent the type of harm the defendant's act or omission caused, the plaintiff must be a member of the class of persons the statute or regulation was designed to protect, and the violation must have been the proximate cause of the injury.

■ PROCEDURAL BASIS

State supreme court consideration of the lower court's grant of summary judgment in the defendants' favor.

■ FACTS

Two of the O'Guins' (P) children were killed while playing at the county landfill when a section of the pit wall collapsed and crushed them. They had entered the landfill after passing through an unlocked gate at the back of their schoolyard and crossing an empty, privately owned field. The landfill was closed on the day in question and no employees were present. The O'Guins (P) sued the county (D) and others for negligence, claiming that the county (D) was negligent per se based on its violations of an Idaho statute and a federal regulation regarding landfills. The trial court granted the county's motion for summary judgment and the O'Guins (P) appealed.

■ ISSUE

Did the trial court properly grant summary judgment in the defendants' favor on the plaintiffs' negligence per se claim?

■ DECISION AND RATIONALE

(Trout, J.) No. In order to replace a common law duty of care with a duty of care from a statute or regulation, the statute or regulation must clearly define the required standard of conduct, the statute or regulation must have been intended to prevent the type of harm the defendant's act or omission caused, the plaintiff must be a member of the class of persons the statute or regulation was designed to protect, and the violation must have been the proximate cause of the injury. Here, the laws clearly define the county's (D) standard of conduct by requiring the county (D) to fence or otherwise block access to the landfill when an attendant is not on duty. The county (D) failed to meet this standard. The state statute indicates that it was intended to protect human health and safety, and the relevant section from the Code of Federal Regulations states the same thing. Clearly, the O'Guin children were in the class of unauthorized persons who could gain access to an unsecured landfill that the statute and regulation intended to protect. And finally, there is at least a question of fact as to whether the county's (D) violations led to the children's death. Accordingly, the court improperly granted summary judgment in the defendants' favor. Reversed.

■ DISSENT

(Eismann, J.) The statute and regulation considered in this case were intended to prevent illegal dumping of wastes that are dangerous to human health, not unauthorized access by pedestrians who may injure themselves.

Analysis:

The court explains in this case that the effect of establishing negligence per se through the violation of a statute is to conclusively establish the first two elements of a cause of action in negligence: that is, the elements of duty and breach are effectively taken away from the jury. The application of negligence per se thus lessens the plaintiff's burden only on the issue of the defendant's departure from the standard of conduct required of a reasonable person. As this opinion demonstrates, however, the plaintiff is not entirely relieved of his or her burden, and in fact negligence per se itself requires demonstration of the four requisite elements.

■ CASE VOCABULARY

NEGLIGENCE PER SE: Negligence established as a matter of law, so that breach of the duty is not a jury question. Negligence per se usually arises from a statutory violation.

Impson v. Structural Metals, Inc.

(Car Driver) v. (Truck Driver)

487 S.W.2d 694 (Tex.1972)

A LEGALLY SUFFICIENT EXCUSE MAY ALSO PERMIT A PARTY TO AVOID THE NEGLIGENCE PER SE DOCTRINE

■ **INSTANT FACTS** A truck driver attempted to pass a car within 100 feet of an intersection in violation of a statute, but hit the car when the car turned left.

■ **BLACK LETTER RULE** When there is evidence that a party has violated a statutory standard of care, the court has no duty to submit the issue of negligence to the jury where there is no evidence of a legally acceptable excuse or justification.

■ PROCEDURAL BASIS

Appeal after judgment in personal injury and wrongful death actions for damages.

■ FACTS

The driver of Structural Metals, Inc.'s (Structural Metals) (D) truck attempted to pass Impson's (P) car within 100 feet of an intersection, but the car turned left and the truck hit the car. Because a statute prohibits passing within 100 feet of an intersection, the trial judge found negligence as a matter of law and entered judgment for Impson (P). Structural Metals (D) argued that the court should excuse its driver's violation because he forgot the existence of the intersection; the sign marking it was small; there were no "no passing" lines on the road; and the driver was watching the car, which was partly off the road on the right, rather than looking for intersection signs. The Court of Appeals held that a jury must decide the negligence issue because Structural Metals (D) offered some excuses.

■ ISSUE

When there is evidence that a party has violated a statutory standard of care, but the party offers evidence of some excuse, must the court submit the issue of negligence to the jury?

■ DECISION AND RATIONALE

(Greenhill) No. Not all excuses or justifications are legally acceptable. In other cases we have accepted excuses including a tire blowout, unavoidable skidding on wet streets, and the impossibility of stopping a truck within the prescribed distance from a railroad track. However, we did not address the legal sufficiency of the excuse in any of these cases. The *Restatement of Torts (Second) § 288A* [lists some categories of excuses for statutory violations] states that an excused violation of a statute is not negligence. Although not exclusive, this section lists some excusable situations, including: (a) incapacity, such as blindness, a heart attack, or young age; (b) reasonable lack of knowledge of the need for compliance, such as when a tail light unexpectedly goes out without the driver's knowledge; (c) inability after reasonable diligence to comply, such as when it is impossible to stop a truck within a certain distance; (d) an emergency not due to the person's own misconduct, such as an unexpected tire blowout or brake failure; and (e) a greater risk of harm from compliance, such as when a law requires pedestrians to walk on one side of the road, but circumstances make this more dangerous than walking on the other side. We approve the Restatement's general treatment of legally acceptable excuses. However, the excuses Structural Metals (D) offered for its driver's violation all fell within the realm of ordinary care. The driver acted deliberately, with knowledge of the law and at least notice of the presence of the intersection. There was no impossibility, emergency, incapacity, or greater risk of harm from compliance with the law to excuse the driver's violation. Because there was no evidence offered of any legally acceptable excuse or justification, this was, in law, an unexcused violation which, when coupled with the jury's finding of proximate cause, entitled Impson (P) to judgment. Court of Appeals judgment reversed, trial court judgment affirmed.

Analysis:

This case discusses some of the categories of situations that courts usually find legally sufficient to excuse the violation of a standard-setting statute. In *Impson,* Structural Metals' (D) driver violated a statute that prohibited passing within 100 feet of an intersection and collided with a car turning left into the intersection. The trial court did not submit the issue of negligence to the jury. The court of appeals agreed that the statutory violation constituted negligence per se, but held that because Structural Metals (D) offered evidence of justification or excuse, the trial court had a duty to submit the issue of negligence to the jury. The Supreme Court of Texas disagreed. Because it found that none of the excuses Structural Metals (D) offered was legally acceptable, it held that the trial court was correct in deciding that the violation was unexcused as a matter of law, and that the issue of negligence therefore did not require submission to the jury. In *Impson,* the court explained that mere ordinary care does not necessarily constitute a legally acceptable excuse.

■ CASE VOCABULARY

EXCUSE: A reason for exemption from a duty of care.

INCAPACITY: A lack of physical or mental abilities that makes a person unable to exercise ordinary care.

JUSTIFICATION: A legally sufficient reason for conduct that frees a person from liability where his conduct would otherwise be tortious.

CHAPTER SIX

Breach of Duty

Pipher v. Parsell

Instant Facts: When three sixteen-year-olds were driving in a pick-up, the passenger-side rider unexpectedly grabbed the wheel two times, and the second time it happened the truck left the road and Pipher (P) was injured.

Black Letter Rule: When the actions of a passenger that cause an accident are not foreseeable, there is no negligence attributable to the driver, but when the actions of a passenger that interfere with the driver's safe operation of his vehicle are foreseeable, the failure to prevent such conduct may be a breach of the driver's duty to other passengers or the public.

Indiana Consolidated Insurance Co. v. Mathew

Instant Facts: Mr. Mathew (D) started his brother's lawnmower to cut his brother's lawn and the lawnmower caught fire damaging his brother's garage.

Black Letter Rule: The standard of care to adjudge negligent conduct is whether a person exercised the duty to use care that an ordinary prudent person would exercise under the same or similar circumstances.

Stinnett v. Buchele

Instant Facts: Employee hired to paint a barn roof falls from the roof while painting it and injuries himself.

Black Letter Rule: An employer does not breach a duty to its employee to provide a reasonably safe place to work and reasonably safe tools for doing the work when the employee injures himself during the scope of his employment and the employee's knowledge of the dangers to be incurred while working is equal to or exceeds the knowledge of the employer.

Bernier v. Boston Edison Co.

Instant Facts: Mr. Bernier (P) was injured when an electric light pole fell on him after it was struck by an automobile that was involved in a minor traffic accident.

Black Letter Rule: Failure to take reasonable steps to prevent unreasonable risk of injury from reasonably foreseeable accidents is negligence.

United States v. Carroll Towing Co.

Instant Facts: A barge, without a bargee on broad broke adrift, was carried by wind into a tanker whose propeller broke a hole in barge's bottom, and barge lost its cargo and sank.

Black Letter Rule: Absence a reasonable excuse, barge owner's failure to take reasonable steps to prevent unreasonable risk of barge breaking away in busy wartime harbor by manning barge with bargee is negligence.

Santiago v. First Student, Inc.

Instant Facts: Santiago (P) was injured while riding a bus operated by First Student, Inc. (D).

Black Letter Rule: A plaintiff bears the burden of proving a defendant's actions were the proximate cause of her injuries.

Upchurch v. Rotenberry

Instant Facts: Automobile passenger is injured when automobile strikes a tree after automobile driver attempts to avoid an animal on the roadway.

Black Letter Rule: It is the duty of the jury to determine whether a defendant in a negligence case exercised reasonable care under the circumstances.

Thoma v. Cracker Barrel Old Country Store, Inc.

Instant Facts: Restaurant patron sustains injuries from a fall in a restaurant.

Black Letter Rule: Proof of negligent conduct in a slip and fall case requires a finding by the jury that the owner of or employees at the premises either created a dangerous condition or had knowledge of the dangerous condition that lead to the fall and resulting injuries.

The T. J. Hooper

Instant Facts: Large barge filled with coal and the tugboat which was its tow were lost at sea during heavy weather.

Black Letter Rule: Notwithstanding a custom of usage or the lack thereof, there are precautions so imperative that even their universal disregard will not excuse their omission.

Byrne v. Boadle

Instant Facts: Barrel of flour falls on a man as he passes a flour shop.

Black Letter Rule: Under certain circumstances, the fact that an accident occurred can support an inference or presumption of negligence.

Warren v. Jeffries

Instant Facts: Six-year old boy jumped out of a car when it begins to roll backward. When the boy jumped he fell, and the front wheel of the car rolled over his chest, killing him.

Black Letter Rule: Pure speculation is not a basis for applying the doctrine of res ipsa loquitur.

Giles v. City of New Haven

Instant Facts: Elevator operator is injured when chain of elevator she was operating became hooked on the rail bracket in the elevator shaft.

Black Letter Rule: Use by the plaintiff of the instrumentality that caused her injury does not preclude a finding that the defendant had control of the instrumentality.

Pipher v. Parsell

(Injured Passenger) v. (Driver)

930 A.2d 890 (Del. 2007)

A DRIVER MAY FACE LIABILITY WHEN A PASSENGER'S FORESEEABLE ACTIONS CAUSE AN ACCIDENT

■ **INSTANT FACTS** When three sixteen-year-olds were driving in a pick-up, the passenger-side rider unexpectedly grabbed the wheel two times, and the second time it happened the truck left the road and Pipher (P) was injured.

■ **BLACK LETTER RULE** When the actions of a passenger that cause an accident are not foreseeable, there is no negligence attributable to the driver, but when the actions of a passenger that interfere with the driver's safe operation of his vehicle are foreseeable, the failure to prevent such conduct may be a breach of the driver's duty to other passengers or the public.

■ PROCEDURAL BASIS

State supreme court review of a superior court holding in favor of the defendant.

■ FACTS

Pipher (P), Parsell (D), and another were all riding in the front seat of a pick-up truck. Parsell (D) was driving and Pipher (P) was sitting in the middle. All three were sixteen years old at the time. All of a sudden, the third passenger reached over and grabbed the steering wheel, causing the truck to veer onto the shoulder. Parsell (D) was shocked, he said, but he did nothing the make sure it did not happen again. Pipher (P) actually recalled that the two boys just laughed it off. About thirty seconds later, the passenger grabbed the wheel again, and this time Parsell (D) lost control of the vehicle. The truck left the road, ultimately hitting a tree, and Pipher (P) was injured. She sued Parsell (D). At trial, Parsell (D) admitted he probably could have done more to prevent the second incident, but the trial judge concluded he had no duty to do so. The court entered judgment as a matter of law in Parsell's (D) favor.

■ ISSUE

Did the trial court err when it ruled, as a matter of law, that the defendant driver was not negligent?

■ DECISION AND RATIONALE

(Holland, J.) Yes. When the actions of a passenger that cause an accident are not foreseeable, there is no negligence attributable to the driver, but when the actions of a passenger that interfere with the driver's safe operation of his vehicle are foreseeable, the failure to prevent such conduct may be a breach of the driver's duty to other passengers or the public. A driver owes a duty of care to his passengers because it is foreseeable that they may be injured if, through inattention or otherwise, the driver involves the car he is operating in a collision. In this case, a reasonable jury could have found that Parsell (D) breached his duty to protect Pipher (P) from the actions of the third passenger by preventing him from grabbing the steering wheel a second time. This case involves factual determinations that should have been submitted to the jury. Reversed and remanded.

Analysis:

The case excerpt does not consider whether the passenger who arguably caused the accident may be held liable in this case. Although, statistically speaking, it is more likely a negligent driver will be held liable, under circumstances much like those presented here other courts have held the negligent passenger accountable. *See, e.g., Petway v. McLeod,* 171 S.E. 225 (Ga. Ct. App. 1933) (holding that the jury could infer that the conduct of a passenger in grabbing the steering wheel and swerving the vehicle to one side was grossly negligent); *White v. Parks,* 140 A. 70 (Md. 1928) (affirming judgment for the driver and passenger plaintiffs against a salesperson-passenger who seized the steering wheel and jerked it from the driver's control); *Brainerd v. Stearns,* 284 P. 348 (Wash. 1930) (affirming judgment for the mother-in-law passenger against her son-in-law passenger, who struggled with the driver for control of the car and turned it toward the ravine into which it plunged).

■ CASE VOCABULARY

JUDGMENT AS A MATTER OF LAW: A judgment rendered during a jury trial—either before or after the jury's verdict—against a party on a given issue when there is no legally sufficient basis for a jury to find for that party on that issue. In federal practice, the term *judgment as a matter of law* has replaced both the directed verdict and the judgment notwithstanding the verdict.

Indiana Consolidated Insurance Co. v. Mathew

(Insurance Co. Seeking Damages) v. (Non-Negligent Defendant)

402 N.E.2d 1000 (Ind.App.1980)

INDIANA APPEALS COURT FINDS THAT APPELLEE'S CONDUCT WHILE OPERATING A LAWNMOWER WAS NOT NEGLIGENT

■ **INSTANT FACTS** Mr. Mathew (D) started his brother's lawnmower to cut his brother's lawn and the lawnmower caught fire damaging his brother's garage.

■ **BLACK LETTER RULE** The standard of care to adjudge negligent conduct is whether a person exercised the duty to use care that an ordinary prudent person would exercise under the same or similar circumstances.

■ PROCEDURAL BASIS

Appeal from trial court finding that Mr. Mathew (D) did not act negligently.

■ FACTS

Mr. Mathew (D) and his brother took turns mowing their lawns. When Mr. Mathew's (D) brother was out of town, Mr. Mathew (D) decided to mow his brother's lawn. Mr. Mathew (D) went to his brother's garage to retrieve a twelve-horsepower Toro riding lawnmower to mow the lawn. The lawnmower was in good working condition. Noticing that the lawnmower was low on fuel, Mr. Mathew (D) filled the lawnmower's fuel tank to three-fourths of its capacity. Twenty minutes later, Mr. Mathew (D) returned to the garage and started the lawnmower. Upon starting the lawnmower, Mr. Mathew (D) noticed a flame in the engine area, and he immediately shut the engine off. When Mr. Mathew (D) opened the hood of the lawnmower to investigate, he observed a flame four to five inches tall under the fuel tank. Mr. Mathew (D) then attempted to extinguish the flame with a towel; however, he was unsuccessful. Failing to find a means to extinguish the flame and realizing the lawnmower was spewing fuel, Mr. Mathew (D) left the garage to call the fire department. When he returned, he found the garage engulfed in flames. Indiana Consolidated Insurance Co. (Consolidated) (P), the insurer of Mr. Mathew's (D) brother's garage, brought suit against Mr. Mathew (D) alleging that Mr. Mathew (D) breached a duty owed to his brother to exercise due care in starting the lawnmower. The trial court found that Mr. Mathew (D) had not acted negligently, and Consolidated (P) appealed.

■ ISSUE

Is the standard of care to adjudge negligent conduct whether a person exercised the duty to use care that an ordinary prudent person would exercise under the same or similar circumstances?

■ DECISION AND RATIONALE

(Hoffman) Yes. The standard of care to adjudge negligent conduct is whether a person exercised the duty to use care that an ordinary prudent person would exercise under the same or similar circumstances. The trial court record shows that Mr. Mathew (D) added fuel to the lawnmower's fuel tank in a careful manner. He did not fill the fuel tank to its capacity, nor did he spill any fuel while inserting it into the tank. Under the circumstances, Mr. Mathew (D) did not breach a duty to exercise care that an ordinary prudent person would exercise. Consolidated's (P) contention that Mr. Mathew's (D) conduct of starting the lawnmower in the garage is negligent conduct is without merit. Garages are designed to permit the starting of motorized vehicles and are commonly used for such purposes. It was not reasonably foreseeable that a lawnmower in good working condition would catch fire. Therefore, Mr. Mathew (D) was not negligent when he started the lawnmower in the garage. Consolidated's (P) contention that Mr. Mathew (D) was negligent because he failed to push the flaming lawnmower out of the garage also lacks merit. The flaming lawnmower was spewing fuel, and Mr. Mathew (D) feared for his safety as the fuel tank could explode. Confronted with an emergency, Mr. Mathew (D) chose to call the fire department. Since the law values human life more than it values property, Mr. Mathew's (D) conduct under the circumstance was reasonable. Judgment affirmed.

Analysis:

Negligence is careless conduct under the circumstances. Mr. Mathew (D) did not fill the lawnmower's fuel tank in a careless manner. Since people regularly start lawnmowers in garages, Mr. Mathew (D) was not careless when he started his brother's lawnmower in his brother's garage. Additionally, he was not careless when he called the fire department because he could not extinguish the flames and feared the fuel tank would explode. Under these circumstances, Mr. Mathew (D) did not owe a duty to risk his life to save his brother's garage. Since Mr. Mathew's (D) conduct was not careless under any of the circumstances, he did not act negligently.

Stinnett v. Buchele

(Painter/Employee) v. (Employer)

598 S.W.2d 469 (Ky.App.1980)

EMPLOYEE'S KNOWLEDGE MAY VITIATE CLAIM THAT EMPLOYER BREACHED A DUTY OWED TO THE EMPLOYEE

■ **INSTANT FACTS** Employee hired to paint a barn roof falls from the roof while painting it and injuries himself.

■ **BLACK LETTER RULE** An employer does not breach a duty to its employee to provide a reasonably safe place to work and reasonably safe tools for doing the work when the employee injures himself during the scope of his employment and the employee's knowledge of the dangers to be incurred while working is equal to or exceeds the knowledge of the employer.

■ PROCEDURAL BASIS

Negligence plaintiff appeals lower court summary judgment order.

■ FACTS

Mr. Buchele (D), a practicing physician, hired Mr. Stinnett (P) to paint his barn roof and nail down its edges. Mr. Stinnett (P) had been in the painting business for two years and had painted numerous barns before his employment with Mr. Buchele (D). Mr. Stinnett (P) fell from the barn roof while painting it and severely injured himself. Mr. Buchele (D) provided the coating for the roof, but he did not provide a safety net. Mr. Stinnett (P) did not supply his own safety net, nor did he request a safety net from Mr. Buchele (D). Mr. Stinnett (P) brought a negligence suit against Mr. Buchele (D). The trial court granted summary judgment for Mr. Buchele (D) as it found that Mr. Buchele (D) had not acted in a negligent manner. Mr. Stinnett (P) appealed.

■ ISSUE

Does an employer breach a duty to its employee to provide a reasonably safe place to work and reasonably safe tools for doing the work when the employee injures himself during the scope of his employment and the employee's knowledge of the dangers to be incurred while working is equal to or exceeds the knowledge of the employer?

■ DECISION AND RATIONALE

(Oakes) No. An employer does not breach a duty to its employee to provide a reasonably safe place to work and reasonably safe tools for doing the work when the employee injures himself during the scope of his employment and the employee's knowledge of the dangers to be incurred while working is equal to or exceeds the knowledge of the employer. Mr. Stinnett (P) filed a workmen's compensation claim for his injuries, and the Workmen's Compensation Board denied that claim. He now contends that Mr. Buchele (D) was negligent for failing to comply with occupational and health regulations and for failure to provide a safe place to work. This Court does not find any evidence that Mr. Buchele (D) was negligent in failing to provide to Mr. Stinnett (P) a safe place to work. While an employer has a duty to provide a reasonably safe place to work and reasonably safe tools with which to work, that duty does not extend to the impossible duty of providing an absolutely safe workplace and tools. Even though painting a barn may be dangerous, this Court does not find that Mr. Buchele (D) is liable for negligence because he asked Mr. Stinnett (P) to paint his barn roof. Further, an employer's duty to provide safety devices rests upon the assumption that the employer has more knowledge than the employee. Liability ceases to exist when the employee's knowledge of the dangers to be incurred is equal to the knowledge of the employer. Since Mr. Stinnett (P) is an experienced barn painter, this court does not find that Mr. Buchele (D), as an employer, breached a duty owed to Mr. Stinnett (P). As there is no evidence of negligence to submit to the jury, this Court affirms the trial court's judgment.

Analysis:

Negligence is careless conduct under the circumstances. The circumstances in the instant case do not support a finding of negligence, because Mr. Stinnett (P) is an experienced painter. He knows the danger involved with painting a barn. On the other hand, Mr. Buchele (D) is a physician. There is no evidence that Mr. Buchele's (D) barn painting knowledge equals or exceeds Mr. Stinnett's (P). Therefore, Mr. Buchele (D) was not careless under the circumstances. Contributory negligence on the part of the plaintiff and lack of negligence on the part of the defendant are easily confused in these circumstances. The issue often arises in "open and obvious danger" cases, when the defendant creates a condition that will be dangerous to anyone who ignores it but that is safe enough when people pay reasonable attention.

Bernier v. Boston Edison Co.

(Person Injured When a Utility Pole Fell on Him) v. (Designer/Maintainer of Utility Pole)

380 Mass. 372, 403 N.E.2d 391 (1980)

SUPREME JUDICIAL COURT OF MASSACHUSETTS FINDS THAT PERSONS HAVE A DUTY TO REASONABLY FORESEE ACCIDENTS THAT CREATE AN UNREASONABLE RISK OF HARM

■ **INSTANT FACTS** Mr. Bernier (P) was injured when an electric light pole fell on him after it was struck by an automobile that was involved in a minor traffic accident.

■ **BLACK LETTER RULE** Failure to take reasonable steps to prevent unreasonable risk of injury from reasonably foreseeable accidents is negligence.

■ FACTS

Mr. Bernier (P) was injured when Ms. Ramsdell (D1) lost control of her automobile after she was involved in a minor traffic collision with Mr. Boireau's (D2) automobile. Following the collision between the two vehicles, a collision that resulted from the drivers of the two vehicles failure to correctly negotiate a right turn, Ms. Ramsdell (D1) lost control of her vehicle. Her vehicle then entered and traveled down a sidewalk. While on the sidewalk, Ms. Ramsdell's (D1) vehicle struck and knocked down an electric light pole that Boston Edison Co. (D3) owned. The pole fell on Mr. Bernier's (P) legs. The impact of the pole broke Mr. Bernier's (P) thighs and left shin bone. The break to Mr. Bernier's (P) left shin bone caused a permanent shorting of his left leg. Mr. Bernier (P) and a female friend who was injured after Ms. Ramsdell (D1) lost control of her car brought a negligence cause of action against Ms. Ramsdell (D1), Mr. Boireau (D2), and Edison (D3). The trial court jury rendered an adverse verdict against Ms. Ramsdell (D1) and Edison (D3), and Edison (D3) appealed.

■ ISSUE

Does a person or a corporation have a duty to reasonably foresee accidents that create an unreasonable risk of injury and take reasonable steps to mitigate the risk of injury?

■ DECISION AND RATIONALE

(Kaplan) Yes. A person or a corporation has a duty to reasonably foresee accidents that create an unreasonable risk of injury and take reasonable steps to mitigate the risk of injury. Edison (D3) designed the electric light pole that is the focus of this case. A designer or co-designer and maintainer of such a pole must anticipate the environment in which the pole is used. Further, it must design against reasonably foreseeable risks associated with the use of electric light poles under the circumstances. Trial court evidence shows that there was a risk of automobiles colliding with Edison (D3) poles and that Edison (D3) was aware of this risk. Edison (D3) was aware of the risk because 100 to 120 Edison poles a year are knocked down by automobiles. Therefore, Edison (D3) has a duty to foresee collisions with its poles and the risks that such collisions pose to pedestrians. Trial evidence fails to show that Edison (D3) appreciated the risks. Rather, the evidence shows that Edison (D3) was more concerned with the cost of constructing and maintaining poles than with the risk of harm to pedestrians. When the potential for serious injury exists, consideration of safety measures is warranted, even if the likelihood of accidents is not great. Expert testimony from Mr. Bernier's (P) expert witness revealed that the pole in question in the instant case would collapse when struck by an automobile traveling six m.p.h. Further, the expert testified that Edison (D3) could increase the stability of the pole at low costs. Even Edison (D3) employees offered testimony that suggests that more stable types of poles were known to and available to Edison (D3). Edison (D3) has a duty to reasonably foresee injuries to pedestrians that result from automobile collisions with its electric light poles. The trial jury found that Edison (D3) was negligent in the design and maintenance of the pole that is at issue in the instant case. Since the pole in question will topple when struck by a vehicle traveling at an extremely low speed, the pole creates an unreasonable risk of injury to pedestrians. Judgment affirmed.

Analysis:

In the instant case, Edison (D3) was aware that many of its poles are struck by automobiles and then topple to the ground. A reasonable person would realize that a falling electric light pole poses a serious risk of injury to pedestrians. Edison (D3) was aware of this risk but chose to ignore it. Ignoring a known serious risk of injury to others, a risk that one can reasonably make an effort to mitigate, is careless conduct under the circumstances. Note the balancing that the court had to do in this case. If the pole gives way and falls on impact, the passengers in the car are safer than if they had collided with an immovable object. On the other hand, falling poles may strike pedestrians or others. To make things safer for pedestrians is to make them riskier for car passengers and vice versa. So if the telephone company installs stronger poles to protect the pedestrian, part of the cost of doing so will be borne by car passengers who suffer injury as a result. Note also that an expert testified that the defendant's pole would fall when struck by an automobile driving at only six miles per hour. This kind of testimony is admissible to help the jury estimate how risky the defendant's pole really was.

United States v. Carroll Towing Co.

(Party in Admiralty) v. (Tug Boat Towing Co.)

159 F.2d 169 (C.C.A.2, 1947)

UNITED STATES COURT OF APPEALS FINDS THAT BARGE OWNER AND ITS EMPLOYEES WERE NEGLIGENT WHEN BARGEE WAS ABSENT WHEN BARGE BROKE ADRIFT, LOST HER CARGO, AND SANK

■ **INSTANT FACTS** A barge, without a bargee on broad broke adrift, was carried by wind into a tanker whose propeller broke a hole in barge's bottom, and barge lost its cargo and sank.

■ **BLACK LETTER RULE** Absence a reasonable excuse, barge owner's failure to take reasonable steps to prevent unreasonable risk of barge breaking away in busy wartime harbor by manning barge with bargee is negligence.

■ PROCEDURAL BASIS

Proceedings in admiralty.

■ FACTS

A barge broke adrift from a tugboat that the Carroll Towing Co. (Carroll) (D) operated. Upon breaking adrift, the wind and tide carried the barge against a tanker. The tanker's propeller broke a hole in the barge. As a result, the barge lost its cargo of flour and sank. The trial court found that the owners and operators of the tugboat assigned to the barge were liable for the damages to the barge and then considered if the absence of a bargee on board the barge at the time of the incident reduced the recovery of the owner of the barge.

■ ISSUE

Whether absence a reasonable excuse, barge owner's failure to take reasonable steps to prevent unreasonable risk of barge breaking away in busy wartime harbor by manning barge with bargee is negligence?

■ DECISION AND RATIONALE

(Hand) Yes. Absence a reasonable excuse, barge owner's failure to take reasonable steps to prevent the unreasonable risk of the barge breaking away in the harbor by manning a barge with a bargee is negligence. There is no general rule to determine when the absence of a bargee will make the owner of a barge liable for damages to other vessels. Under certain circumstances, any vessel may break free from her mooring and become a menace to other vessels. Therefore, the duty of a vessel's owner depends upon the probability (P) that the vessel will break free, the gravity of the resulting injury (L) if she does break free, and the burden (B) of adequate precautions to prevent her from breaking free or mitigating damages if she does break free. If the burden of adequate precautions is less than the product of the probability that a vessel will break free and the gravity of the resulting injury if she does ($B < PL$), liability would attach under the appropriate circumstances. Whether a barge will break from her fast and cause damage depends on circumstances such as stormy weather and busy harbor conditions. However, a barge is not a bargee's prison. In the instant case, the bargee left the barge at 5:00 PM on January 3rd. The barge broke away at 2:00 PM on the following day. The bargee was absent, without excuse, from 5:00 PM on January 3rd to 2:00 PM the following day. The bargee's absence occurred in January when the days are short. Further, the incident of the instant case occurred in the full tide of war activity when barges are constantly drilled in an out. Given the weather conditions and the busy nature of the harbor, this court holds that it is reasonable to require a barge owner to have a bargee on board during the working hours of daylight, unless there is a reasonable excuse for the bargee's absence.

Analysis:

Courts routinely apply some form of risk-utility weighing as a means of determining whether conduct was negligent. The structured or rigorous model is usually traced to this opinion. Judge Hand recognized the traditional idea that a weighing of risks and utilities was necessary. The burden of precaution in Judge Hand's formula includes any cost the defendant might have to incur to make things safe enough, but it also includes costs that would be inflicted upon others or upon society at large. Here, the burden or precaution was simple: the increased or marginal cost to the defendant of keeping a bargee on board 24 hours a day. Thinking about costs and benefits in terms of the *Carroll Towing* formula, a judge or juror can compare benefits with costs because they have now been put on a common scale. One of the criticisms of the formula, however, at least as it might be rigorously applied, is that it may do social good without doing individual justice.

Santiago v. First Student, Inc.

(Student) v. (Bus Company)

839 A.2d 550 (R.I.2004)

A PLAINTIFF'S INABILITY TO RECALL DETAILS IS FATAL TO HER CASE

■ **INSTANT FACTS** Santiago (P) was injured while riding a bus operated by First Student, Inc. (D).

■ **BLACK LETTER RULE** A plaintiff bears the burden of proving a defendant's actions were the proximate cause of her injuries.

...ode Island Court of Appeals, affirming summary judgment for the defendant.

■ FACTS

First Student, Inc. (D) operates a school bus that allegedly collided with a car at an intersection that Santiago (P), an injured school-age passenger, could not identify. During her deposition, Santiago (P) testified that she could not remember at which intersection the accident occurred, but she said that she saw an unidentified vehicle approaching the intersection, after which it collided with the bus, causing her face to strike the seatback in front of her. She could not testify as to whether there was a stop sign at the intersection or to the extent of damage to the other vehicle. Because the police did not respond, no report was prepared. The trial court granted First Student's (D) motion for summary judgment.

■ ISSUE

Without evidence of causation, is summary judgment for the defendant appropriate?

■ DECISION AND RATIONALE

(Per curiam.) Yes. While the evidence supports that Santiago (P) was injured in an accident, holding the defendant liable for the accident based on the evidence provided would be pure speculation. The plaintiff has provided no evidence that the bus driver failed to stop at a stop sign or was otherwise negligent. The plaintiff bears the burden of proving the defendant's actions caused her injuries, and her burden cannot be relieved because the nature of the incident renders liability difficult to prove. Affirmed.

Analysis:

In an ordinary negligence case, the plaintiff always bears the burden of proving that the defendant's negligence caused her injuries. Under a special class of negligence cases, however, causation can be inferred under the doctrine of res ipsa loquitur. This doctrine applies when an accident occurs under circumstances that would not otherwise occur absent a defendant's negligence. The doctrine does not apply in this case, because the injuries here could have resulted without any negligence by the defendant.

■ CASE VOCABULARY

BURDEN OF PROOF: A party's duty to prove a disputed assertion or charge.

CAUSATION: The causing or producing of an effect.

PROXIMATE CAUSE: A cause that is legally sufficient to result in liability.

Upchurch v. Rotenberry

(Parent of Deceased Son) v. (Driver of Automobile)

761 So.2d 199 (Miss.2000)

IT IS THE ROLE OF THE JURY TO DETERMINE IF THE DEFENDANT IS NEGLIGENT

■ **INSTANT FACTS** Automobile passenger is injured when automobile strikes a tree after automobile driver attempts to avoid an animal on the roadway.

■ **BLACK LETTER RULE** It is the duty of the jury to determine whether a defendant in a negligence case exercised reasonable care under the circumstances.

■ PROCEDURAL BASIS

Appeal from an adverse jury verdict and denial of motion for judgment notwithstanding the verdict.

■ FACTS

Timothy Adam Upchurch (Adam) was a passenger in Ms. Rotenberry's (D) car. While Adam was a passenger in the car, Ms. Rotenberry (D) lost control of her car and struck a tree. The collision with the tree caused Adam to receive injuries that lead to his death, and Adam's mother, Ms. Upchurch (P) brought a wrongful death action against Ms. Rotenberry (D). Only Ms. Rotenberry (D) witnessed the accident. During the trial, there was conflicting testimony about the speed at which Ms. Rotenberry's car was traveling when it struck the tree and the manner in which the car left the road. Additionally, there was conflicting testimony about whether Ms. Rotenberry (D) was intoxicated at the time of the accident. During the trial, Ms. Rotenberry (D) testified that she did not remember the events leading up to the accident. However, five weeks after the accident, she signed a document that stated a large animal such as a dog or deer ran across the road causing her to swerve to the right to avoid the animal and then leave the road. The jury returned a verdict in favor of Ms. Rotenberry (D), and Ms. Upchurch (P) moved the court for a judgment notwithstanding the verdict. The trial court denied the motion, and Ms. Upchurch (P) appealed.

■ ISSUE

Does a jury have a duty to determine whether a defendant in a negligence case exercised reasonable care under the circumstances?

■ DECISION AND RATIONALE

(Pittman) Yes. It is the duty of the jury to determine whether a defendant in a negligence case exercised reasonable care under the circumstances. This Court will not second-guess a jury's findings regarding the credibility of witnesses, nor will it second-guess its findings of fact; for the jury is the judge of the weight of the evidence and the credibility of witnesses. The jury, in accord with its duty, determined that Ms. Rotenberry (D) acted reasonably in maneuvering her car to avoid an animal. Further, it found that she did not have time to avoid the tree after her car left the road. Absent some clear evidence of juror misconduct, this Court will not interfere with the jury's findings.

Analysis:

Upon first reading the facts, one wonders how this accident could have been caused by anyone other than the defendant. But, some other evidence was presented. The defendant had earlier made a statement that an animal had run in front of her car. If this were true, a reasonably prudent person would swerve the car to avoid the collision. Thus, the cause of the accident may have been the unexpected appearance of the animal and not the negligence of the defendant. Ultimately, the question of negligence is for the jury. In this case, apparently the jury believed that the cause of the accident was the sudden appearance of the large animal. Accordingly, there was no basis for the appellate court to overturn the jury verdict.

Thoma v. Cracker Barrel Old Country Store, Inc.

(Person Who Fell in Restaurant) v. (Restaurant Owner)

649 So.2d 277 (Fla.Dist.Ct.App.1995)

IN A SLIP AND FALL CASE, A PLAINTIFF MUST PROVE THAT THE DEFENDANT CREATED A DANGEROUS CONDITION OR HAD KNOWLEDGE OF SUCH A CONDITION

■ **INSTANT FACTS** Restaurant patron sustains injuries from a fall in a restaurant.

■ **BLACK LETTER RULE** Proof of negligent conduct in a slip and fall case requires a finding by the jury that the owner of—or employees at—the premises either created a dangerous condition or had knowledge of the dangerous condition that lead to the fall and resulting injuries.

■ PROCEDURAL BASIS

Appeal from summary judgment.

■ FACTS

Ms. Thoma (P) slipped and fell in the Cracker Barrel Restaurant (Cracker Barrel) (D) after eating her breakfast. When Ms. Thoma (P) arose to her feet, she noticed drops of clear liquid in a one foot by two feet area. Ms. Thoma (P) claims she slipped on the liquid. Before the fall, Ms. Thoma (P) did not see anyone drop anything on the restaurant floor. A witness to the fall described the area in which Ms. Thoma (P) fell as an area where waitresses would frequently go in and out of the kitchen door. The witness saw waitresses carry beverage pitchers in the area. He did not see customers carrying beverages in the area, nor did he see anyone spill anything in the area. After the fall, the manager of the restaurant inspected the area, and he did not discover any foreign object on the floor. The trial court granted Cracker Barrel (D) summary judgment and Ms. Thoma (P) appealed.

■ ISSUE

Does proof of negligent conduct in a slip and fall case require a finding by the jury that the premises owner or his employees either created a dangerous condition or had knowledge of the dangerous condition that lead to the fall and resulting injuries?

■ DECISION AND RATIONALE

(Kahn) Yes. Proof of negligent conduct in a slip and fall case requires a finding by the jury that the owner of the premises or his employees either created a dangerous condition or had knowledge of the dangerous condition that lead to the fall and resulting injuries. In this case, there is no evidence that Ms. Thoma (P) or the witness to her fall saw anyone drop or spill anything in the area in which Ms. Thoma (P) fell. Since Cracker Barrel (D) waitresses regularly traversed the area to enter and exit the kitchen, the area in which the fall occurred was in their clear view. Further, no one saw anybody, except restaurant employees, carrying beverages in the area of the fall. If a jury had the opportunity to hear the evidence in this case, it could find that there was a liquid in the area in which Ms. Thoma (P) fell and Cracker Barrel (D) employees, through the exercise of due diligence, should have noticed the liquid before the fall. It is the duty of the jury to determine by the preponderance of the evidence whether

Cracker Barrel exercised due diligence in the maintenance of its restaurant floor. Therefore, summary judgment is reversed and this case is remanded to the trial court.

Analysis:

Slip and fall cases and their variants are quite common. The duty of reasonable care is routinely played out in three ways. First, if the defendant negligently creates the dangerous condition, as where a grocery clerk spills a slippery substance on the floor, or the defendant negligently waxes the floor, the defendant will be subject to liability for injuries suffered in the invitee's fall. Second, if the landowner negligently markets goods in such a way that they are likely to be dislodged by other customers with resulting injury to the plaintiff, the trier can find negligence. Finally, as in the situation in this case, if some unknown person creates a condition of danger, by dropping a substance on the floor, for example, the defendant is not negligent in creating the danger, but may be negligent in failing to inspect periodically for such mishaps. Courts often say that the defendant must have actual or constructive knowledge of the danger. Courts tend to say that if the dangerous substance has been present for a long period of time, the trier can infer that the store was negligent in failing to inspect or discover.

The T. J. Hooper

(Unseaworthy Tugboat)

60 F.2d 737 (C.C.A.2, 1932)

EVEN IF A DEFENDANT ACTS ACCORDING TO THE CUSTOM OF HIS INDUSTRY, HE MAY STILL BE LIABLE

■ **INSTANT FACTS** Large barge filled with coal and the tugboat which was its tow were lost at sea during heavy weather.

■ **BLACK LETTER RULE** Notwithstanding a custom of usage or the lack thereof, there are precautions so imperative that even their universal disregard will not excuse their omission.

■ PROCEDURAL BASIS

Appeal from finding that tugboat owner was liable for damages to cargo and barge owners.

■ FACTS

A barge filled with a cargo of coal was lost at sea in heavy weather. The tugboat Hooper (D), the barge's tow, was also lost at sea. The cargo owner brought suit against the owners of the barge and tugboat. The trial court found that all vessels were unseaworthy. The Hooper (D) was found to be unseaworthy because she did not have a radio receiving set on board that was capable of receiving weather forecasts. Tugs do not usually carry such radios. Additionally, the trial court found the tug and the barge jointly liable to the cargo owner. Further, it found that the tug was liable for half of the damages for the loss of the barge. The owner of the Hooper (D) and the barge owner appealed.

■ ISSUE

Is the custom of usage the proper standard to apply in a negligence action?

■ DECISION AND RATIONALE

(Hand) No. Notwithstanding a custom of usage or the lack thereof, there are precautions so imperative that even their universal disregard will not excuse their omission. The Hooper (D) was lost in heavy weather. A radio receiving set was on board the Hooper (D), but this set was her master's personal property. Further, the set was not in working order. Since the radio receiving set was not functioning, the Hooper's (D) master failed to receive radio broadcasts of coming heavy weather. Had he received the broadcasts, he could have sought shelter and save the Hooper (D) and her tow. Radio receiving sets are inexpensive and reliable if maintained properly. However, there is no custom as to the use of radio receiving sets on tugboats. Some tugs have them; others do not. Notwithstanding, there are precautions so imperative that their disregard will not excuse their omission. If the Hooper (D) had a functioning radio receiving set, she would have received the weather forecast and taken appropriate action. Since she did not have such a set, she was unseaworthy and liable for the damages that she caused. Decree affirmed.

Analysis:

Violation of, or compliance with, custom is relevant and admissible but not conclusive on the negligence issue; custom merely provides evidence that may or may not persuade the jury. In this case, the general practice of the tug industry was not the standard of care. It was admissible as evidence but not conclusive, so the tug could properly be held responsible in spite of the fact that it had operated in line with industry practice. Evidence of a custom may be used either as a sword or a shield. As a sword, the plaintiff can show the defendant's violation of a safety custom as some evidence that the defendant failed to act as a reasonable person under the circumstances. As a shield, the defendant can show his compliance with custom as evidence that his conduct was that of a reasonable person.

Byrne v. Boadle

(Man Injured By Falling Barrel of Flour) v. (Flour Shop Owner)

2 H. & C. 722 (1863)

RES IPSA LOQUITUR: THE THING SPEAKS FOR ITSELF

■ **INSTANT FACTS** Barrel of flour falls on a man as he passes a flour shop.

■ **BLACK LETTER RULE** Under certain circumstances, the fact that an accident occurred can support an inference or presumption of negligence.

■ PROCEDURAL BASIS

Appeal from nonsuit judgment in a negligence suit.

■ FACTS

Mr. Byrne (P) was walking in the road and then became unconscious. He then filed a negligence suit. At Mr. Byrne's (P) trial, a witness testified that a barrel of flour fell on Mr. Byrne (P). Mr. Boadle's (D) shop was adjacent to Mr. Byrne (P), and the barrel appeared to have fallen from Mr. Boadle's (D) shop. At his trial, Mr. Byrne (P) failed to produce any direct evidence of negligent conduct, and the trial judge enter judgment of nonsuit for Mr. Boadle (D). Mr. Byrne (P) appealed.

■ ISSUE

Under certain circumstances, can the fact that an accident occurred support an inference or presumption of negligence?

■ DECISION AND RATIONALE

(Pollock) Yes. Under certain circumstances, the fact that an accident occurred can support an inference or presumption of negligence. At trial, Mr. Boadle's (D) attorney argued that Mr. Byrne (P) failed to introduce any direct evidence that connects Mr. Boadle (D) or his employees with the accident. Even if the facts alleged by Mr. Byrne (P) are true, the attorney argued that Mr. Byrne (P) should not prevail as he failed to present affirmative proof of Mr. Boadle's (D) negligent conduct. This is a case of res ipsa loquitur. Some courts have held that in certain cases the fact that an accident occurred is evidence of negligent conduct. Other courts have held that a plaintiff is not entitled to a jury verdict unless he presents some affirmative evidence that the defendant engaged in negligent conduct. It would be incorrect for this Court to hold that a presumption of negligence can never arise from the fact that an accident occurred. It would also be incorrect for this court to hold that a presumption of negligence does not arise in the instant case. Persons who store barrels in a warehouse have a duty to keep the barrel secure in the warehouse. If a barrel escapes, its escape is prima facie evidence of negligence. To require a plaintiff in such a case to call as witnesses the defendant's warehouse employees to present affirmative evidence of negligent conduct is preposterous.

Analysis:

Res ipsa loquitur is a rebuttable presumption or inference that the defendant was negligent, which arises upon proof that the instrumentality causing injury was in the defendant's exclusive control, the accident was one that ordinarily does not happen in the absence of negligence, and the plaintiff did not contribute to his own injuries. Here, the barrel of flour was under the control of Mr. Boadle (D) and his employees. Since barrels of flour do not fly out of windows or doors on their own accord, it is appropriate to presume that negligent conduct caused one of Mr. Boadle's (D) barrels to escape and injure Mr. Byrne (P). Although it was a fair inference that the barrel had come from the defendant's shop, the plaintiff was unable to show that the defendant had been negligent in any particular way. Nevertheless, the court thought the happening spoke for itself and that the jury would be permitted to find that the defendant was negligent. Res ipsa loquitur cases permit the jury to infer negligence without knowing any particular misconduct at all.

■ CASE VOCABULARY

RES IPSA LOQUITUR: Literally, "The thing speaks for itself." Rebuttable presumption or inference that the defendant was negligent, which arises upon proof that the instrumentality causing injury was in the defendant's exclusive control, the accident was one which ordinarily does not happen in the absence of negligence, and the plaintiff did not contribute to his own injuries.

Warren v. Jeffries

(Plaintiff in Wrongful Death Action) v. (Owner of Car That Rolled Over Six-Year-Old Boy)

263 N.C. 531, 139 S.E.2d 718 (1965)

PURE SPECULATION DOES NOT CREATE RES IPSA LOQUITUR

■ **INSTANT FACTS** A six-year old boy jumped out of a car when it begins to roll backward. When the boy jumped he fell, and the front wheel of the car rolled over his chest, killing him.

■ **BLACK LETTER RULE** Pure speculation is not a basis for applying the doctrine of res ipsa loquitur.

■ PROCEDURAL BASIS

Appeal from nonsuit judgment.

■ FACTS

Mr. Jeffries (D) went to Terry Enoch's home to visit his father. Terry was a six-year-old boy. Terry's father was not at home, and Mr. Jeffries (D) decided to wait for him. Mr. Jeffries (D) parked his car on an incline and went into the house. During this time, there were a dozen children, including Terry, in and around the house. About an hour after Mr. Jeffries (D) arrival, he gave Terry's mother the keys to his car so that she could go to the store and purchase some polish for her children. The mother and five children started towards the car, then Terry's mother returned Terry's eyeglasses to the house. The five children entered the rear seat of the car. Terry was the last person to enter the car. The children did not touch any of the car's controls. When Terry closed the car's door, something clicked in the front of the car, and the car began to roll backwards towards a ditch. One of the children opened the car door and told the other children to jump out of the car. Terry was the first to jump. When he did, he fell, and the front wheel of the car ran over his chest. Later, Terry died. Ms. Warren (P) brought a wrongful death action against Mr. Jeffries (D). The trial court rendered a nonsuit judgment, and Ms. Warren (P) appealed.

■ ISSUE

Can pure speculation be a basis for applying the doctrine of res ipsa loquitur?

■ DECISION AND RATIONALE

(Per Curiam) No. Pure speculation is not a basis for applying the doctrine of res ipsa loquitur. Ms. Warren (P) alleges that Mr. Jeffries (D) was negligent because he failed to set the hand brake, engage the transmission, and maintain adequate brakes. However, Ms. Warren (P) failed to produce any evidence in support of these allegations. No one examined the car after the accident. This Court can only speculate as to what caused the car to make a clicking sound and roll backwards. Pure speculation does not support the application of the doctrine of res ipsa loquitur. Judgment affirmed.

Analysis:

The court states here that the cause of the accident is pure speculation; therefore, re ipsa loquitur does not apply. A closer reading of this case reveals that Ms. Warren's (P) attorney may be at fault. The complaint does not allege "the thing speaks for itself." Rather, it alleges three specific negligent acts: failure to set the hand brake, engage the transmission, and maintain adequate brakes. However, Ms. Warren (P) failed to produce any evidence in support of her allegations. The nature of Ms. Warren's (P) allegations runs counter to the doctrine of res ipsa loquitur, therefore, the Court found that the doctrine did not apply in this case.

Giles v. City of New Haven

(Lady Injured in Elevator) v. (Representative for Otis Elevator Co.)

228 Conn. 441, 636 A.2d 1335 (1994)

RES IPSA LOQUITUR: THE DIMINISHING ROLE OF EXCLUSIVE CONTROL

■ **INSTANT FACTS** Elevator operator is injured when chain of elevator she was operating became hooked on the rail bracket in the elevator shaft.

■ **BLACK LETTER RULE** Use by the plaintiff of the instrumentality that caused her injury does not preclude a finding that the defendant had control of the instrumentality.

■ PROCEDURAL BASIS

Appeal from an appellate court decision holding that the trial court should not have granted the defendant a directed verdict.

■ FACTS

Otis Elevator Company (Otis) (D) installed and maintained an elevator that Ms. Giles (P) had operated for fourteen years. One day while ascending in her elevator, Ms. Giles (P) was injured when the elevator's chain became entangled with a bracket on the wall of the elevator shaft. The chain then tightened and broke, and the elevator cab began to shake and shudder. Fearing for her safety, Ms. Giles (P) reversed the direction of the elevator and directed it to the nearest floor so she could escape. Ms. Giles (P) brought suit, and the trial court entered a directed verdict for Otis (D). Ms. Giles (P) appealed and the appellate court reversed the trial court's decision. Otis (D) appealed the appellate court's decision.

■ ISSUE

Does use by the plaintiff of the instrumentality that caused her injury preclude a finding that the defendant had control of the instrumentality?

■ DECISION AND RATIONALE

(Katz) No. Use by the plaintiff of the instrumentality that caused her injury does not preclude a finding that the defendant had control of the instrumentality. During the appellate court's proceedings, the parties agreed that the accident would not have occurred in the absence of negligence. However, Otis (D) contends that the doctrine of re ipsa loquitur does not apply to this case because Ms. Giles (P) failed to show that Otis (D) had exclusive control over the elevator. It is true that Ms. Giles (P) operated the elevator and controlled the sway of the chain. However, these facts do not automatically preclude the application of the doctrine of res ipsa loquitur. The element of control by the defendant is intended to limit the application of res ipsa loquitur to a situation in which a defendant's negligence was more probably than not the cause of a plaintiff's injuries. Therefore, use of the instrumentality by the plaintiff is not an automatic bar against the application of the doctrine. Rather than a fixed rule, control is a flexible term. Control may exist if a defendant has the right or power of control and the opportunity to exercise it. Many jurisdictions now de-emphasize the role of exclusive control. For example, an inference of negligence may be drawn against a defendant who shares control with another. Otis (D) was in control of the maintenance and repair of the elevator and its parts, and operation of the elevator by Ms. Giles (P) was tantamount to the elevator's use. To avoid liability, Otis (D) argues that even though it controlled the elevator chain, Ms. Giles (P) controlled its sway. Ms. Giles (P) operation of the elevator may diminish the exclusivity of Otis's (D) control; however, a jury could find that her operation of the elevator did not vitiate Otis's (D) control of the chain and its condition, which resulted in excessive sway. Appellate court judgment affirmed.

Analysis:

Res ipsa loquitur is a rebuttable presumption or inference that arises upon proof that the instrumentality causing injury was in the defendant's exclusive control. For res ipsa loquitur to apply, a defendant need only have a degree of control or responsibility such that his negligence was more probably than not the cause of the plaintiff's injuries. In the instant case, Otis (D) had control of the maintenance of the elevator and its parts. Ms. Giles (P) operated the elevator and its chain. The court reasoned that if Otis (D) had maintained the elevator and the chain properly, the chain would not have hooked on a shaft wall bracket. This assessment appears reasonable since Ms. Giles (P) had operated the elevator for fourteen years without incident. Courts have generally reformulated the rule such that the control required is control at the time of the negligence rather than the time of the injury; or it is the right or authority to control, not actual physical control that counts; or the test ultimately is not so much control per se but "management" or "responsibility." Other courts continue to state the exclusive control test, but determine "control" on the basis of an estimate of probabilities that the defendant rather than another person had control at the relevant time.

CHAPTER SEVEN

Harm and Factual Cause

Right v. Breen

Instant Facts: The plaintiff was rear-ended and claimed no injuries at the scene, but later brought suit for personal injuries; the defendant argued that the plaintiff's injuries resulted from his five previous motor-vehicle accidents, not the present one, and that not even nominal damages should be awarded.

Black Letter Rule: When a plaintiff's rights have been intentionally invaded, vindication in court through the award of nominal and even exemplary damages serves the policy of deterrence, but when the action sounds in negligence, no purpose would be served by a nominal damages award.

Hale v. Ostrow

Instant Facts: A pedestrian stepped into the street to avoid an obstacle created by bushes overgrowing the sidewalk in front of the Ostrows' (D) property, and when she did she tripped and fell on a chunk of concrete in front of a business; she sued the Ostrows (D), who contended that the business owner and the city were liable.

Black Letter Rule: A negligence claim requires proof by a preponderance of the evidence of both causation in fact and proximate causation, and both kinds of causation generally involve questions of fact that must be resolved by the jury, unless the uncontroverted facts and all reasonable inferences to be drawn therefrom make the case so clear that all reasonable persons would agree on the outcome.

Salinetro v. Nystrom

Instant Facts: Dr. Nystrom (D) took x-rays of Salinetro (P) when, unbeknownst to her, she was pregnant, and as a result she chose to have an abortion.

Black Letter Rule: If the injury would not have occurred but-for the defendant's negligence, causation exists.

Landers v. East Texas Salt Water Disposal Co.

Instant Facts: Two independent companies caused salt and oil to flow into Lander's (P) lake killing the fish, and both were jointly and severally liable.

Black Letter Rule: Where the independent tortious acts of two or more wrongdoers join to produce an indivisible injury, which from its nature cannot be apportioned with reasonable certainty to the individual wrongdoers, all of the wrongdoers are jointly and severally liable for the entire damages.

Lasley v. Combined Transport, Inc.

Instant Facts: A Combined Transport (D) truck lost a load of large glass panes on the freeway; Lasley's (D) son was caught up in the ensuing traffic jam when his pickup was hit by a vehicle driven by Clemmer (D), which caused his truck to erupt into a fire in which the son died. The issue in this case concerned the exclusion of evidence of Clemmer's (D) intoxication at the time of the collision.

Black Letter Rule: Factual cause exists if someone examining the event without regard to legal consequences would conclude that the allegedly faulty conduct or condition in fact played a role in its occurrence.

Summers v. Tice

Instant Facts: Two hunters, acting independently of each, negligently fired guns, only one of which hit Summers (P).

Black Letter Rule: Where two or more tortfeasors are negligent, but only one could have caused the harm to an injured third party, the tortfeasors are jointly and severally liable even absent proof as to which one actually caused the injury.

Mohr v. Grantham

Instant Facts: Mohr (P) suffered brain damage allegedly as a result of delayed medical treatment, but the court granted summary judgment in the doctors' favor; she and her husband appealed.

Black Letter Rule: The loss of a less-than-even chance is a loss worthy of redress.

Right v. Breen

(Personal-Injury Plaintiff) v. (Defendant Driver)

277 Conn. 364, 890 A.2d 1287 (2006)

IN NEGLIGENCE CASES, NO LOSS MEANS NO NOMINAL DAMAGES

■ **INSTANT FACTS** The plaintiff was rear-ended and claimed no injuries at the scene, but later brought suit for personal injuries; the defendant argued that the plaintiff's injuries resulted from his five previous motor-vehicle accidents, not the present one, and that not even nominal damages should be awarded.

■ **BLACK LETTER RULE** When a plaintiff's rights have been intentionally invaded, vindication in court through the award of nominal and even exemplary damages serves the policy of deterrence, but when the action sounds in negligence, no purpose would be served by a nominal damages award.

■ PROCEDURAL BASIS

On certified appeal to the state supreme court following appellate court affirmance of an award of nominal damages to the plaintiff.

■ FACTS

The plaintiff was stopped at a red light when his vehicle was hit from behind by a car driven by the defendant. There was only minor damage to the plaintiff's vehicle, and no injuries were reported at the scene. Later, however, the plaintiff brought suit claiming that he suffered bodily injuries, and seeking both economic and noneconomic damages. At trial, the defendant presented evidence that the injuries resulted from the plaintiff's five previous motor-vehicle damages, not the present accident. The jury returned a verdict of zero economic and zero noneconomic damages. The plaintiff filed a motion to set aside the verdict, arguing that he was entitled at least to nominal damages under Connecticut law. The trial court agreed and awarded the plaintiff one dollar and her attorneys' fees. The defendant appealed. The court of appeals felt constrained by precedent on nominal damages awards, so it affirmed. This certified appeal followed.

■ ISSUE

Was the plaintiff entitled to nominal damages?

■ DECISION AND RATIONALE

(Katz, J.) No. When a plaintiff's rights have been intentionally invaded, vindication in court through the award of nominal and even exemplary damages serves the policy of deterrence, but when the action sounds in negligence, no purpose would be served by a nominal damages award. Indeed, Connecticut common law requires proof of actual damages to support a cause of action sounding in negligence. Our common law reflects a clear distinction between intentional and negligent acts, allowing recovery of nominal damages only when a plaintiff's right has been *intentionally* invaded, but allowing recovery only upon proof of causation and actual damages when a plaintiff's right has been *negligently* invaded. Conduct that is merely negligent, without proof of an actual injury, is not considered to be a significant interference with the public interest such that there is any right to complain of it, or to be free from it. Reversed and remanded.

Analysis:

Nominal damages may be awarded for the infraction of a legal right, when the extent of the loss is not shown, or when the right is one not dependent on loss or damage. In negligence cases, however, if the plaintiff fails to establish a loss, the action will be dismissed. An award of nominal damages is, in essence, a judicial declaration that the plaintiff's right has been violated. The practical significance of a judgment for nominal damages is that the plaintiff thereby establishes a legal right. The judgment may deter future infringements, or it may enable the plaintiff to obtain an injunction to restrain a repetition of the wrong. An award of nominal damages will also, in many cases, entitle a plaintiff to costs, or it might serve as a peg upon which to hang an award of exemplary damages.

■ CASE VOCABULARY

EXEMPLARY DAMAGES: Damages awarded in addition to actual damages when the defendant acted with recklessness, malice, or deceit; specifically, damages assessed by way of penalizing the wrongdoer or making an example to others. Punitive damages, which are intended to punish and thereby deter blameworthy conduct, are generally not recoverable for breach of contract. The Supreme Court has held that three guidelines help determine whether a punitive-damages award violates constitutional due process: (1) the reprehensibility of the conduct being punished; (2) the reasonableness of the relationship between the harm and the award; and (3) the difference between the award and the civil penalties authorized in comparable cases.

NOMINAL DAMAGES: A trifling sum awarded when a legal injury is suffered but when there is no substantial loss or injury to be compensated.

Hale v. Ostrow

(Injured Pedestrian) v. (Property Owners)

166 S.W.3d 713 (Tenn. 2005)

A CAUSE IN FACT NEED NOT BE THE ONLY CAUSE OF AN ACCIDENT

■ **INSTANT FACTS** A pedestrian stepped into the street to avoid an obstacle created by bushes overgrowing the sidewalk in front of the Ostrows' (D) property, and when she did she tripped and fell on a chunk of concrete in front of a business; she sued the Ostrows (D), who contended that the business owner and the city were liable.

■ **BLACK LETTER RULE** A negligence claim requires proof by a preponderance of the evidence of both causation in fact and proximate causation, and both kinds of causation generally involve questions of fact that must be resolved by the jury, unless the uncontroverted facts and all reasonable inferences to be drawn therefrom make the case so clear that all reasonable persons would agree on the outcome.

■ PROCEDURAL BASIS

State supreme court review of an appellate court decision affirming summary judgment for the Ostrows (D).

■ FACTS

Hale (P) was walking home from the bus stop when she noticed that the sidewalk ahead was obstructed by overgrown bushes. She also noticed that the sidewalk had "crumbled." As she looked into the street to see if she could safely step off the sidewalk to avoid the obstruction, she tripped and fell on a loose chunk of concrete. Hale (P) broke her hip and required extensive medical care.

The property with the overgrown bushes was owned by the Ostrows (D), but the crumbled sidewalk where Hale (P) actually fell was in front of a business owned by someone else. Hale (P) sued both property owners, as well as the city. The Ostrows (D) moved for summary judgment, arguing that Hale's (P) injury was caused by the defective sidewalk, not their overgrown bushes. The trial court granted the Ostrows' (D) motion and the court of appeals affirmed. Hale (P) appealed to the state supreme court.

■ ISSUE

Did the court properly grant summary judgment in the Ostrows' (D) favor?

■ DECISION AND RATIONALE

(Anderson, J.) No. A negligence claim requires proof by a preponderance of the evidence of both causation in fact and proximate causation, and both kinds of causation generally involve questions of fact that must be resolved by the jury, unless the uncontroverted facts and all reasonable inferences to be drawn therefrom make the case so clear that all reasonable persons would agree on the outcome. A defendant's conduct is the cause in fact of an injury if it directly contributed to the injury. In a case like this, we must ask whether the plaintiff's injury would have happened but for the defendant's act. If not, then the defendants' conduct is a cause in fact. It is not necessary that the defendants' act be the *sole* cause of the plaintiff's injury, only that it be *a* cause. Here, there is at least a question of fact as to whether the overgrown bushes were a cause in fact of Hale's (P) injury. Had she not needed to avoid the obstruction, Hale (P) would not have stepped into the street. Would she have tripped on the concrete chunk anyhow? Maybe, but on a defendant's motion for summary judgment, the evidence must be viewed in the light most favorable to the plaintiff. Summary judgment for the defendants reversed.

Analysis:

The court's inquiry does not end once it is determined that the plaintiff's injury would not have happened but for the defendant's breach of duty. The next question is whether the defendant's breach was a proximate cause of the plaintiff's injury, which is very different from a cause in fact. Proximate cause puts a limit on the causal chain, such that defendants will not be held liable for injuries that were not *substantially* caused by their conduct, or that were not reasonably foreseeable results of their conduct. In order for proximate cause to exist, (1) the defendant's conduct must have been a "substantial factor" in bringing about the harm; (2) there must be no rule or policy that should relieve the wrongdoer from liability because of the manner in which the negligence resulted in harm; and (3) the harm giving rise to the action must have been reasonably foreseeable or anticipated by a person of ordinary intelligence and prudence.

■ CASE VOCABULARY

BUT-FOR CAUSE: The cause without which the event could not have occurred.—Also termed *actual cause*; *cause in fact*; *factual cause*.

PROXIMATE CAUSE: A cause that is legally sufficient to result in liability; an act or omission that is considered in law to result in a consequence, so that liability can be imposed on the actor; a cause that directly produces an event and without which the event would not have occurred.

Salinetro v. Nystrom

(Pregnant Patient) v. (Negligent Doctor)

341 So.2d 1059 (Fla.Dist.Ct.App.1977)

BUT-FOR CAUSATION TEST IS NOT ALWAYS HELPFUL

■ **INSTANT FACTS** Dr. Nystrom (D) took x-rays of Salinetro (P) when, unbeknownst to her, she was pregnant, and as a result she chose to have an abortion.

■ **BLACK LETTER RULE** If the injury would not have occurred but-for the defendant's negligence, causation exists.

■ PROCEDURAL BASIS

Appeal from judgment following directed verdict in medical malpractice action seeking damages.

■ FACTS

Salinetro (P) was in an auto accident and underwent a medical examination in connection with back injuries sustained. Dr. Nystrom (D) took x-rays of her lower back and abdominal areas. Unknown to Salinetro (P), at the time the x-rays were administered, she was approximately four to six weeks pregnant. Dr. Nystrom (D), his receptionist and his x-ray technician failed to inquire whether or not Salinetro (P) was pregnant or the date of her last menstrual period. After the pregnancy was confirmed, Salinetro's (P) gynecologist advised her to terminate her pregnancy because of the possible damage to the fetus by the x-rays. Salinetro (P) underwent a therapeutic abortion and the pathology report stated that the fetus was dead at the time of the abortion. Salinetro (P) sued Dr. Nystrom (D) for medical malpractice. At the close of all evidence, Dr. Nystrom (D) moved for a directed verdict on the ground that Salinetro (P) failed to make a prima facie case of medical malpractice. The trial judge granted the motion, and judgment was entered for Dr. Nystrom (D).

■ ISSUE

If the injury would not have occurred but-for the defendant's negligence, does causation exist?

■ DECISION AND RATIONALE

(Per Curiam) Yes. The but-for causation test provides that if the injury would not have occurred but-for the defendant's negligence, causation exists. Even if we were to assume that Dr. Nystrom's (D) conduct fell below the standard of care in the medical community, the failure to inquire about pregnancy or last menstrual period was not the cause of the injury. Salinetro (P) testified that even if she had been asked about being pregnant, she would have answered in the negative. She also testified that being a few days late with her menstrual period was not unusual and did not indicate to her that she may have been pregnant. Six days prior to her visit to Dr. Nystrom (D), Salinetro (P) had seen her gynecologist and he had found no evidence that she was pregnant. Simply because Salinetro (P) was late with her period would not in and of itself mean that she was pregnant because further tests were required to ascertain if she was pregnant. Thus, this point is without merit.

Analysis:

Without using the words, this case examines the *but-for test* of causation. The court believed that since Salinetro (D) did not know that she was pregnant at the time of the x-rays, had the doctor acted in a non-negligent manner and asked her if she was pregnant, her response would have been "no." Thus, in the court's view, the result would have been the same. However, the court's analysis is somewhat flawed. Perhaps if the doctor had asked the question, it would have caused Salinetro (D) to inquire about the risk of x-rays if she was pregnant. If the doctor said that x-rays could cause serious consequences, it may have prompted her to have a pregnancy test. The court's opinion is really based on speculation about whether the injury could have been avoided if the doctor had not been negligent.

■ CASE VOCABULARY

ARGUENDO: For sake of argument, but without admitting the truth of the statement.

DIRECTED VERDICT: Judge entering judgment for one party before return of jury verdict.

PER CURIAM: An opinion by the whole court, rather than one judge.

PRIMA FACIE CASE: When the evidence is sufficient to prove the case, unless contrary evidence is presented by the other side.

Landers v. East Texas Salt Water Disposal Co.

(Lake Owner) v. (Salt Polluter)

151 Tex. 251, 248 S.W.2d 731 (1952)

WRONGDOERS CAN BE LIABLE JOINTLY AND SEVERALLY FOR SAME INJURY

■ **INSTANT FACTS** Two independent companies caused salt and oil to flow into Lander's (P) lake killing the fish, and both were jointly and severally liable.

■ **BLACK LETTER RULE** Where the independent tortious acts of two or more wrongdoers join to produce an indivisible injury, which from its nature cannot be apportioned with reasonable certainty to the individual wrongdoers, all of the wrongdoers are jointly and severally liable for the entire damages.

■ PROCEDURAL BASIS

Appeal from lower court ruling regarding sufficiency of pleading for negligence and damages.

■ FACTS

Landers (P) owned a small lake and stocked it with fish at considerable expense. He sued East Texas Salt Water Disposal Co. (Salt Water) (D1) alleging that its pipe lines broke and thousands of barrels of salt water flowed into the lake, killing the fish. Landers (P) also sued Sun Oil Company (Oil Co.) (D2) alleging that on or about the same day it caused large quantities of salt water and oil to flow into the lake, killing the fish. [This was not a good day to be fishing.] He alleged that both Salt Water (D1) and Oil Co. (D2) were negligent and liable for the damages resulting from the loss of the fish.

■ ISSUE

Where the independent tortious acts of two or more wrongdoers join to produce an indivisible injury, which from its nature cannot be apportioned with reasonable certainty to the individual wrongdoers, are all of the wrongdoers jointly and severally liable for the entire damages?

■ DECISION AND RATIONALE

(Calvert) Yes. We hold that where the independent tortious acts of two or more wrongdoers join to produce an indivisible injury, which from its nature cannot be apportioned with reasonable certainty to the individual wrongdoers, all of the wrongdoers are jointly and severally liable for the entire damages. We overrule the holding of *Sun Oil Co. v. Robicheaux*, which stated that an action cannot be maintained against several defendants jointly, where each acts independently of the other and there is no concert or unity of design between them, and a defendant is liable only for the damages from his own act. This rule has made it impossible for gravely injured plaintiffs to obtain damages through joint and several judgments against all wrongdoers whose independent tortious acts have joined in producing an injury. The plaintiffs in these suits were denied relief because they were unable to apportion the injury attributable to each defendant. From the pleadings in this case, it appears that there was neither concert of action nor unity of design between Salt Water (D1) and Oil Co. (D2) in the commission of their alleged tortious acts. [Strange coincidence that two separate companies polluted the lake with salt on the same day.] However, their alleged wrongful acts produced the death of the fish, which is an indivisible injury that cannot be apportioned among the wrongdoers. Therefore, Salt

Water (D1) and Oil Co. (D2), if established by the evidence, can be held jointly and severally liable for Landers' (P) damages.

Analysis:

Joint and several liability is the topic of this case. However, the case also demonstrates a problem with the *but-for* test. Applying the but-for test separately to both Salt Water (D1) and Oil Co. (D2), it is clear that two sets of negligence *caused* a single injury. Since either negligent act alone could have killed the fish, a strict interpretation of the but-for test would prohibit liability against either wrongdoer. In this situation, most courts apply a substantial factor test, so that all defendants who are substantial factors in the harm are causes in fact. If both wrongdoers may be held liable, the issue becomes whether to apply joint and several liability, or proportionate fault liability. Since the death of the fish cannot be apportioned, both wrongdoers will be held liable. Note that if there was evidence the Oil Co. (D2) only released oil into the lake and it killed a certain type of fish, and Salt Water's (D1) release of salt killed plant life, then the damages to Landers (P) could be apportioned between both wrongdoers.

■ CASE VOCABULARY

JOINTLY AND SEVERALLY LIABLE: A form of liability where the injured party may sue one or more wrongdoers separately, or all together, and enforce the judgment obtained against one or all.

Lasley v. Combined Transport, Inc.

(Father of Decedent) v. (Trucking Company)

261 P.3d 1215 (Or. 2011)

EVIDENCE OF INTOXICATION WAS NOT RELEVANT AS TO CAUSATION, BUT IT WAS RELEVANT WITH REGARD TO ALLOCATION OF FAULT

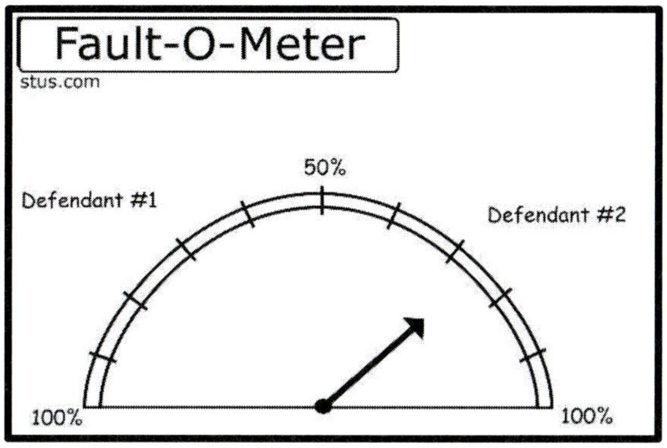

■ **INSTANT FACTS** A Combined Transport (D) truck lost a load of large glass panes on the freeway; Lasley's (D) son was caught up in the ensuing traffic jam when his pickup was hit by a vehicle driven by Clemmer (D), which caused his truck to erupt into a fire in which the son died. The issue in this case concerned the exclusion of evidence of Clemmer's (D) intoxication at the time of the collision.

■ **BLACK LETTER RULE** Factual cause exists if someone examining the event without regard to legal consequences would conclude that the allegedly faulty conduct or condition in fact played a role in its occurrence.

■ PROCEDURAL BASIS

State supreme court review of a court of appeals decision concluding that the trial court erred in excluding evidence of Clemmer's (D) intoxication.

■ FACTS

A truck owned by Combined Transport (D) lost part of its load, consisting of large panes of glass, on the freeway, which caused the following traffic to back up. Lasley's (P) son was stopped in his pickup truck in the traffic tie-up when he was hit by a vehicle driven by Clemmer (D). The collision caused a fuel leak and fire in Lasley's (P) son's vehicle, and the son died in the fire. Clemmer (D) admitted her negligence in driving at an unreasonable speed and failing to maintain a proper lookout and control, and that her negligence was a cause of the decedent's death. The court granted Clemmer's (D) motion in limine to exclude evidence of her intoxication at the time of the collision. The jury returned a verdict against both Combined Transport (D) and Clemmer (D), finding the trucking company 22% at fault and Clemmer (D) 78% at fault. Combined Transport (D) appealed and the court of appeals reversed, concluding that the trial court erred in excluding the evidence of Clemmer's (D) intoxication because the evidence was relevant both as to whether Combined Transport's (D) negligence was a substantial factor in causing the decedent's death, and as to how to apportion fault between the defendants.

■ ISSUE

Did the trial court err in excluding evidence of Clemmer's (D) intoxication as relevant to the issue of causation?

■ DECISION AND RATIONALE

(Walters, J.) No. Factual cause exists if someone examining the event without regard to legal consequences would conclude that the allegedly faulty conduct or condition in fact played a role in its occurrence. When the negligence of multiple tortfeasors combines to produce harm, each tortfeasor whose negligence was a cause of the harm may be held liable. It is factual, not legal, cause that is at issue in this case. The "substantial factor" test is a test for factual cause. It may be possible to imagine a circumstance in which one defendant's conduct is a factual cause of the plaintiff's harm in the sense that the harm would not have occurred absent the defendant's conduct, but in which the defendant's conduct is so insignificant when contrasted with that of another that the first defendant's conduct should not be deemed a cause of the plaintiff's harm. However, that is not the situation here. In this case, the conduct of each defendant was a substantial factor in contributing to the decedent's death. The evidence that Clemmer (D) was intoxicated would not make Clemmer's (D) conduct more significant or Combined Transport's (D) conduct less significant in terms of a causation analysis. Combined Transport (D) confuses causation and negligence. Combined Transport (D) argues that evidence of Clemmer's (D) intoxication would show that she would have collided with the decedent's pickup truck and killed him even if he had not been stopped on the freeway, but the trucking company offers no evidence to support this abstract assertion. The intoxication evidence was irrelevant to the issue of causation.

Analysis:

The court held that evidence of Clemmer's intoxication was not relevant on the issues of causation, liability, or damages, but it was relevant to determine the degree of fault of both Clemmer (D) and Combined Transport (D). Moreover, the court said, the trucking company should have raised Clemmer's (D) intoxication as an affirmative defense in its answer. However, the court construed Combined Transport's (D) counter-claim for contribution as the equivalent of an affirmative defense, because it put Lasley (P) on notice of Combined Transport's (D) theory that Clemmer was intoxicated and that therefore a higher degree of fault should be attributed to her.

■ CASE VOCABULARY

AFFIRMATIVE DEFENSE: A defendant's answer to a complaint that does not deny the facts of the charge or the plaintiff's complaint, but presents evidence or arguments in favor of the defendant that mitigate or excuse the defendant's actions (*e.g.,* insanity, self-defense, and duress are pleas used in criminal cases that are affirmative defenses).

CONTRIBUTION: That which one person does or gives to meet his share of a jointly held responsibility; the right to demand a person bear his portion of a shared burden, such as a jointly held debt or a concurrently caused injury.

IN LIMINE: [Latin.] On the threshold; in the beginning. Motions in limine are brought before trial, often to decide evidentiary issues.

Summers v. Tice

(Shot in the Face Victim) v. (Negligent Hunter)

33 Cal.2d 80, 199 P.2d 1 (1948)

ALTERNATIVE CAUSATION RULE ESTABLISHED WHEN TWO PEOPLE ARE NEGLIGENT BUT ONLY ONE COULD HAVE CAUSED THE INJURY

■ **INSTANT FACTS** Two hunters, acting independently of each, negligently fired guns, only one of which hit Summers (P).

■ **BLACK LETTER RULE** Where two or more tortfeasors are negligent, but only one could have caused the harm to an injured third party, the tortfeasors are jointly and severally liable even absent proof as to which one actually caused the injury.

■ PROCEDURAL BASIS

Appeal from judgments entered following court trial in action for negligence seeking personal injury damages.

■ FACTS

Summers (P), Tice (D1) and another hunter (D2) were quail hunting on an open range when Summers (P) was struck by birdshot discharged from a shotgun. Summers (P) sued Tice (D1) and the other hunter (D2) for negligence for personal injuries to his right eye and face. The trial judge found that both Tice (D1) and the other hunter (D2) were using the same type of shotgun and shells. They both shot at a quail in a negligent manner. [Why were they negligent you ask? The bird was only 10 feet off the ground between them and Summers (P), and they knew Summers (P) was only 75 yards away.] Summers (P) was struck in his right eye and in his upper lip, but the shot to the eye caused the most damage. The shot to the eye could only have come from one gun, not both. Judgment was entered against both Tice (D1) and the other hunter (D2). They both appealed [trying to make Summers (P) prove who fired the damaging shot].

■ ISSUE

Where two or more tortfeasors are negligent, but only one could have caused the harm to an injured third party, are the tortfeasors jointly and severally liable absent proof as to which one actually caused the injury?

■ DECISION AND RATIONALE

(Carter) Yes. We hold that where two or more tortfeasors are negligent, but only one could have caused the harm to an injured third party, the tortfeasors are jointly and severally liable even absent proof as to which one actually caused the injury. Other cases have held that where two defendants negligently act in concert and cause injury to a third person, both are liable, even though only one of them could have caused the injury and the injured party is unable to prove which one caused the injury. If this were not the case, both tortfeasors would be exonerated from liability even though each was negligent and the injury resulted from such negligence. It is clear that the burden of proof on the subject should be shifted to the negligent wrongdoers. They are the negligent ones who brought about the injury, and hence it should rest with them each to absolve himself if he can. It would be unfair to require the injured party to point to who caused the harm. Thus, we affirm the decision of the lower court holding both Tice (D1) and the other hunter (D2) liable for Summers' (P) injuries. Summers (P) is not required to prove which hunter shot him in the eye. The burden shifts to Tice (D1) and the other hunter (D2) to try to absolve one or the other from liability. Affirmed.

Analysis:

This famous case created the *alternative causation rule.* The rule extends joint and several liability so that where both tortfeasors are negligent, but only one of them causes the injury, both will be held liable. In such situations, the burden of proof shifts to the defendants to exculpate themselves, if possible, from liability. The rationale is that the negligent defendants should bear the loss rather than the innocent plaintiff. It should be noted, however, that virtually all courts reject the alternative causation rule in products liability cases with numerous defendants.

■ CASE VOCABULARY

CONSOLIDATED: Combing two different cases for trial at the same time before the same judge.

REMEDILESS: Being without redress or ability to enforce a right.

TRIER OF FACT: Either the judge or a jury who decides the disputed factual matters at trial.

Mohr v. Grantham

(Accident Victim) v. (Physician)

262 P.3d 490 (Wash. 2011)

THE COURT RECOGNIZES THE LOSS OF CHANCE DOCTRINE

■ **INSTANT FACTS** Mohr (P) suffered brain damage allegedly as a result of delayed medical treatment, but the court granted summary judgment in the doctors' favor; she and her husband appealed.

■ **BLACK LETTER RULE** The loss of a less-than-even chance is a loss worthy of redress.

■ FACTS

Mohr (P) was driving when she suffered a hypoglycemic event, causing her to run into a utility pole. At the hospital, Dr. Grantham (D) observed lacerations on Mohr's (P) face and decided to run some neurological tests. The results of the tests were normal. Even so, Mohr (P) began suffering neurological symptoms while at the hospital, and Grantham told one of Mohr's (P) sons, who was also a doctor, that he would run more neurological tests. He failed to do so. Instead, Grantham (D) discharged Mohr (P), prescribing a strong narcotic but not providing discharge instructions on head injuries. Mohr (P) continued to suffer symptoms at home and was transported back to the hospital by ambulance the next day. Even after Mohr's (P) two physician sons insisted on a CT angiogram, treatment was delayed. The eventual angiogram showed a dissected carotid artery, but again there was a delay in administering anticoagulant therapy. Mohr (P) suffered permanent brain damage. She and her husband sued, arguing that the doctors' negligence substantially diminished her chance of recovery. Her two physician sons and two other doctors testified on Mohr's (P) behalf, presenting evidence that if she had received non-negligent treatment she would have had a 50 to 60% chance of a better outcome. The court granted summary judgment for the defendants on the basis that the Mohrs (P) did not show "but for" causation, and the Mohrs (P) appealed.

■ ISSUE

In the medical malpractice context, is there a cause of action for the lost chance of a better outcome?

■ DECISION AND RATIONALE

(Owens, J.) Yes. The loss of a less-than-even chance is a loss worthy of redress. In the *Herskovits* case, which involved the failure to diagnose lung cancer, we recognized a cause of action for the loss of a chance. The opinion in that case explained that to decide otherwise would be a blanket release from liability for doctors and hospitals any time there was a less than 50% chance of survival, regardless of how flagrant the negligence. We hold that *Herskovits* applies to lost chance claims where the ultimate harm is some serious injury short of death. We also formally adopt the reasoning of the *Herskovits* plurality that a plaintiff bears the burden to prove duty, breach of duty, and that such breach proximately caused a loss of chance of a better outcome. The next issue for consideration is damages. Treating the loss of chance as a cognizable injury permits plaintiffs to recover for the loss of an opportunity for a better outcome, an interest that should be compensable, but properly valued. *Herskovits* adopted a proportional damages approach, holding that, if the loss was a 40% chance of survival, the plaintiff could recover only 40% of what would be compensable under the ultimate harm of death or disability (i.e., 40% of traditional tort recovery). This percentage of loss is a question for the jury. The Mohrs (P) have made a prima facie case under the lost chance doctrine. Summary judgment for the defendants is reversed and the case is remanded to the trial court for further proceedings.

■ DISSENT

(Madsen, C.J.) It is a fundamental principle in a medical malpractice action that the plaintiff must prove causation of the plaintiff's actual physical or mental injury before tort liability will be imposed. No matter how the lost chance cause of action is characterized, the plaintiff is freed of the requirement of proving causation. If there is to be any change in the law, it should come from the legislature.

Analysis:

The court explained that the appropriate framework for considering a lost chance claim was the substantial factor theory of causation. The substantial factor test is an exception to the general rule of providing but-for causation and requires that a plaintiff prove that the defendant's alleged act or omission was a substantial factor in causing the plaintiff's injury, even if the injury could have occurred anyway. As held in *Herskovits*, traditional all-or-nothing causation in lost chance cases would subvert the deterrence objective of tort law.

■ CASE VOCABULARY

BUT-FOR CAUSATION: A rule of causation that considers whether the injury would not have occurred but for the defendant's negligent act.

SUBSTANTIAL FACTOR TEST: A formula used to determine proximate cause that considers whether the defendant's conduct was a substantial factor in producing the harm.

CHAPTER EIGHT

Scope of Liability (Proximate Cause)

Thompson v. Kaczinski

Instant Facts: The defendants left unsecured parts from their disassembled trampoline in their yard for a few weeks; when a storm erupted, strong winds blew the top of the trampoline into the road and Thompson (P) was injured when he swerved to avoid hitting it.

Black Letter Rule: Tort law does not impose liability on an actor for all harm factually caused by the actor's tortious conduct.

Palsgraf v. Long Island Railroad Co.

Instant Facts: A passenger waiting for a train was injured on a railroad platform after railway employees dislodged from the arm of another passenger who they were negligently helping jump onto a moving train, a package of fireworks that exploded when it fell on the tracks, the shock from which caused scales to fall on the plaintiff.

Black Letter Rule: The risk reasonably to be perceived defines the duty to be obeyed.

Hughes v. Lord Advocate

Instant Facts: While playing in and around an unguarded open manhole, two young boys accidentally knocked a kerosene lantern into the manhole, breaking the lantern and causing an unforeseeable explosion.

Black Letter Rule: The fact that the defendant's negligence causes a known harm in an unforeseeable manner does not relieve him of liability.

Marcus v. Staubs

Instant Facts: Staubs' (P) daughters were involved in an accident, killing one of them and seriously injuring another, after Marcus (D) provided the minors with alcohol and took them to a party; Marcus (D) argued that the fact that the girls stole a truck and drove themselves home after consuming alcohol relieved him of liability.

Black Letter Rule: A tortfeasor whose negligence is a substantial factor in bringing about injuries is not relieved from liability by the intervening acts of third persons if those acts were reasonably foreseeable by the original tortfeasor at the time of his negligent conduct.

Delaney v. Reynolds

Instant Facts: Delaney (P) shot herself with an unlocked, loaded gun kept in the house she shared with a police officer, and in her negligence suit against him the officer claimed that Delaney's (P) suicide attempt was a superseding cause of her injuries.

Black Letter Rule: When an intervening occurrence was foreseeable by the defendant, the causal chain of events remains intact and the defendant's original negligence remains a proximate cause of the plaintiff's injury.

Derdiarian v. Felix Contracting Corp.

Instant Facts: A road worker was injured after a man negligently drove his car through the work site and struck a boiling cauldron of enamel that was negligently left unguarded from traffic, causing the enamel to splatter and burn the worker.

Black Letter Rule: An intervening act may not serve as a superseding cause, and relieve an actor of responsibility, where the risk of the intervening act occurring is the very same risk which renders the actor negligent.

Ventricelli v. Kinney System Rent A Car, Inc.

Instant Facts: A man was struck by a moving vehicle while trying to shut the defective trunk lid on the vehicle he rented.

Black Letter Rule: A rental car company could not have foreseen that a driver would strike its client while the client was attempting to shut the trunk lid negligently left in disrepair by the company.

Marshall v. Nugent

Instant Facts: A man that was struck while attempting to warn oncoming traffic of an obstruction in the road, sued the truck driver that caused the obstruction.

Black Letter Rule: In a traffic mix-up due to negligence, before the waters have become placid and normal again, the unfolding of events between the culpable act and the plaintiff's eventual injury may be bizarre indeed; yet the defendant may be liable for the result.

Thompson v. Kaczinski

(Injured Driver) v. (Trampoline Owner)

774 N.W.2d 829 (Iowa 2009)

LIABILITY MAY ATTACH IF A REASONABLE JURY COULD FIND THAT THE PLAINTIFF'S INJURIES AROSE FROM A RISK POSED BY THE DEFENDANT

"Foreseeability" is tricky.
You should leave it for the jury to decide.

■ **INSTANT FACTS** The defendants left unsecured parts from their disassembled trampoline in their yard for a few weeks; when a storm erupted, strong winds blew the top of the trampoline into the road and Thompson (P) was injured when he swerved to avoid hitting it.

■ **BLACK LETTER RULE** Tort law does not impose liability on an actor for all harm factually caused by the actor's tortious conduct.

■ PROCEDURAL BASIS

Review by the state supreme court of the court of appeals' decision affirming the trial court's summary judgment for the defendants.

■ FACTS

Kaczinski (D) and Lockwood (D) disassembled their outdoor trampoline and placed the pieces in their yard, thirty-eight feet from the road, for later disposal. Before they got rid of it, a storm erupted, and the top of the trampoline blew into the roadway. That same morning, Thompson (P) was driving down the road in front of Kaczinski's (D) home and came upon the debris. When he swerved to avoid it, Thompson (P) lost control of his vehicle, went into the ditch, and rolled several times. Thompson (P) and his wife sued Kaczinski (D) and Lockwood (D) for the injuries he sustained, but the court awarded summary judgment in the defendants' favor, concluding that the displacement of the trampoline's top to the surface of the road was not foreseeable. Thompson (P) appealed and the court of appeals affirmed. The state supreme court granted the application for further review.

■ ISSUE

Did the trial court properly rule that the defendants were not liable as a matter of law?

■ DECISION AND RATIONALE

(Hecht, J.) No. Tort law does not impose liability on an actor for all harm factually caused by the actor's tortious conduct. An actor's liability is limited to those physical harms that result from the risks that made the actor's conduct tortious. This "risk standard" is intended to prevent the unjustified imposition of liability by confining the scope of liability to the reasons for holding the actor liable in the first place. In other words, the scope of liability issue is fact intensive and requires consideration of the risks that made the actor's conduct tortious, as well as a determination of whether the harm at issue is a result of any of those risks. Foreseeability has long been relevant in a negligence analysis, and is still relevant in a scope of liability determination. Both the risk standard and a foreseeability test exclude liability for harms that were sufficiently unforeseeable at the time of the actor's tortious conduct that they were not among the potential harms that made the actor negligent. But a foreseeability test risks being misunderstood because of uncertainty about what must be foreseen, by whom, and at what time. Accordingly, we adopt the Restatement's scope of liability analysis and apply the risk standard as articulated therein.

We must next consider whether the trial court erred in concluding that the harm suffered by Thompson (P) was outside the scope of the risk of the defendants' conduct as a matter of law. We hold that the question of whether a serious injury to a motorist was within the range of harms risked by disassembling the trampoline and leaving it untethered for a few weeks in the yard, less than forty feet from the road, is not so clear as to justify deciding the issue at the summary judgment stage. A reasonable juror could determine that the defendants should have known occasional high winds could displace the unsecured part. They were in their home for several hours after the storm passed and did not discover the debris on the roadway, remove it, or warn approaching motorists. Viewed in the light most favorable to Thompson (P), we conclude a reasonable factfinder could find that the harm he suffered resulted from the risks that made the defendants' conduct negligent. Reversed and remanded.

Analysis:

The plaintiff's burden in a tort case is to establish both cause in fact and legal, or proximate, cause, the latter of which requires a policy determination of whether the law must require the defendant to be legally responsible for the injury. The court held here that a reasonable possibility existed that the defendants could be held legally responsible. The issue was one for the finder of fact, not the court, so the trial court erred in deciding in the defendants' favor as a matter of law.

Palsgraf v. Long Island Railroad Co.

(Injured Bystander) v. (Railway Company)

248 N.Y. 339, 162 N.E. 99 (1928)

A DEFENDANT IS NOT LIABLE FOR UNFORESEEABLE HARMS

■ **INSTANT FACTS** A passenger waiting for a train was injured on a railroad platform after railway employees dislodged—from the arm of another passenger whom they were negligently helping to jump onto a moving train—a package of fireworks. The fireworks exploded when it fell on the tracks, and the shock from the explosion caused scales to fall on the plaintiff.

■ **BLACK LETTER RULE** The risk reasonably to be perceived defines the duty to be obeyed.

■ PROCEDURAL BASIS

Appeal to the New York Court of Appeals, challenging the decision of the Appellate Division upholding a jury verdict for the plaintiff.

■ FACTS

Ms. Palsgraf (P) was standing on a platform waiting for her train to arrive. While waiting, another train was disembarking. A man carrying a package of unidentified contents jumped onto the moving train, but seemed unsteady, as if about to fall. Two railway officials, one on the train the other on the platform, helped the man regain balance, but in the process dislodged the package from the man's arm. The package was filled with fireworks, which began to explode when they fell. The shock of the explosion threw some scales down. The scales fell on Ms. Palsgraf (P) and caused her injuries, for which she sued. The jury found for Mrs. Palsgraf (P) and the Appellate Division affirmed.

■ ISSUE

Does a defendant owe a duty of care to a plaintiff whose injury was the result of an unforeseeable risk?

■ DECISION AND RATIONALE

(Cardozo, J.) No. The risk reasonably to be perceived defines the duty to be obeyed. Negligence is not actionable unless it involves the invasion of a legally protected interest, the violation of a right. The conduct of the railway official may have been a wrong to the man carrying the package, but was not a wrong in relation to Mrs. Palsgraf (P), standing far away. Nothing gave notice that the falling package had the ability to injure those standing at such a distance. This case does not turn on the issue of proximate cause, for that question arises only after it has been established that the defendant violated a duty to the plaintiff. We can assume that negligence in relation to the plaintiff would entail liability for any and all consequences, no matter how extraordinary. But the issue of consequences is rooted in a wrong, which we do not find in this case. Reversed.

■ DISSENT

(Andrew, J.) This case turns not on the issue of negligence, but on whether the Long Island Railway Co.'s agent proximately caused Ms. Palsgraf's (P) injury. The majority holds too narrow a view of negligence. It is true that negligence is relational. That relationship, however, is not merely, as the majority holds, between a man and those whom he might reasonably expect his act would injure. Rather, the relationship is between a man and those to whom he does in fact injure. Simply stated, every one owes to the world at large the duty to refrain from those acts that may unreasonably threaten the safety of others. But liability is not endless, for it is limited by proximate cause, which is determined by several factors. Probable cause is a line arbitrarily drawn by the law so as to conveniently determine the point at which liability for negligence will cease. In deciding proximate cause the court must ask itself several questions. Was there a natural and continuous sequence between cause and effect? Was the act a substantial factor in producing the harm? Was there a direct connection between them, without too many intervening causes? Is the cause likely to produce the result? Could the result have reasonably been foreseen? Is the cause too remote in space and time? Applying these factors to the present case leads me to conclude that the act of knocking a package onto the ground proximately caused Ms. Palsgraf's injury. The explosion was a substantial factor in causing the injury. The events were the result of a natural and continuous sequence. There was no remoteness of time, and very little remoteness of space. It is also obvious that the explosion would foreseeably cause injury to anyone on the platform.

Analysis:

This is one of those few cases where both the majority and dissenting opinions are often cited for their propositions. Justice Cardozo's opinion focused on the duty owed to the plaintiff and essentially ties the scope of this duty to the foreseeability of the harm caused and the injured plaintiff. If the harm caused was not a foreseeable risk of the defendant's action, then no duty was owed to the plaintiff. Similarly, if an injury occurs to a person whom no one could have foreseen being injured, the defendant is not liable because there is no duty owed to unforeseeable plaintiffs. Justice Andrews, however, saw the issue in terms of proximate cause. In rejecting the majority's narrow view of negligence and the duty owed, Justice Andrews states that everyone owes to the world at large a duty to refrain from acts that unreasonably threaten the safety of others. Most courts have rejected this view, choosing to adopt Justice Cardozo's foreseeability inquiry. But Justice Andrews's dissent is still valid for its elucidation on proximate cause. Andrews refused to limit the issue of proximate cause to an inquiry of foreseeability alone. Instead, he lists several factors that are essential to determining whether proximate cause exists, such as the continuity of space and time, whether the negligent act was a substantial factor in the injury, and the foreseeability of the result.

Hughes v. Lord Advocate

(Injured Child) v. (Government Tortfeasor)

A.C. 837 (H.L.) (1963)

A HARM IS NOT OUTSIDE THE SCOPE OF RISK SIMPLY BECAUSE IT OCCURS IN AN UNEXPECTED MANNER

■ **INSTANT FACTS** While playing in and around an unguarded open manhole, two young boys accidentally knocked a kerosene lantern into the manhole, breaking the lantern and causing an unforeseeable explosion.

■ **BLACK LETTER RULE** The fact that the defendant's negligence causes a known harm in an unforeseeable manner does not relieve him of liability.

■ PROCEDURAL BASIS

Not provided.

■ FACTS

While on break, Post Office employees working on a telephone cable left unguarded an open manhole, covered with a tent and kerosene lamps. Two boys found the unguarded site and descended into the hole, tying one of the lamps to a rope. The boys climbed out with no problem, but once out of the whole, they knocked a kerosene lamp into the hole, breaking the lamp. Some of the kerosene unforeseeably vaporized and came into contact with the open flame, causing an explosion. The Hughes (P) boy fell into the hole as a result of the shock created by the explosion and suffered severe burns.

■ ISSUE

May a defendant escape liability on the ground that the harm caused, while foreseeable, occurred in an unforeseeable manner?

■ DECISION AND RATIONALE

(Lord Reid) No. The fact that the defendant's negligence causes a foreseeable harm in an unforeseeable manner does not relieve him of liability. It is agreed that the accident was so unlikely as to be unforeseeable. But the mere fact that the way in which an accident happened could not be anticipated is not enough to relieve the defendant of liability. The cause of this accident was a known source of danger, the lamp, but it behaved in an unpredictable way. In my judgment that affords no defense.

■ CONCURRENCE

(Lord Guest) I find unacceptable the argument that liability should not be had because although the burns suffered were a foreseeable risk from the lamps, the explosion which caused the burns was unforeseeable. An explosion is nothing more than one way which burning might be caused by a potentially dangerous lamp.

■ CONCURRENCE

(Lord Pearce) The explosion did not create an accident and damage of a different type from the misadventure and damage that was foreseeable. The accident was but a variant of the foreseeable. The harm which resulted was neither greater than nor different in kind from that which was foreseeable.

Analysis:

The "manner of injury" rule identifies the "foreseeability" that should be applicable to the proximate cause analysis adopted in *Medcalf v. Washington Heights Condominium Ass'n, Inc.* and *Palsgraf v. Long Island Railroad Co.* The law, essentially, does not require that a defendant have foreseen the manner in which an injury occurred. Rather, for proximate cause, the foreseeability that is controlling is the foreseeability of the particular type of harm or injury that occurred. The fact that the foreseeable harm occurs as the result of an unforeseeable sequence of events does not absolve the negligent actor of liability. Therefore, the court here held that because burns were a foreseeable harm of leaving kerosene lamps unattended, it did not matter that the burns to Hughes (P) were caused by an unforeseeable explosion caused by the kerosene lamps.

Marcus v. Staubs

(Provider of Alcohol to Minors) v. (Mother of Injured Girls)

___ S.E.2d ___, 2012 WL 5834579 (W. Va. 2012)

INTERVENING ACTS DO NOT ALWAYS BREAK THE CHAIN OF CAUSATION

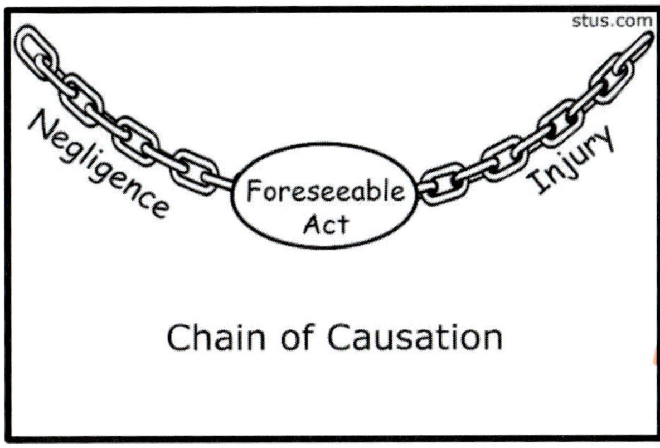

■ **INSTANT FACTS** Staubs' (P) daughters were involved in an accident, killing one of them and seriously injuring another, after Marcus (D) provided the minors with alcohol and took them to a party; Marcus (D) argued that the fact that the girls stole a truck and drove themselves home after consuming alcohol relieved him of liability.

■ **BLACK LETTER RULE** A tortfeasor whose negligence is a substantial factor in bringing about injuries is not relieved from liability by the intervening acts of third persons if those acts were reasonably foreseeable by the original tortfeasor at the time of his negligent conduct.

■ PROCEDURAL BASIS

State appellate court review of the trial court's denial of Marcus's (D) motion for summary judgment and granting of Staubs' (P) motion for summary judgment.

■ FACTS

The thirteen- and fourteen-year-old Staubs sisters were drinking at a house party. Their friend Marcus (D) had driven them to the party and provided the alcohol. When a parent arrived home and told the girls they could not spend the night, they called Marcus (D) for a ride home but he declined. The sisters and two friends left the house and stole a truck from the neighbor. A fourteen-year-old friend drove the truck. On the way home, the vehicle hit an embankment. One of the Staubs sisters was killed and the other sustained a head injury. The Staubs sisters' mother (P) brought suit against Marcus (D) and others, alleging that Marcus (D) was liable because he had provided the alcohol to the minors. Marcus (D) argued that the illegal consumption of alcohol by the minors, the theft of the vehicle, and the young driver's reckless operation of the vehicle without a license and while intoxicated were all intervening causes relieving him of liability.

■ ISSUE

Did the trial court properly grant summary judgment in the plaintiff's favor?

■ DECISION AND RATIONALE

(Per curiam.) No. A tortfeasor whose negligence is a substantial factor in bringing about injuries is not relieved from liability by the intervening acts of third persons if those acts were reasonably foreseeable by the original tortfeasor at the time of his negligent conduct. Marcus (D) argues that the criminal acts in this case were not reasonably foreseeable and therefore break the chain of causation. We find it properly within the province of the jury to determine the measure of the defendant's knowledge of and participation in the procurement of the alcohol, whether the alcohol was "furnished" to the minors, and then, if so, whether given the facts and circumstances leading up to those events, the subsequent acts of the minors and their friends were reasonably foreseeable. We therefore find that the trial court's award of summary judgment improperly invaded the province of the jury in determining whether Marcus's (D) actions were the proximate cause of the accident and whether the subsequent criminal actions were intervening causes and, as such, was error.

Analysis:

The defendant claimed in this case that he did not legally cause the plaintiff's alleged injury because that injury was produced, in material part, by a superseding or intervening cause. A superseding or intervening cause is any intentionally harmful act, force of nature, or criminal event, unforeseeable by the defendant, that intervenes in the sequence of events leading from the defendant's alleged negligence to the plaintiff's alleged injury and proximately causes that injury. Under the law, the intervention of such a superseding cause relieves the defendant from liability for the plaintiff's injury on the ground that, due to such superseding cause, the defendant did not legally cause the injury, even though his or her negligence was a substantial factor in bringing the injury about. When a claim of superseding cause is made at trial, the plaintiff must disprove at least one essential element of that claim in order to prove its own conflicting claim of legal causation.

■ CASE VOCABULARY

INTERVENING CAUSE: An event that occurs after the initial act leading to an accident, and substantially causes the accident; the intervening cause relieves the party whose act started the series of events that led to the accident from liability, because the original negligence is no longer the proximate cause.

Delaney v. Reynolds

(Self-Inflicted Gunshot Victim) v. (Police Officer)

63 Mass.App.Ct. 239, 825 N.E.2d 554 (2005)

SUICIDE MAY OR MAY NOT BE A SUPERSEDING CAUSE OF INJURY

■ **INSTANT FACTS** Delaney (P) shot herself with an unlocked, loaded gun kept in the house she shared with a police officer, and in her negligence suit against him the officer claimed that Delaney's (P) suicide attempt was a superseding cause of her injuries.

■ **BLACK LETTER RULE** When an intervening occurrence was foreseeable by the defendant, the causal chain of events remains intact and the defendant's original negligence remains a proximate cause of the plaintiff's injury.

■ PROCEDURAL BASIS

Appellate court review of the trial court's entry of summary judgment in the defendant's favor.

■ FACTS

Delaney (P) and Reynolds (D) lived together. Reynolds (D), a police officer, stored a loaded and unlocked gun in the bedroom, even though he knew Delaney (P) was depressed and had a substance abuse problem. One night, when Delaney (P) had been drinking heavily and smoking crack cocaine, Reynolds (D) ordered her out of his house. While packing her belongings, Delaney (P) took the loaded gun from the bedroom. She ran toward the living room in which Reynolds (D) was sitting and fired twice toward the window, but the gun did not go off. She then ran back upstairs, with Reynolds (D) in pursuit. When she reached the bedroom, Delaney (P) put the gun under her chin and pulled the trigger, and this time the gun went off, seriously injuring Delaney (P). She sued Reynolds (D) for negligence, but he argued that her attempted suicide was a superseding cause of her injuries. The trial judge agreed and granted summary judgment in Reynolds's (D) favor.

■ ISSUE

Did the trial court properly grant summary judgment in Reynolds's (D) favor on Delaney's (P) negligence claim?

■ DECISION AND RATIONALE

(Judge Undisclosed.) No. When an intervening occurrence was foreseeable by the defendant, the causal chain of events remains intact and the defendant's original negligence remains a proximate cause of the plaintiff's injury. This formulation is not altered when the original negligent act is followed by an independent act or event that actively operates in bringing about the plaintiff's injury. To prevail on a claim of negligence, the plaintiff must prove that the defendant was negligent and that his negligence was a proximate cause of her injury. Negligent conduct is the proximate cause of an injury if the injury was a foreseeable result of the defendant's negligent conduct. The question in this case is whether suicide is such an extraordinary event as to not be foreseeable. Recent decisions by this and other courts indicate no ironclad rule that suicide constitutes an intervening and superseding cause as a matter of law. In this case, Delaney (P) argued that whether she intended to kill herself was a question of fact, given that the gun had misfired twice before she shot herself. We agree. We also think that the jury should be able to consider whether the risk that Delaney (P) would use Reynolds's (D) unsecured gun to injure herself was foreseeable, and that Reynolds's (D) failure to secure the gun was therefore a proximate cause of Delaney's (P) injuries. Reversed.

Analysis:

In this case, the facts favor a finding of foreseeability. Delaney (D) was known by Reynolds (D) to be a depressed substance abuser, which supports an argument that he—especially given that he was a police officer—should have known better than to leave an unlocked, loaded gun handy. It is also more likely, and thus more foreseeable, that a person suffering from depression will attempt suicide. If Reynolds's (D) roommate were a happy-go-lucky, mentally healthy teetotaler, Reynolds's (D) actions may have been deemed less negligent because misuse of the gun would have been less foreseeable. Here, however, given the facts, at a minimum the jury had a right to consider the issues, and the trial court therefore erred in granting summary judgment in the defendant's favor.

■ CASE VOCABULARY

INTERVENING CAUSE: An event that comes between the initial event in a sequence and the end result, thereby altering the natural course of events that might have connected a wrongful act to an injury. If the intervening cause is strong enough to relieve the wrongdoer of any liability, it becomes a *superseding cause*.

SUPERSEDING CAUSE: An intervening act or force that the law considers sufficient to override the cause for which the original tortfeasor was responsible, thereby exonerating that tortfeasor from liability.

Derdiarian v. Felix Contracting Corp.

(Injured Road Worker) v. (General Contractor)

51 N.Y.2d 308, 434 N.Y.S.2d 166, 414 N.E.2d 666 (1980)

THE FACT THAT A THIRD PARTY NEGLIGENTLY TRIGGERED THE HARM CREATED BY THE DEFENDANT'S NEGLIGENCE DOES NOT AUTOMATICALLY PRECLUDE RECOVERY FROM THE DEFENDANT

■ **INSTANT FACTS** A road worker was injured after a man negligently drove his car through the work site and struck a boiling cauldron of enamel that was negligently left unguarded from traffic, causing the enamel to splatter and burn the worker.

■ **BLACK LETTER RULE** An intervening act may not serve as a superseding cause, and relieve an actor of responsibility, where the risk of the intervening act occurring is the very same risk which renders the actor negligent.

■ PROCEDURAL BASIS

Appeal to the New York Court of Appeals, challenging the decision of the Appellate Division to uphold a jury verdict for the plaintiff.

■ FACTS

Felix Contracting Corp. (Felix) (D) was installing an underground gas main alongside a road. Mr. Derdiarian (P) was in charge of a kettle filled with liquid enamel, boiling to 400 degrees at the job site. Felix (D) insisted that the kettle be set on the west side of the excavation, facing oncoming traffic. The work site, including the kettle, was protected only by a single wooden horse. Testimony established that the work site was improperly protected. While driving eastbound, Mr. Dickens (D) lost control of his vehicle when he suffered an epileptic seizure brought on by his failure to take medication at the proper time. Mr. Dickens' (D) vehicle crashed into Mr. Derdiarian (P) and the kettle, causing the latter to splatter over the former's face and body.

■ ISSUE

Does a third party intervening act invariably break the causal link between the defendant's negligence and the harm caused?

■ DECISION AND RATIONALE

(Cooke, C.J.) No. An intervening act may not serve as a superseding cause, and relieve an actor of responsibility, where the risk of the intervening act occurring is the very same risk which renders the actor negligent. It is well settled that a plaintiff need not show that the precise manner in which an accident occurred was foreseeable. Where the acts of a third party intervene between the defendant's conduct and the plaintiff's injury, the question of liability turns upon whether the intervening act is a normal or foreseeable consequence of the situation created by the defendant's negligence. Although foreseeability can often be a question of law, especially where only one conclusion could be reached, the question is often left to the trier of fact. We cannot say as a matter of law that Dickens' (D) negligence was a superseding cause which interrupted the link between Felix's (D) negligence and Mr. Derdiarian's (P) injury. A prime hazard associated with failing to secure a roadwork site is that a driver will negligently enter the site and cause injury. The finder of fact could have concluded that the foreseeable result of the risk created by Felix (D) was the injury of a worker caused by a driver negligently entering the work site.

Analysis:

Courts often use the term "superseding cause" when the negligence of a second actor renders the first actor not liable. This case illustrates that the existence of an intervening actor does not always serve to supersede the negligence of the first actor. As with most issues related to proximate cause, foreseeability is the crucial factor in determining the extent of liability. If foreseeable, the intervening act will not supersede the negligence of the first actor. In this case, the intervening act—Mr. Dickens (D) negligently crashing into the work site—was the exact risk created by Felix's (D) negligence. The court here holds of no consequence the fact that the negligence was caused by a failure to take medicine and not an inability to drive safely. The exact harm that was foreseeable—injury to workers—was the harm that occurred.

Ventricelli v. Kinney System Rent A Car, Inc.

(Injured Lessee) v. (Rental Car Company)

45 N.Y.2d 950, 411 N.Y.S.2d 555, 383 N.E.2d 1149 (1978)

THE FORESEEABILITY OF AN INTERVENING ACT CAN BE A QUESTION OF LAW OR FACT, DEPENDING ON THE CIRCUMSTANCES

■ **INSTANT FACTS** A man was struck by a moving vehicle while trying to shut the defective trunk lid on the vehicle he rented.

■ **BLACK LETTER RULE** A rental car company could not have foreseen that a driver would strike its client while the client was attempting to shut the trunk lid negligently left in disrepair by the company.

■ PROCEDURAL BASIS

Appeal to the Court of Appeal of New York, challenging the decision of the Appellate Division reversing and dismissing the verdict against the rental car company.

■ FACTS

Mr. Ventricelli (P) rented from Kinney System Rent A Car, Inc. (Kinney) (D) a vehicle that had a defective trunk lid that did not close properly. While he and a passenger were attempting to shut the trunk, Ventricelli was struck by a car driven by Mr. Maldonado (D). At the time of the accident, Ventricelli (P) was "safely" in a parking space.

■ ISSUE

Could Kinney (D) have foreseen that a driver would negligently strike its client while the latter was attempting to shut the trunk negligently maintained by Kinney?

■ DECISION AND RATIONALE

(Memorandum) No. The immediately effective cause of Ventricelli's (P) injuries was the negligence of Maldonado (D). It was certainly foreseeable that Kinney's (D) negligence would lead to Ventricelli's repeated attempts to close the lid. What was not foreseeable was the collision between vehicles both parked a brief interval before the accident. Ventricelli (P) was in a relatively safe parking space, not in an actively traveled lane. He might have been in that situation independent of any negligence on the part of Kinney (D). Under these circumstances, to hold the accident a foreseeable consequence of Kinney's (D) negligence is to stretch the concept of foreseeability beyond acceptable limits. Affirmed.

■ DISSENT

(Fuchsberg, J) Not only was it foreseeable, but it was a reasonable expectation that a driver confronted with a trunk lid with a penchant for flying open would alight and promptly proceed to the rear of the car to attempt to secure the lid manually so that he might continue on his way without further danger. Kinney's (P) negligence thrust upon Ventricelli (P) a choice between the danger from the defective lid and the danger of being struck while attempting to close the trunk.

Analysis:

The court concludes as a matter of law that the accident was not a foreseeable consequence of Kinney's (P) failure to properly maintain the trunk lid. This case could be seen as an application of the rule, eventually adopted by this court in *Sheehan v. City of New York*, that an actor has not proximately caused an accident if his negligence merely furnishes the condition or occasion for the occurrence of an event. The court considered it important that Ventricelli (P) was "safely" parked, and that Ventricelli (P) could have been in that same position for any number of reasons, e.g., loading and unloading the trunk. The court could have reached the exact opposite result under the "manner of harm" rule. The court could have held immaterial the fact that Mr. Ventricelli (D) was struck while the car was parked, because a car accident is a foreseeable result of a faulty trunk lid. This case thus illustrates the arbitrary line that is "proximate cause."

Marshall v. Nugent

(Injured Pedestrian/Passenger) v. (Intervening Negligent Driver)

222 F.2d 604 (1st Cir. 1955)

THE SCOPE OF RISK FROM A DEFENDANT'S NEGLIGENCE CAN BE EXTENDED TEMPORALLY AND GEOGRAPHICALLY, DEPENDING ON THE CIRCUMSTANCES

■ **INSTANT FACTS** A man that was struck while attempting to warn oncoming traffic of an obstruction in the road, sued the truck driver that caused the obstruction.

■ **BLACK LETTER RULE** In a traffic mix-up due to negligence, before the waters have become placid and normal again, the unfolding of events between the culpable act and the plaintiff's eventual injury may be bizarre indeed; yet the defendant may be liable for the result.

■ PROCEDURAL BASIS

Appeal to the Second Circuit, challenging the decision of the district court denying the defendant's motion for a directed verdict.

■ FACTS

Marshall (P) was a passenger in a vehicle that was forced off the road by a truck that was partly in both lanes. The truck stopped to help pull the vehicle back onto the road, an effort that partly blocked the road. In an effort to warn oncoming vehicles, Marshall (P) walked toward the top of a hill, but was struck by Nugent's (D) vehicle before reaching the top. Marshall (P) sued Nugent (D) and the truck driver, Prince (D). The jury found against the truck driver, who appealed arguing that he was not the proximate cause.

■ ISSUE

Must a defendant's negligence immediately precede the harm to the plaintiff?

■ DECISION AND RATIONALE

(Magruder, J.) No. In a traffic mix-up due to negligence, before the waters have become placid and normal again, the unfolding of events between the culpable act and the plaintiff's eventual injury may be bizarre indeed; yet the defendant may be liable for the result. We find semantic the argument that Prince's (D) negligence was "merely a condition" to the accident and not the proximate cause thereof. The issue of proximate cause requires a flexible approach in defining the risk, or risks, narrowly, or more broadly, as seems appropriate to an individual case. With regard to motor vehicle accidents, the possibilities are endless. It is often impossible for a defendant to predict how his negligent act will work out. When the issue of proximate cause arises in a borderline case, we leave it to the jury to decide. Consequently, the district court did not err in refusing to direct a verdict for Prince (D). Marshall (P) was a passenger in the vehicle Prince (D) ran off the road. Prince's negligence was a breach of duty to Marshall; and although the act of negligence was over and done with, its consequences were still attendant.

Analysis:

This case serves as an example that the temporal scope of risk attendant to a negligent act is often broad, which, of course, increases the possibility of an intervening cause. The court refused to accept the "merely a condition" argument that was adopted in *Sheehan v. City of New York*, holding that the conclusion that an act is merely a condition to an event is simply another way of stating there was no proximate cause. Instead, the court adopts what it deems a flexible approach that broadens or narrows the scope of risk depending on the circumstances. The court gives lip service to the idea that proximate cause is an effort to define foreseeability. But the opinion fails to mention the foreseeability of Nugent's (D) negligent driving. Rather, the court holds that the possibilities for harm arising from a traffic mishap are too numerous to be foreseeable. The point to be taken from this case is that scope of harm can be stretched both temporally and geographically, depending on the circumstances.

CHAPTER NINE

Fault of the Plaintiff

Butterfield v. Forrester

Instant Facts: Butterfield (P) was thrown from his horse and was injured after encountering an obstruction which Forrester (D) had placed in the road.

Black Letter Rule: When a plaintiff's lack of ordinary care contributes to an accident, he cannot recover for injuries sustained.

Pohl v. County of Furnas

Instant Facts: Pohl (P) sued the county (D) alleging that injuries he sustained when he went off the road could have been avoided had the county (D) properly placed an appropriately reflective sign warning of the sharp curve ahead; the county (D) argued that Pohl's (P) excessive speed caused, or at least worsened, his injuries.

Black Letter Rule: An intervening cause cuts off a tortfeasor's liability only when it is not foreseeable.

Bexiga v. Havir Manufacturing Corp.

Instant Facts: A machine operator sued the manufacturer of the machine after his hand was crushed, resulting in the loss of fingers and deformity of his hand.

Black Letter Rule: In negligence cases the defense of contributory negligence has been held to be unavailable where considerations of policy and justice dictate.

Christensen v. Royal School District No. 160

Instant Facts: A student was sexually abused by her teacher, and she and her parents brought suit; the school district and principal attempted to assert a defense of contributory fault because the relationship was purportedly consensual.

Black Letter Rule: Contributory fault may not be assessed against a thirteen-year-old child based on her failure to protect herself from being sexually abused when the defendant stands in a special relationship to the child and has a duty to protect the child.

Butterfield v. Forrester

(Horseback Rider) v. (House Repairman)

11 East. 59, 103 Eng. Rep. 926 (1809)

A PLAINTIFF CANNOT RECOVER FOR INJURY FROM AN ACCIDENT WHEREIN HE DID NOT USE ORDINARY CARE

■ **INSTANT FACTS** Butterfield (P) was thrown from his horse and was injured after encountering an obstruction which Forrester (D) had placed in the road.

■ **BLACK LETTER RULE** When a plaintiff's lack of ordinary care contributes to an accident, he cannot recover for injuries sustained.

■ PROCEDURAL BASIS

Plaintiff appeals from the jury's judgment for the defendant.

■ FACTS

Forrester (D), while making repairs to his house, put a pole across the part of the road which was close to his home. Free passage was left by another road, however. Butterfield (P), who had just left a tavern [drunk riding?], was riding his horse very fast down the road and did not see the obstruction. He was thrown by his horse and was injured [but did he spill his beer?]. A witness testified that, although darkness was approaching, there was enough light left to see the obstruction from 100 yards away, and if Butterfield (P) had not been riding so fast he might have observed and avoided it. There was no evidence that Butterfield (P) was intoxicated at the time [didn't have breathalyzers back then!]. The jury found for Forrester (D), and this appeal followed.

■ ISSUE

Can a plaintiff recover for personal injury when his lack of ordinary care contributed to the accident?

■ DECISION AND RATIONALE

(Bayley, J. and Ellenborough, C.J.) No. When a plaintiff's lack of ordinary care contributes to an accident, he cannot recover for injuries sustained. Butterfield (P) was riding his horse as fast as he could go through the streets. If he had used ordinary care he would have seen the obstruction and been able to avoid it. One person being in fault will not dispense with another's using ordinary care for himself. Application for a new trial is denied.

Analysis:

Contributory negligence is an affirmative defense that must be raised and proved by the defendant in a case. In general, the same rules and tests apply to determine whether conduct is contributorily negligent as are used to determine if conduct is negligent, except that the duty here is not owed to any other person. Rather, it is a duty to exercise ordinary care in the circumstances to avoid one's own injury at the hands of another. Also, there is no requirement of an "act"—the duty of self-protection always exists and is often violated by unreasonable inaction in the face of danger. At common law, the plaintiff's contributory negligence was an absolute and complete bar to any recovery for the negligence of the defendant, no matter how slight the negligence of the plaintiff as compared to the negligence of the defendant. However, contributory negligence is a defense only to negligence; it is no defense at all to an intentional tort, nor to "reckless" or "willful" misconduct.

■ CASE VOCABULARY

CONTRIBUTORY NEGLIGENCE: Conduct on the part of the plaintiff that is a contributing cause to his own injuries.

INTENTIONAL TORT: A wrong or injury caused by the purposeful actions of the defendant.

IPSO FACTO: In and of itself.

ORDINARY CARE: Care which is reasonably commensurate with a known danger.

PRIMA FACIE: Not requiring further support to establish existence, validity or credibility.

Pohl v. County of Furnas

(Injured Driver) v. (County)

682 F.3d 785 (8th Cir. 2012)

THE FACTFINDER IS IN THE BEST POSITION TO DECIDE ISSUES OF INTERVENING CAUSE AND COMPARATIVE FAULT

■ **INSTANT FACTS** Pohl (P) sued the county (D) alleging that injuries he sustained when he went off the road could have been avoided had the county (D) properly placed an appropriately reflective sign warning of the sharp curve ahead; the county (D) argued that Pohl's (P) excessive speed caused, or at least worsened, his injuries.

■ **BLACK LETTER RULE** An intervening cause cuts off a tortfeasor's liability only when it is not foreseeable.

■ PROCEDURAL BASIS

Appeal by both sides from a trial court judgment partially favoring each party.

■ FACTS

Pohl (P) was driving to a friend's farmhouse when he mistakenly turned onto Drive 719 instead of Road 719. Unlike Road 719, which continued in a straight line, Drive 719 was a gravel road with a ninety-degree curve. There was no posted speed limit, but Drive 719 was subject to a general statutory limit of fifty miles per hour. Pohl (P) was traveling at over sixty miles per hour when he came upon the sign warning of the curve, but he braked too late and went off the road. His car hit an embankment, rolled, and came to rest upside down in a culvert. Pohl (P) lost consciousness. When he came to, he realized he could not move his legs. He waited until daybreak but no help had arrived, so Pohl (P) dragged himself to a nearby farmhouse, where the residents called an ambulance. Pohl (P) had suffered a fracture and cord compression in his thoracic spine. He sued the county, arguing that the sign was negligently placed and maintained. Pohl's (P) expert testified at trial that because of its placement and lack of reflectivity, the sign failed to provide motorists with enough notice of the curve, and that even if Pohl (P) had been traveling at fifty miles per hour, he still would have left the roadway. The county's (D) expert testified that had Pohl (P) been traveling at the legal speed, he could have safely negotiated the curve, or at least had a less severe accident. The district court found that the county (D) was 60% negligent based on a combination of the sign's lack of retro-reflectivity and its placement, and that Pohl (P) was 40% negligent based on his driving over the speed limit, and it reduced his damages accordingly. Both sides appealed.

■ ISSUE

Was Pohl's (P) excessive speed an intervening cause that was itself a proximate cause of his injuries?

■ DECISION AND RATIONALE

(Murphy, J.) No. An intervening cause cuts off a tortfeasor's liability only when it is not foreseeable. In such cases, the new and independent conduct of a third person is itself the proximate cause of the injury and breaks the causal connection between the original conduct and the injury. Here, however, testimony at trial indicated that traffic engineers assume drivers will exceed the speed limit by ten to fifteen miles per hour on a fifty-mile-per-hour road. Thus, Pohl's (P) travel in excess of the speed limit by thirteen miles per hour was readily foreseeable and not an intervening cause relieving the county (D) of liability.

In addition, the county (D) argues that the district court undervalued Pohl's (P) contributory negligence. The county's (D) expert's testimony conflicted with Pohl's (P) expert's on this point. When there are two permissible views of the evidence, the factfinder's choice between them cannot be clearly erroneous. Nor did the district court clearly err in finding that Pohl's negligence at the time of the crash was a proximate cause of his injuries, or in its apportionment of negligence to Pohl (P). Apportionment of negligence is purely a matter for the factfinder, and its decision will not be disturbed on appeal if it is supported by credible evidence and bears a reasonable relationship to the elements of negligence proved at trial. Accordingly, we affirm the judgment of the district court.

Analysis:

Although the court sometimes uses the term "contributory negligence" in this case, it is actually applying the comparative negligence doctrine. Under the contributory negligence doctrine, the plaintiff's recovery is completely barred if the damages suffered were partly the plaintiff's own fault. Most states have abolished contributory negligence and have adopted a comparative-negligence analysis. Comparative negligence is the principle that reduces a plaintiff's recovery proportionally to the plaintiff's degree of fault, rather than barring recovery completely. In modified comparative negligence states, liability for negligence is apportioned in accordance with the percentage of fault that the factfinder assigns to each party, and the plaintiff's recovery is reduced by the percentage of negligence assigned him or her, but the plaintiff's recovery is barred if his or her percentage of fault is 50% or more.

■ CASE VOCABULARY

COMPARATIVE NEGLIGENCE: A plaintiff's own negligence that proportionally reduces the damages recoverable from the defendant.

CONTRIBUTORY NEGLIGENCE: A plaintiff's own negligence that played a part in causing the plaintiff's injury and that is significant enough to bar the plaintiff from recovering damages.

Bexiga v. Havir Manufacturing Corp.

(Machine Operator) v. (Machine Manufacturer)

60 N.J. 402, 290 A.2d 281 (1972)

WHERE CONSIDERATIONS OF JUSTICE AND POLICY DICTATE, CONTRIBUTORY NEGLIGENCE IS UNAVAILABLE AS A DEFENSE TO EITHER NEGLIGENCE OR STRICT LIABILITY CLAIMS

■ **INSTANT FACTS** A machine operator sued the manufacturer of the machine after his hand was crushed, resulting in the loss of fingers and deformity of his hand.

■ **BLACK LETTER RULE** In negligence cases the defense of contributory negligence has been held to be unavailable where considerations of policy and justice dictate.

■ PROCEDURAL BASIS

Appeal from the Appellate Division's affirmance of the trial court's dismissal of the action at the close of the plaintiff's case.

■ FACTS

This is a products liability case. Bexiga (P), a minor, was operating a power punch press for his employer when his right hand was crushed by the machine, resulting in the loss of fingers and deformity of his hand. Bexiga (P) mistakenly placed his hand under the ram at the same time the foot pedal was depressed, and no safety devices were in place to prevent this action. His father brought this suit on behalf of Bexiga (P) against Havir Manufacturing Corp. (D), the manufacturer of the machine. Bexiga's (P) expert, Andrew Gass, a mechanical engineer, testified that the machine amounted to a "booby trap" because there were no safety devices in its basic design and none were installed prior to the accident. Gass described two "basic types" of protective safety devices, both of which were known in the industry at the time of the manufacture and sale. These and other safety devices were available from companies specializing in safety equipment. The trial court dismissed the action at the close of Bexiga's (P) case. The Appellate Division affirmed and this appeal followed.

■ ISSUE

Can contributory negligence be used as a defense in a case where the injury was the very eventuality the duty owed was designed to protect against?

■ DECISION AND RATIONALE

(Proctor, J.) No. In negligence cases the defense of contributory negligence has been held to be unavailable where considerations of policy and justice dictate. We think this case presents a situation where the interests of justice dictate that contributory negligence be unavailable as a defense to either the negligence or strict liability claims. The asserted negligence of Bexiga (P)—placing his hand under the ram while at the same time depressing the foot pedal—was the very eventuality the safety devices were designed to guard against. It would be anomalous to hold that Havir (D) has a duty to install safety devices but a breach of that duty results in no liability for the very injury the duty was meant to protect against. We hold that under the facts presented to us in this case the defense of contributory negligence is unavailable. The judgment of the Appellate Division is reversed and the cause is remanded for a new trial.

Analysis:

This case can be understood as holding that when a defendant undertakes to protect a plaintiff from his own fault, or when the law imposes such a duty, the entire responsibility for care by definition falls upon the defendant, and the plaintiff's fault cannot be held against him. That is logical enough, but when should the law impose such a duty if it is not one voluntarily undertaken by the defendant? A reasonable rule would be that such a duty is imposed when the defendant imposes a risk upon the plaintiff, but that plaintiff's fault imposes no similar risk upon the defendant. In other words, the risks are not reciprocal or mutual. Perhaps, additionally, the plaintiff's vulnerability might play a part in determining responsibility, such as when the defendant knows of a plaintiff's disability that prevents or inhibits the plaintiff's care for himself, or when the plaintiff's risky conduct endangers himself but not others.

■ CASE VOCABULARY

PRODUCTS LIABILITY: A doctrine holding a manufacturer liable when an article is placed into the market with a defect which causes an injury.

STRICT LIABILITY: Liability imposed without regard to fault.

Christensen v. Royal School District No. 160

(Student) v. (Teacher's Employer)

156 Wash.2d 62, 124 P.3d 283 (2005)

SCHOOLS HAVE A DUTY TO PROTECT THEIR STUDENTS

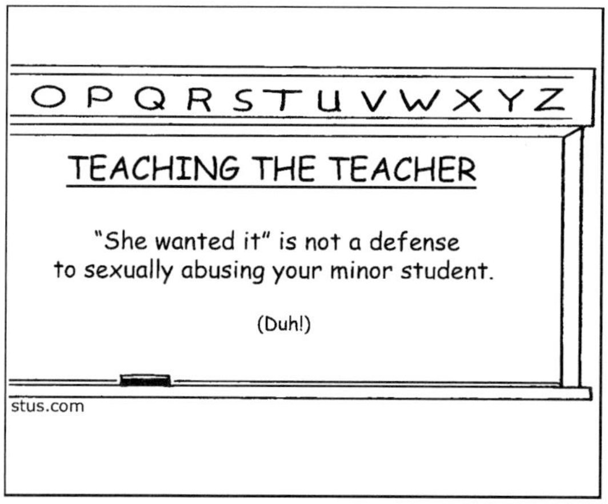

■ INSTANT FACTS A student was sexually abused by her teacher, and she and her parents brought suit; the school district and principal attempted to assert a defense of contributory fault because the relationship was purportedly consensual.

■ BLACK LETTER RULE Contributory fault may not be assessed against a thirteen-year-old child based on her failure to protect herself from being sexually abused when the defendant stands in a special relationship to the child and has a duty to protect the child.

■ PROCEDURAL BASIS

State supreme court consideration of a certified question from the trial court.

■ FACTS

Diaz, a twenty-six-year-old teacher, engaged in sexual relations with Christensen (P), his thirteen-year-old student, in Diaz's classroom. Diaz claimed that the relationship was consensual, but Christenson (P) and her parents sued the school district, alleging negligent hiring and supervision. The district (D) and the school's principal (D) asserted an affirmative defense of contributory fault based on Christenson's (P) purported voluntary participation. The student (P) moved for partial summary judgment on the contributory fault issue, and the trial court certified to the state supreme court the question of whether a thirteen-year-old victim of sexual abuse can be contributorily at fault for her participation in the relationship.

■ ISSUE

Can contributory fault be asserted against a thirteen-year-old victim of sexual abuse for her participation in the relationship?

■ DECISION AND RATIONALE

(Alexander, C.J.) No. Contributory fault may not be assessed against a thirteen-year-old child based on her failure to protect herself from being sexually abused when the defendant stands in a special relationship to the child and has a duty to protect the child. Because we recognize the vulnerability of children in the school setting, as a matter of public policy children do not have a duty to protect themselves from sexual abuse by their teachers. A school has a special relationship with the students in its custody and a duty to protect them from reasonably anticipated dangers. The principal (D) and the district (D) had a clear duty to protect students in their custody, and this duty included an obligation to supervise and control Diaz. This does not mean, however, that the district cannot defend itself against the negligent hiring and supervision claim. If they were thwarted in their attempts to ascertain whether Christensen (P) was abused by her teacher as a result of Christensen's (P) denial when asked about the relationship, that fact would likely be relevant to the issue of the district's negligence. That being said, a child lacks the capacity to consent to sexual abuse and is under no duty to protect herself from being abused.

■ DISSENT

(Sanders, J.) Washington law holds minors responsible for contributory negligence in many contexts, and there is no reason why sexual misconduct should be any different. Contributory negligence is a question of fact for the jury. The school district (D) took steps to protect this student. Officials met with Christensen (P) and her parents, but the girl lied about her involvement with the teacher. Yes, school districts must protect their students, but if a student undermines the district's efforts, she must bear at least some of the fault for the resulting injury. If Christensen (P) lied, this is contributory negligence and a proper defense for the district.

Analysis:

The dissent's position is a bit hard to understand. Generally speaking, child victims of sexual abuse will be reluctant to admit, in front of their parents and school officials, that they were involved in a sexual relationship with a teacher, perhaps out of embarrassment or shame, or maybe even because the teacher told them not to tell. A teacher is an authority figure, and young students are vulnerable to that authority. Students are coached from an early age to do what the teacher says without question, so it seems incongruous to argue that a child should be held accountable for her actions when the teacher abuses his or her position of authority and takes sexual advantage of the student, as the dissent would have it here.

CHAPTER TEN

Assumption of the Risk

Moore v. Hartley Motors

Instant Facts: After Moore (P) signed a release to participate in an ATV safety course, she was injured when thrown from an ATV.

Black Letter Rule: A court may invalidate a release as against public policy upon consideration of such factors as the type of service performed and whether the party seeking exculpation has a decisive advantage in bargaining strength because of the essential nature of the service.

Avila v. Citrus Community College District

Instant Facts: A community college baseball player was hit in the head by a pitch thrown by the opposing team's pitcher, and he sued, but the college argued that the player assumed the risk of his injury.

Black Letter Rule: Primary assumption of the risk arises when, as a matter of law and policy, a defendant owes no duty to protect a plaintiff from particular harms.

Moore v. Hartley Motors

(Safety Course Participant) v. (Landowner)

36 P.3d 628 (Alaska 2001)

THE SCOPE OF A RELEASE IS DETERMINED BY THE PARTIES' INTENT

■ **INSTANT FACTS** After Moore (P) signed a release to participate in an ATV safety course, she was injured when thrown from an ATV.

■ **BLACK LETTER RULE** A court may invalidate a release as against public policy upon consideration of such factors as the type of service performed and whether the party seeking exculpation has a decisive advantage in bargaining strength because of the essential nature of the service.

■ PROCEDURAL BASIS

On appeal to review summary judgment for the defendants.

■ FACTS

When Moore (P) purchased a four-wheel ATV, the seller offered a rebate if Moore (P) would complete a safety course conducted on the property of Hartley Motors (D). Before the course, Moore (P) executed a consent form and release. During the course, Moore (P) was thrown from the ATV and was injured on a rock concealed by grass. Moore (P) sued Hartley Motors (D), the seller, and the course instructor, alleging they failed to provide a safe training course and location. After the court granted the defendants' motion for summary judgment, Moore (P) appealed.

■ ISSUE

Did a genuine issue of material fact exist concerning whether the plaintiff executed a valid release of the defendants' negligence?

■ DECISION AND RATIONALE

(Fabe, C.J.) Yes. While releases are usually upheld as valid, a court may invalidate a release as against public policy upon consideration of such factors as the type of service performed and whether the party seeking exculpation has a decisive advantage in bargaining strength because of the essential nature of the service. Because the ATV course is not an essential service, the defendants did not have a bargaining advantage over Moore (P) because she had a choice as to whether to take the class. Accordingly, the release does not violate public policy. However, the court failed to consider the scope of the release. The contract released the defendants from liability for bodily injuries and property damage arising out of Moore's (P) participation in the course, but did not mention a release of negligence generally. A reasonable reading of the release demonstrates Moore's (P) intent to release claims for negligence related to the inherent risks of ATV riding, but not for injuries caused by unreasonably dangerous defects on the property. Because the release does not address these claims, a genuine issue of material fact exists concerning the danger associated with the ATV course and the application of the release. Reversed and remanded.

Analysis:

The key to the court's decision that the release does not violate public policy was Moore's (P) meaningful choice whether to accept the terms of release. Because the ATV course was not required of her by law, public policy does not forbid the release. If the course were required by law, such as in the case of motorcycle training in certain states, public policy may forbid a waiver.

■ CASE VOCABULARY

ASSUMPTION OF THE RISK: The act or an instance of a prospective plaintiff's taking on the risk of loss, injury, or damage.

RELEASE: Liberation from an obligation, duty, or demand; the act of giving up a right or claim to the person against whom it could have been enforced.

Avila v. Citrus Community College District

(College Baseball Player) v. (Opposing Team's School)

38 Cal.4th 148, 41 Cal.Rptr.3d 299, 131 P.3d 383 (2006)

BASEBALL PLAYERS ASSUME THE RISK OF GETTING HIT BY A BALL

■ **INSTANT FACTS** A community college baseball player was hit in the head by a pitch thrown by the opposing team's pitcher, and he sued, but the college argued that the player assumed the risk of his injury.

■ **BLACK LETTER RULE** Primary assumption of the risk arises when, as a matter of law and policy, a defendant owes no duty to protect a plaintiff from particular harms.

■ PROCEDURAL BASIS

State supreme court consideration of the court of appeals' decision reversing the trial court's granting of the defendant's demurrer.

■ FACTS

Avila (P) played baseball for the Rio Hondo Community College Roadrunners. During a pre-season road game against Citrus College (D), a Roadrunners pitcher hit a Citrus College (D) batter with a pitch. When Avila (P) was next up at bat, and the Citrus College (D) pitcher threw a ball that hit Avila (P) in the helmet, cracking it and injuring Avila (P). Avila (P) contended that the pitch was a "beanball" thrown in retaliation for the previous Roadrunners pitch, or, at a minimum, that it was thrown negligently. Avila (P) sued various entities, including Citrus College (D), which demurred. The trial court granted the demurrer, but the court of appeals reversed.

■ ISSUE

Did Avila (P) assume the risk of his injury?

■ DECISION AND RATIONALE

(Werdegar, J.) Yes. Primary assumption of the risk arises when, as a matter of law and policy, a defendant owes no duty to protect a plaintiff from particular harms. In the sporting context, it precludes liability for injuries arising from those risks deemed inherent in a sport. A court need not ask what risks a particular plaintiff subjectively knew of and chose to encounter, but instead must evaluate the fundamental nature of the sport and the defendant's role in or relationship to that sport, in order to determine whether the defendant owes a duty to protect a plaintiff from the particular risk of harm. In the co-participant context, as in this case, the host school's role is a mixed one. Co-participants themselves have a duty not to act recklessly outside the bounds of the sport, and coaches and instructors have a duty not to increase the risks inherent in sports participation. That is, the host school owes a duty to participants, both home and visiting players, at a minimum not to increase the risks inherent in the sport.

Avila (P) alleges that Citrus College (D) breached this duty, but we disagree. Whether or not pre-season games are allowed, hosting one only subjected Avila (P) to the risks inherent in playing baseball. Being hit by a pitch simply is an inherent risk of the game. It is well known that pitchers will even *intentionally* throw balls at batters for a variety of reasons, so even being intentionally hit, while a violation of the official rules, is inherent in the sport. It is true that an athlete does not assume the risk of a co-participant's intentional or reckless conduct totally outside the range of the ordinary activity involved in the sport, but the pitcher's conduct in this case did not fall outside that range. While the provision of umpires might have decreased the risk to Avila (P), the district (D) had a duty not to increase the risk, not a duty to *decrease* the risk. Nor did Citrus College (D) breach its duty to Avila (P) by failing to provide medical care after he was hit, because the district (D) did not cause Avila's (P) injury, he was not helpless, and his own coaches and trainers were there to assist him. Reversed.

Analysis:

As Justice Kennard points out in his concurring opinion, under traditional assumption-of-risk analysis, even sports participants owe each other a duty to refrain from unreasonably risky conduct that may cause harm. Intentionally hitting another person in the head with a hard object thrown at a high speed is highly dangerous, and should be deemed potentially tortious, he says, no matter whether the object is a ball thrown on a baseball field or a rock thrown on a city street. Accordingly, if the district (D) were complicit in a decision by the pitcher to hit Avila (P) in the head with the baseball, it should be held liable for Avila's (P) injuries, but only if Avila (P) had alleged that coaches employed by the district (D) either advised or condoned such an act. Because he did not, the trial court properly sustained the district's demurrer.

■ CASE VOCABULARY

DEMURRER: A pleading stating that although the facts alleged in a complaint may be true, they are insufficient for the plaintiff to state a claim for relief and for the defendant to frame an answer. In most jurisdictions, such a pleading is now termed a *motion to dismiss*, but the demurrer is still used in a few states, including California, Nebraska, and Pennsylvania.

CHAPTER ELEVEN

Defenses Not on the Merits

Crumpton v. Humana, Inc.

Instant Facts: A woman was injured when her nurse improperly attempted to lower her hospital bed after surgery.

Black Letter Rule: The statute of limitations commences running from the date of injury, and there is no authority to suggest that the statute of limitations should be tolled during the time when the parties were negotiating a settlement.

Lincoln Electric Co. v. McLemore

Instant Facts: McLemore (P) sued Lincoln Electric (D) for injuries he sustained after prolonged exposure to welding fumes, and Lincoln (D) claimed that the lawsuit was time barred.

Black Letter Rule: A plaintiff's cause of action accrues at the point at which he discovered, or by reasonable diligence should have discovered, the injury.

Vreeland v. Ferrer

Instant Facts: The personal representative of the estate of a deceased aircraft passenger sued the owner of the aircraft under state law, but the defendant aircraft owner argued that federal law, under which it would not be liable, preempted the plaintiff's state law claims.

Black Letter Rule: When a federal law does not expressly preempt state law, preemption may be inferred only when the scheme of federal regulation is sufficiently comprehensive to make reasonable the inference that Congress left no room for supplementary state regulation.

Crumpton v. Humana, Inc.

(Injured Hospital Patient) v. (Hospital's Insurance Co.)

99 N.M. 562, 661 P.2d 54 (1983)

THE STATUTE OF LIMITATIONS COMMENCES RUNNING FROM THE DATE OF INJURY, AND IS NOT TOLLED DURING SETTLEMENT NEGOTIATIONS

■ **INSTANT FACTS** A woman was injured when her nurse improperly attempted to lower her hospital bed after surgery.

■ **BLACK LETTER RULE** The statute of limitations commences running from the date of injury, and there is no authority to suggest that the statute of limitations should be tolled during the time when the parties were negotiating a settlement.

■ PROCEDURAL BASIS

Appeal from the trial court's grant of summary judgment in favor of the defendant.

■ FACTS

On February 8, 1979, Wanda Crumpton (P) underwent surgery at a Medical Center. Three days later, when a nurse attempted to lower her hospital bed, she alleged that she sustained injuries to her neck and legs. Her suit was filed more than three years later [oops!] on February 15, 1982. The trial court granted a motion for summary judgment on the ground that the suit was barred by the three year statute of limitations.

■ ISSUE

Is a statute of limitations tolled during a time of negotiations between the parties?

■ DECISION AND RATIONALE

(H. Vern Payne, C.J.) No. Crumpton (P) argues that her injury was not ascertainable until some time after the accident occurred [delayed reaction?]. Further, she contends that the statute of limitations should have been tolled during the time the parties were negotiating. These arguments are entirely without merit. Crumpton (P) plainly testified in her deposition that her injuries occurred on February 11, 1979. She also testified that the problems she continues to have are attributable to the February 11, 1979 accident. In our view, the fact that she had continuing treatments and hospitalizations after the injury does not necessarily make the date of the injury unascertainable. The statute of limitations commences running from the date of injury. Crumpton (P) cites no authority for her argument that the statute should be tolled during the time the parties were negotiating a settlement. Humana (D) did not fraudulently lead Crumpton (P) to believe that the case would be settled at some future date; in fact, in May, 1981, Humana (D) sent Crumpton a letter making a final offer for a compromise settlement of the case. Accordingly, we affirm the trial court's grant of summary judgment against Crumpton (P). Because we determine this appeal to be frivolous and entirely without merit, costs and attorney's fees are to be borne by Crumpton (P) [take that!].

Analysis:

Statutes of limitation are not limited to torts cases. Almost every type of claim must be brought within a period of time specified by the applicable statute of limitations. The time limit imposed may vary depending upon the tort, and once the action is properly brought, the statute of limitations has no other function. It merely requires commencement of the action within a certain period of time; it does not impose requirements on the actual commencement of the trial. The cause of action generally accrues when an injury results in cases of negligence; thus, the statute of limitations was properly deemed to have begun to "run" at the time Crumpton (P) was injured.

■ CASE VOCABULARY

DEPOSITION: A pre-trial witness statement made under oath taken in question and answer form.

FRIVOLOUS APPEAL: Clearly lacking in substance, and insufficient as a matter of law.

MERITLESS ARGUMENT: No validity or credibility of a cause.

STATUTE OF LIMITATIONS: A statutorily set period of time beyond which an action may not be brought.

TOLL: To stop the running of the statute of limitations.

Lincoln Electric Co. v. McLemore

(Welding Product Company) v. (Welder)

54 So. 3d 833 (Miss. 2010)

THE COURT DID NOT ACCEPT THE JURY'S FINDING ON THE CLAIM'S ACCRUAL DATE

■ **INSTANT FACTS** McLemore (P) sued Lincoln Electric (D) for injuries he sustained after prolonged exposure to welding fumes, and Lincoln (D) claimed that the lawsuit was time barred.

■ **BLACK LETTER RULE** A plaintiff's cause of action accrues at the point at which he discovered, or by reasonable diligence should have discovered, the injury.

■ PROCEDURAL BASIS

State supreme court review of a judgment in the plaintiff's favor.

■ FACTS

McLemore (P) had been working as a welder for many years when, in 2001, he began experiencing slowness in his left hand and arm. He went to a chiropractor, who sent him to a neurologist. The physician told McLemore (P) he had Parkinsonism, which could have been related to welding. McLemore (P) then went to see a lawyer who had done previous legal work for him. After that, McLemore (P) saw six more doctors, one of whom advised McLemore, in 2002, to stop welding. McLemore (D) sued. His main expert witness at trial testified that McLemore (D) had manganism, a syndrome with features atypical of Parkinsonism that is caused by exposure to manganese. McLemore (P) testified that he first learned he suffered from manganism in 2005. However, McLemore (P) had filed various lawsuits claiming neurological injuries from welding products as early as February 2004. Lincoln Electric (D) had been named as a defendant in a 2004 and a 2005 complaint, but those complaints were never served on Lincoln (D).

In 2006, Lincoln (D) was served with an amended complaint naming it as a defendant. Lincoln (D) moved for summary judgment, claiming that McLemore's (P) claim against it was filed outside the statute of limitations. The trial court denied the motion and awarded McLemore (P) nearly $2 million in damages. Lincoln (D) appealed, arguing that McLemore knew that he had an injury in September 2002 when he was diagnosed with Parkinsonism and that his condition may have been related to welding. Accordingly, Lincoln (D) contended, the complaint should have been filed by September 2005, but McLemore (P) did not file his cause of action until November 2005. McLemore (P) countered that his claim accrued in October 2005, when he was diagnosed with manganism, and that until that time he did not know that welding fumes had caused his damages.

■ ISSUE

Did McLemore (P) bring his lawsuit within the three-year statute of limitations?

■ DECISION AND RATIONALE

(Chandler, J.) No. A plaintiff's cause of action accrues at the point at which he discovered, or by reasonable diligence should have discovered, the injury. We have held that the plain language of the statute of limitations supports an interpretation that the cause of action accrues upon discovery of the injury, not discovery of the injury and its cause. McLemore (P) knew of his injury in September 2002. Thereafter, he sought legal advice and filed a complaint alleging a serious neurological injury related to manganese exposure. These events show that McLemore (P) knew or should have known, no later than September 2002, that he had an injury. Reversed.

■ DISSENT

(Kitchens, J.) The statute of limitations commences upon discovery of an injury, which is an issue of fact to be decided by the jury when there is a genuine dispute. Only if reasonable minds could not differ may the question be decided by the court. Here, the jury found that McLemore (P) discovered, or should have discovered, his claimed injury of manganism in October 2005. The jury's conclusion should not be disturbed on appeal.

Analysis:

The accrual of a personal injury claim resulting from exposure to a toxic substance can be a tricky question. Here, the court concluded that the claim accrued when McLemore (P) learned he had a disease that could be related to welding, not when he learned that he actually had manganism, which was a different diagnosis. As the dissent pointed out, in most instances when two or more reasonable conclusions or inferences can be drawn from the facts, the jury's finding is the one that counts. The court in this case must have determined that only one reasonable conclusion could be drawn from the facts, and that conclusion was that McLemore (P) knew about his injury more than three years before he filed suit against Lincoln Electric (D), so his claim was time-barred.

■ CASE VOCABULARY

DISCOVERY RULE: A legal doctrine that suspends the running of the statute of limitations during periods of time in which the plaintiff did not discover, or by the exercise of reasonable diligence, could not have discovered, the injuries that would lead to his or her claim against the defendant.

STATUTE OF LIMITATIONS: Statutes that limit the period of time during which civil and criminal cases may be initiated, which are designed to prevent fraudulent and stale claims from arising after the evidence has been lost or after the facts have become obscure through the passage of time or the defective memory, death, or disappearance of witnesses.

Vreeland v. Ferrer

(Personal Representative of Vreeland Estate) v. (Plane Lessee)

71 So. 3d 70 (Fla. 2012)

STATE LAW IS NOT PREEMPTED WHEN THERE IS NO EXPRESS PREEMPTION IN OR CONFLICT WITH THE FEDERAL STATUTE

■ **INSTANT FACTS** The personal representative of the estate of a deceased aircraft passenger sued the owner of the aircraft under state law, but the defendant aircraft owner argued that federal law, under which it would not be liable, preempted the plaintiff's state law claims.

■ **BLACK LETTER RULE** When a federal law does not expressly preempt state law, preemption may be inferred only when the scheme of federal regulation is sufficiently comprehensive to make reasonable the inference that Congress left no room for supplementary state regulation.

■ PROCEDURAL BASIS

State supreme court review of an appellate court decision affirming the trial court ruling on preemption.

■ FACTS

Ferrer (D) leased a plane from Aerolease of America (D). The plane crashed and the pilot and his passenger, Martinez, were killed. Vreeland (P), the administrator and personal representative of the Martinez estate, filed a wrongful death case against Aerolease (D) asserting various state law claims. Aerolease (D) moved for summary judgment, arguing that federal law preempted Florida law. The federal law provided, in relevant part, that an owner or lessor of an aircraft is liable for personal injury, death, or property damage on land or water only when the aircraft is in the actual possession or control of the owner or lessor and the accident occurs because of the aircraft, engine, or propeller, or the flight of the aircraft—i.e., not the negligence of the pilot, as was alleged in this case. Under Florida state law, by contrast, known as the dangerous instrumentality doctrine, the owner or lessor of an aircraft is vicariously liable for the negligent conduct of a pilot. The trial court entered summary judgment in Aerolease's (D) favor, finding that the federal law preempted the state law, and the court of appeals affirmed in part and reversed in part. Vreeland (P) filed a petition with the state supreme court seeking review of the appellate court's decision.

■ ISSUE

Did the court correctly find that federal law preempted Florida's dangerous instrumentality doctrine?

■ DECISION AND RATIONALE

(Lewis, J.) No. When a federal law does not expressly preempt state law, preemption may be inferred only when the scheme of federal regulation is sufficiently comprehensive to make reasonable the inference that Congress left no room for supplementary state regulation.

Preemption may be either express or implied and is compelled whether Congress's command is explicitly stated in the statute's language or implicitly contained in its structure and purpose. Preemption of a whole field will be inferred if the field is one in which the federal interest is dominant.

Even when Congress has not completely displaced state regulation, state law is nullified to the extent it actually conflicts with federal law. Such a conflict exists when compliance with both state and federal requirements is impossible, or when the state law poses an obstacle to the accomplishment of the objectives of Congress. Here, there is no express preemption language in the federal statute, so preemption, if it applies at all, can only be implied. To determine whether it should be, we look closely at the language of the federal statute. Every version of that statute in effect since its enactment in 1948 has referenced injury, death, or property damage that occurs on land or water, or on the surface of the earth. These words may be read to specify that the limitation on liability only applies to death, injury, or damage that is caused to people or property that are physically on the ground or in the water, not in the plane. We conclude that Congress did not intend to preempt state law with regard to injuries to passengers or aircraft crew. Florida's dangerous instrumentality doctrine imposes vicarious liability on owners and lessors of aircraft, even when the aircraft is not within their immediate control or possession at the time of the loss. The wrongful death action is therefore not preempted.

■ DISSENT

(Polston, J.) Federal law preempts Florida's dangerous instrumentality doctrine. The majority's "on the ground" distinction defies reality. Even though Martinez was in the aircraft when he died, his death occurred on land, not in the aircraft prior to hitting the ground. The plain meaning of the statute requires preemption.

Analysis:

The preemption doctrine has its roots in the Constitution's Supremacy Clause, which states that the Constitution and the laws of the United States are the supreme law of the land. As noted in this opinion, preemption can be either express or implied. Implied preemption presents more challenging issues. If the federal statute does not expressly state that it preempts state law, the court looks beyond the statute's language to determine whether Congress chose to occupy the field of law at issue, whether the state law directly conflicts with the federal law, or whether enforcement of the state law would frustrate Congressional purposes.

■ CASE VOCABULARY

PREEMPTION DOCTRINE: The doctrine based on the Supremacy Clause of the Constitution that holds that certain matters are of such a national, as opposed to local, character that federal laws take precedence over state laws.

CHAPTER TWELVE

Carriers, Host-Drivers, and Landowners

Gladon v. Greater Cleveland Regional Transit Authority

Instant Facts: A man sued a transit authority for negligence for failing to exercise care when the train ran him over after he was forced onto the tracks by his assailants.

Black Letter Rule: Once an invitee goes outside the area of invitation, his status becomes one of a licensee or trespasser, depending on the circumstances.

Bennett v. Stanley

Instant Facts: Bennett's (P) wife and son drowned when the son was playing with frogs near Stanley's (D) unenclosed pool.

Black Letter Rule: Under the attractive-nuisance doctrine, a landowner is liable for injuries to an unknowing child trespasser caused by an artificial condition if (1) the landowner knows or has reason to know that children are likely to trespass on his land and that the condition is reasonably likely to cause injury or death to child trespassers, (2) the child trespasser does not discover or appreciate the danger of the condition, (3) the landowner's burden of safeguarding the condition is not outweighed by the degree of risk to the child, and (4) the landowner fails to reasonably eliminate the danger.

Kentucky River Medical Center v. McIntosh

Instant Facts: A paramedic (P) tripped on a raised curb while wheeling a patient into the ER at the hospital (D) and broke her hip; the hospital (D) argued that it was not liable because the danger was open and obvious.

Black Letter Rule: A possessor of land is not liable to his invitees for physical harm caused to them by an activity or condition on the land whose danger is known or obvious to them, unless the possessor should have anticipated the harm despite such knowledge or obviousness.

Minnich v. Med-Waste, Inc.

Instant Facts: Minnich (P) was injured on the job while attempting to stop a truck from rolling into a public street.

Black Letter Rule: The firefighter's rule bars tort recovery by a firefighter or police officer for on-the-job injuries sustained during the discharge of his or her duties.

Rowland v. Christian

Instant Facts: A guest in an apartment sued his host after the guest sliced his hand on a broken faucet.

Black Letter Rule: A landowner owes a duty of reasonable care to all who enter upon his land.

Pagelsdorf v. Safeco Insurance Co. of America

Instant Facts: A tenant's guest sued the owner of the building after the guest fell off the second story balcony due to a faulty railing.

Black Letter Rule: A landlord is under a duty to exercise ordinary care in the maintenance of the premises.

Gladon v. Greater Cleveland Regional Transit Authority

(Injured Passenger) v. (Metro Operator)

75 Ohio St.3d 312, 662 N.E.2d 287 (1996)

THE STATUS OF THE PERSON WHO ENTERS UPON THE LAND DEFINES THE SCOPE OF THE DUTY THAT THE LANDOWNER OWES TO THE ENTRANT

■ **INSTANT FACTS** A man sued a transit authority for negligence for failing to exercise care when the train ran him over after he was forced onto the tracks by his assailants.

■ **BLACK LETTER RULE** Once an invitee goes outside the area of invitation, his status becomes one of a licensee or trespasser, depending on the circumstances.

■ PROCEDURAL BASIS

Appeal challenging the trial court's instruction to the jury that the plaintiff was an invitee as a matter of law, and the trial court's denial of the defendant's motion for a directed verdict.

■ FACTS

After mistakenly exiting a Greater Cleveland Regional Transit Authority (RTA) (D) at the wrong station, Robert Gladon (P) was assaulted on the platform, ending up on the train tracks either by force or in an effort to evade his assailants. While Gladon (P) lay on the tracks, an RTA (D) train approached the station. Mary Bell (D), the train's operator, first observed a tennis shoe and then Gladon's (P) leg on the tracks. Bell (D) pulled the control handle and then hit the emergency brake. Gladon (P) sued RTA (D) and Bell (D) alleging negligence in operation of the train; specifically, that Bell (D) negligently failed to bring the train to a stop after the point she perceived or should have perceived Gladon's (D) peril. The trial court overruled RTA's (D) motion for a directed verdict. The court also instructed the jury that Gladon was an invitee as a matter of law, which required RTA (D) to use ordinary care to discover and to avoid danger.

■ ISSUE

Is the status of an invitee absolute?

■ DECISION AND RATIONALE

(Cook, J.) No. Once an invitee goes outside the area of invitation, his status becomes one of a licensee or trespasser, depending on the circumstances. If he goes outside the area with consent, he becomes an invitee, otherwise he becomes a trespasser for purposes of determining the liability of the landowner. RTA's (D) invitation to Gladon (P) did not extend to the area on or around the tracks, as evidenced by the rule disallowing the public in that very area. Although Gladon (P) argues that he retained his status as an invitee because he did not intentionally enter the restricted area, the Restatement holds that the manner of entry is immaterial, unless entry is privileged. We find it unnecessary to decide whether Gladon (P) became a trespasser or licensee upon entering the tracks because each is owed an identical duty—to refrain from willful, wanton, or reckless conduct which is likely to harm the entrant. There is no duty to anticipate or prevent the presence of licensees or trespassers. However, when a trespasser or licensee is discovered in a position of peril, the landowner is required to use ordinary care to avoid injuring him. This duty arises only after the landowner knows or should know of the licensee or trespasser's presence. Accordingly, we remand for a new trial. Furthermore, we find that, because reasonable minds could differ on the issues of wanton and willful conduct and failure to use reasonable care, the trial court did not err in refusing to direct a verdict. Reversed and remanded.

Analysis:

This case illustrates the somewhat archaic common law rules with regard to a landowner's duty of care toward those who enter upon his land. Under those rules, a landowner's liability was based on the status of the entrant as either an invitee, a licensee, or a trespasser. Essentially, an invitee is a person that is on the land for the benefit of the landowner, or on premises generally held open for the public. The greatest duty of care is owed to invitees. Licensees include all those who had consent to be on the land, but did not qualify as an invitee. A trespasser is, of course, a person whose entrance was not consented to or is unprivileged. Lesser duties of care are owed to both licensees and trespassers. The issue in this case was whether Gladon (P), who held the status of an invitee as a train passenger, lost that status by reason of ending up on the train tracks after his assault. The court notes that an entrant's status as an invitee is subject to change when he ventures away from the area he is entitled to be in. Relying on the Restatement (Second) of Torts, the court refuses to modify this rule when the invitee ventures off through no fault of his own, in this case by reason of an assault. In such a case the invitee becomes either a licensee or a trespasser, a distinction that was of no import in this case because under Ohio law licensees and trespassers were owed the same duty. As a licensee or trespasser, Gladon (P) was owed only a duty of reasonable care when Bell (D) became aware or should have become aware of the situation. The issue of reasonableness being one for the jury, the court remanded for a new trial.

Bennett v. Stanley

(Father) v. (Pool Owner)

92 Ohio St.3d 35, 748 N.E.2d 41 (2001)

THE ATTRACTIVE-NUISANCE DOCTRINE REQUIRES A HIGHER DUTY OF CARE TO CHILD TRESPASSERS

■ **INSTANT FACTS** Bennett's (P) wife and son drowned when the son was playing with frogs near Stanley's (D) unenclosed pool.

■ **BLACK LETTER RULE** Under the attractive-nuisance doctrine, a landowner is liable for injuries to an unknowing child trespasser caused by an artificial condition if (1) the landowner knows or has reason to know that children are likely to trespass on his land and that the condition is reasonably likely to cause injury or death to child trespassers, (2) the child trespasser does not discover or appreciate the danger of the condition, (3) the landowner's burden of safeguarding the condition is not outweighed by the degree of risk to the child, and (4) the landowner fails to reasonably eliminate the danger.

■ PROCEDURAL BASIS

On appeal to review a decision of the Ohio Court of Appeals affirming summary judgment for the defendant.

■ FACTS

Stanley (D) purchased a home with a swimming pool that had not been used by the previous owners. The pool was enclosed by a fence and a brick wall and covered with a tarp. After moving in, Stanley (D) drained the pool and removed the tarp and fencing around the pool. Over time, the pool filled with rainwater and became pond-like, containing frogs and snakes. Thereafter, Bennett (P) and his family moved in next door. Between Stanley's (D) property and Bennett's (P) property was a fence with an eight-foot gap. Stanley (D) was aware that Bennett (P) had young children, but, having no concern that children would get into the pool, never posted any warnings. One day, Bennett's (P) young son was playing by Stanley's (D) pool and fell in. Attempting to save the child, Bennett's (P) wife drowned, along with the son. Bennett (P) sued Stanley (D) for negligence, arguing that the pool created an unreasonable risk of harm to his children, who could not realize the danger. The court granted summary judgment to Stanley (D), finding that the child was a trespasser to whom Stanley (D) owed only a duty "to refrain from wanton and wilful conduct." On appeal, the Ohio Court of Appeals affirmed.

■ ISSUE

Is a landowner liable for injuries caused by artificial conditions on his land that present a foreseeable risk of danger to unknowing child trespassers?

■ DECISION AND RATIONALE

(Pfeifer, J.) Yes. While ordinarily a landowner owes a trespasser only a duty to refrain from wanton and wilful conduct, children have a special status in tort law. Because of their youth and inexperience, children are owed a higher duty of care to protect them from dangers they may be unable to appreciate. Ohio law has long recognized the dangerous instrumentality exception to a landowner's duty to trespassers, by which the landowner is under a higher duty to a child trespasser when he actively and negligently operates hazardous machinery or other apparatus, the danger of which may not be apparent to a child. The Restatement (Second) of Torts § 339 offers a similar doctrine. Under this attractive-nuisance doctrine, a landowner is liable for injuries to a child trespasser caused by an artificial condition if (1) the landowner knows or has reason to know that children are likely to trespass on his land and that the condition is reasonably likely to cause injury or death to child trespassers, (2) the child trespasser does not discover or appreciate the danger of the condition, (3) the landowner's burden of safeguarding the condition is not outweighed by the degree of risk to the child, and (4) the landowner fails to reasonably eliminate the danger.

The court adopts the attractive-nuisance doctrine. In so doing, the differences between a duty owed by a landowner to different classes of land users are not abandoned, but rather the special duty owed to children is recognized when the condition presents a foreseeable and unreasonable risk of danger or serious bodily harm to children. The doctrine does not automatically impose liability whenever children are injured or killed on another's land, but simply requires a landowner to act with ordinary care to remove any foreseeable dangers on his land to which unknowing children may foreseeably be exposed. By adopting the attractive-nuisance doctrine, a plaintiff need only allege negligence rather than wanton and wilful conduct to establish a cause of action. Reversed and remanded.

Analysis:

Despite the attractive-nuisance doctrine, the outcome of the case may have been different had Stanley (D) taken precautions in advance of the accident to protect children from the pool. Had Stanley (D) maintained the fencing around the pool and repaired the gap in the fence between the neighboring properties, it would be arguable that children's presence on his property was not foreseeable and that he had reasonably eliminated any danger to children. By failing to take such precautions, however, Stanley (D) breached his duty under the attractive-nuisance doctrine.

■ CASE VOCABULARY

ATTRACTIVE-NUISANCE DOCTRINE: The rule that a person who owns property on which there is a dangerous thing or condition that will foreseeably lure children to trespass is under a duty to protect those children from the danger.

DANGEROUS INSTRUMENTALITY: An instrument, substance, or condition so inherently dangerous that it may cause serious bodily injury or death without human use or interference.

TRESPASSER: One who commits a trespass; one who intentionally and without consent or privilege enters another's property.

Kentucky River Medical Center v. McIntosh

(Hospital) v. (Paramedic)

319 S.W.3d 385 (Ky. 2010)

THE TRADITIONAL OPEN AND OBVIOUS DOCTRINE AND PRINCIPLES OF COMPARATIVE FAULT ARE INCOMPATIBLE

■ **INSTANT FACTS** A paramedic (P) tripped on a raised curb while wheeling a patient into the ER at the hospital (D) and broke her hip; the hospital (D) argued that it was not liable because the danger was open and obvious.

■ **BLACK LETTER RULE** A possessor of land is not liable to his invitees for physical harm caused to them by an activity or condition on the land whose danger is known or obvious to them, unless the possessor should have anticipated the harm despite such knowledge or obviousness.

■ PROCEDURAL BASIS

Supreme Court consideration of whether the case should have been decided in the defendant's favor as a matter of law.

■ FACTS

McIntosh (P), a paramedic, transported a critically ill patient to the hospital (D). As she guided the stretcher to the emergency room door, which she had done about 400 times at this hospital (D) in the past, she tripped on the curb and broke her hip. McIntosh (P) was focused at the time of her fall on making sure the patient was doing all right and that the IV lines did not get tangled. McIntosh (P) sued the hospital (D) for her injuries. At trial, she testified that the defendant hospital (D) was the only one she transported patients to that had such an uneven surface between the ambulance dock and the ER doors. An EMT testified along the same lines. The jury found the hospital (D) liable and awarded damages. The hospital (D) appealed and the appellate court affirmed, because the hospital (D) could reasonably expect that a paramedic treating a critically ill patient could be distracted and forget, if she ever observed it, that the curb was uneven, and could fail to protect herself against it. The state supreme court granted discretionary review to determine whether the open and obvious doctrine should have completely barred the plaintiff's cause of action.

■ ISSUE

Could the court decide this case as a matter of law based on the open and obvious doctrine?

■ DECISION AND RATIONALE

(Noble, J.) No. A possessor of land is not liable to his invitees for physical harm caused to them by an activity or condition on the land whose danger is known or obvious to them, unless the possessor should have anticipated the harm despite such knowledge or obviousness. Under the traditional open and obvious doctrine, land possessors could not be held liable to invitees who were injured by open and obvious dangers. But the trend of courts in this country is against the rule absolving, ipso facto, owners and occupiers of land from liability for injuries resulting from known or obvious conditions, and rather to allow the jury to evaluate the comparative fault of the parties. The open and obvious doctrine, as an automatic bar to recovery, is incompatible with principles of comparative fault. If the land possessor could foresee the injury, but still failed to take reasonable precautions to prevent it, he can be held liable, based not only on his superior knowledge, but also because the land possessor is in a unique position as the only person who can eliminate the danger. In this case, the hospital (D) had good reason to expect that a paramedic would be distracted as she approached the ER entrance. Even though the curb may have been open and noticeable to some extent, the possessor had reason to expect that the invitee's attention may be distracted. After all, McIntosh (P) was rushing a critically ill patient into a hospital (D). Even so, she, too, had a duty to act reasonably to ensure her own safety. In addition, she was familiar with the location. Thus, genuine issues of material fact as to comparative fault were properly submitted to the jury, and the court cannot decide this case as a matter of law.

■ DISSENT

(Schroder, J.) The curb was open and obvious. It was not an OSHA violation. It appears the hospital (D) is being held liable for violating a duty to build its emergency entrance like all other hospitals. There is no such duty.

Analysis:

The hospital (D) had moved for summary judgment on the open and obvious issue, but the trial court denied the motion. As the Restatement emphasizes, whether a danger was known and appreciated by the plaintiff, whether the risk was obvious to a person exercising reasonable perception, intelligence, and judgment, and whether there was some other reason for the defendant to foresee the harm are all relevant considerations. These are generally factual determinations, and as such require consideration by a factfinder, not a decision as a matter of law by the court.

■ CASE VOCABULARY

IPSO FACTO: By that very fact or act; an inevitable result.

OSHA: Occupational Safety and Health Administration. Under the Occupational Safety and Health Act, employers are responsible for providing a safe and healthful workplace. OSHA's mission is to assure safe and healthful workplaces by setting and enforcing standards, and by providing training, outreach, education and assistance. Employers must comply with all applicable OSHA standards.

Minnich v. Med-Waste, Inc.

(Public Safety Officer) v. (Medical Waste Hauler)

349 S.C. 567, 564 S.E.2d 98 (2002)

THE SOUTH CAROLINA SUPREME COURT REFUSES TO ADOPT THE FIREFIGHTER'S RULE

■ **INSTANT FACTS** Minnich (P) was injured on the job while attempting to stop a truck from rolling into a public street.

■ **BLACK LETTER RULE** The firefighter's rule bars tort recovery by a firefighter or police officer for on-the-job injuries sustained during the discharge of his or her duties.

■ PROCEDURAL BASIS

Consideration of a certified question from a federal district court.

■ FACTS

Minnich (P) was working as a public safety officer for the Medical University of South Carolina when he was called upon to assist in loading medical waste onto a truck owned by Med-Waste, Inc. (D). When the truck began to roll toward a public street, Minnich (P) ran to the truck and stopped it. In the process, Minnich (P) suffered injuries allegedly due to the acts and omissions of the defendant's employees. Minnich (P) sued Med-Waste (D) in federal court. The defendants contended that Minnich's (P) claims were barred by the firefighter's rule, which precludes firefighters and certain other public employees from recovering against a negligent defendant for injuries sustained in the course of their employment. The federal court certified to the South Carolina Supreme Court the question of the application of the firefighter's rule to emergency professionals.

■ ISSUE

Does the firefighter's rule bar an emergency professional's claim for injuries sustained in the course of his duties as a result of a defendant's negligence?

■ DECISION AND RATIONALE

(Pleicones, J.) No. Historically, the firefighter's rule was adopted to bar a firefighter's claims for injuries sustained while controlling a fire that was caused by a homeowner's negligence. The firefighter's rule has been justified by firefighters' and police officers' assumption of the known and inherent risks associated with their duties. Public policy also supports the firefighter's rule, in that any on-the-job injuries are compensable by workers' compensation, and firefighters and police officers often enter private property unannounced such that the level of care owed to invitees or licensees would be unreasonable.

Across the country, states vary on the proper application of the firefighter's rule. Some courts permit recovery for injuries caused by a defendant's wanton and wilful conduct resulting in the injuries, while others permit recovery for negligence unrelated to the specific reason the firefighter was originally called to the scene. Some states have enacted legislation to abolish the firefighter's rule altogether. South Carolina has never recognized the firefighter's rule in any situation, much less applied it to emergency professionals. South Carolina tort law adequately addresses negligence claims brought against third parties arising out of the discharge of a firefighter's duties, and it applies equally to other emergency professionals.

Analysis:

In theory, the firefighter's rule is largely based on public policy. Because firefighters and police officers have a duty to protect the public from danger, often placing themselves in harm's way to save others, it would be inequitable to permit such public servants to recover for injuries sustained while knowingly performing their duties. In some circumstances, the threat of civil liability may even prompt individuals not to seek needed assistance.

Rowland v. Christian

(Injured Guest) v. (Homeowner)

69 Cal.2d 108, 70 Cal.Rptr. 97, 443 P.2d 561 (1968)

A LANDOWNER OWES A GENERAL DUTY OF CARE TO ALL THOSE WHO ENTER UPON HIS LAND

■ **INSTANT FACTS** A guest in an apartment sued his host after the guest sliced his hand on a broken faucet.

■ **BLACK LETTER RULE** A landowner owes a duty of reasonable care to all who enter upon his land.

■ PROCEDURAL BASIS

Appeal from the trial court's grant of summary judgment for the defendant.

■ FACTS

James Rowland (P), a social guest at Nancy Christian's (D) apartment, severed his hand on the porcelain handle of a bathroom faucet. Christian (D) knew the faucet was broken, but failed to warn Rowland (P).

■ ISSUE

Does liability for negligence of a possessor of land depend on whether the plaintiff is classified as a trespasser, licensee or invitee?

■ DECISION AND RATIONALE

(Peters, J.) No. A landowner owes a duty of reasonable care to all who enter upon his land. With regard to the liability of a possessor of land for injuries to persons who have entered upon that land, courts have often departed from the fundamental rule of liability for negligence by classifying the plaintiff as a trespasser, licensee or invitee, and then adopting special rules as to the duty owed to each. Whatever the historical justifications, these distinctions are not justified in light of our modem society. Although the rules are simple, complexity and confusion have been caused by attempts to apply this ancient terminology in our modern society. The classifications, with their corresponding immunities and exceptions, are often irrelevant to the factors that determine liability. These factors include the connection between the defendant's conduct and the injury, the defendant's culpability, the policy of preventing future harm, and the availability of insurance. A man's life or limb does not become less worthy under the law simply because he has come upon land without permission, or with permission but no business purpose. Reasonable people do not ordinarily vary their conduct upon such matters. The common law rules obscure rather than illuminate the proper considerations which should be govern the question of duty. Reversed.

■ DISSENT

(Burke, J.) I find that the common law rules supply a workable approach to the problems involved, one which provides the degree of stability and predictability so highly prized in the law. The majority's approach has left the question to a case by case analysis, with no principles to guide.

Analysis:

With this case, the activist California Supreme Court of the 1960s was the first to abolish the common law categories upon which landowner liability was based. At the time this case was decided, in most jurisdictions the trial court would have found for Rowland (P) on the ground that his status as a licensee required Christian (D) to warn him of all concealed dangers, the broken faucet being one such danger. Under the rules in place in California, however, a licensee was owed the same duty as a trespasser. The court here bases its decision on modern social mores and humanitarian values, and the fact that the distinctions between trespassers, licensees, and invitees is often arbitrary. In place of these distinctions, the court lists several factors that should determine liability, such as foreseeability, the connection between the injury and the defendant's conduct, and the availability of insurance.

Pagelsdorf v. Safeco Insurance Co. of America

(Injured Tenant Guest) v. (Landlord's Insurer)

91 Wis.2d 734, 284 N.W.2d 55 (1979)

ALTHOUGH THE COMMON LAW RELIEVES LANDLORDS FROM LIABILITY FOR INJURIES TO HIS TENANTS AND THEIR VISITORS RESULTING FROM DEFECTS IN THE PREMISES, THE MODERN TREND IS TO APPLY GENERAL PRINCIPLES OF NEGLIGENCE

■ **INSTANT FACTS** A tenant's guest sued the owner of the building after the guest fell off the second story balcony due to a faulty railing.

■ **BLACK LETTER RULE** A landlord is under a duty to exercise ordinary care in the maintenance of the premises.

■ PROCEDURAL BASIS

Not provided.

■ FACTS

While James Pagelsdorf (P) was helping the Blattners move from their home in a two-story duplex, he fell off the second-story balcony after the railing gave way. Pagelsdorf (P) sued Mahnke (D), the owner of the duplex. An inspection showed that the wood which formed the railing suffered from dry rot, a defect that was not apparent to the eye. Although Mahnke (D) had contracted to keep the premises in repair, that duty was limited to known or reported defects.

■ ISSUE

Is a landlord liable for injuries suffered by tenants and their guests as a result of the landlord's negligence in keeping the premises in disrepair?

■ DECISION AND RATIONALE

(Callow, J.) Yes. A landlord is under a duty to exercise ordinary care in the maintenance of the premises. Under the traditional rule, a landlord is not liable for injuries to his tenants and their visitors resulting from defects in the premises. This rule is based on the notion that a lease is a conveyance of property under which the landlord transfers possession and control of the premises. There are, however, exceptions to the rule of nonliability. A landlord is liable if he contracts to repair defects, or if knowing of a defect at the time of the lease, the landlord conceals it from a tenant who could not reasonably be expected to discover it. There are further exceptions where the premises are leased for public use, or are retained by the landlord, or where the landlord negligently makes repairs. It does not appear as if any of these exceptions are applicable in this case. Under the traditional rule, Mahnke (D) would be held not liable as a matter of law. But we reject this approach, and instead adopt a rule requiring a landlord to exercise ordinary care in the maintenance of the premises. Reversed.

Analysis:

This case illustrates just one avenue courts have taken to avoid applying the common law rule that relieved landlords from liability for injuries that occur on the premises while the tenant is in possession. The court imposes upon landlords a duty to exercise reasonable care to the tenant and his guests. The opinion, however, discusses some of the traditional exceptions to the general rule of nonliability. Some courts have also imposed an implied warranty of habitability, which requires a landlord to keep the premises in good condition. However, these implied warranties usually form the basis of actions for breach of contract, not actions in tort. Legislatures have also enacted statutes that impose certain affirmative duties on landlords. In total, the rule of nonliability still remains, but the exceptions have become numerous.

CHAPTER THIRTEEN

Duties of Medical and Other Professionals

Walski v. Tiesenga

Instant Facts: A patient who suffered vocal paralysis during surgery sought to establish the negligence of her surgeon through the use of an expert's testimony, the thrust of which was that the expert would have performed the surgery differently.

Black Letter Rule: It is insufficient for a plaintiff to establish a prima facie case of medical malpractice merely to present testimony of another physician that he would have acted differently from the defendant.

Vergara v. Doan

Instant Facts: The parents of a newborn injured during delivery sued the small town doctor who performed the delivery, claiming that he failed to meet the medical standard of care.

Black Letter Rule: A physician must exercise that degree of care, skill, and proficiency exercised by reasonably careful, skillful, and prudent practitioners in the same class to which he belongs, acting under the same or similar circumstances.

States v. Lourdes Hospital

Instant Facts: While undergoing surgery for the removal of an ovarian cyst, States' (P) arm was injured, allegedly due to Lourdes Hospital's (D) negligence in administering anesthesia.

Black Letter Rule: The doctrine of res ipsa loquitur permits a factfinder to find negligence simply from the fact that an injury occurred, when the injury is of a kind that ordinarily does not occur absent negligence.

Ybarra v. Spangard

Instant Facts: A patient that suffered minor paralysis during an appendectomy sought to recover against every doctor and nurse in whose care he was placed during the surgery, arguing that the doctrine of res ipsa loquitur allowed an inference against of negligence against each defendant.

Black Letter Rule: Where a plaintiff receives unusual injuries while unconscious and in the course of medical treatment, the doctrine of res ipsa loquitur may be used to infer negligent conduct on the part of all those defendants that had control over him or the instrumentalities which might have caused the injuries.

Harnish v. Children's Hospital Medical Center

Instant Facts: After undergoing a procedure that resulted in the total loss of tongue function, a patient sued her doctor and the hospital for negligently failing to inform her before surgery of the risk of loss of tongue function.

Black Letter Rule: A physician owes to his patient the duty to disclose in a reasonable manner all significant medical information that the physician possesses or reasonably should possess that is material to an intelligent decision by the patient whether to undergo a proposed procedure.

Lewellen v. Schneck Medical Center

Instant Facts: A driver was injured in a one-car accident and taken to the hospital, where the staff failed to detect a fractured spine.

Black Letter Rule: A hospital must provide appropriate medical screening within the capability of the hospital's emergency department to determine whether an emergency medical condition exists, and if it does, the patient may not be discharged until he has received stabilizing treatment or has been appropriately transferred.

Horizon/CMS Healthcare Corp. v. Auld

Instant Facts: The administratrix of nursing home's former patient brought suit against the home, claiming that the decedent was subjected to negligent medical care.

Black Letter Rule: Investigation reports written by state officials may be used as evidence of a defendant's subjective knowledge of the peril his conduct creates.

Walski v. Tiesenga

(Injured Patient) v. (Surgeon)

72 Ill.2d 249, 21 Ill.Dec. 201, 381 N.E.2d 279 (1978)

ONE ELEMENT OF A CAUSE OF ACTION FOR MEDICAL MALPRACTICE IS PROOF OF THE STANDARD OF CARE, ESTABLISHED THROUGH EXPERT TESTIMONY, BY WHICH THE DEFENDANT PHYSICIAN'S CONDUCT IS TO BE MEASURED

■ **INSTANT FACTS** A patient who suffered vocal paralysis during surgery sought to establish the negligence of her surgeon through the use of an expert's testimony, the thrust of which was that the expert would have performed the surgery differently.

■ **BLACK LETTER RULE** It is insufficient for a plaintiff to establish a prima facie case of medical malpractice merely to present testimony of another physician that he would have acted differently from the defendant.

■ PROCEDURAL BASIS

Appeal to the Illinois Supreme Court, challenging the decision of the appellate court affirming the directed verdict issue by the trial court in favor of the defendant.

■ FACTS

Dr. Marvin Tiensenga (D) operated to perform a thyroidectomy on Ms. Harriet Walski (P). The procedure carried with it the risk of damaging the laryngeal nerves, resulting in a loss of voice. Although Dr. Teinsenga (D) made a cut wide enough to avoid the area where the nerves were thought to be, he in fact severed the nerves, paralyzing Ms. Walski's (P) vocal chords. As part of her case against Dr. Tiensenga (D), Ms. Walski (P) offered expert testimony from Dr. Berger, who stated that he was taught to perform, and would have in fact performed the surgery in a different manner than that chosen by Dr. Tiensenga (D). When confronted with a quotation from a medical textbook that indicated there existed a certain amount of controversy concerning the procedures available, Dr. Berger testified that he did not agree. At the conclusion of the trial, the court directed a verdict for Dr. Tiensenga (D). The appellate court affirmed.

■ ISSUE

May a plaintiff establish a prima facie case of medical malpractice merely by offering testimony from an expert who states that he would have acted differently?

■ DECISION AND RATIONALE

(Kluczynski, J.) No. It is insufficient for a plaintiff to establish a prima facie case of medical malpractice merely to present testimony of another physician that he would have acted differently from the defendant. A plaintiff in a cause of action for medical malpractice must first establish, through expert testimony, the standard of care owed by the defendant doctor. Once the standard has been established, the plaintiff must prove that the defendant doctor departed from that standard. Ms. Walski (P) has failed to establish the proper standard of care. Dr. Berger testified only concerning his own personal preference in performing a thyroidectomy. He in no way testified that such a preference was the generally accepted medical standard of care.

In contrast, Dr. Tiensenga (D) testified that although a medical treatise advised using a different procedure, his course of action was based on the fact that Ms. Walski (P) had previous surgeries which necessitated a departure from the procedure indicated in the treatise. Differences in opinions are consistent with the exercise of due care. Affirmed.

Analysis:

A physician normally must possess the skill and ability of other physicians. Exactly what that skill entails must be established by expert testimony. In this case the court holds that Dr. Berger's testimony did not establish the standard of care, but rather merely expressed his opinion. This court held, as have most courts, that a mere disagreement with the defendant's conduct does not establish the standard of care. There is a subtle difference between an expert's opinion on what constitutes the standard of care and his opinion on what should have been done. In effect, Dr. Berger's testimony can be summarized in one sentence: "I would have done things differently." But what courts require is a statement to the effect of, "under the established medical practice, things should have been done differently." The expert's opinion should go to the standard of care, not necessarily the care he would provide.

Vergara v. Doan

(Parents of Injured Newborn) v. (Doctor)

593 N.E.2d 185 (Ind.1992)

THE STANDARD OF CARE OWED BY A PHYSICIAN DOES NOT NECESSARILY DEPEND ON THE SIZE OF THE COMMUNITY THE PHYSICIAN PRACTICES IN

■ **INSTANT FACTS** The parents of a newborn injured during delivery sued the small town doctor who performed the delivery, claiming that he failed to meet the medical standard of care.

■ **BLACK LETTER RULE** A physician must exercise that degree of care, skill, and proficiency exercised by reasonably careful, skillful, and prudent practitioners in the same class to which he belongs, acting under the same or similar circumstances.

■ PROCEDURAL BASIS

Appeal to the Supreme Court of Indiana, challenging the decision of the Court of Appeals affirming the jury verdict in favor of the defendant.

■ FACTS

During birth, Javier Vergara (P) suffered severe and permanent injuries. His parents sued Dr. John Doan (D), the doctor who delivered Javier (P), for medical malpractice. At trial, Dr. Doan's (D) conduct was measured against the standard of care given in similar localities. The jury found for Dr. Doan (D), and the Court of Appeals affirmed.

■ ISSUE

Is the standard of care owed by a doctor to a patient dependent on the locality where the medical services are rendered?

■ DECISION AND RATIONALE

(Shepard, C.J.) No. A physician must exercise that degree of care, skill, and proficiency exercised by reasonably careful, skillful, and prudent practitioners in the same class to which he belongs, acting under the same or similar circumstances. The strict locality rule measured a doctor's conduct against that of other doctors in the same community. Under modified locality rule, heretofore adhered to by this Court, the standard of care was that degree of care, skill, and proficiency which is commonly exercised by ordinarily careful, skillful, and prudent physicians, at the time of the operation and in similar localities. We believe the modified rule is no longer applicable in today's society. The reasons for the locality rule, in either of its forms, was that there was a great disparity between rural and urban areas with respect to medical opportunities, equipment, facilities, and training. Travel and communication were also difficult. Thus the locality rule was intended to prevent the inequity that would result from holding rural doctors to the same standard as doctors in large cities. However, with advances in communication, travel, and medical education, those disparities have significantly diminished. Moreover, the modified locality rule has a major drawback. It permits a lower standard of care to be exercised in smaller communities because other communities are likely to have the same care. Under the rule we adopt today, locality is only one factor to be considered in determining whether a doctor acted reasonably. Other factors include advances in the profession, availability of facilities, and whether the doctor is a specialist or general practitioner. Applied to the present case, we find that the new rule would not have changed the way the case was tried. The Vergaras (P) medical expert, a doctor from Pittsburgh, offered testimony that the standard of care in small communities required Dr. Doan (D) to perform a cesarean section, and required the presence of an anesthesiologist, or like professional. Evidently the jury disagreed and found Dr. Doan's (D) conduct reasonable. Affirmed.

Analysis:

The locality rule persisted for years, but with today's advances in transportation, communications, and medical training, the rule has become difficult to justify. The rule adopted by this court alleviates the locality rule's major drawback: that doctors in small communities were given an incentive to refrain from becoming acquainted with the latest medical techniques if they were held to the standards of similar communities. Nevertheless, the court's disposition of the case is somewhat questionable. The court notes that the application of the modified locality rule did not prejudice the Vergaras (P). It reasoned that, because the Vergaras' (P) expert, a doctor from a big city, testified that the standards of the smaller community required Dr. Doan (D) to perform a cesarean section, the verdict merely reflected the jury's disagreement with the Vergaras' (P) expert. But it is just as reasonable to think that the verdict reflected the jury's opinion that Dr. Doan (D), being an urban doctor, was unfamiliar with the standards of a small community. If that indeed was the case, then the Vergaras (P) were prejudiced by the application of the modified locality rule, because the standards of a small community are irrelevant under the generally applicable standard adopted by the court.

States v. Lourdes Hospital

(Patient) v. (Hospital)

100 N.Y.2d 208, 792 N.E.2d 151, 762 N.Y.S.2d 1 (2003)

EXPERT MEDICAL TESTIMONY MAY CLARIFY THE APPLICATION OF RES IPSA LOQUITUR

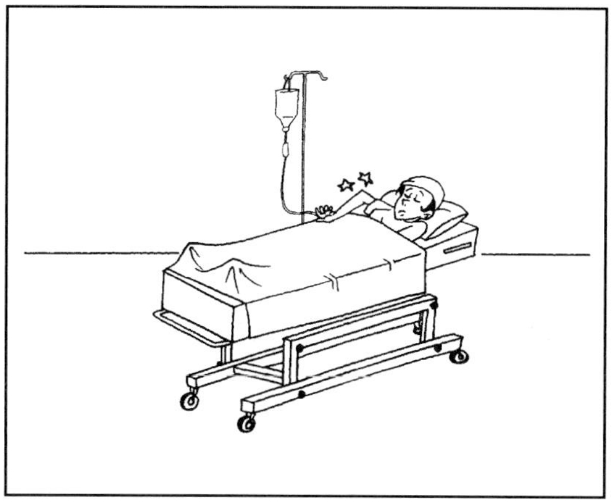

■ **INSTANT FACTS** While undergoing surgery for the removal of an ovarian cyst, States' (P) arm was injured, allegedly due to Lourdes Hospital's (D) negligence in administering anesthesia.

■ **BLACK LETTER RULE** The doctrine of res ipsa loquitur permits a factfinder to find negligence simply from the fact that an injury occurred, when the injury is of a kind that ordinarily does not occur absent negligence.

■ PROCEDURAL BASIS

On appeal to review a decision of the New York Appellate Division reversing a trial court denial of summary judgment.

■ FACTS

States (P) successfully underwent surgery at Lourdes Hospital (D) to remove an ovarian cyst. Before the procedure, States' (P) arm was placed on a board, rotated, and connected to an IV tube. States (P) complained of pain and discomfort, but there were no complications during surgery. Upon awakening from anesthesia, States (P) complained of increasing pain in her arm and shoulder. States (P) sued the hospital for medical malpractice. At the close of discovery, the defendant moved for summary judgment based on a lack of direct evidence of negligence by the anesthesiologist. States (P) responded that, despite the absence of direct evidence, expert medical testimony could establish that her injuries would not have occurred absent negligence, thus invoking res ipsa loquitur. The motion for summary judgment was denied, but the New York Appellate Division reversed, holding that the injury was not of the kind that a jury could draw upon its common experience and knowledge to establish an inference of negligence. States (P) appealed.

■ ISSUE

May expert medical testimony be introduced to a jury to establish the likelihood that the injury would not have occurred absent negligence?

■ DECISION AND RATIONALE

(Ciparick, J.) Yes. When appropriate, the doctrine of res ipsa loquitur permits a factfinder to draw an inference of negligence by the fact that an injury occurred. To establish res ipsa loquitor, the plaintiff must prove not only that the injury would not occur absent negligence, but also that the injury was caused by an agent or instrumentality exclusively in the defendant's control and that the plaintiff contributed to the injury in no way. Once these three elements are established, a factfinder may infer the defendant's negligence.

Addressing the first element, the defendant here contends that the jury may only rely on its common everyday experiences to determine whether the injury would occur absent negligence. The plaintiff counters that expert medical testimony may be offered to inform the jury's decision.

Restatement of Torts § 328D supports the plaintiff's position. Under the Restatement, the jury may consider the issue through not only its common knowledge, but also through evidence offered by the parties, including expert testimony in matters requiring specialized knowledge. Expert testimony reliably establishes the probability that negligence occurred to the same extent that layperson knowledge establishes matters of common understanding. Expert testimony is offered for the purpose of educating and assisting the jury, but the ultimate inference must be drawn by the jury on the basis of its understanding of the case. The burden remains on the plaintiff to establish the elements of res ipsa loquitur and prove the defendant's liability, albeit by reasonable inference. Because the plaintiff is free to offer expert medical testimony in support of its theory, summary judgment was appropriately denied. Reversed.

Analysis:

The doctrine of res ipsa loquitur permits an inference that negligence occurred. Many courts, however, state that res ipsa loquitur creates just a presumption of negligence. Courts often mistakenly interchange the inference of negligence and the presumption of negligence, but the distinction is not subtle. With an inference, a jury is permitted to conclude that negligence occurred, while with a presumption, the jury is compelled to find negligence absent rebuttable evidence offered by the defendant.

■ CASE VOCABULARY

INFERENCE: A conclusion reached by considering other facts and deducing a logical consequence from them.

PRESUMPTION: A legal inference or assumption that a fact exists, based on the known or proven existence of some other fact or group of facts. A presumption shifts the burden of production or persuasion to the opposing party, who can then attempt to overcome the presumption.

RES IPSA LOQUITUR: The doctrine providing that, in some circumstances, the mere fact of an accident's occurrence raises an inference of negligence so as to establish a prima facie case.

Ybarra v. Spangard

(Injured Patient) v. (Head Surgeon)

25 Cal.2d 486, 154 P.2d 687 (1944)

WHEN A MEDICAL PATIENT SUFFERS AN INJURY WHICH COULD NOT HAVE BEEN CAUSED IN THE ABSENCE OF NEGLIGENCE, BUT WHOSE SOURCE THE PLAINTIFF CANNOT IDENTIFY, AN INFERENCE OF NEGLIGENT CONDUCT MAY BE RAISED AGAINST THOSE CAREGIVERS THAT ASSISTED THE PLAINTIFF

■ **INSTANT FACTS** A patient who suffered minor paralysis during an appendectomy sought to recover against every doctor and nurse in whose care he was placed during the surgery, arguing that the doctrine of res ipsa loquitur allowed an inference against of negligence against each defendant.

■ **BLACK LETTER RULE** Where a plaintiff receives unusual injuries while unconscious and in the course of medical treatment, the doctrine of res ipsa loquitur may be used to infer negligent conduct on the part of all those defendants that had control over him or the instrumentalities which might have caused the injuries.

■ PROCEDURAL BASIS

Appeal to the Supreme Court of California, challenging the trial court's decision to enter a judgment of nonsuit as to all the defendants.

■ FACTS

Mr. Ybarra (P) was diagnosed with appendicitis by his physician, Dr. Tilley (D), who recommended that he undergo an appendectomy. The surgery was to be performed by Dr. Spangard (D) at a hospital owned and managed by Dr. Swift (D). After Ybarra (P) was wheeled into the operating room by Nurse Gisler (D), Dr. Resser (D), the anesthetist, pulled him toward the head of the operating table, laying him against two hard objects at the top of his shoulders. Shortly thereafter, the surgery was performed, with Ybarra remaining unconscious throughout the procedure. When he awoke, Ybarra, who was being attended in his room by Nurse Thompson (D), complained of a pain between his neck and shoulder. Dr. Tilley (D) gave him appropriate treatment, but the pain persisted. Ybarra (P) eventually developed paralysis and atrophy of the muscles around the shoulder. The medical evidence established that the injury was caused by some trauma, pressure or strain applied between the shoulder and neck. Ybarra (P) sued every doctor and nurse in whose care he was placed, seeking a *res ipsa loquitor* instruction against each. The trial court entered a judgment of nonsuit as to all the defendants.

■ ISSUE

May an inference of negligence be raised against those defendants that had control over a medical patient who suffered unusual injuries during his care?

■ DECISION AND RATIONALE

(Gibson, C.J.) Yes. Where a plaintiff receives unusual injuries while unconscious and in the course of medical treatment, the doctrine of res ipsa loquitur may be used to infer negligent conduct on the part of all those defendants that had control over him or the instrumentalities which might have caused the injuries. The present case is one that comes within the reason and spirit of the doctrine of res ipsa loquitur perhaps more than any other. It is difficult to see why the doctrine should not apply to a patient, who submits himself to the care and custody of doctors and nurses, is rendered unconscious, and receives an injury from instrumentalities used in his treatment. An opposite rule would restrict a patient who suffered severe injuries from recovering for negligent treatment unless the doctors and nurses volunteered to disclose the identity of the negligent person. It is argued that the doctrine is inapplicable in this case because Ybarra has failed to show which instrumentality caused his injury and which defendant has exclusive control over that instrumentality. First, we believe that, in order to meet the instrumentality requirement, it should be enough that Ybarra (P) can show an injury resulting from an external force applied when he lay unconscious in the hospital. This rule is consistent with those cases that have created an exception to the instrumentality requirement when strict application would defeat the policies behind the doctrine. As to the issue of control, considering that Ybarra (P) was rendered unconscious by Spangard (D) and the others, it is manifestly unreasonable for them to insist that Ybarra (P) identify the person who committed the negligent act. The burden lies upon the defendants to make an initial explanation. It is also argued that the doctrine, if applicable, cannot be applied to all the defendants, for it is unreasonable to believe that each committed the negligent act which caused Ybarra's (P) injury. But every defendant in whose custody the plaintiff was placed for any period was bound to exercise ordinary care to see that no unnecessary harm came to him and each would be liable for failure in this regard. Reversed.

Analysis:

The doctrine of res ipsa loquitur concerns a rational inference of negligence from the facts. But the issue here was not about whether the defendants were negligent, but rather which defendant was negligent. The court did not suggest that the facts supported a conclusion that the injury would not have occurred in the absence of negligence, a finding that is essential to the application of the doctrine. Instead, the court focused on the duty owed to patients and the patient's lack of information. The court essentially holds each defendant hostage with the threat of liability, until one comes forward with the necessary information. This rule could be justified on the ground that the caregivers are in the best position to provide the necessary information, assuming every caregiver has knowledge of the incident.

Harnish v. Children's Hospital Medical Center

(Injured Patient) v. (Hospital)

387 Mass. 152, 439 N.E.2d 240 (1982)

DOCTORS OWE THEIR PATIENT A DUTY TO DISCLOSE MATERIAL INFORMATION THAT IS RELEVANT TO THE PATIENT'S DECISION TO UNDERGO TREATMENT

■ **INSTANT FACTS** After undergoing a procedure that resulted in the total loss of tongue function, a patient sued her doctor and the hospital for negligently failing to inform her before surgery of the risk of loss of tongue function.

■ **BLACK LETTER RULE** A physician owes to his patient the duty to disclose in a reasonable manner all significant medical information that the physician possesses or reasonably should possess that is material to an intelligent decision by the patient whether to undergo a proposed procedure.

■ PROCEDURAL BASIS

Appeal to the Massachusetts Supreme Court, challenging the decision of the trial court dismissing the action on the grounds of inadequate proof.

■ FACTS

Ms. Harnish (P) underwent an operation to remove a tumor in her neck. During the operation, a nerve was severed, causing a permanent and total loss of tongue function. Harnish (P) sued her doctor and the Children's Hospital Medical Center (Hospital) (D) on the ground that they neglected to inform her of the risk of loss of tongue function, which she alleged was a foreseeable and material risk of the operation. There is no claim that the surgery was performed negligently. The trail court dismissed the action for a lack of proof.

■ ISSUE

Must a doctor disclose the risks of treatment to a patient?

■ DECISION AND RATIONALE

(O'Connor, J.) Yes. A physician owes to his patient the duty to disclose in a reasonable manner all significant medical information that the physician possesses or reasonably should possess that is material to an intelligent decision by the patient whether to undergo a proposed procedure. It is well established that every person has a strong interest in being free from nonconsensual invasion of bodily integrity. Courts have protected this interest by requiring a doctor to obtain his patient's consent before giving treatment or performing a procedure. That consent, however, must be informed. Yet there are limits to what a person can expect from his doctor in this regard. The information a physician should possess is that information possessed by the average qualified physician or, in the case of a specialty, by the average qualified specialist. In either case, what the physician should know must ordinarily be proved by expert testimony. The extent to which the physician must share information depends on what information he should reasonably recognize is material to a reasonable patient's decision. Materiality is an issue that lay persons are qualified to judge upon without expert testimony. The types of information a doctor is expected to disclose include the nature of the patient's condition, the benefits to be expected, the inability to predict results, the irreversibility of the procedure, the likely result of no treatment, and the availability of alternatives, including their risks and benefits. A doctor may, in certain circumstances, withhold otherwise material information. Although we do not find it necessary to discuss the contours of the privilege of nondisclosure, we note that a physician may not withhold information simply because he believes the patient would refuse necessary treatment. Finally, turning to the issue of causation, the plaintiff must show that neither she nor a reasonable person in similar circumstances would have undergone the procedure. Reversed in part, and affirmed in part.

Analysis:

Informed consent embodies the idea that individuals have a right to be free from bodily intrusions and that consent is valid only if it is informed. The rule adopted by the court here creates a cause of action with five elements. First, the plaintiff must prove that the physician failed to disclose required information. A doctor is required to disclose information the he should reasonably believe the patient would find material. Some courts have held that what a doctor should reasonably believe must be established by expert testimony. Second, the plaintiff must prove through expert testimony that the physician knew or should have known the undisclosed information. Third, the plaintiff must prove that the undisclosed information would be materially relevant to a reasonable person in deciding whether to undergo treatment. The court provides a laundry list of the kinds of information that must usually be disclosed. With respect to the materiality and relevance of these kinds of information, the court expressly excludes the need for expert testimony, permitting the jury to decide what is and is not reasonably material. Materiality is to be judged with reference to the "reasonable patient," and not the plaintiff, unless the physician is aware that the plaintiff attached some special importance to a matter. For example, a physician usually will not need to disclose a risk of loss of voice if it has only a one in ten million chance of occurring; but if the physician knows the patient is a professional opera singer, then he may have a duty to disclose that particular minute risk. The fourth element is that of causation, which involves an inquiry that is both subjective and objective. To prove cause in fact, the plaintiff must show, given the undisclosed information, that a reasonable person would not have undergone the treatment in those particular circumstances. The plaintiff must also show that she herself would not have undergone the treatment. The fifth element, not discussed by the court, is proof of damages, which is essential to any cause of action.

Lewellen v. Schneck Medical Center

(Accident Victim) v. (Treating Hospital)

2007 WL 2363384 (S.D. Ind. 2007)

HOSPITALS MAY NOT SEND UNSTABLE PATIENTS OUT THE DOOR WITHOUT RISKING LIABILITY

The quality of this X-ray is terrible.
I should wait for better films, but instead I'm just gonna hope for the best and discharge you.

■ **INSTANT FACTS** A driver was injured in a one-car accident and taken to the hospital, where the staff failed to detect a fractured spine.

■ **BLACK LETTER RULE** A hospital must provide appropriate medical screening within the capability of the hospital's emergency department to determine whether an emergency medical condition exists, and if it does, the patient may not be discharged until he has received stabilizing treatment or has been appropriately transferred.

■ PROCEDURAL BASIS

Federal trial court consideration of the defendant's motion for summary judgment.

■ FACTS

Lewellen (P) was driving home from visiting his cousin when his vehicle left the road, rolled, and ended up in the ditch. Lewellen (P) had been drinking. In fact, three hours later, his blood-alcohol level was nearly four times the legal limit. After the accident, Lewellen (P) was admitted to Schneck Medical Center (D), where he complained of lower back pain. X-rays were taken, but they were of poor quality. The staff, believing Lewellen (P) to be fine—just drunk—began the discharge process, even before the last of his x-rays were printed. Lewellen (P) was in too much pain to even stand or walk, and he was uncooperative with regard to his discharge. Trooper Drew, one of the officers who had arrived at the scene of the accident, also refused to sign the discharge papers. Given Lewellen's (P) condition, Drew felt he had no choice but to transport Lewellen (P) to jail. Before they actually left the hospital, the last of the x-rays came off the printer. A doctor on duty made a notation on the ER chart that the x-rays revealed no fracture, but that they were of poor quality due to Lewellen's (P) supposed lack of cooperation. (Several doctors who later reviewed his x-rays had no trouble detecting the fracture.)

Two hours after Lewellen (P) was discharged, a radiologist, pursuant to the hospital's standard quality control process, reviewed the x-rays once more, concluding that a fracture could not be ruled out because of the poor quality of the x-rays, but he contacted no one about this conclusion. In reality, Lewellen (P) had a burst fracture in his spine, and his condition worsened while he was in jail. An officer at the jail observed Lewellen (P) in great distress and called the hospital. A nurse that he spoke with said that a review of the x-rays indicated an abnormality, but she did not suggest that Lewellen (P) be brought back to the hospital or otherwise provide instructions as to proper treatment. Being unsatisfied with that result, the officer talked to the jail commander and an ambulance was called. Lewellen (P) was taken back to Schneck (D), where a CT scan showed the extent of his injuries. Despite an operation, Lewellen (P) remained seriously and permanently injured, unable to urinate or defecate on his own. Lewellen (P) brought suit against Schneck (D) under the Emergence Medical Treatment and Active Labor Act (EMTALA). The defendant moved for summary judgment.

■ ISSUE

Was Schneck (D) entitled to summary judgment on Lewellen's (P) EMTALA claim?

■ DECISION AND RATIONALE

(Tinder, J.) No. A hospital must provide appropriate medical screening within the capability of the hospital's emergency department to determine whether an emergency medical condition exists, and if it does, the patient may not be discharged until he has received stabilizing treatment or has been appropriately transferred. If the hospital fails to adhere to either of these requirements, the patient may sue. EMTALA is a "disparate treatment" statute—that is, a patient must show that he was treated differently from other patients. A hospital is not liable under EMTALA if it provides a patient with an examination comparable to the one offered to other patients presenting with similar symptoms, unless the examination is so cursory that it is not designed to identify acute and severe symptoms that alert the doctor to the need for immediate treatment to prevent serious bodily injury. The plaintiff here did not present evidence that the screening performed on him differed from other patients' screenings. However, a reasonable jury could conclude that the screening was so cursory that it was not designed to identify acute and severe symptoms, and thus did not satisfy EMTALA. If the last of the x-rays were just printing as Lewellen (P) was being discharged, how could his screen be designed to identify acute and severe symptoms? His stay at the hospital was alarmingly brief considering Lewellen's (P) complaints of pain, and the fact that he could not sit or stand. Lewellen (P) had a bleeding gash in his arm that still had grass and dirt in it even after he arrived at the jail. This scenario is so grave that a jury could conclude that the screening requirement was not met. Motion for summary judgment denied.

Analysis:

The Emergency Medical Treatment and Active Labor Act governs when and how a patient may be refused treatment or transferred from one hospital to another when he is in an unstable medical condition. The avowed purpose of the statute is to prevent hospitals from rejecting patients, refusing to treat them, or transferring them to other hospitals because they are unable to pay or are covered under the Medicare or Medicaid programs. EMTALA was passed as part of the Consolidated Omnibus Budget Reconciliation Act of 1986, and it is sometimes referred to as "the COBRA law." A number of laws fall under that general name, including the statute governing continuation of medical insurance benefits after termination of employment.

Horizon/CMS Healthcare Corp. v. Auld

(Nursing Home) v. (Administratrix of Deceased Patient's Estate)

985 S.W.2d 216 (Tex.App.1999)

SUBSTANDARD NURSING CARE AND ELDER ABUSE IS AN OFTEN NEGLECTED PROBLEM

■ **INSTANT FACTS** The administratrix of nursing home's former patient brought suit against the home, claiming that the decedent was subjected to negligent medical care.

■ **BLACK LETTER RULE** Investigation reports written by state officials may be used as evidence of a defendant's subjective knowledge of the peril his conduct creates.

■ PROCEDURAL BASIS

Appeal from the jury verdict for the plaintiff, claiming that the trial court mistakenly admitted into evidence written investigation reports made by state officials.

■ FACTS

From August 1994 to August 1995, Martha Hary was a resident of Heritage Western Hills Nursing Home, which was owned by Horizon/CMS Healthcare Corp. (Horizon) (D). During that year, Martha's body developed pressure sores, some of which rotted her skin to the point of leaving the bone exposed, and suffered contractures in all extremities. Lexa Auld (P), alleged that Ms. Harry's ailments were the result of Heritage's (D) failure to provide her with medical care and treatment within the acceptable standard of care. The evidence showed that Auld had established that the nursing home failed to: (1) regularly turn and reposition Ms. Hary for a total of 1,680 hours; (2) feed Ms. Harry regularly (she missed 238 total meals); (3) provide incontinent care by not keeping Ms. Hary's skin clean and dry for a total of 1,728 hours; and (4) treat Ms. Harry with passive range of motion exercises. Heritage's own records reflected these deficiencies. The evidence also established that these deficiencies were the cause of Ms. Hary's ailments. At trial, the judge admitted into evidence written investigation reports made by the Texas Department of Human Services to determine compliance with state and federal requirements. A jury found for Ms. Auld (P), awarding $2,371,000 in actual damages, and $90,000,000 in punitive damages, an amount later reduced to just under $9.5 million. Horizon appealed on the ground that the surveys did not establish whether Horizon (D) deviated from the proper standard of care.

■ ISSUE

Did the court properly admit into evidence investigation reports written by state officials to determine compliance with state and federal requirements?

■ DECISION AND RATIONALE

(Holman, J.) Yes. Investigation reports written by state officials may be used as evidence of a defendant's subjective knowledge of the peril his conduct creates. Because gross negligence was an issue at trial, that subjective knowledge was essential to Ms. Auld's case. The information contained in the reports showed that the state did bring the deficient conditions to

Horizon's (D) attention. Thus we conclude that the trial court did not abuse its discretion. Affirmed.

Analysis:

The size of the damages awarded here is not surprising, considering that nursing home care is a highly profitable business, with some corporate enterprises reporting revenues in the billions. This case just might illustrate how nursing homes manage to make that kind of money, i.e., by cutting corners and providing substandard care. But this case is really an anomaly, for most abuse and neglect goes unreported. Moreover, few causes of action are brought because actual damages are limited by the fact that the elderly have short life expectancies, and bed-ridden patients are not deprived of an active life.

CHAPTER FOURTEEN

Family Members and Charities

Neel v. Sewell

Instant Facts: Neel (P), who was seventeen, sued his dad (D) to recover for injuries he sustained when he and his dad (D) were cleaning out Neel's (P) step-grandma's house, and his dad (D) moved for summary judgment on the ground of parental immunity.

Black Letter Rule: Claims of negligent supervision are properly viewed as involving the exercise of reasonable parental authority over a child, and are thus barred by parental immunity.

Neel v. Sewell

(Son/Step-Grandson) v. (Step-Grandmother)

834 F. Supp. 2d 648 (E.D. Mich. 2011)

PARENTAL IMMUNITY HAS BEEN ABROGATED, SUBJECT TO IMPORTANT EXCEPTIONS

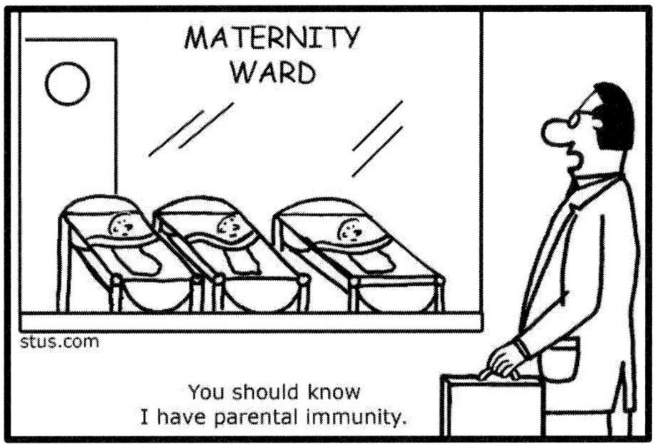

■ **INSTANT FACTS** Neel (P), who was seventeen, sued his dad (D) to recover for injuries he sustained when he and his dad (D) were cleaning out Neel's (P) step-grandma's house, and his dad (D) moved for summary judgment on the ground of parental immunity.

■ **BLACK LETTER RULE** Claims of negligent supervision are properly viewed as involving the exercise of reasonable parental authority over a child, and are thus barred by parental immunity.

■ PROCEDURAL BASIS

Federal district court consideration of the defendant father's motion for summary judgment.

■ FACTS

Neel (P), his dad (D), and his aunt were helping his step-grandmother, Sewell (D), clean out her house. A fire was started in the yard to dispose of the garbage that had accumulated. Neel (P), who was seventeen years old at the time, was placing plastic milk jugs on the fire when a bag containing an aerosol can exploded. Neel (D) was severely burned. He sought to recover from his father (D), Evans, on the ground that his father had negligently supervised him. Evans (D) moved for summary judgment, arguing that he was immune from liability for claims of negligent supervision brought by his son.

■ ISSUE

Was Evans (D) entitled to parental immunity?

■ DECISION AND RATIONALE

(Rosen, C.J.) Yes. Claims of negligent supervision are properly viewed as involving the exercise of reasonable parental authority over a child, and are thus barred by parental immunity. Michigan has abrogated the common law doctrine of parental immunity. Accordingly, a child may maintain a lawsuit against his parent for injuries suffered as a result of the alleged ordinary negligence of the parent. There are, however, two important exceptions: (1) when the alleged negligent act involves the exercise of reasonable parental authority over the child; and (2) when the alleged negligent act involves an exercise of reasonable parental discretion with respect to the provision of food, clothing, housing, medical and dental services, and other care. Evans (D) argues that this case falls within the first exception. We agree. Other decisions have refused to allow claims for negligent parental supervision. The claim that Evans (D) failed to properly watch over Neel (D) are like those rejected by other courts, where a two-year-old fell into a construction hole and a three-year-old drowned while her father went to the restroom. The defendant's motion for summary judgment is therefore granted.

Analysis:

Parental immunity did not exist at English common law. Rather, it was created by American courts, first arising in Hewellette v. George, 9 So. 885 (Miss. 1891). Many courts, including those of Michigan, have abolished the doctrine for some purposes, such as in actions by unemancipated minors against their parents to recover for injuries sustained in motor-vehicle accidents, or here, actions for negligent supervision against the parent. Nor does parental immunity apply when the injury is inflicted by the parent or child through willful, wanton, or criminal conduct. Note that the parent-child immunity doctrine works both ways; that is, it also encompasses the principle that parents cannot sue their children.

■ CASE VOCABULARY

The immunity doctrine holding that children cannot sue their parents, and that parents cannot sue their children, in tort.

CHAPTER FIFTEEN

Governmental Entities, Officers, and Employees

United States v. Olson

Instant Facts: Miners injured in a mine accident sued the government based on the alleged negligence of federal mine inspectors, and the district court held that the suit was barred by the FTCA, but the Ninth Circuit reversed.

Black Letter Rule: The FTCA requires a court to look to the state law on the liability of private entities, not to those of public entities, when assessing the government's liability under the FTCA in the performance of activities that private persons do not perform.

Purcell v. United States

Instant Facts: Despite being warned that Purcell intended to commit suicide and had a gun, military personnel allowed him to go to the bathroom with a friend, where Purcell fatally shot himself in the chest; his family (P) sued the government (D), which argued for immunity under the *Feres* doctrine.

Black Letter Rule: Under the *Feres* doctrine, the government is not liable under the FTCA for injuries to servicemen where the injuries arise out of or are in the course of activity incident to service.

Whisnant v. United States

Instant Facts: An employee was exposed to mold at a government-run commissary and he sued the government (D) for his resultant health problems, but the federal district court dismissed the case under the discretionary function exception to the FTCA; the employee appealed.

Black Letter Rule: Because removing an obvious health hazard is a matter of safety rather than policy, the government's alleged failure to do so is not protected under the discretionary function exception.

Riss v. City of New York

Instant Facts: Riss (P) sued City (D) for negligence due to the police failing to provide protection from attacker who had previously threatened her on numerous occasions.

Black Letter Rule: A municipality is not liable for failure to provide special police protection to a member of the public who was repeatedly threatened with personal harm and eventually suffered injuries for lack of protection.

Harry Stoller and Co., Inc. v. City of Lowell

Instant Facts: Firefighters negligently failed to use sprinkler system to fight fire, relying only on the fire hoses, and Stoller (P) sued City (D) for destruction of buildings and contents.

Black Letter Rule: In order for the discretionary function exception to apply to governmental acts, the conduct must involve making a policy or planning judgment.

Sama v. Hannigan

Instant Facts: Sama (P), an inmate, underwent a hysterectomy after advising her doctors that she would prefer to keep her remaining ovary in order to harvest eggs in the future, but the doctors removed the ovary anyhow and Sama (P) sued; the doctors claimed that they were entitled to qualified immunity.

Black Letter Rule: Qualified immunity shields government officials performing discretionary functions, such as the administration of medical care, from liability for civil damages insofar as their conduct does not violate clearly established statutory or known constitutional rights of which a reasonable person would have been aware.

Navarro v. Block

Instant Facts: Domestic violence victim called 911 to report that estranged husband was in route to her home to kill her, but operator did not dispatch police, and victim was killed.

Black Letter Rule: A municipality may be liable for civil rights violations if there is proof of the existence of a custom or informal policy with repeated constitutional violations for which municipal officials were not discharged or reprimanded, even if the official policy-makers did not have actual knowledge of the custom and practice.

United States v. Olson

(Government) v. (Injured Mine Worker)

546 U.S. 43, 126 S.Ct. 510, 163 L.Ed.2d 306 (2005)

THE GOVERNMENT MAY BE LIABLE IF PRIVATE ENTITIES WOULD BE LIABLE UNDER LIKE CIRCUMSTANCES

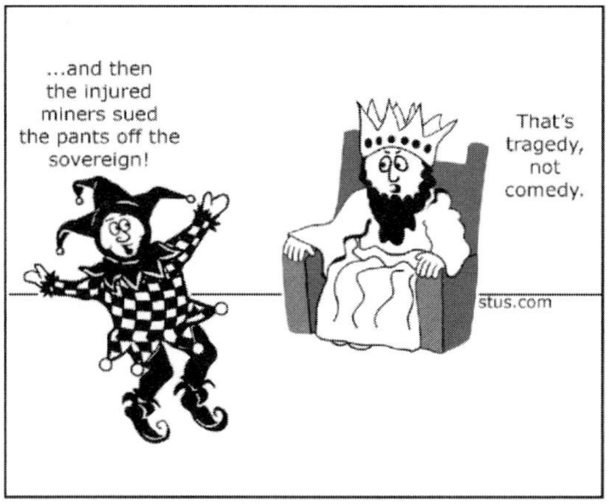

■ **INSTANT FACTS** Miners injured in a mine accident sued the government based on the alleged negligence of federal mine inspectors, and the district court held that the suit was barred by the FTCA, but the Ninth Circuit reversed.

■ **BLACK LETTER RULE** The FTCA requires a court to look to the state law on the liability of private entities, not to those of public entities, when assessing the government's liability under the FTCA in the performance of activities that private persons do not perform.

■ PROCEDURAL BASIS

Supreme Court review of a Ninth Circuit decision reversing a federal district court dismissal of the plaintiff's FTCA claim.

■ FACTS

The Federal Tort Claims Act (FTCA) authorizes private tort actions against the United States under circumstances where the U.S., if a private person, would be liable in accordance with the law of the place where the act or omission occurred. In this case, two injured mine workers sued the United States, claiming that the negligence of federal mine inspectors helped bring about a serious mine accident in Arizona. The federal district court dismissed the suit, in part on the ground that the allegations failed to show that Arizona law would impose liability on a private person under similar circumstances. The Ninth Circuit reversed, holding that where unique governmental functions are at issue, the FTCA waives sovereign immunity if a state or municipal entity would be subject to liability under the same circumstances. The case went to the United States Supreme Court.

■ ISSUE

Did the Ninth Circuit apply the proper standard for holding the government liable under the FTCA for injuries sustained in a mine accident?

■ DECISION AND RATIONALE

(Breyer, J.) No. The FTCA requires a court to look to the state law on the liability of private entities, not to those of public entities, when assessing the government's liability under the FTCA in the performance of activities that private persons do not perform. The Ninth Circuit reads into the FTCA something that is not there. The Act says that it waives sovereign immunity under circumstances where the United States, if a *private person*—not the United States, if it were a *state or municipal entity*—would be liable. We have consistently stuck to this private person standard. The Ninth Circuit's reading of the FTCA errs in another way as well. The FTCA makes the Unites States liable in the same manner and to the same extent as a private individual would be under *like* circumstances, not the *same* circumstances. The judgment of the court of appeals is therefore vacated and the case is remanded so the district court can decide this case in the first instance.

Analysis:

This case had a long and arduous history and, obviously, did not end here. Initially, the federal district court had granted the government's motion to dismiss. The miners appealed, and the Ninth Circuit Court of Appeals reversed and remanded. Certiorari was granted. The Supreme Court, in the excerpt reprinted in the casebook, vacated and remanded the case back to the lower courts. On remand, the federal district court dismissed the action once again, and the miners once again appealed to the Ninth Circuit. The court of appeals reversed and remanded—again. After a bench trial, the federal district court ultimately held that the conduct of the field office supervisor in evaluating anonymous complaints about conditions in the mine was protected under the FTCA's discretionary-function exception, and that the manner in which the inspector conducted his inspections was protected under the discretionary-function exception as well.

■ CASE VOCABULARY

DISCRETIONARY FUNCTION: A deed involving an exercise of personal judgment and conscience.

SOVEREIGN IMMUNITY: A government's immunity from being sued in its own courts without its consent. Congress has waived most of the federal government's sovereign immunity in the Federal Tort Claims Act.

Purcell v. United States

(Family of Dead Serviceman) v. (Government)

656 F.3d 463 (7th Cir. 2011)

FERES CREATES AN EXCEPTION TO THE GOVERNMENT'S WAIVER OF SOVEREIGN IMMUNITY

■ **INSTANT FACTS** Despite being warned that Purcell intended to commit suicide and had a gun, military personnel allowed him to go to the bathroom with a friend, where Purcell fatally shot himself in the chest; his family (P) sued the government (D), which argued for immunity under the *Feres* doctrine.

■ **BLACK LETTER RULE** Under the *Feres* doctrine, the government is not liable under the FTCA for injuries to servicemen where the injuries arise out of or are in the course of activity incident to service.

■ PROCEDURAL BASIS

Federal appellate court review of a district court decision in favor of the defendant.

■ FACTS

Navy (D) and Department of Defense (DOD) (D) personnel were called to Purcell's barracks and informed he planned to kill himself and had a gun. They did not find the gun, but allowed him to go to the bathroom with a friend. Upon entering, Purcell pulled the gun from his waistband and committed suicide by shooting himself in the chest. His family (P) sued under the Federal Tort Claims Act (FTCA), arguing that the defendants' actions were contrary to standard operating procedures. The court found the case barred by the *Feres* doctrine, which provides that the government is not liable under the FTCA for injuries to servicemen where the injuries arise out of or are in the course of activity incident to service.

■ ISSUE

Was the government immune from suit under the *Feres* doctrine?

■ DECISION AND RATIONALE

(Flaum, J.) Yes. Under the *Feres* doctrine, the government is not liable under the FTCA for injuries to servicemen where the injuries arise out of or are in the course of activity incident to service. The FTCA provides generally that the United States is liable in the same manner and to the same extent as a private individual under like circumstances. Excepted from this waiver of sovereign immunity, however, are claims arising out of the combatant activities of the military or naval forces during the time of war. The *Feres* doctrine expands upon this exception, extending immunity to cases in which the injuries arose out of or in the course of an activity incident to service. The *Feres* doctrine is not without controversy. However, *Feres* remains the law. At the time Purcell committed suicide in his on-base residential building, Purcell was on active duty, living in the barracks on a military base, experiencing problems that developed shortly after he enlisted, and deliberately avoided Navy and DOD personnel who were sent to Purcell's barracks to help him. Purcell stood in the type of relationship to the military at the time of his death that the occurrences causing his injury arose out of activity incident to military service, and thus *Feres* bars his suit. Affirmed.

Analysis:

When the Supreme Court reaffirmed *Feres*, it discussed three rationales in support of the doctrine: (1) the need to protect the uniquely federal relationship between the government and the armed forces, which could be adversely affected by applying differing tort laws (e.g., from different states); (2) the existence of statutory compensatory schemes; and (3) the need to avoid interference with military discipline and effectiveness. The dispositive inquiry in *Feres* cases is whether the service member stands in the type of relationship to the military at the time of his or her injury that the occurrences causing the injury arose out of activity incident to military service. In this case, the court held, he did.

■ CASE VOCABULARY

SOVEREIGN IMMUNITY: The doctrine that holds that a government or sovereign is immune or exempt from tort liability because of its status in society. Most jurisdictions have waived tort immunity to a certain extent.

Whisnant v. United States

(Injured Employee) v. (Government)

400 F.3d 1177 (9th Cir. 2005)

COURTS APPLY A TWO-PART TEST TO DETERMINE WHETHER THE DISCRETIONARY FUNCTION EXCEPTION APPLIES

■ **INSTANT FACTS** An employee was exposed to mold at a government-run commissary and he sued the government (D) for his resultant health problems, but the federal district court dismissed the case under the discretionary function exception to the FTCA; the employee appealed.

■ **BLACK LETTER RULE** Because removing an obvious health hazard is a matter of safety rather than policy, the government's alleged failure to do so is not protected under the discretionary function exception.

■ PROCEDURAL BASIS

Federal circuit court review of a district court decision dismissing the plaintiff's case.

■ FACTS

Whisnant (P) worked for a company that provided seafood to the commissary of a naval base. The commissary was operated by a government agency (D). Regulations required periodic safety inspections of the commissary, but the agency's employees could decide how and when to conduct these inspections. The government (D) contracted out maintenance work at the base to Johnson Controls. In 1997, Johnson's inspections revealed that mold had accumulated in the meat department of the commissary. Over the next three years, several commissary employees and customers became ill. Tests conducted in 2000 proved that toxic molds were present, and the government (D) closed down the meat department. Whisnant's (P) exposure to the mold caused him to suffer from pneumonia, headaches, swollen glands, a sore throat, a persistent cough, and other health problems. He sued the government (D) under the Federal Tort Claims Act (FTCA), and the government (D) moved to dismiss on the ground that the suit was barred by the discretionary function exception, which provides that the FTCA does not apply to any claim based on the exercise or performance, or the failure to exercise or perform, a discretionary function or duty on the party of an agency or employee of the government, whether or not the discretion was abused. The federal district court granted the defendant's motion, and the plaintiff appealed.

■ ISSUE

Was the plaintiff's suit barred by the discretionary function exception?

■ DECISION AND RATIONALE

(Fletcher, J.) No. Because removing an obvious health hazard is a matter of safety rather than policy, the government's alleged failure to do so is not protected under the discretionary function exception. In determining the applicability of the discretionary function exception, courts must ask whether the challenged action was discretionary in the first place—that is, was it governed by a mandatory statute, policy, or regulation? If the action is not discretionary, it obviously cannot be shielded under the exception. Second, courts must ask whether the action is the type Congress meant to protect—that is, does the action involve a decision susceptible to social, economic, or political policy analysis? It is the government's burden to demonstrate the applicability of the discretionary function exception.

In this case, the first question is easily answered. No statute, policy, or regulation mandates the specific manner in which the commissary was to be inspected, so the function at issue was discretionary. The second question is more difficult to answer. We have held that the *design* of a course of governmental action is shielded by the discretionary function exception—that is, it is susceptible to social, economic, or political policy analysis—whereas the *implementation* of that course of action is not. We have also held that matters of scientific and professional judgment—particularly those concerning safety—are rarely considered to be susceptible to social, economic, or political policy. Under these principles, Whisnant's (P) suit is not barred. He does not allege that the government (D) was negligent in designing its safety inspection procedures; rather, he charges the government (D) with negligence in following through on those procedures to safeguard the health of employees and customers of the commissary. Moreover, cleaning up mold involves professional and scientific judgment, not decisions on social, economic, or political policy.

The government (D) argues that it was constrained by budgetary concerns, but we decline to permit the government (D) to use these concerns as a shield against allegedly negligent conduct. While the government (D) has the discretion to decide how to carry out its responsibility to maintain safe and healthy premises, it does not have discretion to abdicate that responsibility. Whisnant (P) has alleged negligence in the implementation rather than the design of government safety regulations, and the decisions of the government (D) that Whisnant (P) claims were negligent concerned technical and professional judgments about safety, rather than broad questions of social, economic, or political policy. Therefore, the discretionary function exception to the FTCA does not bar Whisnant's (P) suit. Reversed and remanded.

Analysis:

As this case explains, when a federal statute, regulation, or policy specifically prescribes a course of action embodying a fixed or readily ascertainable standard, a government employee's conduct does not fall within the discretionary function exception. In other words, when a government employee violates a mandatory regulation, there is no shelter from liability under the FTCA's discretionary function exception, because there is no room for choice and the action is plainly contrary to policy. Where, however, the government official must act without reliance on a fixed or readily ascertainable standard, the decision he or she makes is deemed discretionary, and possibly falls within the exception. Among the factors that a court may consider are the nature of the conduct, whether Congress intended the conduct to be shielded from tort liability, whether the actions of the government regulate the conduct of private individuals, the underlying basis for the discretionary function exception, and whether a tort suit provides the relevant standard of care for evaluating the governmental decision.

Riss v. City of New York

(Victim of Attack) v. (City)

22 N.Y.2d 579, 293 N.Y.S.2d 897, 240 N.E.2d 860 (1968)

CITY IS IMMUNE FROM LIABILITY WHERE POLICE OFFICERS FAILED TO PROVIDE PROTECTION

■ **INSTANT FACTS** Riss (P) sued City (D) for negligence due to the police failing to provide protection from attacker who had previously threatened her on numerous occasions.

■ **BLACK LETTER RULE** A municipality is not liable for failure to provide special police protection to a member of the public who was repeatedly threatened with personal harm and eventually suffered injuries for lack of protection.

■ PROCEDURAL BASIS

Appeal following dismissal of action after presentation of the evidence in negligence action seeking damages for personal injuries.

■ FACTS

Riss (P) sued the City of New York (D) for negligence alleging that the city police failed to provide police protection. Riss (P) had been terrorized for months by a rejected suitor who threatened to kill or maim her. She repeatedly sought protection from the police. Thereafter, she received a phone call warning that it was her "last chance." She again called the police but nothing was done. The next day, the rejected suitor hired someone to throw lye into Riss' (P) face, causing blindness in one eye, loss of a portion of vision in the other eye, and permanent facial scarring. The trial court [recognizing that the law is not always fair] dismissed Riss' (P) complaint at the end of all the evidence and the appellate division affirmed. Riss (P) appealed.

■ ISSUE

Is a municipality liable for failure to provide special police protection to a member of the public who was repeatedly threatened with personal harm and eventually suffered injuries for lack of protection?

■ DECISION AND RATIONALE

(Breitel) No. The municipality is not liable for failing to provide police protection to a member of the general public. We first must distinguish certain types of governmental activities where liability may be found. Activities that displace or supplement traditionally private enterprises may lead to liability, such as rapid transit systems, hospitals and places of public assembly. Activities that provide services and facilities for the use of the public may also lead to liability, such as highways, public buildings and the like. The basis for liability is that the services or facilities are for the direct use of members of the public. This case involves governmental protection services from external hazards, such as controlling the activities of criminal wrongdoers. [This is certainly an impossible task.] If we were to permit tort liability for those who seek police protection based on specific hazards, it would cause a determination as to how the limited resources of the community should be allocated and without predictable limits. We should not so dictate the allocation of the resources and it should be left to the legislature to make the determination concerning the scope of public responsibility. Imposing liability in such situations will not cure the problem of crime in cities [and would bankrupt the city]. It is not for the courts, in the absence of legislation, to carve out an area of tort liability for police protection to members of the public. This case is distinguishable from the situation where the police authorities undertake responsibilities to particular members of the public and expose them, without adequate protection, to the risks that then materialize into actual losses. Judgment is affirmed.

Analysis:

This case examines immunities under state, as opposed to federal, law. States have adopted various types of statutes, abolishing sovereign immunity. Accordingly, there are many situations whereby a municipality may be liable under principles of ordinary tort law. However, as with the Federal Tort Claims Act, there are exceptions in certain circumstances. This case demonstrates that the police are not liable for failing to provide protection to the public, even if they negligently fail to do so. The court's reasoning is that there is no statutory basis that would provide for such liability, and it was unwilling to judicially create such liability. Note that the court's decision also distinguished the situation of the police undertaking responsibility to particular members of the public, which could lead to liability for negligently failing to act. The difference is that a special relationship has developed with a certain member of the public, as distinguished from the public at large.

Harry Stoller and Co., Inc. v. City of Lowell

(Burned Business) v. (City)

412 Mass. 139, 587 N.E.2d 780 (1992)

DISCRETIONARY FUNCTION EXCEPTION DOES NOT APPLY WHEN FIREFIGHTERS USE INADEQUATE METHODS TO FIGHT A FIRE

■ **INSTANT FACTS** Firefighters negligently failed to use sprinkler system to fight fire, relying only on the fire hoses, and Stoller (P) sued City (D) for destruction of buildings and contents.

■ **BLACK LETTER RULE** In order for the discretionary function exception to apply to governmental acts, the conduct must involve making a policy or planning judgment.

■ PROCEDURAL BASIS

Appeal from judgment entered notwithstanding the verdict in negligence action seeking damages.

■ FACTS

Harry Stoller and Co., Inc. (Stoller) (P) sued the City of Lowell (City) (D) for the destruction of its buildings and their contents due to fire. The firefighters, in violation of accepted practice, chose not to use the sprinkler system to fight the fire, relying instead on the fire hoses. [Bad choice.] The jury awarded damages to Stoller (P) but the trial judge granted judgment notwithstanding the verdict for City (D) under the state's statutory discretionary immunity. Stoller (P) appeals contending that the decision by the firefighters to not use the sprinkler system was not a discretionary act involving making a policy or planning judgment.

■ ISSUE

Does the discretionary function exception require that the conduct involve making a policy or planning judgment?

■ DECISION AND RATIONALE

(Wilkins) Yes. In order for the discretionary function exception to apply to governmental acts, the conduct must involve making a policy or planning judgment. In the past, we have declined to apply the discretionary function exception to various governmental acts. Examples include a police officer deciding whether to remove an intoxicated driver from the road, a city physician treating a patient in the emergency room, and failing to provide adequate information to allow the protection of one's property from a client of the mental health department. These acts do not involve discretionary functions that amount to making a policy or planning judgment. With respect to firefighting, certain conduct does have a planning or policy basis. Determining the number and location of fire stations, the amount of equipment to buy, the size of the department, the number and location of hydrants, and the quantity of water supply involve policy considerations, especially the allocation of financial resources. The conduct involved in this case however is different. The negligence of the firefighters in choosing not to use the sprinkler system did not involve planning or policy considerations. Although it may have been discretionary to choose whether to put water through the sprinkler system or through hoses, it was not based on a policy or planning judgment. Thus, the discretionary functions exception does not shield the City (D) from liability. [If it did, everything would be considered discretionary and municipalities would always win.] Reversed.

Analysis:

Recall that if the government acts in a discretionary manner, it will generally be immune from liability. This case concerns the discretionary function exemption as applied to municipalities. It clarifies that in order for the discretionary function exception to apply, the conduct must involve a policymaking or planning judgment. The court of appeal held here that the conduct did not rise to the level of a discretionary function involving policy making or judgment and thus the City (D) could be held liable. Note that the firefighters, in responding to the fire, used inadequate methods to fight the fire. The court concluded that the firefighters exercised discretion in choosing not to use the sprinklers, but such discretion did not involve a choice regarding public policy and planning.

■ CASE VOCABULARY

JUDGMENT N.O.V.: Latin initials for judgment non obstante veredicto; otherwise known as judgment notwithstanding the verdict, obtained through a motion made post-verdict to have judgment rendered in favor of one party notwithstanding a verdict in favor of the other party.

Sama v. Hannigan

(Prisoner/Patient) v. (Government Physician)

669 F.3d 585 (5th Cir. 2012)

FOR A RIGHT TO BE "CLEARLY ESTABLISHED," THERE MUST BE ONLY ONE REASONABLE CONCLUSION AS TO ITS APPLICATION

■ **INSTANT FACTS** Sama (P), an inmate, underwent a hysterectomy after advising her doctors that she would prefer to keep her remaining ovary in order to harvest eggs in the future, but the doctors removed the ovary anyhow and Sama (P) sued; the doctors claimed that they were entitled to qualified immunity.

■ **BLACK LETTER RULE** Qualified immunity shields government officials performing discretionary functions, such as the administration of medical care, from liability for civil damages insofar as their conduct does not violate clearly established statutory or known constitutional rights of which a reasonable person would have been aware.

■ PROCEDURAL BASIS

Federal circuit court review of a district court judgment in the defendants' favor.

■ FACTS

Sama (P) was diagnosed with cervical cancer while in prison. She had previously undergone removal of her right ovary. Sama (P) was referred to the University of Texas Medical Branch for treatment. Hannigan (D) was her primary doctor. A radical hysterectomy was recommended, but Sama (P) requested that she keep her left ovary if possible. During surgery, the doctors observed the ovary to be abnormal and dysfunctional, so they removed it. Sama (P) sued, and the doctors moved for summary judgment on qualified immunity grounds. The trial court granted the motion and Sama (P) appealed.

■ ISSUE

Were the physicians entitled to qualified immunity?

■ DECISION AND RATIONALE

(Owen, J.) Yes. Qualified immunity shields government officials performing discretionary functions, such as the administration of medical care, from liability for civil damages insofar as their conduct does not violate clearly established statutory or known constitutional rights of which a reasonable person would have been aware. Once raised, the burden shifts to the plaintiff, who may rebut entitlement to immunity by demonstrating that the official's allegedly wrongful conduct violated clearly established law. For a right to be clearly established, existing law must truly compel the conclusion for every like-situated, reasonable government agent that what the defendant is doing violates federal law in the circumstances. Here, we consider precedent with regard to a patient's right to refuse unwanted medical treatment. In the prison context, we must also consider the state's countervailing interest in providing appropriate, necessary medical treatment to inmates. Here, Sama (P) consented to a radical hysterectomy. However, she maintains that she did not and would not consent to a necessary part of that procedure—removal of her ovary. Her alleged non-consent to the removal of her ovary was qualified by her purpose, which was to attempt to harvest eggs at some point in the future. When the physicians observed the scar tissue, cysts, and abnormality of Sama's (P) ovary, they relied on their medical judgment to conclude it was nonfunctional. Their decision to remove it did nothing to foreclose Sama's (P) ability to have a child; her pre-existing condition prevented her from having a biological child. Moreover, the doctors thought that leaving the ovary in place would be life-threatening. Sama (P) did not say that she would rather die than have an ovary removed. In light of these circumstances, we cannot say that the law is clearly established such that a reasonable official in the doctors' position would understand that their conduct violated Sama's (P) due process rights. Sama (P) had the duty to negate qualified immunity, and she failed to do so. The law on Fourteenth Amendment claims involving unwanted medical treatment in the prison context is far from certain. Given the dearth of case law and the existence of at least some cases indicating the doctors' conduct was not contrary to clearly established law, Sama (P) failed to rebut the defendants' entitlement to qualified immunity. Affirmed.

Analysis:

The discretionary function exception to the Federal Tort Claims Act precludes government liability for claims based on the exercise or performance of, or the failure to exercise or perform, a discretionary function or duty on the part of an employee of the government, whether or not the discretion involved may be abused. The discretionary function exception does not apply, however, if a statute, regulation, or policy prescribes a specific course of conduct, since in such a case there is no rightful option but to adhere to the directive. In other words, if the employee violates the mandatory statute, regulation, or policy, there is no shelter from liability because there is no room for a choice. Government conduct cannot be discretionary, for purposes of the FTCA immunity, if it violates the constitution, a statute, or an applicable regulation.

■ CASE VOCABULARY

DISCRETIONARY FUNCTION: An act involving the exercise of personal judgment and conscience.

DUE PROCESS: The fair and orderly administration of justice.

QUALIFIED IMMUNITY: The immunity from civil liability of a public official who is performing a discretionary function, as long as his or her conduct does not violate clearly established constitutional or statutory rights.

Navarro v. Block

(Family of Murdered Woman) v. (Sheriff)

72 F.3d 712 (9th Cir.1995)

A MUNICIPALITY MAY BE LIABLE FOR CIVIL RIGHTS VIOLATIONS IF THERE EXISTS A DISCRIMINATORY CLASSIFICATION THAT AFFECTS PERSONS IN A MANNER NOT RATIONALLY RELATED TO LEGITIMATE GOVERNMENTAL OBJECTIVES

■ **INSTANT FACTS** Domestic violence victim called 911 to report that estranged husband was in route to her home to kill her, but operator did not dispatch police, and victim was killed.

■ **BLACK LETTER RULE** A municipality may be liable for civil rights violations if there is proof of the existence of a custom or informal policy with repeated constitutional violations for which municipal officials were not discharged or reprimanded, even if the official policy-makers did not have actual knowledge of the custom and practice.

■ PROCEDURAL BASIS

Appeal from summary judgment entered in action for damages for wrongful death under 42 U.S.C. § 1983.

■ FACTS

Maria Navarro received a telephone call one night from the brother of her estranged husband who said that her husband was on his way to her house to kill her and others. Maria called 911 for help and the 911 dispatcher told her to call back if he arrived. [They didn't want the police to sit around just waiting for the killer to arrive.] Fifteen minutes later the estranged husband arrived and shot and killed Maria and others. Maria's family, Navarro (P) filed suit against the County (D1) and the Sheriff, Block, (D2) whose department handled 911 calls. The basis for the claims was that victims of domestic violence were classified as non-emergency calls, thereby being denied equal protection under the law. The trial court granted summary judgment for the County (D1) and Block (D2).

■ ISSUE

Can a municipality be held liable for civil rights violations if there is proof of the existence of a custom or informal policy with repeated constitutional violations for which municipal officials were not discharged or reprimanded, even if the official policy-makers did not have actual knowledge of the custom and practice?

■ DECISION AND RATIONALE

(Pregerson) Yes. We hold that a municipality may be liable for a custom or policy of civil rights violations even if the official policy-makers did not have actual knowledge of the custom and practice. Under *Monell v. Dept. of Social Services* [municipalities may not be liable under 42 U.S.C. § 1983 unless constitutional violation results from an official municipal policy, custom or official decision], the Supreme Court held that a municipality may also be sued for constitutional deprivations pursuant to governmental custom, even though such custom has not received formal approval through the governmental body's official decision making channels.

Thus, if there is proof of the existence of a custom or informal policy with repeated constitutional violations for which municipal officials were not discharged or reprimanded, a municipality may be liable for its custom even if the official policy-makers did not have actual knowledge of the custom and practice. Navarros (P) claim that the County (D1) carried out a policy and practice of not treating 911 domestic violence calls as "emergency" calls. The 911 operator stated that it was the practice of the Sheriff's (D2) department not to classify domestic violence 911 calls as Code 2 or "emergency procedure" calls, although there was no written policy or procedure that precluded sending patrol cars to the scene, or gave them less priority than other calls. We hold that the district court erred in holding that there were no genuine issues of material fact as to whether the County (D1) had a policy or custom of not classifying the domestic violence calls as an emergency. The County (D1) argues that even if there was such a policy or custom, there was no evidence that discrimination against women was a motivating factor behind the alleged policy. The Navarros (P) contend that treating domestic calls differently from non-domestic 911 calls impermissibly discriminates against abused women. Even though such custom may be gender neutral on its face, a discriminatory application of a facially neutral law violates the Constitution. However, there must be proof of discriminatory intent or motive. [Isn't not taking victims of domestic violence seriously a discriminatory intent or motive? The argument is that since males could be victims too, it's not gender based.] In the present case, no such evidence has been offered. There is only a conclusionary allegation to that effect. Nevertheless, even in the absence of evidence of gender discrimination, the equal protection claim survives because the Navarros (P) could prove that the domestic violence/non-domestic violence classification fails the rationality test. The district court did not review the rationality of the County's (D1) domestic violence/non-domestic violence classification and thus the matter should be remanded for a proper determination. We affirm the holding that the Navarros (P) did not offer any evidence to support the claim that the Sheriff's (D2) department failed to train dispatchers properly to avoid an indifference to the equal protection rights of abused women. However, we reverse the granting of summary judgment on the equal protection claim because there are genuine issues of material facts as to whether the County (D1) had a custom of not classifying domestic violence 911 calls as emergencies. If on remand the Navarros (P) prove the existence of a discriminatory custom against victims of domestic violence, the district court must review the rationality of such a custom.

Analysis:

This case looks at the liability of municipalities under 42 U.S.C. § 1983. The United States Supreme Court ruled in *Monell v. Department of Social Services* that a municipality may be liable under § 1983 only if the constitutional right violation is due to some policy or custom of the municipality. Second, a facially neutral policy that discriminates must have a rational basis. In this case, the district court did not consider the issue of whether there was a rational basis for the County's (D1) objectives. The court of appeals therefore remanded the case so that the district court could determine if there were issues as to whether the County (D1) had a custom of not classifying domestic violence 911 calls as emergencies. On remand of the case, the trial judge concluded that the Sheriff's (D2) policy excluded domestic violence cases because they were usually cases of violence not yet in progress; thus, it gave them lower priority than violence-in-progress calls. A second appeal was filed and the court of appeals held that domestic violence calls could not be equated with not-in-progress calls because some may involve violence in progress.

■ **CASE VOCABULARY**

DEPOSITION: Pre-trial discovery method whereby person is questioned, under oath and in the presence of a court reporter, by attorneys for the parties to the action.

GENUINE ISSUES OF MATERIAL FACT: Also referred to as a triable issue of fact or question of fact, which will defeat a motion for summary judgment, so that the matter may proceed to trial.

SUMMARY JUDGMENT: Judgment entered after granting a legal motion for summary judgment in which party requests that the judge enter judgment, before trial, on the grounds that the action has no merit or there is no defense to the action.

CHAPTER SIXTEEN

Nonfeasance

Estate of Cilley v. Lane

Instant Facts: Lane (D) broke up with Cilley, and when he went to visit her after the break-up she asked him to leave; he shot himself in the stomach, purportedly by accident, and Lane (D) failed to immediately call an ambulance; Cilley eventually arrived at the hospital about five to ten minutes too late to be resuscitated, and his estate sued Lane (D).

Black Letter Rule: Maine law does not impose a general obligation to protect others from harm not created by the actor.

Wakulich v. Mraz

Instant Facts: Elizabeth Wakulich died after Michael and Brian Mraz (D) bet her she couldn't drink a full bottle of alcohol without losing consciousness or vomiting.

Black Letter Rule: One who voluntarily undertakes to render services to another is liable for bodily harm caused by his failure to perform such services with due care or with such competence and skill as he possesses.

Farwell v. Keaton

Instant Facts: Friend of beating victim failed to seek immediate medical attention for, or inform anyone of, the victim-friend's whereabouts.

Black Letter Rule: Social companions have a duty to aid one another in situations of peril.

Podias v. Mairs

Instant Facts: Three young men were in a car that hit a motorcycle. They left the motorcycle driver on the roadway, and the victim was run over by another vehicle and died; at no time did the three men summon assistance. The victim's estate sued all three. The trial court granted summary judgment to the two passengers in the first car, finding they had no duty to the deceased.

Black Letter Rule: Although the common law has persistently refused to impose on a stranger the moral obligation to go to the aid of another human being who is in danger, an exception exists for a failure to render assistance when there is some definite relation between the parties of such a character that social policy justifies the imposition of a duty to act.

DeShaney v. Winnebago County Dept. of Social Services

Instant Facts: Child was severely beaten by his father while in his custody, and social workers monitoring the family following cessation of temporary custody knew of prior abuse but did nothing.

Black Letter Rule: A public entity must have custody of another in order to hold it liable for depriving the person of federal due process rights by failing to prevent harm caused by a third person.

Estate of Cilley v. Lane

(Estate of Decedent/Former Boyfriend) v. (Former Girlfriend)

985 A.2d 481 (Me. 2009)

THE COURT REFUSED TO CREATE A NEW "SPECIAL RELATIONSHIP" BASED ON WITNESSING AN INJURY

■ **INSTANT FACTS** Lane (D) broke up with Cilley, and when he went to visit her after the break-up she asked him to leave; he shot himself in the stomach, purportedly by accident, and Lane (D) failed to immediately call an ambulance; Cilley eventually arrived at the hospital about five to ten minutes too late to be resuscitated, and his estate sued Lane (D).

■ **BLACK LETTER RULE** Maine law does not impose a general obligation to protect others from harm not created by the actor.

■ PROCEDURAL BASIS

State appellate court review of the trial court decision granting the plaintiff's motion to dismiss.

■ FACTS

Cilley and Lane (D) were in an on-again-off-again relationship. After one break-up, Lane (D) told Cilley that they could still be friends. Thereafter Cilley went to Lane's (D) house trailer to visit her, but Lane (D) immediately asked him to leave. Cilley then either left and got a rifle, or picked up a rifle that was already in Lane's (D) trailer. Lane (D) left the trailer and heard a loud pop. She looked back and saw Cilley fall to the floor, saying, "It was an accident" and "was not supposed to happen." Lane did not see any blood but did not investigate or attempt to determine whether Cilley was hurt; instead, she went to a friend's trailer and told two people there that Cilley had pretended to shoot himself inside her trailer. The friends looked out the window and saw Cilley lying on the steps to Lane's (D) trailer, halfway out the door. They went to Cilley, who mumbled that "it was an accident." One friend noted that Cilley was turning white and was having difficulty breathing. The other friend called 911. Cilley could not be resuscitated at the hospital, although the doctor who treated him said he could have been resuscitated had he arrived at the hospital just five to ten minutes sooner. Cilley died from a single gunshot wound to his abdomen. Cilley's estate (P) sued Lane (D), alleging negligent failure to assist. Lane (D) moved to dismiss the claim and the court granted her motion. The estate (P) appealed.

■ ISSUE

Did the plaintiff state a valid claim for negligent failure to assist?

■ DECISION AND RATIONALE

(Gorman, J.) No. Maine law does not impose a general obligation to protect others from harm not created by the actor. Nonetheless, the estate (P) makes two arguments as to why Lane (D) did have a duty to act and contact emergency assistance in this case. First, the estate (P) argues that a duty existed because Lane (D) was a social host and Cilley was her guest. But a licensee who is asked to leave and refuses to do so becomes a trespasser. Therefore, Lane's (D) only duty to Cilley was to refrain from wanton, willful, or reckless behavior. Her failure to summon emergency assistance immediately after she heard the popping sound does not rise to this level. Second, the estate (P) urges the court to recognize a new common law duty to seek affirmative emergency assistance through reasonable means. We have held that a party does not have an affirmative duty to aid or warn another person in peril unless the party created the danger, or the two people had a special relationship that society recognizes as sufficient to create the duty. Such relationships include common carrier/passenger, employer/employee, parent/child, and innkeeper/guest. The estate (P) asks us to add a new relationship based on witnessing an injury. We decline to do so. Maine has a firm "no duty to rescue" rule. The estate (P) asked the legislature to enact a law imposing sanctions for failure to render reasonable assistance to a person in danger, or to immediately report a crime, as other states have done. But the legislature chose not to, and we must also decline. We are reluctant to create a duty that would impose liability for the failure to act. We choose instead to adhere to established precedent and conclude that absent a special relationship or conduct that has endangered another, a person owes no duty to call aid for an injured person. Affirmed.

Analysis:

As the opinion notes, in response to a few notorious instances of bystander inaction (e.g., the Kitty Genovese murder), some state legislatures enacted laws imposing criminal or civil liability for the failure to render reasonable assistance to a person in danger, or to immediately report a crime that has been committed. The Maine court in this case refused to do so. The court acknowledged that there are very limited types of relationships on which the law will impose a duty to render aid, and this case did not fall within any of those recognized classes. The court followed the state legislature's lead in declining to change the "no duty to rescue" rule.

Wakulich v. Mraz

(Decedent's Family) v. (Young Men)

322 Ill.App.3d 768, 751 N.E.2d 1, 255 Ill.Dec. 907 (2001)

ONCE A DUTY IS VOLUNTARILY ASSUMED, IT MUST BE CARRIED OUT IN A REASONABLE MANNER

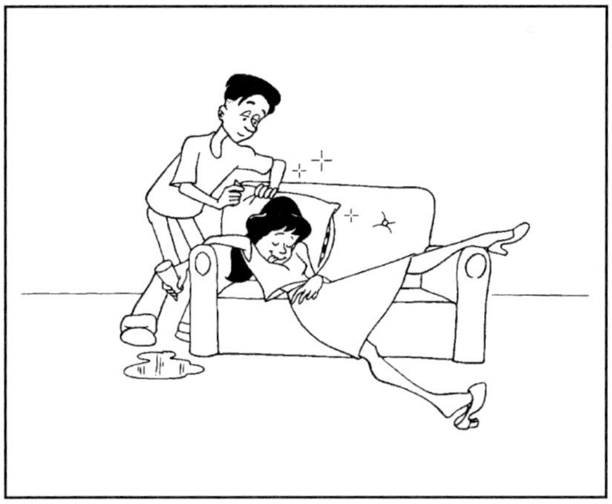

■ **INSTANT FACTS** Elizabeth Wakulich died after Michael and Brian Mraz (D) bet her she couldn't drink a full bottle of alcohol without losing consciousness or vomiting.

■ **BLACK LETTER RULE** One who voluntarily undertakes to render services to another is liable for bodily harm caused by his failure to perform such services with due care or with such competence and skill as he possesses.

■ PROCEDURAL BASIS

On appeal to review a decision dismissing the plaintiff's complaint for failure to state a claim for relief.

■ FACTS

Sixteen-year-old Elizabeth Wakulich died when Michael and Brian Mraz (D), twenty-one and eighteen years old, respectively, bet her that she could not drink a bottle of Goldschlager without losing consciousness or vomiting. After finishing the bottle, Wakulich began vomiting and lost consciousness. The defendants placed Elizabeth on a couch, provided her with a pillow, and removed her vomit-soaked clothing, but did not seek medical attention and prevented others in the house from calling 911. Wakulich's family (D) sued Michael and Brian Mraz (D) and their father, who was in the house at the time of death. Their complaint was dismissed for failure to state a claim because Illinois law does not recognize social host liability for the provision of alcohol to another. Wakulich (P) appealed.

■ ISSUE

Did the plaintiff sufficiently allege a cause of action for failure to exercise due care for Elizabeth's safety?

■ DECISION AND RATIONALE

(McBride, J.) Yes. "One who voluntarily undertakes to render services to another is liable for bodily harm caused by his failure to perform such services with due care or with such competence and skill as he possesses." Here, when Michael and Brian (D) observed Elizabeth, provided her with a pillow, and removed clothing, they voluntarily assumed a duty to care for her. From the allegations in the complaint, a reasonable jury could determine that the actions taken by the defendants, including their preventing others from calling for medical help, constituted negligence. The plaintiff's complaint states a claim upon with relief may be granted. Reversed and remanded.

Analysis:

The excerpt focuses on the defendants' conduct after Elizabeth had consumed the alcohol and fallen unconscious. In some states, one who provides alcohol to a minor may be criminally liable under the state's dram shop act. Here, Michael Mraz (D), an adult, was convicted of a misdemeanor for contributing to the delinquency of a minor. The dram shop act preempted any civil cause of action for social-host liability against the defendants.

■ CASE VOCABULARY

DRAM-SHOP ACT: A statute allowing a plaintiff to recover damages from a commercial seller of alcoholic beverages for personal injury caused by an intoxicated customer.

Farwell v. Keaton

(Heirs of Deceased Teenager) v. (Not Stated)

396 Mich. 281, 240 N.W.2d 217 (1976)

SPECIAL RELATIONSHIPS CREATE DUTY TO AID IN TIMES OF PERIL

■ **INSTANT FACTS** Friend of beating victim failed to seek immediate medical attention for, or inform anyone of, the victim-friend's whereabouts.

■ **BLACK LETTER RULE** Social companions have a duty to aid one another in situations of peril.

■ PROCEDURAL BASIS

Appeal to state Supreme Court after reversal of judgment following jury trial for wrongful death action.

■ FACTS

Farwell's heirs (P) sued for his death resulting from the failure of his friend, Siegrist, to obtain medical assistance for, or to inform of the whereabouts of, Farwell. Farwell and Siegrist, teenaged boys, were friends. While having a few beers, they attempted without success to engage in conversation with some teenaged girls that had walked by. The girls [obviously not interested in the two] complained to friends that they were being followed. Six boys chased Farwell and Siegrist, and Farwell was severely beaten. Siegrist, who escaped injury, put Farwell in the car with ice on his head, and drove around for two hours. Farwell "went to sleep" in the back of the car and later that night Siegrist drove him to his grandparents' home, where he left him in the car after a failed attempt to arouse him. Farwell died three days later from the beating. There was evidence that prompt medical attention could have prevented his death. The jury found for Farwell's heirs (P). The court of appeals reversed on the ground that Siegrist had not assumed any duty to aid his friend Farwell. The matter was appealed to the Michigan Supreme Court.

■ ISSUE

Do social companions have a duty to aid one another in situations of peril?

■ DECISION AND RATIONALE

(Levin) Yes. Social companions have a duty to aid one another in situations of peril. There is a clearly recognized duty of every person to avoid any affirmative acts that may make a situation worse. If one attempts to aid another and fails to use reasonable care in connection therewith, the person will be held liable. The reason is that the person has voluntarily entered into a relationship by taking charge and control of the situation and such relationship is attended with responsibility. In this case, Farwell and Siegrist were companions on a social venture. Implicit in such a common undertaking is the understanding that one will render assistance to the other when he is in peril, if he can do so without endangering himself. Siegrist knew or should have known when he left Farwell badly beaten and unconscious in the back of the car that no one would find him until morning. [Maybe in thought his friend had just had a few too many beers.] Accordingly, because the two companions were engaged in a common undertaking, a special relationship existed between them. Reversed.

Analysis:

Although there is no general duty to render aid to a person in peril, if a special relationship exists a duty may be created. The Supreme Court of Michigan held in this case that being social companions engaged in a common undertaking is sufficient to create such a special relationship. Also, consider whether the conduct of Siegrist put Farwell in a worse condition than he had been in. For example, if Siegrist had left Farwell at the location of the beating, rather than placing him in the car and leaving him unattended overnight, would Farwell have been discovered sooner? Perhaps it is also arguable that Siegrist began to care for Farwell by placing him in his car and transporting him, but failed to act reasonably in that effort. The Restatement of Torts imposes liability on one who discontinues aid only if the defendant has left the victim in a "worse position." The Restatement expressly sets forth five types of relationships that require the use of reasonable care for one's safety, including reasonable affirmative efforts to rescue. They are: (1) carrier-passenger, (2) innkeeper-guest, (3) landowner-invitee, (4) custodian-ward, and (5) employer-employee. Although the two teenage boys in this case did not have a preexisting recognized status with respect to each other, they did have a special relationship for that evening. As the court noted, to claim that Siegrist had no duty to Farwell under the circumstances would be " 'shocking to humanitarian considerations' and fly in the face of the commonly accepted code of social conduct.' "

Podias v. Mairs

(Estate of Deceased Motorcyclist) v. (Drunk Driver)

394 N.J.Super. 338, 926 A.2d 859 (2007)

THOSE UNINJURED IN AN ACCIDENT MAY HAVE A DUTY TO SUMMON HELP FOR THE INJURED

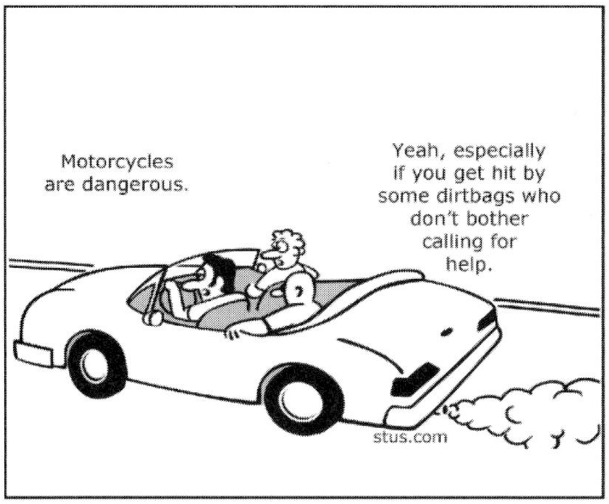

■ **INSTANT FACTS** Three young men were in a car that hit a motorcycle. They left the motorcycle driver on the roadway, and the victim was run over by another vehicle and died; at no time did the three men summon assistance. The victim's estate sued all three. The trial court granted summary judgment to the two passengers in the first car, finding they had no duty to the deceased.

■ **BLACK LETTER RULE** Although the common law has persistently refused to impose on a stranger the moral obligation to go to the aid of another human being who is in danger, an exception exists for a failure to render assistance when there is some definite relation between the parties of such a character that social policy justifies the imposition of a duty to act.

■ PROCEDURAL BASIS

State appellate court review of a trial court decision granting summary judgment to the two passenger-defendants.

■ FACTS

Eighteen-year-old Mairs (D) was drinking beer at the home of a friend. He eventually left with two other friends, and they headed back to the university where they were all students. Mairs (D) was driving. Mairs (D) lost control of the car and hit a motorcycle driven by Podias. One of Mairs's (D) passengers observed Podias on the roadway and told the others he thought Podias (D) was dead. Despite the fact that all three young men had cell phones, no one called for assistance. (They did, however, make dozens of other cell phone calls within a short time of the accident.) A few minutes after the accident, the three left the scene together in Mairs's (D) vehicle, and the two passengers talked about how there was no need to get them in trouble, and that they preferred to be left out of the situation. Meanwhile, another vehicle drove over Podias, who died as a result of those injuries. Podias's (P) estate sued Mairs (D) and the two friends who were passengers, and the trial court granted summary judgment in favor of the friends. The estate (P) appealed.

■ ISSUE

Did the trial court properly dismiss the two passenger-defendants from the lawsuit?

■ DECISION AND RATIONALE

(Parrillo, J.) No. Although the common law has persistently refused to impose on a stranger the moral obligation to go to the aid of another human being who is in danger, an exception exists for a failure to render assistance when there is some definite relation between the parties of such a character that social policy justifies the imposition of a duty to act. This "relational" focus mirrors evolving notions of duty, which are no longer tethered to rigid formalisms or static historical classifications. The assessment of duty thus necessarily requires an examination of the relationships between and among the parties. The fundamental question is whether the plaintiff's interests are entitled to legal protection against the defendant's conduct. The determination of the existence of a duty is ultimately a question of fairness and public policy, which in turn draws on notions of fairness, common sense, and morality.

There are enough facts in the summary judgment record in this case from which a reasonable jury could find that the passenger-defendants breached a duty that proximately caused the decedent's death. Not only did the passengers know of the danger of leaving the injured body in the roadway, the risk of harm from their failure to summon help was also readily foreseeable. They also knew of the risk of harm posed by Mairs's (D) driving while drunk. Juxtapose this foreseeability of harm with the ease with which it could have been prevented. All three young men had cell phones, which they used for their own purposes rather than to call for aid. The passenger-defendants appeared lucid enough to comprehend the severity of the risk of their inaction. They had both the opportunity and the ability to help prevent an obviously foreseeable risk of severe and potentially fatal consequence, yet they failed to act. Under these circumstances, imposition of a duty does not offend notions of fairness and common decency, and is in accord with public policy. Although Mairs (D) clearly created the initial risk, the friends at a minimum acquiesced in the conditions that may have helped create that risk, and subsequently in the conditions that further endangered the victim. They therefore bear some relationship not only to the primary wrongdoer, but also to the incident itself, and it is this nexus that distinguishes this case from those in which a mere presence on the scene of an accident requires no action. It is the degree of the passengers' involvement in the situation, coupled with the serious peril and threat of imminent death to another that might have been avoided with a little effort and inconvenience, that creates a sufficient relationship to impose a duty of action. Reversed and remanded.

Analysis:

The court not only found a potential basis for liability on the part of the passenger-defendants based on their failure to render aid, it also found that they potentially breached a duty by preventing Mairs (D), the primary defendant, from causing the harm. Restatement (Second) of Torts § 876 provides that one may be subject to liability for harm resulting to a third person from the tortious conduct of another if he (a) performs a tortious act in concert with the other or pursuant to a common design with him; (b) knows that the other's conduct constitutes a breach of duty and gives substantial assistance or encouragement to the other so to conduct himself; or (c) gives substantial assistance to the other in accomplishing a tortious result and his own conduct, separately considered, constitutes a breach of duty to the third person. The court found that the aiding-and-abetting aspect of § 876(b) was a potential source of liability in the present case.

DeShaney v. Winnebago County Dept. of Social Services

(Abused Child) v. (Social Services)

489 U.S. 189, 109 S.Ct. 998, 103 L.Ed.2d 249 (1989)

STATE'S CUSTODY OF ANOTHER WILL CREATE A SPECIAL RELATIONSHIP THAT IMPOSES AN AFFIRMATIVE DUTY TO PREVENT HARM TO THE PERSON

■ **INSTANT FACTS** Child was severely beaten by his father while in his custody, and social workers monitoring the family following cessation of temporary custody knew of prior abuse but did nothing.

■ **BLACK LETTER RULE** A public entity must have custody of another in order to hold it liable for depriving the person of federal due process rights by failing to prevent harm caused by a third person.

■ PROCEDURAL BASIS

Appeal to United States Supreme Court following the affirming of summary judgment in action for violation of *42 U.S.C. § 1983.*

■ FACTS

A brain-damaged child and his mother, DeShaney (P), sued Winnebago County Dept. of Social Services (Social Services) (D) claiming that their failure to act deprived the DeShaney (P) boy of his liberty in violation of the Due Process Clause of the Fourteenth Amendment to the U.S. Constitution. Social Services (D) received complaints that the DeShaney (P) boy was being abused by his father, with whom he lived, following his parents' divorce. Social Services (D) took temporary custody of the boy, but returned him to his father after an agreement was reached with the father in which he promised to cooperate in accomplishing certain measures designed to protect the boy. Social Services (D) continued to monitor the boy at his father's home. Evidence of further abuse and noncompliance with the agreement was noted, but Social Services (D) did not act to remove the boy from the father's custody. Thereafter, the boy was so severely beaten by his father that he suffered severe and permanent brain damage rendering him profoundly retarded. The boy and his mother, DeShaney (P), filed suit under *42 U.S.C. § 1983* [depriving one of a right or privilege protected by the federal Constitution or federal law while acting under color of law] contending that Social Services (D) denied the boy due process. The trial court [having the awful job of correctly interpreting the law against DeShaney (P)] granted summary judgment for Social Services (D), the court of appeal affirmed, and an appeal was taken to the United States Supreme Court.

■ ISSUE

Must a public entity have custody of another in order to hold it liable for depriving the person of federal due process rights by failing to prevent harm caused by a third person?

■ DECISION AND RATIONALE

(Rehnquist) Yes. We hold that a public entity must have custody of another in order to hold it liable for depriving the person of federal due process rights by failing to prevent harm caused by a third person. The Due Process Clause of the Fourteenth Amendment provides that "[n]o State shall deprive any person of life, liberty, or property, without due process of law." DeShaney (P) contends that Social Services (D) is liable for failing to provide the boy with adequate protection against his father's violence. However, the Due Process Clause does not impose affirmative duties on the State to protect the life, liberty, and property of its citizens against invasion by private actors. Although the Clause forbids the State itself from depriving individuals of life, liberty, and property without due process of law, its language cannot be extended to impose any affirmative duty to ensure that those interests are not harmed through other means. Thus, a State's failure to protect an individual against private violence does not constitute a violation of the Due Process Clause. The DeShaneys (P) also contend that a "special relationship" existed between the boy and the State because it knew that the boy faced special danger of abuse by his father and it proclaimed its intention to protect him against that danger. We reject this contention. In limited circumstances, the State has an affirmative duty to care and protect particular individuals. See, *Estelle v. Gamble* [State is required to provide adequate medical care to incarcerated prisoners] and *Youngberg v. Romeo* [State is required to provide involuntarily committed mental patients with such services as are necessary to ensure reasonable safety from themselves and others]. However, such affirmative duty arises when the State takes a person into its custody and holds him there against his will. In these circumstances, the Constitution imposes upon the State a duty to assume some responsibility for the person's safety and general well being. These cases have no application to the case at bar. Although the State took temporary custody of the boy, when it returned him to his father's custody it placed him in no worse position than that in which he would have been had it not acted at all. [But shortly thereafter, the boy was in a much worse condition.] We note that it may well be that in voluntarily undertaking to protect the boy, the State acquired a duty under *state tort law* to provide him with adequate protection against that danger. However, the claim before us is one based on the Due Process Clause of the Fourteenth Amendment. The conduct involved does not constitute a violation of the Due Process Clause. Affirmed.

■ DISSENT

(Brennan) I would recognize that the State's knowledge of an individual's predicament and its expressions of intent to help can amount to a limitation of his freedom to act on his own or to obtain help from others. I would read the holdings of *Youngberg* and *Estelle* to stand for the proposition that if a State cuts off private sources of aid and then refuses aid itself, it should be held responsible. Members of the public, other than those working for Social Services (D), would feel that their job was done as soon as they reported the suspicions of child abuse. If Social Services (D) then ignores or dismisses these suspicions, it has thus effectively confined the boy within the walls of the father's violent home. Conceivably, children in this situation are made worse off when the social service entities fail to do their jobs. I disagree with the Majority for its failure to see that inaction can be every bit as abusive of power as action, that oppression can result when a State undertakes a vital duty and then ignores it.

■ DISSENT

(Blackmun) The facts in this case involve not mere passivity, but active state intervention in the life of the boy. This intervention triggered a fundamental duty to aid the boy once the State learned of the severe danger to which he was exposed.

Analysis:

The United States Supreme Court's decision in this famous case stands for the proposition that in order for a civil rights violation to exist that will impose liability upon the State, the State must have *custody* of the victim. In order for an exception to "the no duty to act" rule to apply, there must be a special relationship. The special relationship necessary for a constitutional claim is the public entity's *custody* of the victim. Note, however, that this case concerns violations of federal constitutional rights. Liability may exist under state tort law in non-custodial situations. For example, a medical doctor may be under a duty to report child abuse, and some state statutes create a special relationship or direct duty of reasonable care by the protective agency to an abused child. The majority concluded that Social Services (D) placed the boy in no worse position than that in which he would have been had it not acted at all. However, Justice Brennan's dissent stated that he believed that the inaction by Social Services (D) amounted to taking away further possible aid by the public, and then ignoring it. This, he said, makes children in this situation worse off. Justice Blackmun concluded that there was active state intervention in the life of the boy. Thus, the Court was divided as to whether nonfeasance or misfeasance occurred.

CHAPTER SEVENTEEN

Contract and Duty

Affiliated FM Ins. Co. v. LTK Consulting Services, Inc.

Instant Facts: SMS contracted with the city of Seattle to operate certain aspects of the Seattle Monorail system and was responsible for insuring the trains; two trains were damaged in a fire and the insurance company, after paying for the loss, sought to recover from the engineering firm that had performed electrical work on the monorail system.

Black Letter Rule: The economic loss rule, a doctrine that has attempted to describe the dividing line between the law of torts and the law of contracts, should not be treated as a bright line rule of general application that holds that any time there is an economic loss, there can be no recovery in tort.

Spengler v. ADT Security Services, Inc.

Instant Facts: Spengler (P) contracted with ADT (D) to provide security services to his mother, but when she pressed a distress button ADT (D) gave the wrong address to emergency personnel, and Spengler's (P) mother died.

Black Letter Rule: Under Michigan law, in order for an action in tort to arise out of a breach of contract, the act complained of must constitute (1) a breach of duty separate and distinct from the breach of contract, and (2) active negligence or misfeasance.

Diaz v. Phoenix Lubrication Service, Inc.

Instant Facts: A few weeks after Diaz (P) took the family car to Jiffy Lube (D) for an oil change, he lost control of the vehicle on the roadway and was seriously injured; the plaintiffs alleged that worn tires caused the accident, and that Jiffy Lube (D) should have noticed the wear when it serviced the vehicle, but the court disagreed and granted Jiffy Lube's (D) motion for summary judgment.

Black Letter Rule: The existence of a duty may be based on public policy considerations or on the relationship between the parties, including relationships based on contract, family relations, or conduct undertaken by the defendant.

H.R. Moch Co. v. Rensselaer Water Co.

Instant Facts: The Water Co. (D) contracted with the city to provide water for city fire hydrants. A building caught fire and Rensselaer (D) failed to provide enough water to the fire-hydrant which resulted in the fire spreading to a warehouse owned by Moch (P).

Black Letter Rule: A party cannot maintain an action in torts based on a contract to which they are neither a party nor an intended third party beneficiary.

Florence v. Goldberg

Instant Facts: A six-year-old child was severely injured after being struck by a car at an unguarded street crossing while walking to school alone.

Black Letter Rule: A police department, having assumed a duty to a special class of persons, and having gone forward with performance of that duty in the past, has an obligation to continue its performance.

Affiliated FM Ins. Co. v. LTK Consulting Services, Inc.

(Insurance Company) v. (Engineering Firm)

243 P.3d 521 (Wash. 2010)

IF THE INSURED COULD BRING A TORT CLAIM, THE INSURER, STANDING IN THE INSURED'S SHOES, MAY BRING THAT CLAIM

■ **INSTANT FACTS** SMS contracted with the city of Seattle to operate certain aspects of the Seattle Monorail system and was responsible for insuring the trains; two trains were damaged in a fire and the insurance company, after paying for the loss, sought to recover from the engineering firm that had performed electrical work on the monorail system.

■ **BLACK LETTER RULE** The economic loss rule, a doctrine that has attempted to describe the dividing line between the law of torts and the law of contracts, should not be treated as a bright line rule of general application that holds that any time there is an economic loss, there can be no recovery in tort.

■ PROCEDURAL BASIS

Certified question to the state supreme court from the Ninth Circuit, after the federal district court granted the defendant's motion to dismiss.

■ FACTS

In May 2004, the Seattle Monorail blue train caught on fire due to an electrical problem. All four blue train cars were burned or were engulfed in smoke. The red train stopped to render assistance and help passengers escape. As a result, the red train was also damaged by smoke. Ten years before the fire, the city of Seattle had entered into an agreement with SMS, which granted rights to SMS related to the operation of the monorail. The agreement also allocated responsibility between SMS and the city for maintaining the monorail. Pursuant to the agreement, SMS was required to carry insurance to cover certain risks, including fire.

In 1999, the city had contracted with LTK (D), an engineering firm, to examine the monorail system and recommend repairs. LTK (D) completed its work in 2002. After the fire, SMS's insurer, AFM (P), paid over $3.2 million to SMS to cover its losses. AFM (P) then brought suit against LTK (D), claiming that LTK (D) was negligent in changing the electrical ground system for the blue and red trains. LTK (D) moved for summary, arguing that SMS's losses were purely economic, and that it could not be liable in tort for purely economic losses. According to LTK (D), SMS did not have a property interest in the Seattle Monorail, so its damages could only be economic. The federal district court granted the defendant's motion for summary judgment, and AFM (P) appealed to the Ninth Circuit, which certified the following question.

■ ISSUE

Could SMS, which did not own the monorail, bring a tort action against the engineering firm that worked on monorail maintenance before the fire for negligently causing the fire?

■ DECISION AND RATIONALE

(Fairhurst, J.) Yes. The economic loss rule, a doctrine that has attempted to describe the dividing line between the law of torts and the law of contracts, should not be treated as a bright line rule of general application that holds that any time there is an economic loss, there can be no recovery in tort. We need to ask in this case whether an engineering firm that undertakes to perform engineering services assumes a tort law duty of reasonable care independent of its contractual obligations. We believe that it does; that is, engineers who undertake engineering services are under a duty of reasonable care independent of their contractual obligations. That duty of care is necessarily limited to the level of care that is reasonable in the particular circumstances. An engineer must exercise that degree of care, skill, and learning expected of a reasonably prudent engineer in the state of Washington acting in the same or similar circumstances. The next question in this case is whether an engineer's duty of care extends to safety risks of physical damage to the property on which the engineer works. We hold that it does. Moreover, the scope of an engineer's duty of care extends to all persons who hold legally protected interests in the property, including, in this case, SMS. SMS has property interests in using the Seattle Monorail, and thus SMS was within the scope of LTK's (D) duty of care. Standing in SMS's shoes, AFM (P), its insurer, may claim damages necessary to return SMS to the position it would have been in had the negligence not occurred. We conclude that SMS may sue LTK (D) for negligence, because LTK (D), by undertaking engineering services, assumed a duty of reasonable care, which extended to risks of physical damage to the monorail. SMS enjoyed a legally protected interest in the monorail, and LTK's (D) duty encompassed this interest. By subrogation to SMS's rights, AFM (P) may pursue a claim for negligence against LTK (D).

Analysis:

One way courts have attempted to draw a line between tort and contract claims is to bar tort recovery for purely "economic losses"—as opposed to losses based on physical injury or property damage. In some states this common law rule is called the "economic loss doctrine." Many states recognize an exception to the rule when the defendant commits fraud or negligent misrepresentation, or when a special relationship exists between the parties.

■ CASE VOCABULARY

CERTIFIED QUESTION: A point of law on which a federal court of appeals seeks guidance from either the United States Supreme Court or the highest state court by the procedure of certification.

SUBROGATION: The placement of one person in the place of another so that he or she succeeds to the original person's rights and obligations with respect to a third person.

Spengler v. ADT Security Services, Inc.

(Deceased's Son) v. (Security Service Provider)

505 F.3d 456 (6th Cir. 2007)

WHEN THE BREACHED DUTY ARISES OUT OF CONTRACT, THE REMEDY LIES IN A BREACH OF CONTRACT CLAIM

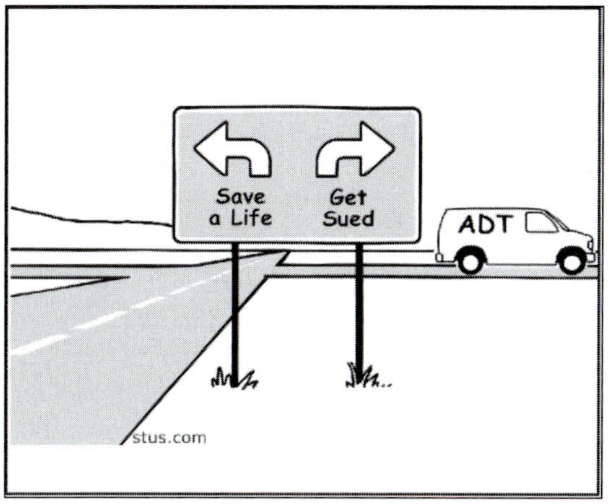

■ **INSTANT FACTS** Spengler (P) contracted with ADT (D) to provide security services to his mother, but when she pressed a distress button ADT (D) gave the wrong address to emergency personnel, and Spengler's (P) mother died.

■ **BLACK LETTER RULE** Under Michigan law, in order for an action in tort to arise out of a breach of contract, the act complained of must constitute (1) a breach of duty separate and distinct from the breach of contract, and (2) active negligence or misfeasance.

■ PROCEDURAL BASIS

Federal appellate court consideration of the district court's dismissal of the plaintiff's tort claim.

■ FACTS

Spengler (P) contracted with ADT (D) to install and monitor a security alarm at his mother's home. The agreement included a call button that his mother could activate when in distress. Spengler's (P) mother could not speak due to cancer of the larynx. ADT (D) received an alarm call from Spengler's (P) mother, but due to an error in the address that ADT (D) gave to the dispatchers, emergency medical services were delayed by about sixteen minutes, and by the time the EMTs arrived, Spengler's (P) mother was asystolic. She never regained consciousness and died in the hospital. Spengler (P) sued ADT (D), alleging that by providing an erroneous address to the dispatcher, ADT (D) committed misfeasance, subjecting it to tort liability. The district court granted partial summary judgment to ADT (D), finding that the defendant breached no duty independent of the parties' agreement. The court also granted partial summary judgment to Spengler (P), finding that ADT (D) breached its contract, but the court limited damages to the amount stated in the parties' agreement—a mere $500. Spengler (P) appealed, arguing that the case sounded in tort and that the contractual limitation of liability clause was unconscionable and unenforceable.

■ ISSUE

Did the court properly dismiss the plaintiff's tort claim on the ground that the case sounded in contract and not in tort?

■ DECISION AND RATIONALE

(Martin, J.) Yes. Under Michigan law, in order for an action in tort to arise out of a breach of contract, the act complained of must constitute (1) a breach of duty separate and distinct from the breach of contract, and (2) active negligence or misfeasance. The duty prong is the threshold inquiry. Where the only violation involved is that of a broken promise to perform a contract, and there exists no independent duty outside the contract, liability, if any, must rest solely on a breach of the contract. ADT's obligation to promptly and correctly dispatch emergency services arose only from the contract, not the common law, and thus no tort liability is available. Having found no independent duty, we need not consider whether ADT's actions constituted misfeasance or negligence. And because the unconscionability of the limitations of damages clause is raised for the first time before this court, we refuse to consider it. Affirmed.

Analysis:

Note that the plaintiff may have had a viable argument that a contract term limiting ADT's (D) damages to $500 was unconscionable, but he failed to raise that argument in the trial court. Generally speaking, new issues cannot be raised for the first time in the appellate court. Had the court found the clause to be unconscionable, it could have refused to enforce it and awarded the plaintiff his actual damages caused by the breach, which, it could be argued, were substantially more than $500.

■ CASE VOCABULARY

UNCONSCIONABILITY: 1. Extreme unfairness. Unconscionability is normally assessed by an objective standard: (1) one party's lack of meaningful choice, and (2) contractual terms that unreasonably favor the other party. 2. The principle that a court may refuse to enforce a contract that is unfair or oppressive because of procedural abuses during contract formation or because of overreaching contractual terms, especially terms that are unreasonably favorable to one party while precluding meaningful choice for the other party. Because unconscionability depends on circumstances at the time the contract is formed, a later rise in market price is irrelevant.

UNCONSCIONABLE: Showing no regard for conscience; affronting the sense of justice, decency, or reasonableness.

UNCONSCIONABLE AGREEMENT: An agreement that no promisor with any sense, and not under a delusion, would make, and that no honest and fair promisee would accept.

Diaz v. Phoenix Lubrication Service, Inc.

(Volvo Owner) v. (Jiffy Lube)

230 P.3d 718 (Ariz. Ct. App. 2010)

A DUTY WILL NOT BE IMPOSED BASED ON A CONTRACTUAL RELATIONSHIP WHEN THE CONTRACT DOES NOT SUGGEST SUCH A DUTY

■ **INSTANT FACTS** A few weeks after Diaz (P) took the family car to Jiffy Lube (D) for an oil change, he lost control of the vehicle on the roadway and was seriously injured; the plaintiffs alleged that worn tires caused the accident, and that Jiffy Lube (D) should have noticed the wear when it serviced the vehicle, but the court disagreed and granted Jiffy Lube's (D) motion for summary judgment.

■ **BLACK LETTER RULE** The existence of a duty may be based on public policy considerations or on the relationship between the parties, including relationships based on contract, family relations, or conduct undertaken by the defendant.

■ PROCEDURAL BASIS

State appellate court review of the trial court decision granting the defendant's motion for summary judgment.

■ FACTS

Diaz (P) took the Volvo owned by his parents to Jiffy Lube (D) for an oil change. Although Jiffy Lube (D) offers a separate tire rotation service and inspection for an additional fee, Diaz (P) did not request the additional work. A few weeks later, Diaz (P) lost control of the Volvo on a wet roadway; the car left the road and rolled over. He suffered serious injuries, including paralysis. The Diaz family (P) filed suit against many possible defendants, all of whom except for Jiffy Lube (D) were eventually dismissed from the case. Jiffy Lube (D) moved for summary judgment, arguing that it had no duty to inspect the inside tread on the Volvo's tires. The court granted the motion and the Diazes (P) appealed.

■ ISSUE

Did Jiffy Lube (D) owe a legal duty to the plaintiffs in regard to the allegedly worn tires?

■ DECISION AND RATIONALE

(Gemmill, J.) No. The existence of a duty may be based on public policy considerations or on the relationship between the parties, including relationships based on contract, family relations, or conduct undertaken by the defendant. None of those bases exists in this case. The plaintiffs argue that the contractual relationship between the parties gave rise to a duty on the party of Jiffy Lube (D) to inspect the tires. We disagree, because the oil change agreement included only a check of the air pressure in the tires, not an overall tire inspection. Nor did public policy warrant a conclusion that Jiffy Lube (D) owed a duty of care to perform a safety inspection of the tires. We have recognized that an actor has a duty to exercise reasonable care when the actor's conduct creates a risk of physical harm, but here, Jiffy Lube's (D) actions did not create the risk resulting from the worn tires. An actor whose conduct has not created a risk of physical harm to another has no duty of care to the other unless there is some other affirmative basis for the existence of a duty. There was no duty here based on public policy or contract, given Jiffy Lube's (D) limited undertaking. Affirmed.

Analysis:

The plaintiffs also argued in this case that a duty arose because the standard in the industry called for service and maintenance businesses like Jiffy Lube (D) to inspect all visible vehicle components for hazards during the performance of their service work. But, the court explained, the *existence* of a duty is the threshold legal question that must be determined by the court. Standard industry practices, by contrast, address primarily whether there has been a *breach* of duty. If Jiffy Lube (D) did not owe the plaintiffs a duty in the first place, the standard of care and the potential breach thereof were irrelevant.

■ CASE VOCABULARY

PUBLIC POLICY: A flexible term often meaning "what is good for (or will not harm) the general public"; the principle of law that no person can do that which has a tendency to harm the general public.

H.R. Moch Co. v. Rensselaer Water Co.

(Warehouse Owner/Third Party) v. (Water Company/Contractor)

247 N.Y. 160, 159 N.E. 896 (1928)

A CONTRACTUAL PROMISE DOES NOT CREATE LIABILITY TO THIRD PARTY NON-INTENDED BENEFICIARIES

■ **INSTANT FACTS** The Water Co. (D) contracted with the city to provide water for city fire hydrants. A building caught fire and Rensselaer (D) failed to provide enough water to the fire-hydrant which resulted in the fire spreading to a warehouse owned by Moch (P).

■ **BLACK LETTER RULE** A party cannot maintain an action in torts based on a contract to which they are neither a party nor an intended third party beneficiary.

■ PROCEDURAL BASIS

Appeal to the Court of Appeals of New York after the Appellate Division reversed the decision by the trial court to deny the motion to dismiss the complaint.

■ FACTS

The Rensselaer Water Company (the Water Co.) (D) contracted with the City of Rensselaer (city) to supply water for the city's needs and also to private customers at an agreed upon rate. Included in this contract was the requirement that the Water Co. (D) provide water to the city's fire hydrants at a rate of $42.50 each per year. While the contract was in force a building caught fire. The Water Co. (D) was notified of the fire but failed to provide adequate water to allow it to be extinguished before the fire spread. H.R. Moch Co. (Moch) (P) owned a warehouse that was totally destroyed by the fire after it spread. Moch (P) brought suit against the Water Co. alleging a cause of action based on a breach of contract, and a cause of action under common-law tort. The Water Co. (D) brought a motion to dismiss the complaint. This was denied by the trial court, but this denial was then reversed by the Appellate Division.

■ ISSUE

Can an action in tort be maintained based on a contract to which the injured party is neither a party nor an intended third party beneficiary?

■ DECISION AND RATIONALE

(Cardozo) No. The city has no general duty to protect its citizens from fire. [That's news.] That being so the Water Co. (D) when it contracted to supply water to the hydrants did not contract to assume a duty owed by the city to its citizens. It is true that every city contract should properly be entered into for the benefit of the public. But to maintain an action based on the breach of contract a more specific intent to benefit Moch (P) would have to be shown. It would be necessary to show a benefit that was so immediate and clear that the Water Co. (D) could be said to have assumed the risk of such a duty. That is not the case here. If all those who contracted with the city were to be assumed to have assumed such general risks the cost of city services would become astronomical. Thus there is no liability here for breach of contract. There is also no liability here under tort. It is true that once a party assumes to act they have undertaken a duty to act with care. Moch (P) argues that there should be liability in this case under that principle. But the key question here is whether the Water Co. (D) has actually undertaken to act, such that any relationship of duty exists between them. Moch (P) argues that the Water Co (D) entered into such a relationship with them, and any other who might have benefited by the supply of water when it entered into its contract with the city. We believe that this would again create too great an extension of liability. Under this logic any wholesaler would be liable to any retail customer who claimed injury from its failure to provide the retailer with goods. Everyone making a promise having the quality of a contract would be liable not only to the party promised but to an infinite number of potential beneficiaries once the performance of that promise had begun. Thus we find no tort liability for the failure to provide water to the city in this case. (What is the intended purpose of supplying water to fire hydrants if not to allow the city to put out fires?)

Analysis:

One way to look at this case is that it is simply a nonfeasance case; as the Water Company (D) never started to provide water to the hydrant, it never took any affirmative action that would make it liable for negligence in not providing adequate water. However, this case is not really that simple. Supplying the water to the hydrant at adequate pressure seems to be very closely linked to the bigger action of correctly running a water company. It is clear that the Water Co. (P) did undertake to run a water company, and even undertook to provide water to some hydrants. Having taken this action, isn't it reasonable to say that it was negligent in not doing so in a way that was adequate to prevent Moch's (P) warehouse from burning down? What the court seems to be saying is that there must be a limit to the liability assumed by entering into a contract so that the burden of potential liability does not bring commerce to a halt. Thus, the case is apparently more a question of the scope of duty than the difference between misfeasance and nonfeasance.

■ CASE VOCABULARY

ASSUMPTION OF A DUTY: The agreement to take upon oneself a duty that primarily belongs to someone else.

MAINTAIN AN ACTION: The act of continuing or pursuing an action or suit at law. When a suit survives a motion to dismiss it has been maintained, though it has not yet been won.

NON-INTENDED THIRD-PARTY BENEFICIARY: A person who derives benefit from a contract, though not a party to the contract, when the parties to the contract did not directly intended him to benefit.

Florence v. Goldberg

(Run-Over Child) v. (Car Driver and City)

44 N.Y.2d 189, 404 N.Y.S.2d 583, 375 N.E.2d 763 (1978)

A PARTY WILL BE LIABLE FOR THE FAILURE TO PERFORM A DUTY, WHICH WAS VOLUNTARILY AND REGULARLY ASSUMED, IF THAT FAILURE RESULTS IN INJURY TO ANOTHER

■ **INSTANT FACTS** A six-year-old child was severely injured after being struck by a car at an unguarded street crossing while walking to school alone.

■ **BLACK LETTER RULE** A police department, having assumed a duty to a special class of persons, and having gone forward with performance of that duty in the past, has an obligation to continue its performance.

■ PROCEDURAL BASIS

Appeal from the Appellate Division's judgment in favor of the plaintiffs.

■ FACTS

Florence (P) took her six-year-old child to school each day for two weeks, during which time the city police had stationed a guard at a street crossing. Florence (P), having observed this protection, ceased to take the child to school. On the day in question, the crossing guard regularly assigned there called in sick. Departmental regulations called for sending a substitute if possible and, if not, to cover the most dangerous crossings. No substitute was sent and the principal of the school was not notified. The child was struck at the unguarded crossing and suffered severe brain damage. Florence (P) recovered against the city (D) and those responsible for the operation of the car (D). The city (D) appeals.

■ ISSUE

Does a police department have a duty to supervise school crossings if it voluntarily assumed the regular performance of that duty in the past?

■ DECISION AND RATIONALE

(Jasen, J.) Yes. There is little question that the police department voluntarily assumed a particular duty to supervise the school crossing. Significantly, the duty assumed by the police department was a limited one: a duty intended to benefit a special class of persons—viz., children crossing designated intersections while traveling to and from school at scheduled times. Having witnessed the regular performance of this special duty for a two-week period, Florence (P) relied upon its continued performance. The police department, having assumed a duty to a special class of persons, and having gone forward with performance of that duty in the past, had an obligation to continue its performance. Had the police department not assumed a duty to supervise school crossings, Florence (P) would not have permitted her child to travel to and from school alone. The department's failure to perform this duty placed the child in greater danger than he would have been had the duty not been assumed, since Florence (P) would not have had reason to rely on the protection afforded her child and would have been required, in her absence, to arrange for someone to accompany her child to and from school. [The court found that there was also proof that the city (D) was negligent in failing to provide a guard] The order of the Appellate Division should be affirmed, with costs.

Analysis:

Undertakings can create a duty to act affirmatively and with reasonable care. Liability may be imposed if the plaintiff suffers physical harm from the defendant's negligent performance and only if one of two other conditions is met: either the defendant's negligent performance (or withdrawal from performance) must increase the risk to the plaintiff, or else the plaintiff must have relied upon performance. In this case, the child was struck in an unguarded crosswalk where guards had always been provided. Liability for negligently failing to provide the guard follows because the parent relied on the guard. Reliance is possible only when the parent has knowledge of the undertaking and a choice whether to provide some other means of protection. Thus, in this case, testimony that the parent knew that a guard was regularly provided, and that she would have taken the child to school herself if she had known that the guard would not be there, is enough evidence to show reliance and therefore permits recovery.

■ CASE VOCABULARY

REASONABLE CARE: That degree of care which a person of ordinary prudence would exercise in the same or similar circumstances.

VIZ.: That is to say.

CHAPTER EIGHTEEN

The Duty to Protect from Third Persons

Iseberg v. Gross

Instant Facts: A disgruntled former business partner blamed his losses on Iseberg (P), and told two other business partners that he wanted to kill Iseberg (P), but they failed to warn him about the threats; the disgruntled former partner ultimately shot Iseberg (P) four times, and Iseberg (P) sued the other partners for failing to warn him, but the court dismissed the claim and Iseberg (P) appealed.

Black Letter Rule: An affirmative duty to warn or protect against the criminal conduct of a third party may be imposed on one for the benefit of another only if there exists a special relationship between them.

Posecai v. Wal-Mart Stores, Inc.

Instant Facts: A woman sued a store for failing to provide security guards after she was attacked and robbed in the store's parking lot.

Black Letter Rule: A very high degree of foreseeability is required to give rise to a duty to post security guards, but a lower degree or foreseeability may support a duty to implement lesser security measures.

Marquay v. Eno

Instant Facts: Three former high school girls sued the school district for sexual abuse which certain teachers allegedly committed against them.

Black Letter Rule: Failure to report abuse in accordance with the statute could give rise to liability, provided the plaintiff can show that reporting would have prevented the subsequent abuse.

Ward v. Inishmaan Assocs. Ltd. Partnership

Instant Facts: One apartment resident attacked another resident of the same building, and the injured resident sued the building owner and management company, arguing that they failed to protect her from assault by her neighbor.

Black Letter Rule: Generally speaking, landlords have no duty to protect tenants from criminal attack by third parties.

Tarasoff v. Regents of University of California

Instant Facts: A murdered woman's parents sued the University (D) because therapists employed there failed to warn their daughter of death threats made towards her by a patient.

Black Letter Rule: Once a therapist does in fact determine, or under applicable professional standards reasonably should have determined, that a patient poses serious danger of violence to others, he bears a duty to exercise reasonable care to protect the foreseeable victim of that danger.

Brigance v. Velvet Dove Restaurant, Inc.

Instant Facts: A minor who was injured in a car accident is suing the restaurant who served the minor-driver of the car alcoholic beverages.

Black Letter Rule: One who sells intoxicating beverages for on the premises consumption has a duty to exercise reasonable care not to sell liquor to a noticeably intoxicated person.

Iseberg v. Gross

(Lawyer/Business Partner) v. (Business Partner)

227 Ill.2d 78, 316 Ill.Dec. 211, 879 N.E.2d 278 (2007)

THERE IS NO DUTY TO WARN ANOTHER ABOUT A THIRD PARTY'S THREATS TO KILL HIM, UNLESS A SPECIAL RELATIONSHIP EXISTS

■ **INSTANT FACTS** A disgruntled former business partner blamed his losses on Iseberg (P), and told two other business partners that he wanted to kill Iseberg (P), but they failed to warn him about the threats; the disgruntled former partner ultimately shot Iseberg (P) four times, and Iseberg (P) sued the other partners for failing to warn him, but the court dismissed the claim and Iseberg (P) appealed.

■ **BLACK LETTER RULE** An affirmative duty to warn or protect against the criminal conduct of a third party may be imposed on one for the benefit of another only if there exists a special relationship between them.

■ PROCEDURAL BASIS

State supreme court consideration of an order dismissing with prejudice the plaintiff's failure-to-warn claim against the defendants.

■ FACTS

Slavin and Gross (D) started a business together in 1995. Shortly thereafter, Gross (D) contacted Iseberg (P), a lawyer and real estate broker who was in the process of acquiring land to develop into a strip mall. Frank (D) and Iseberg (P) formed a corporation to complete the process. The business owned by Slavin and Gross (D) formed a partnership with the corporation formed by Iseberg (D) and Frank (D). A dispute arose among the partners, and the partnership dissolved. Slavin lost his entire investment and allegedly became mentally unbalanced; he focused his anger on Iseberg (P). Slavin told Gross (D) several times that he wanted to kill Iseberg (P) and then commit suicide. Gross (D) told Frank (D) about the threats, but neither of them told Iseberg (P). In 2000, Slavin rang Iseberg's (P) doorbell and shot him four times when he answered the door, rendering him a paraplegic. Iseberg (P) brought suit against Gross (D) and Frank (D), alleging that they had a duty to warn him that Slavin, their former mutual business partner, had made threats against Iseberg's (P) life. The trial court dismissed the negligence claim with prejudice, and the plaintiffs (Iseberg (P) and his wife) appealed.

■ ISSUE

Did the defendants have a duty to warn the Iseberg (P) about their former mutual business partner's threats against Iseberg's (P) life?

■ DECISION AND RATIONALE

(Burke, J.) No. An affirmative duty to warn or protect against the criminal conduct of a third party may be imposed on one for the benefit of another only if there exists a special relationship between them. Here, no such special relationship existed between the defendants and Iseberg (D). A private person has no duty to act affirmatively to protect another from criminal attack by a third person absent this special relationship between the parties. Four types of special relationships have been recognized: common carrier-passenger, innkeeper-guest, business invitor-invitee, and voluntary custodian-protectee. When an unreasonable risk of physical harm arises within the scope of one of these relationships, an obligation may be imposed on one to exercise reasonable care to protect the other from reasonably foreseeable risk, or to render first aid when it is known that such aid is needed. But the plaintiffs do not allege that one of these special relationships existed; instead, they argue that the special relationship requirement should be abandoned, or that an exception should be applied based on principles of agency. However, the allegations in the complaint fail to establish a principal-agent relationship in this case, and we refuse to abandon the special relationship doctrine, as well as the no-affirmative-duty rule. Both continue to be consistently applied by courts throughout the United States. Affirmed.

Analysis:

The court found here that the facts alleged did not establish an agency relationship between the plaintiff and the defendant, so it did not need to consider whether a principal-agent relationship is special enough to invoke a duty to warn. There are several types of agency relationships, including actual agency and apparent agency. An actual agency is one in which the agent is in fact employed by a principal, and an apparent agency is created by operation of law and established by a principal's actions that would reasonably lead a third person to conclude that an agency relationship exists. Clearly, there may be situations in which mutual business partners act as the agents of each other. The court in this case is not saying that can never be the case, but rather that the allegations in the plaintiffs' complaint did not establish such a relationship here; moreover, even if they had, the court did not seem willing to make new law in this case.

■ CASE VOCABULARY

AGENCY: A fiduciary relationship created by express or implied contract or by law, in which one party (the *agent*) may act on behalf of another party (the *principal*) and bind that other party by words or actions.

AGENT: One who is authorized to act for or in place of another; a representative.

PRINCIPAL: One who authorizes another to act on his or her behalf as an agent.

Posecai v. Wal-Mart Stores, Inc.

(Assaulted Woman) v. (Store)

752 So.2d 762 (La.1999)

IN DECIDING WHETHER TO IMPOSE A DUTY IN A PARTICULAR CASE, THE COURT MUST MAKE A POLICY DECISION IN LIGHT OF THE UNIQUE FACTS AND CIRCUMSTANCES PRESENTED

■ **INSTANT FACTS** A woman sued a store for failing to provide security guards after she was attacked and robbed in the store's parking lot.

■ **BLACK LETTER RULE** A very high degree of foreseeability is required to give rise to a duty to post security guards, but a lower degree or foreseeability may support a duty to implement lesser security measures.

■ PROCEDURAL BASIS

Appeal from the lower court's verdict and award in favor of the plaintiff.

■ FACTS

After Mrs. Posecai (P) finished shopping at Sam's (D), she returned to her car, which was parked in the store's (D) parking lot. A man hiding under her car grabbed her ankle, pointed a gun at her, and robbed her of $19,000 in jewels [pretty fancy for Sam's!]. Posecai (P) sued Sam's (D), claiming it was negligent in failing to provide security guards in the parking lot. Evidence showed that Sam's was adjacent to, but was not in, a high-crime area, and that during the previous six years, there had been three robberies on Sam's premises. During that same time period, there were 83 predatory offenses at 13 businesses in the same block as Sam's (D). The court assessed almost $30,000 in damages against Sam's (D), and this appeal followed.

■ ISSUE

Did the defendant possess the requisite degree of foreseeability for the imposition of a duty to provide security patrols in its parking lot?

■ DECISION AND RATIONALE

(Marcus, J.) No. Jurisdictions have resolved the foreseeability issue in a variety of ways, but four basic approaches have emerged. The specific harm rule, which is now somewhat outdated; a prior similar incidents test, which can lead to arbitrary results; the totality of the circumstances test, which tends to place a greater duty on business owners to foresee the risk of criminal attacks on their property; and finally, a balancing test, which seeks to address the interests of both business proprietors and their customers by balancing the foreseeability of harm against the burden of imposing a duty to protect against criminal acts of third persons. We agree that a balancing test is the best method for determining when business owners owe a duty to provide security for their patrons. The economic and social impact of requiring businesses to provide security on their premises is an important factor. Security is a significant monetary expense for any business and further increases the cost of doing business in high crime areas that are already economically depressed. Moreover, businesses are generally not responsible for the endemic crime that plagues our communities, a societal problem that even our law enforcement and other government agencies have been unable to solve. At the same time, business owners are in the best position to appreciate the crime risks that are posed on their premises and to take reasonable precautions to counteract those risks. The greater the foreseeability and gravity of the harm, the greater the duty of care that will be imposed on the business. A very high degree of foreseeability is required to give rise to a duty to post security guards, but a lower degree of foreseeability may support a duty to implement lesser security measures such as using surveillance cameras, installing improved lighting or fencing, or trimming shrubbery. In the present case, there were only three predatory offenses on Sam's (D) premises in the six and a half years prior to the robbery of Posecai (P). It is also relevant that Sam's only operates during daylight hours and must provide an accessible parking lot to the multitude of customers that shop at its store each year. We conclude that Sam's did not possess the requisite degree of foreseeability for the imposition of a duty to provide security patrols in its parking lot. Reversed.

Analysis:

A threshold issue in any negligence action is whether the defendant owed the plaintiff a duty. Whether a duty is owed is a question of law. In deciding whether to impose a duty in a particular case, the court must make a policy decision in light of the unique facts and circumstances presented. The court may consider various moral, social, and economic factors, including the fairness of imposing liability; the economic impact on the defendant and on similarly situated parties; the need for an incentive to prevent future harm; the nature of the defendant's activity; the potential for an unmanageable flow of litigation; the historical development of precedent; and the direction in which society and its institutions are evolving. The court here looked at each of the four basic approaches to foreseeability, and decided that the balancing test was the most appropriate. The totality of the circumstances test is the most common approach used in other jurisdictions, and it takes additional factors into account, such as the nature, condition, and location of the land, as well as any other relevant factual circumstances bearing on foreseeability. This approach has been criticized, however, as being too broad a standard, effectively imposing an unqualified duty to protect customers in areas experiencing any significant level of criminal activity. The balancing test standard is indeed the best method for determining when business owners owe a duty to provide security for their patrons, as the court decided. In determining the duty that exists, the foreseeability of harm and the gravity of the harm must be balanced against the commensurate burden imposed on the business to protect against that harm.

■ CASE VOCABULARY

FORESEEABILITY: The reasonable anticipation that harm or injury is a likely result from certain acts or omissions.

IMMINENT HARM: Such an appearance of threatened and impending injury as would put a reasonable and prudent man to his instant defense.

PRIOR SIMILAR INCIDENTS TEST: Foreseeability is established by evidence of previous crimes on or near the premises.

SPECIFIC HARM RULE: A landowner does not owe a duty to protect patrons from the violent acts of third parties unless he is aware of specific, imminent harm about to befall them.

TOTALITY OF THE CIRCUMSTANCES TEST: This method takes additional factors into account, such as the nature, condition, and location of the land, as well as any other relevant factual circumstances bearing on foreseeability.

Marquay v. Eno

(Sexually Abused High School Girls) v. (High School Teachers)

139 N.H. 708, 662 A.2d 272 (1995)

SCHOOLS SHARE A SPECIAL RELATIONSHIP WITH STUDENTS ENTRUSTED TO THEIR CARE, WHICH IMPOSES UPON THEM CERTAIN DUTIES OF REASONABLE SUPERVISION

■ **INSTANT FACTS** Three former high school girls sued the school district for sexual abuse which certain teachers allegedly committed against them.

■ **BLACK LETTER RULE** Failure to report abuse in accordance with the statute could give rise to liability, provided the plaintiff can show that reporting would have prevented the subsequent abuse.

■ PROCEDURAL BASIS

The federal district court certified questions to the Supreme Court.

■ FACTS

Three women (P) who were students in the same school district (D) each filed separate complaints alleging that they were exploited, harassed, assaulted, and sexually abused by one or more employees of the school district (D). Each plaintiff also alleges that a host of school employees, including other teachers, coaches, superintendents, principals and secretaries either were aware or should have been aware of the sexual abuse. The women (P) sued the school district (D) and its allegedly abusing employees. The federal district court where the suits were brought certified a number of questions to this Court.

■ ISSUE

Do sexually abused children have a cause of action against the school employees for failure to report abuse about which they either knew or should have known?

■ DECISION AND RATIONALE

(Horton, J.) Yes. The first certified question asks whether the statute which requires that any person "having reason to suspect that a child has been abused or neglected shall report" it, creates a private right of action in favor of abused children against those who have violated the statute's reporting requirement. We hold that the reporting statute does not support a private right of action for its violation because we find no express or implied legislative intent to create such civil liability. First, we note that where the legislature has intended that civil liability flow from the violation of a statute, it has often so provided. Where, as here, civil liability for a statutory violation would represent an abrupt and sweeping departure from a general common law rule of nonliability, we would expect that if the legislature, which is presumed to recognize the common law, intended to impose civil liability it would expressly so provide. Here there was no expressed intent. Nor can we divine any implied intent. We now turn to the negligence per se question. Use of a statute to establish the standard of care is limited to situations where a common law cause of action exists, and then, only if the statute is "applicable." Whether a statutory standard is applicable depends, in part, on whether the type of duty to which the statute speaks is similar to the type of duty on which the cause of action is based. Because the duty to which the statute speaks—reporting of abuse—is considerably different from the duty on which the cause of action is based—supervision of students—we hold that a violation of the reporting statute does not constitute negligence per se in an action based on inadequate supervision of a student. The plaintiffs also argue that all school district employees have a common law duty to protect students whom they know or should know are being sexually abused by another school employee. We hold that some employees owe such a duty while others do not. The duty owed by some defendants is based on their relationship to the students; for other defendants the duty derives from their relationship to the alleged abusers. As a general rule, a person has no affirmative duty to aid or protect another. Such a duty may arise, however, if a special relationship exists. The women (P) argue that a special relationship exists between educators and school children, imposing a duty upon educators to protect students whom they know or should know are being sexually abused by another school employee. We agree with the majority of courts from other jurisdictions that schools share a special relationship with students entrusted to their care, which imposes upon them certain duties of reasonable supervision. The scope of the duty imposed is limited by what risks are reasonably foreseeable. Major factors influencing our conclusion that a special relationship exists between schools and students include the compulsory character of school attendance, the expectation of parents and students for and their reliance on a safe school environment, and the importance to society of the learning activity which is to take place in public schools. For these reasons, we conclude that the social importance of protecting the plaintiffs' interest outweighs the importance of immunizing the defendant from extended liability. While the impairment of protection creates an affirmative duty, it also circumscribes the limits of that duty. Thus the existence of a duty is limited to those periods when parental protection is compromised. That is not to say that employees with a special relationship to a student may not be liable for injuries that occurred off school premises or after school hours, if the student can show that the employee's negligent acts or omissions, within the scope of his or her duty, proximately caused injury to the student. This is a question for the jury. We note that the principal or superintendent rarely has primary supervisory authority over a student. Because, however, it is the school to which parents turn over custody of their children and from which they expect safety, and because the principal and superintendent are charged with overseeing all aspects of the school's operation, we hold that a duty of supervision is owed to each student. Where the principal or superintendent knows or should know that a particular school employee poses a threat to a student, entrustment of the student to the care of that employee will not satisfy the duty of reasonable supervision. Therefore, we hold that employees with supervisory powers of hiring and firing might be liable for negligent hiring or retention of a person they knew or should have known was an abuser, and in this type of action the reporting statute would be applicable. Accordingly, under these circumstances, failure to report abuse in accordance with the statute could give rise to liability, provided the plaintiff can show that reporting would have prevented the subsequent abuse. Remanded.

Analysis:

The doctrine of negligence per se provides that where a cause of action exists at common law, the standard of conduct to which a defendant will be held may be defined as that required by statute, rather than as the usual reasonable person standard. The doctrine of negligence per se, however, plays no role in the creation of common law causes of action. Thus, in many cases, the common law may fail to recognize liability for failure to perform affirmative duties that are imposed by statute. School attendance impairs both the ability of students to protect themselves and the ability of their parents to protect them. It is this impairment of protection from which the special relationship between school and student arises and from which the duty of supervision flows. The court here declined to accept the women's (P) argument that every school employee shoulders a personal duty simply by virtue of receiving a paycheck from the school district. Instead, the duty falls upon those school employees who have supervisory responsibility over students and who thus have stepped into the role of parental proxy. Thus, those employees who share such a relationship with a student and who acquire actual knowledge of abuse or who learn of facts that would lead a reasonable person to conclude a student is being abused are subject to liability if their level of supervision is unreasonable and is a proximate cause of a student's injury.

■ CASE VOCABULARY

CERTIFIED: A method of taking a case from a district court to the Supreme Court in which the former court may request instructions as to any question of law.

EXPRESSED INTENT: Wishes or desires which are stated or declared in direct terms.

IMPLIED INTENT: Wishes or desires are gathered by implication or necessary deduction from the circumstances.

NEGLIGENCE PER SE: The unexcused violation of an applicable statute.

PROXIMATE CAUSE: That which, in a natural and continuous sequence, unbroken by any efficient intervening cause, produces injury, and without which the result would not have occurred.

Ward v. Inishmaan Assocs. Ltd. Partnership

(Apartment Resident) v. (Apartment Owner)

931 A.2d 1235 (N.H. 2007)

THE COURT REFUSED TO HOLD THE LANDLORD LIABLE FOR AN ATTACK ON A RESIDENT, DESPITE NOTICE OF THE NEIGHBORS' ONGOING CONFLICT

■ **INSTANT FACTS** One apartment resident attacked another resident of the same building, and the injured resident sued the building owner and management company, arguing that they failed to protect her from assault by her neighbor.

■ **BLACK LETTER RULE** Generally speaking, landlords have no duty to protect tenants from criminal attack by third parties.

■ PROCEDURAL BASIS

State appellate court review of the trial court's decision denying the defendants' motion for a directed verdict.

■ FACTS

Sommers and Ward (P) lived in the same apartment building owned by Inishmaan (D) and managed by JCM Management (D). Ward (P) had made multiple complaints to the police and JCM (D) personnel about Sommers' harassment of her. In 2002, Sommers attacked Ward (P) outside Ward's (P) apartment, stabbing her several times. Sommers was arrested and charged with attempted murder, but died before the criminal case was heard. Ward (P) sued Inishmaan (D) and JCM (D) for her injuries, alleging that they had failed to protect her from Sommers' assault. The jury returned a verdict in the plaintiff's favor. The defendants moved for a directed verdict, but the court denied the motion and the defendants appealed, arguing that the evidence failed to establish any of the special circumstances required by law to impose liability on a landlord for a criminal assault by a third person.

■ ISSUE

Were the defendants entitled to a directed verdict in their favor?

■ DECISION AND RATIONALE

(Broderick, C.J.) Yes. Generally speaking, landlords have no duty to protect tenants from criminal attack by third parties. We have recognized only two exceptions to this general rule. First, a duty may arise when a landlord has created or is responsible for a known defect in the condition of the premises that foreseeably enhances the risk of criminal attack. Second, a landlord who undertakes to provide security has a duty to act with reasonable care. Where, however, a landlord has made no affirmative attempt to provide security and is not responsible for a physical defect that enhances the risk of crime, there is no duty on the part of a landlord to protect tenants from criminal attack. This case fits neither of the recognized exceptions, so the court erred in denying the defendants' motion for a directed verdict. We vacate the jury's verdict and award and remand the case for entry of judgment in the defendants' favor.

Analysis:

Not all courts would agree with this outcome. In some states, a landlord's liability for the criminal acts of a third party hinge on foreseeability. If that were the case here, it may have been quite possible for the plaintiff to show that her neighbor's attack on her was foreseeable, given her prior complaints to management and the police.

■ CASE VOCABULARY

DIRECTED VERDICT: A jury verdict ordered by the court. In civil cases, a party may receive a directed verdict if the opposite side does not present a prima facie case or a necessary defense.

Tarasoff v. Regents of University of California

(Parents of Murdered Woman) v. (Employer of Therapists)

17 Cal.3d 425, 131 Cal.Rptr. 14, 551 P.2d 334 (1976)

A THERAPIST OWES A LEGAL DUTY NOT ONLY TO HIS PATIENT, BUT ALSO TO HIS PATIENT'S WOULD-BE VICTIM

■ **INSTANT FACTS** A murdered woman's parents sued the University (D) because therapists employed there failed to warn their daughter of death threats made towards her by a patient.

■ **BLACK LETTER RULE** Once a therapist does in fact determine, or under applicable professional standards reasonably should have determined, that a patient poses serious danger of violence to others, he bears a duty to exercise reasonable care to protect the foreseeable victim of that danger.

■ PROCEDURAL BASIS

Appeal from the superior court's ruling which sustained the defendant's demurrers to plaintiffs' second amended complaints without leave to amend.

■ FACTS

Prosenjit Poddar confided his intention to kill Tatiana Tarasoff to a psychologist, Dr. Moore, who was employed by the University of California at Berkley (D). On Moore's request, the campus police briefly detained Poddar, but released him when he appeared rational. Dr. Powelson, Moore's superior, directed that no further action be taken to detain Poddar. No one warned Tatiana of the threats made on her life, and two months later Poddar killed her. Tatiana's parents (P) brought suit against the therapists, the campus police, and the Regents of the University of California as their employer. The superior court concluded that the facts did not set forth causes of action against the defendants, and sustained the defendant's demurrers to the Tarasoffs' (P) second amended complaints without leave to amend. This appeal followed.

■ ISSUE

Does a therapist have a duty to protect a foreseeable victim from dangers posed by their patients?

■ DECISION AND RATIONALE

(Tobriner, J.) Yes. Although the Tarasoffs' (P) pleadings assert no special relation between Tatiana and the therapists (D), they establish as between Poddar and the therapists (D) the special relation that arises between a patient and his doctor or psychotherapist. Such a relationship may support affirmative duties for the benefit of third persons. Thus, for example, a hospital must exercise reasonable care to control the behavior of a patient which may endanger other persons. A doctor must also warn a patient if the patient's condition of medication renders certain conduct, such as driving a car, dangerous to others. The University (D) contends, however, that imposition of a duty to exercise reasonable care to protect third persons is unworkable because therapists cannot accurately predict whether or not a patient will resort to violence. In support of the argument, amicus representing the American Psychiatric Association and other professional societies cite numerous articles which indicate that therapists, in the present state of the art, are unable reliably to predict violent acts; their forecasts, amicus claims, tend consistently to overpredict violence, and indeed are often more wrong than right. We recognize the difficulty that a therapist encounters in attempting to forecast whether a patient presents a serious danger of violence. Obviously we do not require that the therapist in making that determination, render a perfect performance; the therapist need only exercise "that reasonable degree of skill, knowledge, and care ordinarily possessed and exercised by members of that professional specialty under similar circumstances." Within the broad range of reasonable practice and treatment in which professional opinion and judgment may differ, the therapist is free to exercise his or her own best judgment without liability; proof, aided by hindsight, that he or she judged wrongly is insufficient to establish negligence. Amicus contends, however, that even if a therapist does in fact predict that a patient poses a serious danger of violence to others, the therapist should be absolved of any responsibility for failing to act to protect the potential victim. In our view, however, once a therapist does in fact determine, or under applicable professional standards reasonably should have determined, that a patient poses serious danger of violence to others, he bears a duty to exercise reasonable care to protect the foreseeable victim of that danger. While the discharge of this duty of due care will necessarily vary with the facts of each case, in each instance the adequacy of the therapist's conduct must be measured against the traditional negligence standard of the rendition of reasonable care under the circumstances. The ultimate question of resolving the tension between the conflicting interest of patient and potential victim is one of social policy, not professional expertise. In sum, the therapist owes a legal duty not only to his patient, but also to his patient's would-be victim and is subject in both respects to scrutiny by judge and jury. For the foregoing reasons, we find that the Tarasoffs' (P) complaints can be amended to state a cause of action against the therapists and the University, as their employer, for breach of a duty to exercise reasonable care to protect Tatiana. We conclude, however, that the police defendants do not have any such special relationship to either Tatiana or to Poddar sufficient to impose upon them a duty to warn respecting Poddar's violent intentions.

Analysis:

Whenever one person is by circumstances placed in such a position with regard to another that if he did not use ordinary care and skill in his own conduct he would cause danger of injury to the person or property of the other, a duty arises to use ordinary care and skill to avoid such danger. Departure from this fundamental principle only occurs upon the balancing of a number of considerations. The most important of these considerations is foreseeability. As a general principle, a defendant owes a duty of care to all persons who are foreseeably endangered by his conduct, with respect to all risks that make the conduct unreasonably dangerous. However, when the avoidance of foreseeable harm requires a defendant to control the conduct of another person, or to warn of such conduct, the common law has traditionally imposed liability only if the defendant bears some special relationship to the dangerous person or to the potential victim. The court found that the risk that unnecessary warnings may be given is a reasonable price to pay for the lives of possible victims that may be saved.

■ CASE VOCABULARY

AFFIRMATIVE ACTS: Positive, forthcoming actions taken.

AMICUS: A group with a strong interest in or views on the subject matter of an action, but which is not a party to the action.

DEMURRER: An allegation of a defendant, which, admitting the matters of fact alleged by the complaint to be true, shows that as they are therein set forth they are insufficient for the plaintiff to proceed upon.

DUE CARE: That degree of care which an ordinarily prudent person would have exercised under the same or similar circumstances.

Brigance v. Velvet Dove Restaurant, Inc.

(Passenger) v. (Booze Server)

725 P.2d 300 (Okl.1986)

THE OLD COMMON LAW RULE OF A TAVERN OWNER'S NONLIABILITY IS UNREALISTIC AND INCONSISTENT WITH MODERN TORT THEORIES

■ **INSTANT FACTS** A minor who was injured in a car accident is suing the restaurant who served the minor-driver of the car alcoholic beverages.

■ **BLACK LETTER RULE** One who sells intoxicating beverages for on the premises consumption has a duty to exercise reasonable care not to sell liquor to a noticeably intoxicated person.

■ PROCEDURAL BASIS

Appeal from the trial court's dismissal of the plaintiff's claim.

■ FACTS

Jeff Johnson drove a group of minors to the Velvet Dove Restaurant (D), where they were served intoxicating beverages. Johnson was later involved in a one-car accident in which Shawn Brigance (P) was injured. (Presumably, Brigance (P) was a passenger.) Brigance (P) brought suit against the Restaurant (D), alleging that the alcohol served to Johnson caused him to become intoxicated, or increased his earlier intoxication, which in turn caused the car accident. The trial court dismissed the claim, and this appeal followed.

■ ISSUE

Can a tavern owner who furnishes alcoholic beverages to another be held civilly liable for a third person's injuries that are caused by the acts of an intoxicated patron?

■ DECISION AND RATIONALE

(Hodges, J.) Yes. In recent years, many states have retreated from the common law rule of nonliability for a liquor vendor, regarding it as antiquated and illogical. Several states with dram shop laws have also recognized a new common law right of action against a vendor of liquor. Many of the jurisdictions which now recognize a civil right of action do so on the theory that when alcoholic beverages are sold by a tavern keeper to a minor or to an intoxicated person, the unreasonable risk of harm to members of the traveling public may readily be recognized and foreseen. This is particularly evident in current times when traveling by car to and from the tavern is so commonplace and accidents resulting from drinking are so frequent. We find that on the basis of the clear trend in this area we are free to establish a civil cause of action by an injured third person against a commercial vendor of liquor for on the premises consumption. We believe the application of the old common law rule of a tavern owner's nonliability in today's automotive society is unrealistic, inconsistent with modern tort theories and is a complete anachronism within today's society. We thus hold that one who sells intoxicating beverages for on the premises consumption has a duty to exercise reasonable care not to sell liquor to a noticeably intoxicated person. It is not unreasonable to expect a commercial vendor who sells alcoholic beverages for on the premises consumption to a person he knows or should know from the circumstances is already intoxicated, to foresee the unreasonable risk of harm to others who may be injured by such person's impaired ability to operate an automobile. However, even if a commercial vendor for on the premises consumption is found to have breached its duty, a plaintiff must still show the illegal sale of alcohol led to the impairment of the ability of the driver which was the proximate cause of the injury and there was a causal connection between the sale and a foreseeable ensuing injury. In adopting a new rule of liability which creates a civil cause of action, we specifically hold that the law hereby established will be applied prospectively to all causes of action occurring from and after the date the mandate issues herein, except that the rule of liability also applies to the parties in this case. Reversed and remanded.

Analysis:

At common law, a tavern owner who furnished alcoholic beverages to another was not civilly liable for a third person's injuries that were caused by the acts of the intoxicated person. The old common law rule of nonliability has been changed by judicial opinion and statute. Inherent in the common law is a dynamic principle that allows it to grow and to tailor itself to meet changing needs. The development of the law of torts is peculiarly a function of the judiciary. Because duty and liability are matters of public policy, they are subject to the changing attitudes and needs of society.

■ CASE VOCABULARY

CAUSAL NEXUS: A connection which ties the act to the result.

DRAM SHOP LAWS: A State Act which imposes liability on the seller of intoxicating liquors when a third party is injured as a result of the intoxication of the buyer where the sale has caused or contributed to the intoxication.

MANDATE: A judicial command or order issued upon the decision of an appeal.

CHAPTER NINETEEN

Emotional Harm

GTE Southwest, Inc. v. Bruce

Instant Facts: Employees sued their employer for intentional infliction of emotional distress because of the extremely abusive nature of their supervisor.

Black Letter Rule: To establish a cause of action for intentional infliction of emotional distress in the workplace, an employee must prove the existence of some conduct that brings the dispute outside the scope of an ordinary employment dispute and into the realm of extreme and outrageous conduct.

Homer v. Long

Instant Facts: A husband sued his wife's therapist after the therapist used confidential information to seduce the emotionally fragile woman.

Black Letter Rule: There are situations in which conduct directed principally at one person has been regarded as extreme and outrageous as to another, but normally the other person must be present to witness the conduct in order to recover.

Catron v. Lewis

Instant Facts: Catron (P) suffered emotional distress after one of the girls he was pulling on a tube behind his boat was hit by a jet ski and died; he sued the boy riding on the jet ski, the owner of the jet ski, and the state (which operated the recreational area where they were boating), but the court granted summary judgment in the defendants' favor.

Black Letter Rule: When there is no impact or physical injury to the plaintiff, the plaintiff seeking to bring an action for negligent infliction of emotional distress must show that either (1) he or she is a reasonably foreseeably "bystander" victim based on an intimate familial relationship with a seriously injured victim of the defendant's negligence, or (2) the plaintiff was a "direct victim" of the defendant's negligence because the plaintiff was within the zone of danger of the negligence in question.

Boucher v. Dixie Medical Center

Instant Facts: Parents sued the hospital after their son went into a coma and suffered severe brain damage following hand surgery.

Black Letter Rule: The parents of a tortiously injured adult child cannot recover for loss of the child's consortium.

Potter v. Firestone Tire and Rubber Co.

Instant Facts: The Potters (P) sued Firestone (D) after toxic chemicals from the plant were dumped in a landfill and then leached into the drinking water.

Black Letter Rule: A toxic exposure plaintiff need not meet the more likely than not threshold for fear of cancer recovery in a negligence action if the plaintiff pleads and proves that the defendant's conduct in causing the exposure amounts to oppression, fraud, or malice, which authorizes the imposition of punitive damages.

GTE Southwest, Inc. v. Bruce

(Employer) v. (Emotionally Abused Employees)

998 S.W.2d 605 (1999)

GENERALLY, INSENSITIVE OR EVEN RUDE BEHAVIOR DOES NOT CONSTITUTE EXTREME AND OUTRAGEOUS CONDUCT

■ **INSTANT FACTS** Employees sued their employer for intentional infliction of emotional distress because of the extremely abusive nature of their supervisor.

■ **BLACK LETTER RULE** To establish a cause of action for intentional infliction of emotional distress in the workplace, an employee must prove the existence of some conduct that brings the dispute outside the scope of an ordinary employment dispute and into the realm of extreme and outrageous conduct.

■ PROCEDURAL BASIS

Appeal from the Court of Appeals' affirmance of the trial court's judgment for the plaintiff.

■ FACTS

Bruce (P) and several other plaintiffs worked for GTE (D) under Morris Shields. They alleged that over a period of years, Shields engaged in a pattern of grossly abusive, threatening, and degrading conduct, regularly using the harshest vulgarity, verbally threatening and terrorizing them [a real sweetheart!]. He frequently yelled and screamed at the top of his voice, and pounded his fists when requesting the employees to do things [who wouldn't bend over backwards to help?]. He would physically intimidate the employees, charging at them with his fists balled up, stopping very close to their faces. He would force them to clean their offices daily, even though regular janitorial services were provided by others. There was also testimony that he would often call one employee into his office to stand in front of him while he simply stared at her for up to thirty minutes [pervert!]. The testimony detailed many abuses of this kind. The trial court entered judgment on the jury's verdict for Bruce (P) and the other plaintiffs. The Court of Appeals affirmed, and this appeal followed.

■ ISSUE

Was Shields' conduct extreme and outrageous such as to support a claim of intentional infliction of emotional distress?

■ DECISION AND RATIONALE

(Not Stated) Yes. To recover damages for intentional infliction of emotional distress, a plaintiff must prove that: (1) the defendant acted intentionally or recklessly; (2) the conduct was extreme and outrageous; (3) the actions of the defendant caused the plaintiff emotional distress; and (4) the resulting emotional distress was severe. In addition, a claim for intentional infliction of emotional distress cannot be maintained when the risk that emotional distress will result is merely incidental to the commission of some other tort. Accordingly, a claim for intentional infliction of emotional distress will not lie if emotional distress is not the intended or primary consequence of the defendant's conduct. Generally, insensitive or even rude behavior does not constitute extreme and outrageous conduct. Similarly, mere insults, indignities, threats, annoyances, petty oppressions, or other trivialities do not rise to the level of extreme and outrageous conduct. Thus, to establish a cause of action for intentional infliction of emotional distress in the workplace, an employee must prove the existence of some conduct that brings the dispute outside the scope of an ordinary employment dispute and into the realm of extreme and outrageous conduct. Shields' ongoing acts of harassment, intimidation, and humiliation and his daily obscene and vulgar behavior, which GTE (D) defends as his "management style," went beyond the bounds of tolerable workplace conduct. Occasional malicious and abusive incidents should not be condoned, but must often be tolerated in our society. But once conduct such as that shown here becomes a regular pattern of behavior and continues despite the victim's objection and attempts to remedy the situation, it can no longer be tolerated. It is the severity and regularity of Shields' abusive and threatening conduct that brings his behavior into the realm of extreme and outrageous conduct. Affirmed.

Analysis:

In determining whether certain conduct is extreme and outrageous, courts consider the context and the relationship between the parties. In the employment context, some courts have held that a plaintiff's status as an employee should entitle him to a greater degree of protection from insult and outrage by a supervisor with authority over him than if he were a stranger. This approach is based partly on the rationale that, as opposed to most casual and temporary relationships, the workplace environment provides a captive victim and the opportunity for prolonged abuse. In contrast, several courts have adopted a strict approach to intentional infliction of emotional distress claims arising in the workplace. These courts rely on the fact that, to properly manage its business, an employer must be able to supervise, review, criticize, demote, transfer, and discipline employees. This court agreed with the second approach, and, as a result, required that the behavior must be in the realm of extreme and outrageous conduct.

■ CASE VOCABULARY

EXTREME AND OUTRAGEOUS CONDUCT: Above and beyond insulting; shocking to the conscious.

INTENTIONAL INFLICTION OF EMOTIONAL DISTRESS: A tort in which emotional distress is the intended or primary consequence of the defendant's conduct.

Homer v. Long

(Patient's Husband) v. (Patient's Seducer/Therapist)

90 Md.App. 1, 599 A.2d 1193 (1992)

NORMALLY, THIRD PERSONS MUST BE PRESENT TO WITNESS THE EXTREME AND OUTRAGEOUS CONDUCT IN ORDER TO RECOVER FOR SUCH CONDUCT DIRECTED PRINCIPALLY AT ANOTHER PERSON

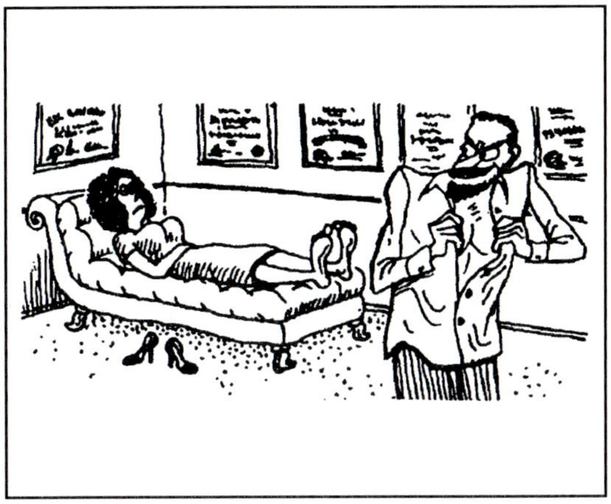

■ **INSTANT FACTS** A husband sued his wife's therapist after the therapist used confidential information to seduce the emotionally fragile woman.

■ **BLACK LETTER RULE** There are situations in which conduct directed principally at one person has been regarded as extreme and outrageous as to another, but normally the other person must be present to witness the conduct in order to recover.

■ PROCEDURAL BASIS

Not Stated.

■ FACTS

Mr. Homer (P) and his wife had been married many years when she was hospitalized for depression. While she was hospitalized, Dr. Long (D), her therapist, used confidential information and took advantage of her dependent, needy and vulnerable condition to seduce her [oh, that should cheer her right up!]. Homer's (P) wife's personality subsequently changed and they were ultimately divorced. Mr. Homer (P) sued Dr. Long (D) for, among other things, intentional or reckless infliction of distress.

■ ISSUE

Can conduct directed principally at one person be regarded as extreme and outrageous as to another person not present to witness the conduct?

■ DECISION AND RATIONALE

(Wilner, C.J.) No. To recover damages for intentional infliction of emotional distress, a plaintiff must prove that: (1) the defendant acted intentionally or recklessly; (2) the conduct was extreme and outrageous; (3) the actions of the defendant caused the plaintiff emotional distress; and (4) the resulting emotional distress was severe. Whether, for purposes of this tort, the conduct is extreme and outrageous depends, at least in part, on the context in which it is viewed. Intrinsically, of course, it is extreme and outrageous; it also violates clear standards set by the medical community itself. But the essence of the requirement is that the conduct must not simply be extreme and outrageous from the perspective of society at large, or from the perspective of someone else, but must also be so as to the plaintiff. Outrageous conduct directed at A does not necessarily give B a cause of action. There are situations in which conduct directed principally at one person has been regarded as extreme and outrageous as to another, but normally the other person must be present to witness the conduct in order to recover. The requirement of presence has been relaxed by some courts in particularly compelling circumstances, as, for example, where a parent sued the defendant for sexually molesting or kidnaping the plaintiff's child. We see no reason not to apply the general rule here. The emotional and economic trauma likely to arise from the seduction of one's spouse is not limited to the case where the seducer is the spouse's therapist. The conduct may be just as outrageous and the harm may be just as great where the seducer is a neighbor, a good friend, a relative, an employee or business associate of Mr. Homer's (P), or indeed anyone in whom Mr. Homer (P) has imposed trust or for whom he or she has special regard.

Analysis:

The Court followed the general rule that allows a third party to recover for extreme and outrageous conduct towards another only if the third party was present to witness the conduct. In this case, it could be assumed that Mr. Homer (P) was not present while his wife was being seduced by Dr. Long (D). Where the extreme and outrageous conduct is directed at a third person, the defendant may know that it is substantially certain, or at least highly probable, that it will cause severe emotional distress to the plaintiff, even if he or she is not present. Since the mental effect can reasonably be anticipated by the defendant, it seems reasonable that he should be held accountable for any harm caused by his actions. The distinction between the wife who sees her husband shot down before her eyes, and the one who hears about it five minutes later, is based on the obvious necessity of drawing a line somewhere.

■ CASE VOCABULARY

CAUSAL CONNECTION: Proof that the wrongful conduct caused the resulting emotional distress.

INTENTIONAL CONDUCT: Purposeful actions.

RECKLESS CONDUCT: Careless, heedless, inattentive to duty.

Catron v. Lewis

(Boater) v. (Owner of Jet Ski)

712 N.W.2d 245 (Neb. 2006)

WHERE THE PLAINTIFF WAS NOT IN THE ZONE OF DANGER, NOR RELATED TO THE VICTIM, THERE WAS NO CLAIM FOR EMOTIONAL DISTRESS

■ **INSTANT FACTS** Catron (P) suffered emotional distress after one of the girls he was pulling on a tube behind his boat was hit by a jet ski and died; he sued the boy riding on the jet ski, the owner of the jet ski, and the state (which operated the recreational area where they were boating), but the court granted summary judgment in the defendants' favor.

■ **BLACK LETTER RULE** When there is no impact or physical injury to the plaintiff, the plaintiff seeking to bring an action for negligent infliction of emotional distress must show that either (1) he or she is a reasonably foreseeably "bystander" victim based on an intimate familial relationship with a seriously injured victim of the defendant's negligence, or (2) the plaintiff was a "direct victim" of the defendant's negligence because the plaintiff was within the zone of danger of the negligence in question.

■ PROCEDURAL BASIS

State appellate court review of the district court decision granting summary judgment in the defendants' favor.

■ FACTS

Catron (P) was pulling his daughters' friends on tubes behind his boat when he noticed two jet skis nearby. When he first saw the jet skis, they were about seventy-five yards away and were going about thirty-five to forty miles per hour; Catron (P) assumed they would avoid hitting the boat. Panek (D) was on one of the jet skis. He ran into Rader, one of the tubers, killing her. After the accident, Catron (P) was diagnosed with major depression and anxiety disorder. He was unable to work. He was eventually diagnosed with post-traumatic stress disorder and prescribed antidepressants. Catron (P) sued the state (which operated the recreational area where they were boating), Panek (D), and Lewis (D) (the owner of the jet ski that Panek (D) was riding) for damages resulting from the emotional distress stemming from his witnessing the accident and his unsuccessful attempt to rescue Rader. The district court granted summary judgment in the defendants' favor and Catron (P) appealed.

■ ISSUE

Did the court properly grant summary judgment in the defendants' favor on the plaintiff's emotional distress claim?

■ DECISION AND RATIONALE

(McCormack, J.) Yes. When there is no impact or physical injury to the plaintiff, the plaintiff seeking to bring an action for negligent infliction of emotional distress must show that either (1) he or she is a reasonably foreseeably "bystander" victim based on an intimate familial relationship with a seriously injured victim of the defendant's negligence, or (2) the plaintiff was a "direct victim" of the defendant's negligence because the plaintiff was within the zone of danger of the negligence in question. Here, Catron (P) was not immediately threatened with physical injury as a result of the alleged negligence that resulted in Rader's death. When Catron (P) observed the jets skis, they were seventy-five yards away, and he testified that he assumed they would either stop or turn to avoid a collision with the boat. Apparently, they did, but Rader was some sixty-one feet behind the boat at the end of the tow rope. Affirmed.

Analysis:

The court describes the zone of danger test as a complement to the basic requirement that persons exercise reasonable care to protect others from injury. Those who breach their basic duty of care to others are required to compensate those who are injured, even when the injuries are not caused by direct impact but by the operation of foreseeable emotional distress. Persons in the zone of danger are foreseeable plaintiffs to the negligent actor, and the fact that the harm results through emotion distress does not protect the actor from liability. Here, however, based on his own testimony, Catron (P) was not in the zone of danger; nor did he have an intimate familial relationship with the victim. Accordingly, the defendants were entitled to summary judgment in their favor.

Boucher v. Dixie Medical Center

(Parents of Quadriplegic) v. (Hospital)

850 P.2d 1179 (Utah 1992)

THERE IS NO RIGHT OF RECOVERY BASED ON THE RELATIONSHIP BETWEEN PARENTS AND THEIR ADULT CHILD IN LOSS OF CONSORTIUM CLAIMS

■ **INSTANT FACTS** Parents sued the hospital after their son went into a coma and suffered severe brain damage following hand surgery.

■ **BLACK LETTER RULE** The parents of a tortiously injured adult child cannot recover for loss of the child's consortium.

■ PROCEDURAL BASIS

Appeal from the trial court's dismissal of the plaintiffs' complaint.

■ FACTS

The Bouchers' (P) eighteen-year-old son, Daniel, was admitted into Dixie Medical Center (D) with a severely injured hand. He lapsed into a coma during the post-operative recovery period following surgery for his hand. He remained in a coma for ten days before awakening as a severely brain-damaged quadriplegic who will need extensive care for the rest of his life [now that's a complication!]. The Bouchers (P) were present at the hospital and observed their son's condition both before and after he awoke from the coma. The Bouchers (P) claimed damaged for (1) negligent infliction of mental distress and (2) loss of their child's consortium or society, in addition to the claim of Daniel Boucher himself. The trial court dismissed the complaint, and this appeal followed.

■ ISSUE

Can the parents of a tortiously injured adult child recover for loss of the child's consortium?

■ DECISION AND RATIONALE

(Hall, J.) No. [The Supreme Court in this opinion concluded that the Boucher (P) parents could not recover for negligent infliction of mental distress because they were not in the zone of danger. The Court then considered the loss of consortium claim as follows.] The Bouchers' (P) second claim presents an issue of first impression in this court: Should Utah judicially adopt a cause of action that allows the parents of a tortiously injured adult child to recover for loss of the child's consortium? Loss of consortium claims are based on the recognition of a legally protected interest in personal relationships. Accordingly, if one member of the relationship is tortiously injured the noninjured party has a cause of action to recover for damage to their relational interest, in other words, the loss of the injured party's company society, cooperation and affection. In the instant case, we are asked to recognize a right of recovery based on the relationship between parents and their adult son. For the reasons set forth below, we decline to adopt such an approach. The majority of jurisdictions that have addressed the issue have declined to recognize a cause of action for loss of filial consortium. Indeed, our research reveals only one jurisdiction that has expressly recognized the specific right the Bouchers (P) urge this court to adopt: a judicially created right to recover for the loss of an adult child's consortium. Utah's Married Woman's Act has been construed to abolish the claim of spousal consortium. Allowing recovery for the loss of an adult child's consortium and denying recovery for the loss of a spouse's consortium would lead to anomalous results. In many instances, the marital relationship is closer and more involved than the relationship between parents and their adult children and therefore should be granted greater or equal protection. However, we cannot recognize a filial consortium claim and extend the same right of recovery to a plaintiff who suffers a loss of consortium because his or her spouse has been tortiously injured. The adoption of the Bouchers' claim, therefore, would invite inequitable applications of the consortium doctrine. The Bouchers (P) also contend that because Utah allows recovery for the loss of society and affection in wrongful death cases, it is logical to extend this theory of damages to cases involving nonfatal injuries. However, we view wrongful death cases as distinguishable from consortium cases. In wrongful death cases, the party that suffers the actual physical injury has no cause of action and the legislature has prescribed the parties who have a right to recover for the loss of the deceased's society and affection. Therefore, there is no danger of expansive liability and no need for the judiciary to attempt to fashion rational limits on relational interests. We decline to adopt a cause of action that allows the parents of a tortiously injured adult child to recover for the loss of consortium. The trial court, therefore, did not err in dismissing the Bouchers' (P) claims of negligent infliction of emotional distress and loss of filial consortium. Affirmed.

Analysis:

At common law, the father of a tortiously injured child did have a cause of action to recover the value of the child's loss of services and the medical expenses incurred on the child's behalf. However, this action was based on a father's right to his minor children's services and a father's obligation to pay his minor children's medical expenses. This right of recovery, therefore, did not extend beyond these two elements of damages, nor did it extend to injuries involving adult or emancipated children. These common law principles have undergone some modification. However, no widely accepted rule has developed that allows recovery in all cases involving adult children. Consortium claims have the potential for greatly expanding the liability that can flow from one negligent act. The recognition of consortium claims may impact the cost and availability of insurance.

■ CASE VOCABULARY

CONSORTIUM: The fellowship, company, cooperation and aid of one another in a relationship.

EMANCIPATED: Freed from the control of another.

WRONGFUL DEATH: A wrongful act, neglect, or default which results in death.

Potter v. Firestone Tire and Rubber Co.

(Contaminated Family) v. (Toxic Waste Dumpers)

6 Cal.4th 965, 25 Cal.Rptr.2d 550, 863 P.2d 795 (1993)

IF A TOXIC EXPOSURE PLAINTIFF PLEADS AND PROVES THAT THE DEFENDANT'S CONDUCT AMOUNTS TO "OPPRESSION, FRAUD, OR MALICE," THE PLAINTIFF NEED NOT MEET THE "MORE LIKELY THAN NOT" THRESHOLD FOR HIS FEAR OF CANCER CLAIM

■ **INSTANT FACTS** The Potters (P) sued Firestone (D) after toxic chemicals from the plant were dumped in a landfill and then leached into the drinking water.

■ **BLACK LETTER RULE** A toxic exposure plaintiff need not meet the more likely than not threshold for fear of cancer recovery in a negligence action if the plaintiff pleads and proves that the defendant's conduct in causing the exposure amounts to oppression, fraud, or malice, which authorizes the imposition of punitive damages.

■ PROCEDURAL BASIS

Appeal from the court of appeal's affirmance of the trial court's award for the plaintiffs.

■ FACTS

Firestone (D) contracted for disposal of industrial wastes produced by its tire manufacturing plant in a Class II sanitary landfill operated by the City. Class II landfills prohibit disposal of toxic substances because of the danger that they will leach into the groundwater. Firestone (D) assured the city that no such waste would be sent to the landfill. Official plant policy required proper disposal of hazardous wastes in a Class I landfill, however that program was costly. When a new production manager came to Firestone (D) to make the plant more profitable, he became angered at the costs of the hazardous waste disposal program [why do things the *right* way when you can do it the *cheap* way instead?]. As a result, Firestone's (D) hazardous waste materials, including serious toxins, were deposited in the landfill. The Potters (P), who lived near the landfill, discovered that toxic chemicals had contaminated their domestic water wells. At least two of the chemicals are known human carcinogens and others are strong suspects. The Potters (P) sued Firestone (D) on theories that included negligent infliction of emotional distress. The trial court awarded $269,500 for psychiatric illnesses and the cost of treating them, $142,975 for the cost of medical monitoring of the Potters (P), and punitive damages of $2.6 million.

■ ISSUE

Does a toxic exposure plaintiff need to meet the more likely than not threshold for fear of cancer recovery in a negligence action?

■ DECISION AND RATIONALE

(Baxter, J.) No. The physical injury requirement is a hopelessly imprecise screening device and, as such, the absence of a present physical injury does not preclude recovery for emotional distress engendered by fear of cancer. We next consider whether recovery of damages for emotional distress caused by fear of cancer should depend upon a showing that the Potter's

(P) fears stem from a knowledge that there is a probable likelihood of developing cancer in the future due to the toxic exposure. This is a matter of hot debate among the parties and amici curiae. We would be very hard pressed to find that, as a matter of law, a plaintiff faced with a 20 to 30 percent chance of developing cancer cannot genuinely, seriously and reasonably fear the prospect of cancer. Nonetheless, we conclude, for public policy reasons, that emotional distress caused by the fear of a cancer that is not probable should generally not be compensable in a negligence action. One concern weighing in favor of a more likely than not threshold is the unduly detrimental impact that unrestricted fear liability would have in the health care field. As amicus curiae California Medical Association points out, access to prescription drugs is likely to be impeded by allowing recovery of fear of cancer damages in negligence cases without the imposition of a heightened threshold. Another policy concern to consider is that allowing recovery to all victims who have a fear of cancer may work to the detriment of those who sustain actual injury and those who ultimately develop cancer as a result of toxic exposure. That is, to allow compensation to all plaintiffs with objectively reasonable cancer fears, even where the threatened cancer is not probable, raises the very significant concern that defendants and their insurers will be unable to ensure adequate compensation for those victims who actually develop cancer or other physical injuries. Another reason in support of the imposition of a more likely than not limitation is to establish a sufficiently definite and predictable threshold for recovery to permit consistent application from case to case. Finally, while a more likely than not limitation may foreclose compensation to many persons with genuine and objectively reasonable fears, it is sometimes necessary to limit the class of potential plaintiffs if emotional injury absent physical harm is to continue to be a recoverable item of damages in a negligence action. Policy considerations aside, we hold that a toxic exposure plaintiff need not meet the more likely than not threshold for fear of cancer recovery in a negligence action if the plaintiff pleads and proves that the defendant's conduct in causing the exposure amounts to oppression, fraud, or malice, which authorizes the imposition of punitive damages. Thus, for instance, fear of cancer damages may be recovered without demonstrating that cancer is probable where it is shown that the defendant is guilty of despicable conduct which is carried on with a willful and conscious disregard of the rights or safety of others. In our opinion, Firestone's (D) conduct brings this case within the "oppression, fraud or malice" exception for recovery of fear of cancer damages. [The Court remanded for reconsideration but not necessarily denial of punitive damages. It approved the award of medical monitoring costs without regard to whether future cancer was more likely than not.]

Analysis:

A carcinogenic or other toxic ingestion or exposure, without more, does not provide a basis for fearing future physical injury or illness. The fact that one is aware that he or she has ingested or been otherwise exposed to a carcinogen or other toxin, without any regard to the nature, magnitude, and proportion of the exposure or its likely consequences, provides no meaningful basis upon which to evaluate the reasonableness of one's fear. Proliferation of fear of cancer claims in the absence of meaningful restrictions might compromise the availability and affordability of liability insurance for toxic liability risks. Unless meaningful restrictions are placed on this potential plaintiff class, the threat of numerous large, adverse monetary awards, coupled with the added cost of insuring against such liability (assuming insurance would be available), could diminish the availability of new, beneficial prescription drugs or increase their price beyond the reach of those who need them most. The general rule that the court announces requires a plaintiff to do more than simply establish knowledge of a toxic ingestion or exposure and a significant increased risk of cancer. The plaintiff must further show that based upon reliable medical or scientific opinion, the plaintiff harbors a serious fear that the toxic ingestion or exposure was of such magnitude and proportion as to likely result in the feared cancer.

■ CASE VOCABULARY

AMICUS CURIAE: A friend of the court; one who gives information to the court on some matter of law which is in doubt.

CARCINOGEN: A cancer-causing agent.

MORE LIKELY THAN NOT THRESHOLD: A greater than fifty percent likelihood of the event occurring.

OPPRESSION, FRAUD, OR MALICE: Intentional deception resulting in injury to another.

TOXIC EXPOSURE PLAINTIFF: A plaintiff who was exposed to toxic substances as the result of the defendant's wrongful conduct.

CHAPTER TWENTY

Prenatal Harms

Remy v. MacDonald

Instant Facts: Remy (P) sued her mother, MacDonald (D), for injuries sustained when MacDonald's (D) negligent operation of an automobile caused her premature birth.

Black Letter Rule: A mother is not liable for her child's prenatal injuries caused by the mother's negligence.

Shull v. Reid

Instant Facts: Parents sued their physician for failure to diagnose CMV in the mother during her pregnancy, and the resulting impact on the child born with and severely affected by CMV.

Black Letter Rule: When medical malpractice results in the birth of a handicapped child, damages are recoverable for the *extraordinary* costs of raising the child to the age of majority or throughout the period of the child's life expectancy, if shorter, but the ordinary costs of raising a healthy child, emotional distress damages, and loss of consortium damages are not recoverable.

Remy v. MacDonald

(Infant) v. (Mother)

440 Mass. 675, 801 N.E.2d 260 (2004)

A MOTHER IS NOT LIABLE FOR HER BABY'S PRENATAL INJURIES

■ **INSTANT FACTS** Remy (P) sued her mother, MacDonald (D), for injuries sustained when MacDonald's (D) negligent operation of an automobile caused her premature birth.

■ **BLACK LETTER RULE** A mother is not liable for her child's prenatal injuries caused by the mother's negligence.

■ PROCEDURAL BASIS

On appeal to review a trial court grant of summary judgment for the defendant.

■ FACTS

MacDonald (D) was thirty-two weeks pregnant when she negligently caused a two-car accident. As a result, Remy (P) was born prematurely and suffered permanent breathing difficulties. Remy (P) sued her mother for her injuries, but a trial court granted MacDonald (D) summary judgment.

■ ISSUE

May a child, born alive, maintain a cause of action in tort against her mother for personal injuries sustained before birth because of the mother's negligence?

■ DECISION AND RATIONALE

(Greaney, J.) No. In order for Remy (P) to succeed on her negligence claims, she must establish MacDonald's (D) legal duty of care. While MacDonald (D) always has a duty to exercise reasonable care to avoid injury to others, the imposition of a precautionary duty upon a mother to her unborn child is "unadvisable or unworkable." During gestation, many personal choices, both dangerous and nondangerous, may risk harm to an unborn fetus, including exposure to chemicals, participation in sports, consumption of medication, or the refusal to take recommended medication. Recognizing a duty to one's unborn child would require courts to analyze the degree of a mother's knowledge of her pregnancy to determine when the duty arises, and to scrutinize the reasonableness of the mother's actions, many of which would be incidents of normal life. The recognition of this duty would threaten to place the unborn fetus's rights ahead of the mother's rights, and no established social policy exists to justify such a duty. While Remy (P) could recover from a third-party for her prenatal injuries, the unique relationship between a mother and her unborn child presents special circumstances that militate against the mother's liability. Accordingly, "there are inherent and important differences between a fetus, in utero, and a child already born, that permits a bright line to be drawn around the zone of potential tort liability of one who is still biologically joined to an injured plaintiff." Affirmed.

Analysis:

The court's denial of prenatal liability against a mother seems to naturally flow from the Supreme Court's 1973 decision in *Roe v. Wade*. Underpinning the court's reasoning is the threat that prenatal liability will have on the mother's rights in light of the rights of her unborn fetus. If the mother owed her unborn child a duty to reasonably protect her from injury, one may argue that abortion, while not criminally sanctionable, would give rise to negligence claims against the mother. Such a result would clearly conflict with the Court's decision in *Roe v. Wade*.

Shull v. Reid

(Parents) v. (Physician)

258 P.3d 521 (Okla. 2011)

THE COURT RECOGNIZES A WRONGFUL BIRTH CASE HERE, BUT A LATER-ENACTED STATUTE WOULD HAVE CHANGED THAT RESULT

■ **INSTANT FACTS** Parents sued their physician for failure to diagnose CMV in the mother during her pregnancy, and the resulting impact on the child born with and severely affected by CMV.

■ **BLACK LETTER RULE** When medical malpractice results in the birth of a handicapped child, damages are recoverable for the *extraordinary* costs of raising the child to the age of majority or throughout the period of the child's life expectancy, if shorter, but the ordinary costs of raising a healthy child, emotional distress damages, and loss of consortium damages are not recoverable.

■ PROCEDURAL BASIS

State supreme court review of a trial court decision granting partial summary judgment in the defendants' favor.

■ FACTS

The Shulls (P) sued Reid (D) for medical malpractice for failing to diagnose Cytomegalovirus during Mrs. Shulls' (P) pregnancy and inform them of the risks to their unborn child. The Shulls (P) alleged that had they known of the risk that their child would be born with the CMV infection, rendering him permanently and completely helpless, they would have terminated the pregnancy. The defendants moved for partial summary judgment, alleging that the only damages recoverable were for the cost of continuing the pregnancy, minus the cost of terminating the pregnancy. The trial court granted the motion.

■ ISSUE

Were the damages in this wrongful birth case limited to the cost of continuing the pregnancy, minus the cost of terminating the pregnancy?

■ DECISION AND RATIONALE

(Combs, J.) No. When medical malpractice results in the birth of a handicapped child, damages are recoverable for the *extraordinary* costs of raising the child to the age of majority or throughout the period of the child's life expectancy, if shorter, but the ordinary costs of raising a healthy child, emotional distress damages, and loss of consortium damages are not recoverable. We first addressed the question of wrongful conception in *Morris v. Sanchez*, where we found that the birth of a healthy child does not constitute a legal harm for which damages are recoverable. Next, we considered the case of *Goforth v. Porter Medical Associates*, in which we again found that the birth of a normal child is not a compensable injury. However, we also explained in *Goforth* that the *Morris* decision cannot be interpreted as precluding claims for other forms of damages that might arise out of the negligent performance of sterilization procedures. In reaching that decision, we relied on a Kansas case, and once again we turn to a Kansas case for guidance. In *Arche v. United States*, the Kansas court held that in a case for the wrongful birth of a handicapped child, the damages recoverable include those costs associated with the handicap, but not those that the parents would have incurred in raising a healthy child. Moreover, emotional damages were not allowable, because the parents were not aware of the injury at the time it occurred, and there was no reason to distinguish a wrongful birth case from other tort cases in this regard. Lastly, the damages recoverable were limited to the period of time of the child's life expectancy or to the age of majority, whichever was shorter.

We hold that in a wrongful birth action alleging medical malpractice, the measure of damages allowable includes the extraordinary medical expenses and other pecuniary losses caused by the defendant's negligence. There is no cause of action for emotional distress, because the injury occurred without human fault during development of the fetus and the parents were unaware of the injury at the time. Loss of consortium is also not allowable, because Oklahoma law does not provide for this type of damage in the instant case. Finally, recovery may be had only for the extraordinary expenses, not the normal and foreseeable coasts of raising a healthy child for the period of the child's life expectancy or until the child reaches the age of majority, whichever is shorter. Reversed and remanded.

Analysis:

After the child in this case was born, the Oklahoma legislature passed a law recognizing wrongful birth actions but not allowing parents to seek economic or noneconomic damages because of a condition that existed at the time of the child's birth, based on a claim that the defendant's act or omission contributed to the mother not terminating the pregnancy. Because the statute was passed after the birth of the child in the *Shull* case, it did not affect the court's holding here, nor would the court apply the statute to any other case arising prior to the statute's enactment in 2008.

■ CASE VOCABULARY

WRONGFUL BIRTH: A medical malpractice claim brought by the parents of a child born with defects, alleging that the defendant's negligence deprived them of the opportunity to avoid or terminate the pregnancy.

WRONGFUL CONCEPTION: A claim brought by parents for the negligently caused birth of their healthy child. In some cases, parents can recover damages directly associated with the pregnancy and the birth, including medical expenses and sometimes emotional distress damages, but most courts do not allow recovery for the cost of raising the child to the age of majority.

WRONGFUL LIFE: A tort action pertaining to childbirth, brought on the child's behalf. In a wrongful life action, the plaintiffs allege that the child would not have been born (or would not have been born with defects) if not for the negligent treatment or advice given by the defendant to one or both parents.

CHAPTER TWENTY-ONE

Wrongful Death and Survival Actions

Weigel v. Lee

Instant Facts: Adult children of the decedent sought damages for her wrongful death, including emotional distress and loss of consortium damages, and the trial court dismissed their claims.

Black Letter Rule: Compensable damages in wrongful death actions specifically include both economic and non-economic damages, the latter of which include mental anguish, emotional distress, and loss of consortium damages.

Weigel v. Lee

(Adult Children of Decedent) v. (Physician)

752 N.W.2d 618 (N.D. 2008)

ADULT CHILDREN MAY RECOVER FOR THEIR PARENTS' WRONGFUL DEATH

■ **INSTANT FACTS** Adult children of the decedent sought damages for her wrongful death, including emotional distress and loss of consortium damages, and the trial court dismissed their claims.

■ **BLACK LETTER RULE** Compensable damages in wrongful death actions specifically include both economic and non-economic damages, the latter of which include mental anguish, emotional distress, and loss of consortium damages.

■ PROCEDURAL BASIS

State supreme court review of a trial court decision dismissing the plaintiffs' claims.

■ FACTS

Rogers died shortly after being admitted to a regular hospital room despite being critically ill. Her adult children sued Dr. Lee (D) and the hospital under North Dakota's wrongful death statute, seeking damages for emotional distress and loss of consortium. The trial court dismissed the case, ruling that adult children do not have a claim for their own emotional distress or loss of their parent's consortium. The court concluded that the kids could only sue for the distress their mother suffered before her death. The plaintiffs appealed.

■ ISSUE

Do adult children have a claim for loss of their parent's consortium and their own emotional distress upon the death of a parent?

■ DECISION AND RATIONALE

(Crothers, J.) Yes. Compensable damages in wrongful death actions specifically include both economic and non-economic damages, the latter of which include mental anguish, emotional distress, and loss of consortium damages. The trial court confused three types of actions here: loss of consortium claims arising out of personal injury actions, survival actions, and wrongful death actions. Although this court has held that children are unable to recover for loss of consortium arising out of personal injury to a parent, that holding should not be construed to prohibit recovery where a parent dies and recovery is allowed under the Wrongful Death Act. North Dakota law also allows for survival actions. A survival action is the continuation of an injured person's claim for personal injury damages after the person dies from those injuries. Although the Weigels (P) could have sought such damages here, they have not.

The Weigels (P) base their claim on and seek recovery under the Wrongful Death Act. Wrongful death actions are intended to compensate the survivors of the deceased for the losses they sustained as a result of a wrongful killing. Persons entitled to recover damages under the Act should not be confused with persons authorized to bring the action in the first place. Those authorized to bring such claims include the decedent's heirs at law, but they bring the claim in a representative capacity for the benefit of the persons entitled to recover. The Wrongful Death Act thus differentiates between the capacity to bring an action and the right to recover damages. Surviving children are eligible to bring an action under the Act if the decedent had no eligible spouse or if the spouse fails to bring a timely action after the children make a demand, but this issue is separate from the children's ability to recover damages. Because the Wrongful Death Act does not exclude the decedent's children from recovering damages thereunder, and because the damages requested are permitted, the Weigels' (P) claim should not have been dismissed. Reversed and remanded.

Analysis:

Loss of consortium damages are often sought in cases involving the death or injury of a person's spouse. Originally, only a husband could sue for loss of his wife's consortium, but in 1950, nearly a century after the enactment of the married women's property acts, a wife's action for negligent impairment of consortium was first recognized. Today nearly every jurisdiction recognizes both a husband's and a wife's right to sue for loss of consortium. As this case shows, damages for the loss of a parent's or a child's consortium are now available as well.

■ CASE VOCABULARY

EMOTIONAL DISTRESS: A highly unpleasant mental reaction (such as anguish, grief, fright, humiliation, or fury) that results from another person's conduct; emotional pain and suffering. Emotional distress, when severe enough, can form a basis for the recovery of tort damages.

LOSS OF CONSORTIUM: A loss of the benefits that one spouse is entitled to receive from the other, including companionship, cooperation, aid, affection, and sexual relations; a similar loss of benefits that one is entitled to receive from a parent or child.

SURVIVAL ACTION: A lawsuit brought on behalf of a decedent's estate for injuries or damages incurred by the decedent immediately before dying. A survival action derives from the claim that a decedent would have had—such as for pain and suffering—if he or she had survived. In contrast is a claim that the beneficiaries may have in a wrongful-death action, such as for loss of consortium or loss of support from the decedent.

WRONGFUL DEATH ACTION: A lawsuit brought on behalf of a decedent's survivors for their damages resulting from a tortious injury that caused the decedent's death.

CHAPTER TWENTY-TWO

Vicarious Liability

Hinman v. Westinghouse Electric Co.

Instant Facts: The defendant was sued after one of its employees, who was driving home from work, ran over a policeman and permanently injured him.

Black Letter Rule: Where the employer and employee have made the travel time part of the working day by their contract, and the employee is using the time for the designated purpose of returning home, the doctrine of respondeat superior is applicable.

Edgewater Motels, Inc. v. Gatzke

Instant Facts: Gatzke (D) negligently started a fire in his hotel room after smoking a cigarette while he filled out his expense account during a business trip.

Black Letter Rule: The smoking of a cigarette, if done while engaged in the business of the employer, is within the employee's scope of employment because it is a minor deviation from the employee's work-related activities, and thus merely an act done incidental to general employment.

Mavrikidis v. Petullo

Instant Facts: The Petullos (D) were performing asphalt work for Clar Pine Servicecenter (D) when Gerald Petullo lost control of his dump truck at an intersection and a load of hot asphalt was dumped on the plaintiff; the jury found Clar Pine (D) vicariously liable for Gerald's (D) negligence and Clar Pine (D) appealed.

Black Letter Rule: Ordinarily, when a person engages a contractor, who conducts an independent business by means of his own employees, to do work not in itself a nuisance, he is not liable for the negligent acts of the contractor in the performance of the contract.

Pusey v. Bator

Instant Facts: Pusey was shot and killed by Bator (D), a security guard assigned to protect private property.

Black Letter Rule: An employer remains liable for injuries caused by its independent contractors when the employer is under a nondelegable duty to take special precautions to prevent a peculiar risk of harm to others.

O'Banner v. McDonald's Corp.

Instant Facts: A man sued a McDonald's restaurant after he slipped and fell in the restroom and injured himself.

Black Letter Rule: In order to recover on an apparent agency theory, a plaintiff would have to show that he actually did rely on the apparent agency in going to the establishment where he was allegedly injured.

Hinman v. Westinghouse Electric Co.

(Run-over Policeman) v. (Crazy Driver's Boss)

2 Cal.3d 956, 88 Cal.Rptr. 188, 471 P.2d 988 (1970)

AN EMPLOYER, HAVING FOUND IT IN THE INTERESTS OF HIS ENTERPRISE TO PAY FOR TRAVEL EXPENSES AND TO GO BEYOND THE NORMAL LABOR MARKET, SHOULD BE REQUIRED TO PAY FOR THE RISKS INHERENT IN HIS DECISION

■ **INSTANT FACTS** The defendant was sued after one of its employees, who was driving home from work, ran over a policeman and permanently injured him.

■ **BLACK LETTER RULE** Where the employer and employee have made the travel time part of the working day by their contract, and the employee is using the time for the designated purpose of returning home, the doctrine of respondeat superior is applicable.

■ FACTS

Herman was employed by Westinghouse Electric Co. (D) as an elevator constructor's helper. His work was assigned from the Westinghouse (D) office and he did not go to the office before or after work; instead he went from home directly to the job site and after work returned home from the job site. For this particular job, Herman received an hour and a half per day as his round-trip travel time and $1.30 for his travel expense. Westinghouse (D) had no control over the method or route of transportation used by Herman. One day, Hinman (P), a Los Angeles policeman, was standing on the center divider of a freeway inspecting a possible road hazard when he was struck by a car driven by Herman. As a result of the accident, Hinman (P) received permanent injuries. The city paid his medical expenses and disability pension. The trial judge refused instructions that Herman was acting within the scope of his employment at the time of the accident and instead instructed the jury that whether he was acting within the scope of his employment depended upon a number of factors including among others "whether his conduct was authorized by his employer, either expressly or impliedly; the nature of the employment, its object and the duties imposed thereby; whether the employee was acting in his discharge thereof; whether his conduct occurred during the performance of services for the employer, either directly or indirectly, or of himself; whether his conduct, even though not expressly or impliedly authorized, was an incidental event connected with his assigned work." Following these instructions, the jury found that Herman was not within the scope of his employment and hence gave a verdict for Westinghouse (D).

■ ISSUE

Is the doctrine of respondeat superior applicable in situations where the employer and employee have made the travel time part of the working day by their contract, and the employee is using the time for the designated purpose of returning home?

■ DECISION AND RATIONALE

(Peters, J.) Yes. Liability of the employer may not be avoided on the basis of the "going and coming" rule. Under the "going and coming" rule, an employee going to and from work is ordinarily considered outside the scope of employment so that the employer is not liable for his torts. The "going and coming" rule is sometimes ascribed to the theory that the employment relationship is "suspended" from the time the employee leaves until he returns or that in commuting he is not rendering service to his employer. Nevertheless, there are exceptions to this rule. Exceptions will be made to the "going and coming" rule where the trip involves an incidental benefit to the employer, not common to commute trips by ordinary members of the work force. Prior case law also indicate that the fact that the employee receives personal benefits is not determinative when there is also a benefit to the employer. There is a substantial benefit to an employer in one area to be permitted to reach out to a labor market in another area or to enlarge the available labor market by providing travel expenses and payment for travel time. It cannot be denied that the employer's reaching out to distant or larger labor markets increases the risk of injury in transportation. In other words, the employer, having found it desirable in the interests of his enterprise to pay for travel time and for travel expenses and to go beyond the normal labor market or to have located his enterprise at a place remote from the labor market, should be required to pay for the risks inherent in his decision. We are satisfied that, where, as here, the employer and employee have made the travel time part of the working day by their contract, the employer should be treated as such during the travel time, and it follows that so long as the employee is using the time for the designated purpose, to return home, the doctrine of respondeat superior is applicable. We conclude that as a matter of law the doctrine is applicable and that the trial court erred in its instructions in leaving the issue as one of fact to the jury.

Analysis:

Earlier authorities sought to justify the respondeat superior doctrine on such theories as "control" by the master of the servant, the master's "privilege" in being permitted to employ another, the third party's innocence in comparison to the master's selection of the servant, or the master's "deep pocket" to pay for the loss. The modern justification for vicarious liability, however, is a rule of policy, a deliberate allocation of a risk. The losses caused by the torts of employees, which as a practical matter are sure to occur in the conduct of the employer's enterprise, are placed upon that enterprise itself, as a required cost of doing business. The employer is better able to absorb these potential losses, and distribute them, through prices, rates, or liability insurance, to the public. As such, the losses are shifted to society and to the community at large.

■ CASE VOCABULARY

EXPRESS AUTHORIZATION: Authorization which has been made known explicitly and in declared terms.

"GOING AND COMING" RULE: An employee going to and from work is ordinarily considered outside the scope of employment such that his employer is not liable for his torts.

IMPLIED AUTHORIZATION: Authorization which is determined by deduction or inference from known facts and circumstances.

RESPONDEAT SUPERIOR: This doctrine stands for the proposition that when an employer is acting through the facility of an employee or agent, and tort liability is incurred during the course of this agency due to some fault of the employee, then the employer must accept the responsibility.

VICARIOUS LIABILITY: The imputation of liability upon one person for the actions of another.

Edgewater Motels, Inc. v. Gatzke

(Fire-Damaged Motel) v. (Fire-Starting Motel Guest)

277 N.W.2d 11 (Minn.1979)

NO HARD AND FAST RULE CAN BE APPLIED TO RESOLVE THE "SCOPE OF EMPLOYMENT" INQUIRY; RATHER, EACH CASE MUST BE DECIDED ON ITS OWN INDIVIDUAL FACTS

■ **INSTANT FACTS** Gatzke (D) negligently started a fire in his hotel room after smoking a cigarette while he filled out his expense account during a business trip.

■ **BLACK LETTER RULE** The smoking of a cigarette, if done while engaged in the business of the employer, is within the employee's scope of employment because it is a minor deviation from the employee's work-related activities, and thus merely an act done incidental to general employment.

■ PROCEDURAL BASIS

Appeal from the trial judge's judgment N.O.V. for the defendant.

■ FACTS

Gatzke (D), a district manager for Walgreen's (D), stayed in the Edgewater Motel (P) while he was in Minnesota supervising the opening of a Walgreen-owned restaurant. Gatzke (D) lived at the Edgewater (P) at the company's expense. He was allowed to call home at company expense, and his laundry, living expenses, and entertainment were all items of reimbursement. There were no constraints as to where he would perform his duties or at what time of day they would be performed. Near midnight one night, Gatzke (D) left work with others on the job. Gatzke (D) and Hubbard went to a restaurant to have a drink. Over the course of an hour, Gatzke (D) consumed a total of four brandy Manhattans, three of which were "doubles." [rough day?] Gatzke (D) and Hubbard spent part of the time discussing the operation of the newly opened restaurant. Gatzke (D) also spoke to the bartender about the mixing and pricing of drinks, as he was interested in learning the bar business because the new Walgreen (D) restaurant served liquor. Around 1:30 a.m., Gatzke (D) and Hubbard walked back to the Edgewater Motel (P). Gatzke (D) apparently looked and acted sober at that time. He went straight to his room, and then "probably" sat down at a desk to fill out his expense account, as was his habit. While Gatzke (D) completed the expense account he "probably" smoked a cigarette. The record indicates Gatzke (D) smoked about two packs of cigarettes per day. A maid testified that the ash trays in Gatzke's (D) room would generally be full of cigarette butts and ashes when she cleaned the room. She also noticed that at times the plastic wastebasket next to the desk contained cigarette butts [now *that's* safe!]. After filling out the expense form, Gatzke (D) went to bed. A fire broke out soon thereafter [surprise!]; Gatzke (D) escaped the burning room, but the fire spread rapidly and caused $330,360 in damages to the motel. Dr. Anderson, a fire reconstruction specialist, testified that the fire started in, or next to, the plastic wastebasket located to the side of the desk in Gatzke's (D) room. He also stated that the fire was caused by a burning cigarette or match. After the fire, the plastic wastebasket was a melted to a "blob." Dr. Anderson stated that x-ray examination of the remains of the basket disclosed the presence of cigarette filters and paper matches. The jury found Gatzke (D) to be guilty of 60% of the negligence and the motel guilty of the remainder. It also found Walgreen (D) liable for Gatzke (D). The trial judge concluded, however, that Gatzke (D) was not within the scope of his employment, and rendered judgment N.O.V. for Walgreen's.

■ ISSUE

Can an employee's smoking of a cigarette constitute conduct within his scope of employment?

■ DECISION AND RATIONALE

(Scott, J.) Yes. The question of whether smoking can be within an employee's scope of employment is a close one, but after careful consideration of the issue we are persuaded by the reasoning of the courts which hold that smoking can be an act within an employee's scope of employment. It seems only logical to conclude that an employee does not abandon his employment as a matter of law while temporarily acting for his personal comfort when such activities involve only slight deviations from work that are reasonable under the circumstances, such as eating, drinking, or smoking. We hereby hold that an employer can be held vicariously liable for his employee's negligent smoking of a cigarette if he was otherwise acting in the scope of his employment at the time of the negligent act. The record contains a reasonable basis from which a jury could find that Gatzke (D) was involved in serving his employer's interests at the time he was at the bar. More importantly, even assuming that Gatzke (D) was outside the scope of his employment while he was at the bar, there is evidence from which a jury could reasonably find that Gatzke (D) resumed his employment activities after he returned to his motel room and filled out his expense account form. The expense account was, of course, completed so that Gatzke (D) could be reimbursed by Walgreens for his work-related expenses. The filling out of the expense form can be viewed as serving a dual purpose; that of furthering Gatzke's (D) personal interests and promoting his employer's business purposes. Accordingly, it is reasonable for the jury to find that the completion of the expense account is an act done in furtherance of the employer's business purposes. Additionally, the record indicates that Gatzke (D) was an executive type of employee who had no set working hours. It was therefore reasonable for the jury to determine that the filling out of his expense account was done within authorized time and space limits of his employment. In light of the above, we hold that it was reasonable for the jury to find that Gatzke (D) was acting within the scope of his employment when he completed his expense account. Accordingly, we set aside the trial court's grant of judgment for Walgreens and reinstate the jury's determination that Gatzke (D) was working within the scope of his employment at the time of his negligent act.

Analysis:

To support a finding that an employee's negligent act occurred within his scope of employment, it must be shown that his conduct was, to some degree, in furtherance of the interests of his employer. Other factors to be considered in the scope-of-employment determination are whether the conduct is of the kind that the employee is authorized to perform and whether the act occurs substantially within authorized time and space restrictions. No hard and fast rule can be applied to resolve the inquiry. Each case must be decided on its own individual facts. The initial question raised by this factual situation is whether an employee's smoking of a cigarette can constitute conduct within his scope of employment. A number of courts have ruled that the act of smoking, even when done simultaneously with work-related activity, is not within the employee's scope of employment because it is a matter personal to the employee that is not done in furtherance of the employer's interest. Other courts have reasoned that the smoking of a cigarette, if done while engaged in the business of the employer, is within an employee's scope of employment because it is a minor deviation from the employee's work-related activities, and thus merely an act done incidental to general employment. This was the view this Court adopted.

■ CASE VOCABULARY

ISSUE OF FIRST IMPRESSION: Refers to the first time a question of law is considered for determination by a court.

JUDGMENT N.O.V.: Literally: notwithstanding the verdict. A judgment which reverses the determination of the jury, and is granted when a judge determines that the jury verdict had no reasonable support in fact or was contrary to law.

NEGLIGENCE: Failure to exercise that degree of care which a reasonable person would exercise under the same circumstances.

REASONABLE PERSON: A hypothetical person who exercises those qualities of attention, knowledge, intelligence and judgment which society requires of its members for the protection of their own interest and the interests of others.

SCOPE OF EMPLOYMENT: An act of a servant done with the intention to perform it as a part of or incident to a service on account of which he is employed.

Mavrikidis v. Petullo

(Accident Victim) v. (Asphalt Contractor)

707 A.2d 977 (N.J. 1998)

WHEN THE CONTRACTEE HAS LITTLE INPUT INTO HOW ITS CONTRACTOR'S WORK IS DONE, IT IS NOT AN EMPLOYER

■ **INSTANT FACTS** The Petullos (D) were performing asphalt work for Clar Pine Servicecenter (D) when Gerald Petullo lost control of his dump truck at an intersection and a load of hot asphalt was dumped on the plaintiff; the jury found Clar Pine (D) vicariously liable for Gerald's (D) negligence and Clar Pine (D) appealed.

■ **BLACK LETTER RULE** Ordinarily, when a person engages a contractor, who conducts an independent business by means of his own employees, to do work not in itself a nuisance, he is not liable for the negligent acts of the contractor in the performance of the contract.

■ PROCEDURAL BASIS

State appellate court review of a trial court decision finding Newark Asphalt (D) vicariously liable for the negligence of the Petullos (D).

■ FACTS

Gerald Petullo (D) drove a dump truck owned by Petullo Brothers, Inc. (D) through a red light and hit Mavrikidis's (P) car. The truck overturned and spilled its load of hot asphalt on Mavrikidis (P). Her injuries, including burns over twenty-one percent of her body, were severe. At the time, Petullo's (D) father, Angelo (D), and Petullo Brother's, Inc. (D) had been hired to do concrete and asphalt work at the Clar Pine Servicecenter (D), a retail gasoline and automotive repair shop. Clar Pine's (D) owner, Pascarello, had limited involvement in the work, other than general supervision, periodic consultation, and paying for three loads of asphalt, including the one involved in the accident. He also directed the Petullos (D) where to lay the asphalt at the service center.

On the morning of the accident, the senior Petullo (D) had ordered twenty tons of asphalt from Newark Asphalt's (D) plant, which was loaded into the truck driven by his son. An expert testified that the truck was overloaded, and that if it had not been, Petullo (D) would have had better control over the vehicle. Mavrikidis (P) sued Angelo and Gerald Petullo (D), Petullo Brothers, Inc. (D), Clar Pine (D), and Newark Asphalt (D). The jury found that the younger Petullo (D) was acting as an agent of his father at the time of the accident, that he drove his truck negligently, that Clar Pine (D) maintained control over the manner and means of performing the inherently dangerous activity of transporting and installing the asphalt, and that Newark Asphalt (D) was negligent in overloading the truck. The jury also found that the Petullos (D) were independent contractors of Clar Pine (D) at the time of the accident, and that Clar Pine (D) was vicariously liable for their negligence. Accordingly, the court entered a judgment against Clar Pine (D) for eighty-nine percent of the damages (which included the seventeen percent attributable directly to Clar Pine, the twenty-four percent attributed to Angelo (D), and the forty-eight percent attributed to Gerald (D)). The remaining eleven percent of the damages was attributed to Newark Asphalt (D). Both of those defendants appealed.

■ ISSUE

Was Clar Pine (D) vicariously liable for the plaintiff's injuries?

■ DECISION AND RATIONALE

(Garibaldi, J.) Yes. Ordinarily, when a person engages a contractor, who conducts an independent business by means of his own employees, to do work not in itself a nuisance, he is not liable for the negligent acts of the contractor in the performance of the contract. It is clear that here the Petullos (D) were independent contractors rather than servants of Clar Pine (D). One who hires an independent contractor has no right of control over the manner in which the work is to be done; it is to be regarded as the contractor's own enterprise, and he, rather than the employer, is the proper party to be charged with the responsibility for preventing the risk. A servant, by contrast, is one who is employed to perform services in the affairs of another, whose physical conduct in the performance is controlled, or is subject to a right of control, by the other.

We must next determine whether this case falls within any exceptions to the general rule of non-liability of principals for the negligence of their independent contractors. There are three recognized exceptions, as set out in the *Majestic* case: (1) where the principal retains control of the manner and means of doing the work, (2) where he engages an incompetent contractor, and (3) where the activity contracted for is inherently dangerous. Under the first exception, supervisory acts performed by the contractee do not give rise to vicarious liability. Here, Pascarello's actions did not exceed the scope of general supervisory powers. Nor was there evidence that the Petullos (D) were unqualified to perform the work. Moreover, the inherently dangerous exception has no application where the injury was caused merely by negligent driving, which is an ordinary risk associated with the transport of materials. Judgment for the plaintiff affirmed, but the case is remanded for a determination of the liability percentages of the Petullos (D) and Newark Asphalt (D).

Analysis:

In determining whether a contractee maintains the right of control, several factors are considered: (1) the extent of control that, by the agreement, the master may exercise over the details of the work; (2) whether the one employed is engaged in a distinct occupation or business; (3) the skill required in that particular occupation; (4) whether the employee or the workman supplies the tools and place of work for the person doing the work; (5) the length of time for which the person is employed; (6) the method of payment (i.e., by time or by the job); (7) whether the work is part of the regular business of the employer; and (8) whether the parties believe they are creating the relationship of master and servant. In this case, the masonry and asphalt work required a skilled individual. Although Pascarello paid for three loads of asphalt, the Petullos (D) provided their own tools and the remainder of the materials. Their work did not involve the regular business of Clar Pine (D), and it spanned only the time it took to lay the asphalt and concrete. The Petullos (D) were independent contractors of Clar Pine (D).

■ CASE VOCABULARY

INDEPENDENT CONTRACTOR: One who undertakes a project for another while retaining control over the means and method by which he accomplishes his goal.

VICARIOUS LIABILITY: The liability of one person for the acts of another; indirect legal responsibility, e.g., the liability of an employer for the acts of its employee.

Pusey v. Bator

(Trespasser) v. (Armed Security Guard)

94 Ohio St.3d 275, 762 N.E.2d 968 (2002)

EMPLOYING ARMED SECURITY GUARDS IS INHERENTLY DANGEROUS

■ **INSTANT FACTS** Pusey was shot and killed by Bator (D), a security guard assigned to protect private property.

■ **BLACK LETTER RULE** An employer remains liable for injuries caused by its independent contractors when the employer is under a nondelegable duty to take special precautions to prevent a peculiar risk of harm to others.

■ PROCEDURAL BASIS

On appeal to review a decision of the Ohio Court of Appeals affirming a directed verdict for the defendant.

■ FACTS

Wilson, on behalf of Greif Brothers, entered into a contract with a security firm to provide uniformed security officers on Greif Brothers' property. The contract did not specify whether the guards were to be armed or unarmed, but upon learning that some of the guards were armed, Wilson never requested that the guards be unarmed. Bator (D) was one of the assigned guards. On the day in question, Bator (D) witnessed Pusey and another man walking through the Greif Brothers parking lot. He radioed another guard working at another location on the property, and then, unarmed, confronted the plaintiffs. After the plaintiffs became angry, Bator (D) returned to his station and retrieved a gun from his briefcase. When he showed the gun to the plaintiffs, Pusey made a quick movement and Bator (D) shot him. Pusey died at the hospital. Pusey's mother (P) sued Bator (D), the security firm, and Greif Brothers for wrongful death. After Bator (D) and the security firm settled, Grief Brothers moved for a directed verdict. The court granted the directed verdict, and the Ohio Court of Appeals affirmed.

■ ISSUE

Is the inappropriate use of a weapon by an armed security guard hired as an independent contractor inherently dangerous, such that an employer is liable for the negligence?

■ DECISION AND RATIONALE

(Douglas, J.) Yes. "[A]n employer is generally not liable for the negligent acts of an independent contractor." However, when the employer owes a nondelegable duty to others, such as when the employer's business involves inherently dangerous activities, the employer may remain liable. An employer's business is inherently dangerous when it creates a peculiar risk of harm to others unless special precautions are taken. To establish a nondelegable duty, the risk of harm must be foreseeable in advance due to the inherent nature of the work, such that special precautions must reasonably be taken.

The use of armed guards to protect private property is inherently dangerous. It is reasonably foreseeable that injuries to others may occur with the inappropriate use of a weapon unless special precautions are taken to avoid the risk of harm. The inappropriate use of a weapon is not a normal, routine matter of customary human activity, but instead presents a special danger arising out of the particular situation. Therefore, "when an employer hires an independent contractor to provide armed security guards to protect property, the inherently-dangerous-work exception is triggered such that if someone is injured by the weapon as a result of a guard's negligence, the employer is vicariously liable even though the guard responsible is an employee of the independent contractor." If the jury determines that Pusey's death was caused by Bator's (D) negligence, Greif Brothers is liable for the damages. Reversed and remanded.

Analysis:

The court's decision to establish armed security services as an inherently dangerous activity as a matter of law has troubled many commentators. While the risk that a trespasser may be shot by an armed security guard may be reasonably foreseeable, wouldn't it also be reasonable to assume that an armed security guard would take reasonable precautions in the discharge of his weapon?

■ CASE VOCABULARY

INDEPENDENT CONTRACTOR: One who is hired to undertake a specific project but who is left free to do the assigned work and to choose the method for accomplishing it.

INHERENTLY DANGEROUS: Requiring special precaution at all times to avoid injury; dangerous per se.

NONDELEGABLE DUTY: A duty that may be delegated to an independent contractor by a principal, who retains primary (as opposed to vicarious) responsibility if the duty is not properly performed.

VICARIOUS LIABILITY: Liability that a supervisory party (such as an employer) bears for the actionable conduct of a subordinate or associate (such as an employee) because of the relationship between the two parties.

O'Banner v. McDonald's Corp.

(Injured Patron) v. (Restaurant)

173 Ill.2d 208, 218 Ill.Dec. 910, 670 N.E.2d 632 (1996)

ACTUAL RELIANCE MUST BE ESTABLISHED IN ORDER TO RECOVER ON AN APPARENT AGENCY THEORY

■ **INSTANT FACTS** A man sued a McDonald's restaurant after he slipped and fell in the restroom and injured himself.

■ **BLACK LETTER RULE** In order to recover on an apparent agency theory, a plaintiff would have to show that he actually did rely on the apparent agency in going to the establishment where he was allegedly injured.

■ PROCEDURAL BASIS

Appeal from the Appellate Court's reversal of the circuit court's grant of summary judgment for the defendant.

■ FACTS

Reginald O'Banner (P) brought an action to recover damages for personal injuries he allegedly sustained when he slipped and fell in the bathroom of a McDonald's (D) restaurant. In his complaint, O'Banner (P) named as defendants McDonald's Corporation and certain "unknown owners." McDonald's (D) promptly moved for summary judgment on the grounds that the restaurant was actually owned by one of its franchisees and that it neither owned, operated, maintained, nor controlled the facility. The circuit court entered summary judgment in favor of McDonald's (D), and O'Banner (P) challenged this decision in the appellate court, theorizing that even though McDonald's (D) was a franchisor, it could nevertheless be held liable for the franchisee's negligence under principles of respondeat superior. O'Banner (P) argued that there was sufficient evidence in the record to establish that the franchisee served as McDonald's (D) actual agent. In the alternative, O'Banner (P) contended that McDonald's (D) could be vicariously liable for the acts and omissions of the franchisee based on the doctrine of apparent agency. The appellate court rejected the actual agency theory based on the documentary evidence, but held that there remained genuine issues of material fact with respect to O'Banner's (P) alternative theory of apparent agency. Accordingly, it reversed and remanded for further proceedings.

■ ISSUE

Did O'Banner (P) establish the required elements enabling him to recover on an apparent agency theory?

■ DECISION AND RATIONALE

(Harrison, J.) No. In this appeal before us, the issue of actual agency has not been pursued. The sole question before us is whether the appellate court erred in reversing and remanding based on the theory of apparent agency. In order to recover on an apparent agency theory, O'Banner (P) would have to show that he actually did rely on the apparent agency in going to the McDonald's (D) where he was allegedly injured. No amount of liberal construction can alter the fact that the record before us is devoid of anything remotely suggesting that the necessary reliance was present here. The pleadings and affidavit submitted by O'Banner (P) in the circuit court state only that he slipped and fell in the restroom of a McDonald's (D) restaurant. They give no indication as to why he went to the restaurant in the first place. The fact that this was a McDonald's may have been completely irrelevant to his decision. For all we know, O'Banner went there simply because it provided the closest bathroom when he needed one or because some friend asked to meet him there. If O'Banner (P) had any basis to support his position, he was obliged to present it to the circuit court. He did not do so, and the time for substantiating any claim of reliance has passed. The appellate court was therefore wrong to reverse the circuit court's entry of summary judgment in McDonald's (D) favor based upon the apparent agency doctrine. For the foregoing reasons, the judgment of the appellate court is reversed, the judgment of the circuit court is affirmed, and the cause is remanded to the circuit court for further proceedings consistent with this opinion. [A dissenting opinion is omitted].

Analysis:

Apparent agency, also known in some states as apparent authority, is based on principles of estoppel. The idea is that if a principal created the appearance that someone is his agent, he should not then be permitted to deny the agency if an innocent third party reasonably relies on the apparent agency and is harmed as a result. Under the doctrine, a principal can be held vicariously liable in tort for injury caused by the negligent acts of his apparent agent if the injury would not have occurred but for the injured party's justifiable reliance on the apparent agency. The fundamental obstacle to O'Banner's (P) recovery in this case concerns this element of reliance. Even if one concedes that McDonald's (D) advertising and other conduct could entice a person to enter McDonald's (D) restaurant in the belief it was dealing with an agent of the corporation itself, that is not sufficient. As the court stated, in order to recover on an apparent agency theory, O'Banner (P) would have had to show that he actually did rely on the apparent agency in going to the McDonald's (D) where he was allegedly injured.

■ CASE VOCABULARY

ACTUAL AGENCY DOCTRINE: A relation in which one person, the agent, acts on behalf of another with the express authority of the latter, the principal.

APPARENT AGENCY DOCTRINE: A doctrine involving the accountability of a principal for the acts of his agent which operates to make a principal liable for actions of the agent on behalf of the principal when a third person in good faith believes that such authority exists.

ESTOPPEL: A bar which precludes a person from denying the truth of a fact which has, in contemplation of law, become settled by the facts and proceedings of judicial or legislative officers, or by the act of the party himself, either by conventional writing, or by representations, expressed or implied.

RELIANCE: Dependence, confidence, trust, repose of mind upon what is deemed sufficient support or authority.

CHAPTER TWENTY-THREE

Common Law Strict Liability

Rylands v. Fletcher

Instant Facts: A mine owner brought a suit for damages against a neighboring mill operator for digging a mill pond, which first flooded abandoned mine shafts and then ultimately flooded the operating mine.

Black Letter Rule: A landowner is strictly liable for damage to adjoining land resulting from the un-natural or abnormal use of his land.

Dyer v. Maine Drilling & Blasting, Inc.

Instant Facts: Homeowners' sued a blasting company for damages to their home sustained as a result of a nearby bridge construction project, alleging strict liability; the court granted the defendant's motion for summary judgment and the plaintiffs appealed.

Black Letter Rule: One who carries on an abnormally dangerous activity is subject to liability for harm to the person, land, or chattels of another resulting from the activity, even if he has exercised the utmost care to prevent the harm.

Rylands v. Fletcher

(Mine Owner) v. (Pond Digger)

L.R. 3 H.L. 330 (House of Lords 1868)

A LANDOWNER WILL BE STRICTLY LIABLE FOR HARMS RESULTING FROM THE UNNATURAL OR ABNORMAL USE OF HIS LAND

■ **INSTANT FACTS** A mine owner brought a suit for damages against a neighboring mill operator for digging a mill pond, which first flooded abandoned mine shafts and then ultimately flooded the operating mine.

■ **BLACK LETTER RULE** A landowner is strictly liable for damage to adjoining land resulting from the unnatural or abnormal use of his land.

■ PROCEDURAL BASIS

Action for damages resulting from the flooding of a mine by a neighboring mill pond. The case was first considered by the Court of Exchequer, then reviewed by the Exchequer Camber and finally reviewed by the House of Lords.

■ FACTS

Rylands (P) operated a mine in Lancaster County in England. Fletcher (D) operated a mill nearby. Fletcher (D) engaged a contractor to dig a reservoir or mill pond to supply water for the operation of the mill. The contractors dug the pond over top of some old abandoned mine shafts. The mine shafts had been filled in, but inadequately, and looked just like solid earth. When the pond was filled with water, the weight of the water caused the filling in the shafts to break down and the shafts were flooded. They in turn led to other mine shafts in an intervening mine, which in turn led to mine shafts in Rylands' (P) mine. Rylands' (P) mine was flooded and damaged. He sought damages for the flooding. The case went before an arbitrator, then was considered by the Court of Exchequer, the Exchequer Chamber and ultimately ruled upon by the House of Lords. At each step, there were separate opinions, which are reflected in the Decision and Rationale Section.

■ ISSUE

Is a landowner liable regardless of fault for damages to another's land resulting from the landowner's unnatural or abnormal use of his own land? [We know the term should technically be "non-natural," but the case says "unnatural" so there it is.]

■ DECISION AND RATIONALE

(In the Court of Exchequer, Bramwell, B.) Yes. It does not matter that Fletcher (D) did not intend to cause the harm. It matters only that Fletcher (D) caused water to flow upon Rylands' (P) property and damage resulted. Such action may be considered either a trespass or a nuisance and liability should result.

(In the Court of Exchequer, Martin, B.) No. There was no trespass, as the damage was not the direct result of Fletcher's (D) activities. It was at most indirect and consequential. There was no nuisance, as nuisance can be understood to mean that the landowner has used his land in a way that was hurtful or injurious to the senses and the use has negatively impacted

his neighbors' ability to use their own land. The making of a pond is a lawful act and is not a nuisance to anyone. There should be no liability in this case.

(In the Exchequer Chamber, Blackburn, J.) Yes. We believe that Baron Bramwell was correct and that Rylands (P) is entitled to recover. The problem is that Fletcher (D) brought onto his property a substance that was harmless enough, but likely to do mischief if it escaped from his property. What is the liability of a landowner who acts in this manner? We believe he has an absolute duty to keep such a substance on his property at his own peril, rather than a duty to merely use all reasonable care to keep it bound within his property. A landowner is prima facie answerable for all damage that results from the escape of a substance upon his land which is likely to do mischief once it escapes. This is the settled law with respect to cattle owners. They keep their cattle at their own peril and are strictly liable for any damage done by an escaped animal, regardless of the precautions they have taken to prevent such an escape. We think the same principle should be applied to a landowner who brings upon his land any substance that will damage his neighbor's property if it escapes, like filth, water or stenches. A landowner is bound to use anything on his own land so that it does not hurt another. We are of the opinion that Rylands (P) is entitled to recover for his damages.

(In the House of Lords, Lord Cairns, L.C.) Yes. The principles upon which this case should be determined are simple. A landowner is entitled to put his land to any lawful, natural use. If, in doing so, an accumulation of water occurs naturally and escapes and causes damage to a neighbor, the landowner will not be liable. But if the accumulation of water or other substances is the result of the non-natural use of the land by the landowner, we are of the opinion that the landowner acts at his own peril.

(In the House of Lords, Lord Cranworth) Yes. The rule was correctly stated by Blackburn, J. in the lower opinion. The rule is if a person brings anything upon his land, which if it escapes is likely to cause damage to his neighbor, that person keeps the substance at his peril. If the substance does escape, regardless of the precautions the landowner took to prevent such an occurrence, the landowner will be strictly liable for the resulting damage.

Analysis:

The rule in *Rylands v. Fletcher* applied regardless of whether the substance involved was inherently dangerous and regardless of any fault or intention on the defendant's part. The basic concept was to compensate those who were injured by a landowner's inconsistent, uncommon, or unusual land use. One way of viewing *Rylands* is that it imposes strict liability on a landowner who brings upon the land something that wouldn't naturally be found there, if the substance escapes and damages another's property. An alternative way of viewing the rule in *Rylands* is that the landowner will be strictly liable for non-natural uses of his land, meaning uses that are inconsistent or abnormal in the surrounding area. Either way, it is clear that *Rylands* imposed strict liability for abnormal or non-natural land uses that caused damage to surrounding property. American courts tended at first to reject *Rylands* and adopt instead the negligence, fault based rules of *Brown v. Kendall*, but there has been a gradual shift to recognize strict liability for abnormally dangerous activities.

■ CASE VOCABULARY

ARBITRATOR: A neutral party chosen by the disputing parties or appointed by the court to hear the facts of the case and render a decision.

PRIMA FACIE: That which appears on the face of something, is presumed from the facts, or is evident at first sight.

Dyer v. Maine Drilling & Blasting, Inc.

(Homeowner) v. (Blasting Company)

984 A.2d 210 (Me. 2009)

BLASTING ACTIVITIES MAY GIVE RISE TO STRICT LIABILITY

■ **INSTANT FACTS** Homeowners' sued a blasting company for damages to their home sustained as a result of a nearby bridge construction project, alleging strict liability; the court granted the defendant's motion for summary judgment and the plaintiffs appealed.

■ **BLACK LETTER RULE** One who carries on an abnormally dangerous activity is subject to liability for harm to the person, land, or chattels of another resulting from the activity, even if he has exercised the utmost care to prevent the harm.

■ FACTS

The Dyers (P) sued Maine Drilling & Blasting (D) for damages to their home caused by nearby blasting performed by Maine Drilling (D) in conjunction with a bridge construction project. The Dyers (P) asserted causes of action in negligence and strict liability. The court granted the defendant's motion for summary judgment and the plaintiffs appealed.

■ ISSUE

Did the trial court properly grant summary judgment in the defendant's favor on the plaintiff's strict liability claim?

■ DECISION AND RATIONALE

(Silver, J.) No. One who carries on an abnormally dangerous activity is subject to liability for harm to the person, land, or chattels of another resulting from the activity, even if he has exercised the utmost care to prevent the harm. Strict liability is limited to the kind of harm, the possibility of which makes the activity abnormally dangerous. At least forty-one states have adopted some form of strict liability for blasting. A person who creates a substantial risk of severe harm to others while acting for his own gain should bear the costs of that activity. We adopt the strict liability approach and remand for a determination of whether the blasting activity in this case was abnormally dangerous. Even under a strict liability analysis, proof of a causal relationship between the blasting and the property damage is still required. We believe the Dyers (P) produced enough evidence on the issue of causation to survive summary judgment. Vacated and remanded.

Analysis:

Under the Restatement approach, adopted by the court here, the following factors are considered in determining whether an activity is abnormally dangerous: (1) the existence of a high degree of risk of some harm to the person, land, or chattels of another; (2) the likelihood that the harm that results will be great; (3) an inability to eliminate the risk by the exercise of reasonable care; (4) the extent to which the activity is not a matter of common usage; (7) the inappropriateness of the activity to the place where it is carried on; and (8) the extent to which its value to the community is outweighed by its dangerous attributes. In this case, the appellate court remanded to the trial court for a determination of whether Maine Drilling & Blasting's (D) activities that caused the plaintiffs' damages were abnormally dangerous.

■ CASE VOCABULARY

ABNORMALLY DANGEROUS: An activity that creates a risk of serious injury to the land or chattels of the plaintiff or to the plaintiff himself, when the risk cannot be eliminated through the exercise of due care and the particular activity is not generally performed in that particular physical area. A judge may determine an activity is abnormally dangerous and thus subject to strict liability.

STRICT LIABILITY: Legal doctrine imposing liability for injuries caused by the defendant's products or acts regardless of the degree of care exercised.

CHAPTER TWENTY-FOUR

Tort Liability for Defective Products

Moorman Manufacturing Co. v. National Tank Co.

Instant Facts: Moorman Manufacturing (P) seeks economic damages ten years after a steel grain storage tank it purchased from National Tank (D) developed a crack.

Black Letter Rule: Damages to a product, caused by a defect in quality and limited to economic losses, may be recovered under contract law theories, but not under the theory of strict tort liability.

Lee v. Crookston Coca-Cola Bottling Co.

Instant Facts: Lee (P) had a Coca-Cola bottle explode in her hand and now seeks damages for her injuries.

Black Letter Rule: A case may be submitted to the jury under both negligence and strict tort liability theories even though all of plaintiff's evidence is circumstantial.

Knitz v. Minster Machine Co.

Instant Facts: Knitz (P) was operating a press when it accidentally activated and severed two of her fingers.

Black Letter Rule: A product design is in a defective condition to the user or consumer if (1) it is more dangerous than an ordinary consumer would expect when used in an intended or reasonably foreseeable manner, or (2) if the benefits of the challenged design do not outweigh the risk inherent in such design.

Honda of America Mfg., Inc. v. Norman

Instant Facts: Karen Norman drowned when her vehicle became submerged in water and she was unable to free herself from the automatic seatbelt mechanism.

Black Letter Rule: Under the common law, to establish products liability, a claimant must prove that an economically and technologically feasible alternative design was available and would have prevented or significantly reduced the risk of death without substantially reducing the utility to the intended users of the product.

McCarthy v. Olin Corporation

Instant Facts: A man boarded a train and began shooting at passengers using a special ammunition specifically designed by its manufacturer to cause as much damage to the victim as possible. The victims are suing the manufacturer for defective design and other claims.

Black Letter Rule: When a product is dangerous by design, the mere fact someone is injured by it will not cause the manufacturer to be liable; there must be something wrong with the product that causes injury, and if nothing is wrong there will be no liability.

Liriano v. Hobart Corporation

Instant Facts: A supermarket worker, Liriano (P), was severely injured by a guardless meat grinder and now sues his employer and the manufacturer for his injuries.

Black Letter Rule: (1) Obvious hazards still require warnings because the warning not only notifies persons of the hazard, it also provides notice of less hazardous alternative ways of proceeding. (2) Cause-in-fact of a plaintiff's injury from an obviously hazardous product will be presumed from the plain fact that the injury occurred in the first place, leaving it to the defendant to rebut the cause-in-fact in order to keep the case from the jury.

Bowling v. Heil Co.

Instant Facts: Bowling (P) was killed when the box on a dump truck descended and crushed him while he was attempting to fix a glitch with the truck.

Black Letter Rule: The comparative fault or negligence of a party who sues a manufacturer for product liability under strict liability in tort shall not be considered in assessing liability or damages, but assumption of risk by the plaintiff is a complete defense.

Hughes v. Magic Chef, Inc.

Instant Facts: Vincent Hughes (P) was severely burned when a stove made by Magic Chef, Inc. exploded due to a buildup of propane gas inside the oven.

Black Letter Rule: (1) Assumption of risk is not to be treated as an affirmative defense when giving a jury instruction, rather it is subsumed by contributory negligence. (2) In instructing on the defense of misuse, the jury is to be instructed to consider the knowledge level of the ordinary user, not the plaintiff's level of knowledge.

Doomes v. Best Transit Corp.

Instant Facts: Injured bus passengers sued the bus manufacturer under state law for the lack of passenger seatbelts, and the bus manufacturer countered that the applicable federal regulation did not require passenger seatbelts.

Black Letter Rule: Under the Supremacy Clause of the United States Constitution, enforcement of a state law is preempted only if (1) the plain language of the federal statute on the subject expressly states that it preempts state law, (2) the federal legislation is so comprehensive that it is inferable the Congress wished to fully occupy the subject matter ("field preemption"), or (3) the state law conflicts with the federal law.

Newmark v. Gimbel's Inc.

Instant Facts: Mrs. Newmark (P) was given a permanent at one of Gimbel's (D) beauty shops. The solution used in giving the permanent caused Newmark's (P) scalp to blister and her hair to fall out.

Black Letter Rule: There is an implied warranty of fitness of the products a retail service provider uses in providing those services the same as if the customer had purchased the product themselves.

Moorman Manufacturing Co. v. National Tank Co.

(Tank Purchaser) v. (Tank Maker)

91 Ill.2d 69, 61 Ill.Dec. 746, 435 N.E.2d 443 (1982)

ECONOMIC DAMAGES TO A PRODUCT CAUSED BY QUALITY DEFECTS IN THAT PRODUCT MAY ONLY BE RECOVERED UNDER CONTRACT LAW

■ **INSTANT FACTS** Moorman Manufacturing (P) seeks economic damages ten years after a steel grain storage tank it purchased from National Tank (D) developed a crack.

■ **BLACK LETTER RULE** Damages to a product, caused by a defect in quality and limited to economic losses, may be recovered under contract law theories, but not under the theory of strict tort liability.

■ PROCEDURAL BASIS

Appeal to the Supreme Court of Illinois after the state appellate court applied strict tort liability in finding for the Defendant.

■ FACTS

Moorman Manufacturing Co. (Moorman) (P) purchased a steel grain storage tank from National Tank Co. (National) (D) for use in Moorman's (P) feed processing plant. About ten years later, a crack developed in the tank. Moorman (P) now sues on theories of strict tort liability, misrepresentation, negligent design and express warranty.

■ ISSUE

Can solely economic damages limited to the purchased product, caused by a defect in quality, and such as to not cause a sudden risk of personal injury or damage to other property, be recovered in strict tort liability?

■ DECISION AND RATIONALE

(Thomas J. Moran, J.) No. The tort law of products liability stems from the contract cause of action for breach of warranty. This theory required that the plaintiff be in privity with the defendant. As the law developed, however, most courts abandoned the privity requirement in implied-warranty actions and ultimately abandoned the fiction of warranty in favor of strict liability in tort. This State formerly adopted strict liability to allow a plaintiff to recover for personal injuries. Whether a consumer could recover under strict liability for solely economic loss is a separate question first addressed in *Santor v. A & M Karagheusian, Inc.* The court in that case held that a plaintiff who'd purchased some carpeting made by the defendant could recover purely economic damages when there was no privity between the parties. However, in *Seely v. White Motor Co.,* the California Supreme Court refused to apply strict liability to allow recovery for solely economic harm. Rather, the court allowed recovery based on express warranty, stating that economic losses are not recoverable in strict tort liability. With respect to the ruling in *Santor,* the California court said, "Only if someone had been injured because the rug was unsafe. . .would there have been any basis for imposing strict liability in tort." Subsequent decisions have gone both ways, with most courts denying recovery in strict tort liability for solely economic losses. We believe the majority of courts are correct and that the language of section 402A should be limited to unreasonably dangerous defects resulting in physical harm to the ultimate user or consumer, or to his property. We believe the framework provided by the Uniform Commercial Code (UCC), including implied and express warranties, rules on disclaimers, notice requirements, limitations on the extent of a manufacturer's liability, and a statute of limitations are adequate. This even though the warranty rules may frustrate just compensation for physical injury. While these rules provide for much flexibility in the commercial setting, they do not allow a manufacturer's strict liability for economic loss to be disclaimed because a manufacturer should not should not be allowed to define the scope of its own responsibility for defective products. Thus, adopting strict liability in tort for economic loss would effectively eviscerate section 2–316 of the UCC. Besides, a large purchaser, such as Moorman (P) in the instant case, can protect itself against the risk of unsatisfactory performance by bargaining for a warranty. Or, it could choose to accept a lower price in lieu of warranty protections. We believe it is better for a consumer to be limited to a comprehensive scheme of remedies under the UCC, rather than to require the consuming public to pay higher prices so the manufacturers can insure against the possibility that some of their products will not meet the business needs of some of their customers. We do hold, however, that strict liability in tort still applies to physical injury to a plaintiff's property, and to personal injury, when a product is defective and unreasonably dangerous. On the other hand, contract law, which protects expectation interests, provides the proper standard when a defect of quality is involved. "Economic loss" has been defined as "damages for inadequate value, costs of repair and replacement of the defective product, or consequent loss of profits—without any claim of personal injury or damage to other property. . ." as well as the "diminution in the value of the product because it is inferior in quality and does not work for the general purposes for which it was manufactured and sold." These definitions are consistent with the policy of warranty law to protect expectations of suitability and quality. We hold that, where only the defective product is damaged, economic losses caused by defects of quality falling under the ambit of a purchaser's disappointed expectations cannot be recovered under a strict liability theory. Here, the damages were limited to the defective tank and were gradual in nature. This was not the type of sudden and dangerous occurrence best served by the policy of tort law that the manufacturer should bear the risk of hazardous products. The damages here are better handled by contract law. [The Court also held that economic losses, though recoverable for intentional misrepresentations, were not recoverable for innocent ones, and that in this case the statute of limitations had run on the warranty claim.] Reversed.

Analysis:

Say X purchases a blender. After using the blender for six months, the motor suddenly burns up and it quits working. X sues the blender manufacturer under strict tort liability. The law of torts usually requires that some wrong has been committed or some duty breached. Certainly, from X's standpoint there has been a wrong perpetrated or a duty shirked. But what if the company is not at fault for the defective blender? In such a situation, the law of torts is not really the perfect fit. Rather, the product will usually be backed by either an express or implied warranty, guaranteeing it will function satisfactorily for a stated length of time, certainly longer than six months. What the Court is saying is that there are other types of law, specifically contract law and the UCC, that were meant for such situations. Strict tort liability can apply, but only if someone has suffered personal injury caused by the defective product, or if there has been some property damage (other than to the defective product itself). Tort law is specifically intended to cover those situations.

■ CASE VOCABULARY

DIMINUTION: To decrease, or cause a decrease, in value, quality, or quantity.

Lee v. Crookston Coca-Cola Bottling Co.

(Injured Waitress) v. (Beverage Bottler)

290 Minn. 321, 188 N.W.2d 426 (1971)

CIRCUMSTANTIAL EVIDENCE ALONE IS SUFFICIENT TO GET A CASE TO THE JURY ON BOTH NEGLIGENCE AND STRICT TORT LIABILITY THEORIES

■ INSTANT FACTS Lee (P) had a Coca-Cola bottle explode in her hand and now seeks damages for her injuries.

■ BLACK LETTER RULE A case may be submitted to the jury under both negligence and strict tort liability theories even though all of plaintiff's evidence is circumstantial.

■ PROCEDURAL BASIS

On appeal from jury verdict in favor of defendant.

■ FACTS

Lee (P) was working as a waitress when a Coca-Cola bottle exploded in her hand. The evidence showed that the bottle had not struck anything, or been subjected to temperature extremes or mishandling. The trial judge refused to submit a claim based on strict tort liability. The jury returned a verdict for Crookston Coca-Cola Bottling Company (Bottler) (D).

■ ISSUE

Is circumstantial evidence alone sufficient to allow a plaintiff's case to be submitted to the jury under both strict tort liability and negligence?

■ DECISION AND RATIONALE

(Rogosheske, J.) Yes. The rule of strict liability imposes liability, without proof of negligence or privity of contract, upon a manufacturer or seller for injury caused by a dangerously defective product. For recovery under strict liability, a plaintiff need only prove that (1) the product was in fact in a defective condition, unreasonably dangerous for its intended use; (2) such defect existed when the product left the control of the defendant; and (3) the defect was the proximate cause of the injury sustained. However, this does not mean a defendant is held liable regardless of circumstances. The mere fact of injury during use of the product is usually insufficient proof to show existence of a defect at the time defendant relinquished control. The narrow question presented here though, is whether circumstantial evidence, the core of the res ipsa loquitur doctrine, is sufficient to take the case to the jury on the theory of strict liability as well as on the theory of negligence. It is certainly evident that the circumstantial evidence in this case is enough to justify submission of the issue of liability on the theory of res ipsa. The Bottler's (D) expert testified that there are three causes of bottle failure: Thermo-shock, internal pressure, and external force. Here, the only possible cause, according to the testimony, was internal pressure. Failure from internal pressure due to excessive carbonation is ordinarily unlikely because the bottle is designed to withstand much greater pressure than is normally applied. However, due to a bottler's customary reuse of bottles, sometimes for years, the capacity of different bottles to withstand internal pressure varies widely. Some bottles could develop defects over longer periods of time because of "rough" handling over the years. This may be only a plausible explanation in this case given the testimony that thermo-shock and external force did not occur. But absent expert opinion, as in a case of this type, circumstantial evidence may be the only available means of establishing a claim of either negligence or defective product. Under strict liability the elements of proof are very simple. The jury need not infer that the bottler (D) was negligent in order to impose liability. It is sufficient that the bottler (D) placed a dangerously defective product on the market. A plaintiff is not required to show exactly what defect caused the accident, but may rely on circumstantial evidence from which a jury may infer that it is more probable than not that the product was defective when it left the control of the defendant. Here the jury could have found, based on the evidence, that the bottler (D) was not negligent. This finding does not preclude recovery under strict liability though. Strict liability does not require negligence, just that the bottle was defective when it was put on the market. Such a finding would compel a verdict for Lee (P), absent any valid defenses. The trial court's refusal to instruct on strict liability deprived Lee (P) of a legitimate choice of theories on which to submit the case and is, thus, reversible error.

Analysis:

The requirements of the doctrine of res ipsa loquitur are that the defendant was in control of the situation; that injury would not normally occur absent some sort of negligence; and that the plaintiff did not contribute to the injury. After these three elements are proved there is an inference of negligence on the part of the defendant. The doctrine is similar to strict tort liability in that it does not require the plaintiff to present specific evidence of negligence by the defendant. Under strict liability, while technically no negligence need be proven, in the truest sense there has to be some sort of "negligence," otherwise the injury would not have occurred. Thus, under strict liability, the defendant may rebut an inference of liability by showing that something material occurred to the product after it left the defendant's control. Similarly, under res ipsa, the requirements of exclusive control by the defendant, and lack of contribution to the injury by the plaintiff, prevent liability when it is less than reasonably certain the defendant caused the injury.

■ CASE VOCABULARY

RES IPSA LOQUITUR: "The thing speaks for itself." The doctrine in tort law that provides that the simple fact that an injury occurred leads to an inference of negligence.

Knitz v. Minster Machine Co.

(Press Operator) v. (Press Maker)

69 Ohio St.2d 460, 432 N.E.2d 814 (1982)

A PRODUCT DESIGN IS DEFECTIVE IF THE BENEFITS OR ADVANTAGES OF THE DESIGN DON'T OUTWEIGH THE RISK INHERENT IN SUCH DESIGN

■ **INSTANT FACTS** Knitz (P) was operating a press when it accidentally activated and severed two of her fingers.

■ **BLACK LETTER RULE** A product design is in a defective condition to the user or consumer if (1) it is more dangerous than an ordinary consumer would expect when used in an intended or reasonably foreseeable manner, or (2) if the benefits of the challenged design do not outweigh the risk inherent in such design.

■ PROCEDURAL BASIS

Appeal to the State Supreme Court from a grant of summary judgment by the trial judge against Knitz (P).

■ FACTS

Minster Machine Company (Minster)(D) manufactured an industrial press originally activated with a two-hand button tripping device that kept the operator's hands out of the danger area. This press was sold by Minster (D) to the Toledo Die and Manufacturing Company (Toledo). Toledo also purchased an optional foot pedal activation device that was in use at the time of the injury. Knitz (P) was a press operator for Toledo. Knitz (P) attempted to move the foot pedal activation device and while doing so leaned on the bottom portion of the die with her hand. Her foot then accidentally activated the foot pedal, causing the press to descend and amputate two of her fingers. There was another safety device intended to pull the operator's hands back, but it was not attached.

■ ISSUE

Is a product defective when it is more dangerous than a consumer would expect when used as intended or in a reasonably foreseeable manner, or when the benefits of the product design do not outweigh the design's inherent risks?

■ DECISION AND RATIONALE

(Brown, William B., J.) Yes. This Court has adopted the rule known as the "consumer expectation test." This test holds that "A product is in a defective condition unreasonably dangerous to the user or consumer if it is more dangerous than an ordinary consumer would expect when used in an intended or reasonably foreseeable manner." The standard reflects the commercial reality that implicit in a product's presence on the market is a representation that it will safely do the jobs for which it was built. However, this rule does not cover situations where the consumer would not know what to expect, because he would have no idea how safe the product could be made. This is the case here. In such cases, the policy underlying strict liability in tort, requires that a product may be found defective in design, even if it satisfies ordinary consumer expectations, if through hindsight the jury determines that the product's design embodies excessive preventable danger, or, in other words, if the jury finds the risk of danger inherent in the challenged design outweighs the benefits of such design. Accordingly, we hold that a product design is in a defective condition to the user if (1) it is more dangerous than an ordinary consumer would expect when used in an intended or reasonably foreseeable manner, or (2) if the benefits of the challenged design do not outweigh the risk inherent in such design. Factors relevant to the evaluation of the defectiveness of the product design are the likelihood that the product design will cause injury, the gravity of the danger posed, and the mechanical and economic feasibility of an improved design. Here, Knitz (P) provided an expert opinion that the press was defective because of the failure of Minster (D) to design the press with adequate guarding that would keep it from being activated with the operator's hands under the press. In light of this, Knitz (P) has made out a genuine issue of fact as to whether the press design was defective. Reversed and remanded.

Analysis:

This opinion represents a change in the law of strict tort liability as it relates to product design defects. The court has formulated what has come to be called the "risk-utility test." This development is largely a result of the work of two people—Page Keeton and Dean John Wade. Dean Wade has advocated the use of seven factors to be applied in the risk-utility test: (1) the usefulness and desirability of the product; (2) probability and magnitude of potential injury; (3) availability of substitutes; (4) manufacturer's ability to eliminate the unsafe characteristic of the product; (5) the consumer's ability to avoid danger; (6) the consumer's probable awareness of the danger; and (7) the manufacturer's ability to spread the loss. The last factor has largely been omitted by most courts adopting the Wade analysis. What the risk-utility test is, in effect, is a cost-benefit analysis form the standpoint of the manufacturer and the user. If a company sells a product that could be rendered much safer at a small cost in both financial terms and utility terms, it is clear under the risk-utility test that liability will exist. However, if the cost of reducing the risk is high and the detriment to the utility of the product is high, liability will most likely not lie.

■ CASE VOCABULARY

SUB JUDICE: Presently before the court; e.g. the "case at bar" or the "instant case."

Honda of America Mfg., Inc. v. Norman

(Car Manufacturer) v. (Decedent's Estate)

104 S.W.3d 600 (Tex.App.Ct.2003)

A RIGHT-HIP SEAT BELT RELEASE MECHANISM IS NO BETTER THAN A LEFT-SHOULDER RELEASE MECHANISM

■ **INSTANT FACTS** Karen Norman drowned when her vehicle became submerged in water and she was unable to free herself from the automatic seatbelt mechanism.

■ **BLACK LETTER RULE** Under the common law, to establish products liability, a claimant must prove that an economically and technologically feasible alternative design was available and would have prevented or significantly reduced the risk of death without substantially reducing the utility to the intended users of the product.

■ PROCEDURAL BASIS

On appeal to review a jury verdict for the plaintiffs.

■ FACTS

Karen Norman accidentally backed her Honda Civic down a boat ramp into the water in Galveston Bay. Norman's vehicle was equipped with an automatic seat belt that engaged mechanically when the doors were closed and a manual lap belt. Unable to free herself from the automatic seatbelt, Norman died as her car sank. At the time of the accident, Norman's blood alcohol exceeded the state limit. The seatbelt mechanism in Karen's car was equipped with a mouse running along the door rail that, when operating properly, moves forward with the door is opened or the ignition is switched off. Additionally, the car was equipped with an emergency release button that permitted the operator to manually disengage the seatbelt. However, the car also had an emergency locking retractor that, when the vehicle experienced rapid deceleration or substantial tilting, would lock the seatbelt in place to secure the occupants in their seats. The Normans (P) sued Honda of America Manufacturing in products liability, alleging that the vehicle had a design defect because when the emergency locking retractor engaged, occupants were unable to reach the emergency release button, and the button was improperly located to enable occupants to release the seatbelt in emergency situations that were likely to occur. A jury found Karen 25% negligent and returned a verdict for the plaintiffs.

■ ISSUE

Did the plaintiffs meet their burden of proving an economically and technologically feasible alternative seat belt and release system?

■ DECISION AND RATIONALE

(Keyes, J.) No. Under the common law, to establish products liability, a claimant must prove that the product was defectively designed so as to be unreasonably dangerous, taking into consideration the utility of the product and the risks involved in its use. To do so, the Normans (P) must show that an economically and technologically feasible alternative seat belt and release system was available and would have prevented or significantly reduced the risk of

Karen's death, without substantially reducing the utility to the intended users of the product. Honda (D) argues the Normans (P) failed to meet this burden.

At trial, the Normans (P) offered the testimony of two experts. Horton, a mechanical engineer, testified that there were three potential alternative designs that could have been used in the vehicle, including a timer programmed to reverse the mouse if it did not travel its entire cycle within an established period of time. Horton, however, failed to state that such a hypothetical alternative was available or economically or technologically feasible. The Normans (P) failed to prove that a timer-controlled mouse was a safer alternative design. The second expert, Laughery, testified that the placement of the emergency button over the driver's left shoulder was not sufficient, because at the time the vehicle was manufactured, Toyota placed the emergency release to the lower right side of the driver's seat, which was easier to access by a restrained driver. From Toyota's earlier use of this alternative, Laughery testified that he knew it was technologically feasible, and he presumed it was economically feasible because of Toyota's decision to utilize that alternative. However, while Toyota's use of the alternative may establish its technological feasibility, it does not establish its economic feasibility. To establish economic feasibility, the plaintiffs must prove the cost of incorporating the technology. The plaintiffs did not meet their burden.

Even if the plaintiffs' evidence could permit a reasonable inference of technological and economic feasibility, they failed to prove that the alternative mechanism would have prevented or significantly reduced the risk of death without imposing an equal or greater risk of harm. The location of the emergency release button was chosen to enable third parties outside the vehicle easier access to the button in the event the driver was immobilized and the vehicle could not be easily accessed. No evidence was offered to prove that the right-hip mechanism would save more lives than the left-shoulder release button. The plaintiffs have not met their burden. Reversed.

Analysis:

The analysis used by the court in this case is often referred to as a risk-utility analysis. Under this approach, a manufacturer need not make its products in the safest manner possible, but rather must only take reasonable measures to ensure that its products are the safest alternative to meet the risks of danger presented while maintaining the utility of the product to the consumer. This principle is driven largely by economics. While a manufacturer can often improve the safety of its product, the cost associated with doing so may only marginally increase safety but make the product too expensive for the consumer.

■ CASE VOCABULARY

DESIGN DEFECT: A product imperfection occurring when the seller or distributor could have reduced or avoided a foreseeable risk of harm by adopting a reasonable alternative design, and when, as a result of not using the alternative, the produce is not reasonably safe.

PRODUCTS LIABILITY: A manufacturer's or seller's tort liability for any damages or injuries suffered by a buyer, user, or bystander as a result of a defective product.

McCarthy v. Olin Corporation

(Shooting Victim) v. (Ammunition Maker)

119 F.3d 148 (2d Cir.1997)

FOR A PRODUCT TO HAVE A DESIGN DEFECT THERE MUST BE SOMETHING WRONG WITH THE PRODUCT'S DESIGN THAT IS NOT CONTEMPLATED BY THE CONSUMER

■ **INSTANT FACTS** A man boarded a train and began shooting at passengers using a special ammunition specifically designed by its manufacturer to cause as much damage to the victim as possible. The victims are suing the manufacturer for defective design and other claims.

■ **BLACK LETTER RULE** When a product is dangerous by design, the mere fact someone is injured by it will not cause the manufacturer to be liable; there must be something wrong with the product that causes injury, and if nothing is wrong there will be no liability.

■ PROCEDURAL BASIS

Appeal from the Federal District Court's granting of Olin Corporation's (D) motion for dismissal for failure to state a claim upon which relief can be granted.

■ FACTS

On December 7, 1993, a man named Colin Ferguson boarded a New York City commuter train and began firing a gun at the passengers. Six people were killed and nineteen others, including Kevin McCarthy (P1) and Maryanne Phillips (P2), were wounded. The assailant's pistol was loaded with Winchester "Black Talons," manufactured by the Olin Corporation (Olin)(D). The injuries to McCarthy (P1) and Phillips (P2) were enhanced because of the special design of the Black Talon bullets. The Black Talon is a hollowpoint bullet designed to bend and spread into six ninety-degree angle razor-sharp petals or "talons" that increase the wounding power of the bullet by stretching, cutting and tearing tissue and bone as it travels through the victim. The Black Talon was designed and manufactured by Olin (D) and went on the market in 1992. It was originally developed for law enforcement agencies, but was also marketed to the general public until a public outcry in 1993 caused Olin (D) to remove the Black Talon from the public market and restrict its sales to law enforcement personnel. The assailant allegedly purchased the ammunition before it was withdrawn by Olin (D).

■ ISSUE

Can a plaintiff assert a valid cause of action for design defect stemming from a product that caused injury when it performed exactly as it was designed to perform?

■ DECISION AND RATIONALE

(Meskill, J.) No. McCarthy (P1) first alleges that Olin (D) is strictly liable because the Black Talon was defectively designed in that the design of the bullets is inherently dangerous and results in enhanced injuries beyond ordinary bullets. The district court rejected this argument because the bullets' performance was an intentional and functional design of the product. We agree. To state a cause of action for design defect, plaintiffs must allege that the bullet was unreasonably dangerous for its intended use. A defectively designed product is one which, at the time it leaves the seller's hands, is in a condition not reasonably contemplated by the ultimate consumer. This rule is tempered by the fact that some products must be dangerous in order to be functional. Here, McCarthy (P1) and Phillips (P2) concede that the bullets performed precisely as intended by the manufacturer and the assailant, Colin Ferguson. Many products, however well designed, may cause death or injury. Guns and bullets are two of them. There must, however, be something wrong with the product, and if nothing is wrong there will be no liability. McCarthy (P1) and Phillips (P2) have not alleged that the bullets were defective. As a matter of law, a product's defect is related to its condition, not its intrinsic function. Here, the Black Talons did exactly what they were intended to do and were therefore not in a defective condition. McCarthy (P1) and Phillips (P2) next allege that under the risk/utility test Olin (D) should be held strictly liable because the risk of harm posed by the Black Talons outweighs the ammunition's utility. But as the district court correctly saw, the risk/utility test is inapplicable because the risks arise from the intended function of the product, not any defect. The risk/utility test requires there be something wrong with the product before determining if it is unreasonably dangerous or defective. Accordingly, we hold that McCarthy (P1) and Phillips (P2) have failed to state a cause of action under New York's strict products liability law. It is also argued that Olin (D) should be held liable in negligence for marketing the ammo to the general public because of its severe wounding power; that Olin (D) should have restricted sales to law enforcement for whom the bullets were originally designed. Also alleged is that Olin (D) should have known that its advertising of the ammo, which highlighted its ripping and tearing capacity, would attract criminals like the assailant here. But New York law doesn't impose a legal duty on manufacturers to control the distribution of potentially dangerous products such as ammunition. Accordingly, even if Olin (D) could foresee the results here, Olin (D) is not legally liable for such misuse. The complaint therefore does not state a valid cause of action in negligence either. Affirmed.

Analysis:

The Plaintiffs in this case were quite obviously attempting to exploit the "deep pockets" of the Olin Corporation (D) because the assailant, Colin Ferguson, was judgment-proof. To do so, they attempted to establish Olin's (D) moral culpability and bootstrap it into a valid cause of action at law. In doing so, McCarthy (P1) and Phillips (P2) allege that the risk of harm posed by the Black Talon outweighs its utility. There is absolutely no rational logic in this assertion. The utility of the product lies solely in the fact that it poses a greater risk, even probability, of harm to those it is used against. This was the specific goal of Olin (D) in designing the ammunition. The reality is that some products are not only inherently dangerous—such as knives—they are also meant to cause harm. The truth of the matter is that whether or not Black Talons were available, Mr. Ferguson would still have been on the train indiscriminately firing on random passengers. As the appeals court recognized, liability cannot be imposed on the manufacturer simply because a person commits a crime with its product.

Liriano v. Hobart Corporation

(Grinder Operator) v. (Grinder Manufacturer)

170 F.3d 264 (2d Cir.1999)

A WARNING HAS TWO PURPOSES: TO CAUSE AWARENESS OF DANGER AND TO POINT OUT LESS DANGEROUS ALTERNATIVES

■ **INSTANT FACTS** A supermarket worker, Liriano (P), was severely injured by a guardless meat grinder and now sues his employer and the manufacturer for his injuries.

■ **BLACK LETTER RULE** (1) Obvious hazards still require warnings because the warning not only notifies persons of the hazard, it also provides notice of less hazardous alternative ways of proceeding. (2) Cause-in-fact of a plaintiff's injury from an obviously hazardous product will be presumed from the plain fact that the injury occurred in the first place, leaving it to the defendant to rebut the cause-in-fact in order to keep the case from the jury.

■ PROCEDURAL BASIS

Appeal from a plaintiff's verdict in a product liability personal injury case, with both issues certified to the New York Court of Appeals before being answered by the Federal Circuit Court herein.

■ FACTS

Luis Liriano (P) was working at Super Associated (Super) (D1), a super market. While working his hand was severely injured by a meat grinder manufactured by Hobart Corporation (Hobart) (D2) and owned by Super (D1). The grinder had been originally sold to Super (D1) equipped with a safety guard, but the guard had been removed while in Super's (D1) possession. The grinder bore no warning indicating it should be operated only with the guard in place. Liriano (P) sued Hobart (D2), who brought a third-party claim against Super (D1). The only claim that went to the jury was the failure-to-warn claim. The jury found for Liriano (P) while attributing a degree of responsibility to all three parties. Both Hobart (D2) and Super (D1) appealed, arguing (1) there was no duty to warn, and (2) even if there was a duty, the evidence was insufficient to get the failure-to-warn claim to the jury. The federal court certified both questions to the New York Court of Appeals, which rejected the first argument and declined to answer the second.

■ ISSUE

(1) Does an injury hazard require a warning despite the hazard being extremely obvious to the user/consumer? (2) Does a plaintiff injured by an extremely obvious hazard that he was not warned of have to prove the failure to warn was the cause-in-fact of his injuries?

■ DECISION AND RATIONALE

(Calabresi, J.) (1) Yes. (2) No. More than a hundred years ago, Judge Oliver Wendell Holmes, Jr., writing for a majority of the Supreme Judicial Court of Massachusetts, held that a pile of coal on the side of a Boston street was warning enough for any and all passersby that there was a coal hole nearby. He held that because of the obviousness of the coal holes existence, given the propensity for Boston residences to have piles of coal next to these holes, that any person who falls into such a whole is bound at their peril to know of the hole. Accordingly, the defendant in that case could, as a matter of law, rely on the plaintiff's responsibility to know of the danger presented. Justice Knowlton disagreed. His opinion delved farther into the facts of the case and showed that the plaintiff's failure to appreciate the peril might have been foreseen by the defendant and hence the failure by the defendant to warn of the hole might constitute negligence, a question a jury should decide. It is this latter view of obvious dangers that has held sway in the intervening years, a view the New York courts have several times endorsed. Looking more closely at the facts at hand, Liriano (P) was only seventeen years old, was a new immigrant to the United States, and had been on the job for only one week. Liriano (P) had never received instruction on operating the meat grinder and had used it only twice or thrice previously. Also, the mechanism that caused the injury was not visible to the operator. It could be argued that such a set of facts was not so remote that a court should say, as a matter of law, that Super (D1) and Hobart (D2) could not have foreseen them and guarded against them by giving a warning. Meat grinders are obviously very dangerous. People may therefore disagree as to whether a failure to warn of such a fact would be enough to raise a jury issue. But warnings do more than simply point out the presence of danger. It can also have the equally important purpose of drawing the user's attention to the existence of alternatives that eliminate or mitigate the danger. It thus follows that the duty to warn is not necessarily obviated merely because a danger is clear. One who grinds meat can therefore benefit not only from being told that his activity is dangerous, but also from being told there is a safer way. Though most people who use grinders will know—as a matter of law—that guardless grinders are dangerous, it doesn't follow that a sufficient number of them will—as a matter of law—also know that protective guards are available, that using them is a realistic possibility, and that they may ask that such guards be used. It is precisely these last pieces of information that the reasonable manufacturer may have a duty to convey even if the danger of using a grinder were itself deemed obvious. Given these facts, a jury could find that providing such a warning is a reasonable and prudent course of action that a manufacturer of meat grinders has a duty to follow. Thus, even if New York would consider the danger of meat grinders to be obvious as a matter of law, that obviousness does not substitute for the warning. Hobart (D2) also raises the argument that Liriano (P) failed to present any evidence that Hobart's (D2) failure to place a warning on the machine was causally related to his injury in that, whether or not there was a warning, Liriano (P) may still have operated the machine as he did and suffered the same injuries. But this argument assumes that Liriano (P) has the burden to show that the failure to warn was a but-for cause of his injury. Liriano (P) does not bear that burden. When it is clear, as a general matter—as it is here—that the kind of negligence the jury attributed to the defendant tends to cause the exact type of injury the plaintiff suffered, rather than require the plaintiff to prove his case is of the ordinary kind, the law presumes normality and requires the defendant to adduce evidence that the case is an exception. Accordingly, it is up to Hobart (D2) to adduce evidence showing that Liriano's (P) injury did not occur as the normally expected result of Hobart's (D2) failure to warn. In other words, here there is a rebuttable presumption that Hobart's (D2) negligence was in fact a but-for cause of Liriano's (P) injury. The district court did not err. Affirmed in all respects.

Analysis:

The Restatement of Products Liability provides that an item is defective when it has a defect of design or manufacture, and also when the maker has failed to provide a warning of foreseeable harm. Warning failures were originally thought of as not only implicating negligence, but also strict liability. The grounds for thinking of warning failures as strict liability cases is that a product that does not carry a reasonable warning when having one could make it safer is an unreasonably dangerous product. However, since the requirement is that the warning meet a standard of reasonableness, the inquiry in such a case essentially collapses into a typical negligence analysis. The end result is that, even though many courts have used the language of strict liability, warning cases are more like negligence cases. A manufacturer's duty to warn means it only has to provide a reasonable warning against foreseeable risks. Accordingly, a manufacturer will be held liable only where the risk could have been mitigated or eliminated by the nonexistent warning *and* if the item without the missing warning was not reasonably safe.

■ CASE VOCABULARY

BUT-FOR CAUSATION: The cause that in the absence of the event in question could not have occurred. Also known as "cause-in-fact" and "actual cause."

Bowling v. Heil Co.

(Man Crushed by Dump Truck Box) v. (Manufacturer of Dump Hoist System)

31 Ohio St.3d 277, 511 N.E.2d 373 (1987)

COMPARATIVE NEGLIGENCE IS NOT CONSIDERED IN A PRODUCT LIABILITY CASE BASED UPON STRICT TORT LIABILITY

■ **INSTANT FACTS** Bowling (P) was killed when the box on a dump truck descended and crushed him while he was attempting to fix a glitch with the truck.

■ **BLACK LETTER RULE** The comparative fault or negligence of a party who sues a manufacturer for product liability under strict liability in tort shall not be considered in assessing liability or damages, but assumption of risk by the plaintiff is a complete defense.

■ PROCEDURAL BASIS

Appeal to the Ohio Supreme Court after the Appeals Court affirmed the ruling of the trial court in allowing the jury to consider Bowling's (P) contributory negligence.

■ FACTS

Heil Co. (Heil) (D) manufactured the dump hoist system (the system that raises and lowers the box on a dump truck) that was installed on a dump truck owned by Rogers. Brashear borrowed the truck for some personal use. He and Bowling (P) had dumped some gravel, but the box would not return to the down position. In order to correct the problem, Bowling (P) leaned in between the overhead box and the truck chassis below to see what was wrong. While in this position Bowling (P) grabbed the control lever on the pump valve assembly and manipulated it, causing the box to rapidly descend and crush Bowling (P), instantly killing him. This action is against Heil (D) and various others involved in the hoist assembly and controls. The jury found that Bowling (P) was guilty of contributory negligence, but not assumed risk and assessed damages at $1.75 million. Included in the verdict was a setoff for the level of Bowling's (P) fault.

■ ISSUE

Is contributory or comparative negligence by a plaintiff in a strict product liability case to be considered by a court in order to reduce the amount of damages awarded the plaintiff?

■ DECISION AND RATIONALE

(Brown, Herbert R., J.) No. Under Ohio law governing products liability, there are two affirmative defenses available, both based upon a plaintiff's misconduct. First, an otherwise strictly liable defendant has a complete defense if the plaintiff assumed the risk caused by the product defect. Second, such a defendant also has a complete defense if the plaintiff misused the product in an unforeseeable manner. The court below held that even though a plaintiff's passive contributory negligence provides no defense to a product liability action, his contributorily negligent affirmative action does provide a defense. Section 402A provides that contributory negligence is not a defense when such negligence is simply a failure to discover a defect, or to guard against the possibility it exists. However, if the user or consumer discovers a defect and is aware of the danger, and nevertheless proceeds unreasonably to make use of the product and is injured by it, he is barred from recovery. The court of appeals has therefore carved out a middle ground: contributory negligence consisting of "affirmative action." There is no such middle ground. "Affirmative action" by the plaintiff is covered because failure to guard against a defect can be "affirmative action." Indeed such would describe the conduct of Bowling (P) in this case. Under section 402A, a plaintiff's contributory negligence amounts to a voluntary assumption of a known risk or it does not. If it does, then the defendant has complete defense. If it does not, the contributory negligence of the defendant provides no defense. The jury found that Bowling (P) was contributorily negligent, but that he had not assumed a known risk. Therefore, Bowling's (P) actions do not provide Heil (D) with a defense to the strict liability claim. As illustrated in comment c to Section 402A, there are several policies and goals underlying the rule in strict liability cases. Most notably, that those who manufacture products have to treat the cost of injuries caused by those products as a part of the costs of production; a cost they can obtain insurance against. Also, as Dean Prosser has stated, the costs of damaging events caused by defective products can best be borne by those who make the products because they have the ability to effect loss spreading by shifting these costs to the consumers who purchase the products by charging higher prices. This is the opposite of the principles of negligence, where the loss is borne by the one that caused it. It must therefore be emphasized that strict liability is at odds with traditional notions of due care. While some courts do consider contributory negligence in strict liability cases, we feel that the better reasoned decisions are those that decline to inject a plaintiff's negligence into the fray. We thus hold that the principles of comparative negligence or comparative fault have no application to a products liability case based upon strict liability in tort. We therefore reverse the judgment of the court of appeals with respect to its reduction of Bowler's (P) verdict by the thirty percent found by the jury to be attributable to contributory negligence.

Analysis:

Justice Brown cites with approval the words of Justice Mosk to support the court's position that in strict liability cases contributory negligence by the plaintiff is irrelevant: "The defective product is comparable to a time bomb ready to explode, it maims its victims indiscriminately, the righteous and the evil, the careful and the careless." But on the facts of this case, the utilization of a little common sense on the part of Bowling (P) would have avoided this tragedy. Why should manufacturers have to pay for the results of the obviously negligent actions of consumers? Also, Ohio law has two affirmative defenses a manufacturer can use in defending a strict product liability case. The first is where the "plaintiff voluntarily and knowingly assumed the risk occasioned by the defect." Bowling (P) knew, or at least should have known, that there was a chance of the dump truck box coming down unexpectedly. By positioning himself between the raised box and the truck chassis he was obviously in a clear danger zone should the box fall. Bowling (P) then "manipulated" the mechanism that controls the up and down motion of the box. At this point, there was a significant chance the box would fall. If these actions do not constitute voluntarily and knowingly assuming the risk occasioned by the defect then what type of conduct would?

■ CASE VOCABULARY

AFFIRMATIVE DEFENSE: A defense that raises new arguments and facts that, if proved true, will defeat a finding of guilt or liability, even if all of the facts or elements alleged by the prosecution or plaintiff are also proved true.

Hughes v. Magic Chef, Inc.

(Injured Cook) v. (Manufacturer of Stove)

288 N.W.2d 542 (Iowa 1980)

MISUSE OF PRODUCT IS NOT AN AFFIRMATIVE DEFENSE; IT IS THE PLAINTIFF'S BURDEN TO PROVE THAT THE USE MADE OF THE PRODUCT BY THE PLAINTIFF WAS REASONABLY FORESEEABLE BY THE MANUFACTURER

■ **INSTANT FACTS** Vincent Hughes (P) was severely burned when a stove made by Magic Chef, Inc. exploded due to a buildup of propane gas inside the oven.

■ **BLACK LETTER RULE** (1) Assumption of risk is not to be treated as an affirmative defense when giving a jury instruction, rather it is subsumed by contributory negligence. (2) In instructing on the defense of misuse, the jury is to be instructed to consider the knowledge level of the ordinary user, not the plaintiff's level of knowledge.

■ PROCEDURAL BASIS

Appeal from a jury verdict for the Defense in a strict product liability suit after the trial court's refusal to grant Plaintiff's motion for a new trial.

■ FACTS

Vincent Hughes (P) was using a stove manufactured by Magic Chef, Inc. (Magic) (D) when the propane tank fueling the stove ran out of gas. After the propane tank was refilled, the two pilot lights on the cook top of the stove were re-lit, but the third inside the oven broiler cavity was not. Two days later when Hughes (P) attempted to use the stove it exploded, severely injuring him. Experts testified that because the third pilot light wasn't lit, the gas that supplied the light built up over the intervening two days and ignited when Hughes (P) tried to use the stove, causing the explosion that caused the injuries. Hughes (P) brought this strict liability action against Magic (D), alleging the stove was unreasonably dangerous. Magic (D) raised the affirmative defenses of assumption of risk and misuse of product.

■ ISSUE

(1) Is misuse of a product to be treated as an affirmative defense in the giving of jury instructions? (2) Did the court err in including a specific reference to what the Plaintiff knew or should have known about the pilot light in its instruction to the jury regarding misuse?

■ DECISION AND RATIONALE

(Uhlenhopp, J.) (1) No. (2) Yes. This Court has previously held in *Rosenau* that in an ordinary negligence case, the defense of assumption of risk is not to be pled and submitted as a separate defense. Instead, the elements of assumed risk are to be included in the contributory negligence instruction. Separate instructions could tend to confuse the jury and cause it to render inconsistent verdicts. Hughes (P) argues that this same reasoning applies to the products liability defenses of misuse of product and assumption of risk. But this argument fails to recognize the different natures of those two issues. Misuse bars recovery when the product is used in a way not reasonably foreseeable to the defendant. Assumption of risk is a defense to a strict liability action when the plaintiff has voluntarily and unreasonably proceeded to encounter a known danger. Misuse has to do with the producer's responsibility. If a product is misused, the maker is not liable from the outset. Assumption of risk has to do with the user's culpability; he is barred from recovering if he proceeds in the face of a known danger. While we recognize that often both misuse and assumption of risk will be present in one case, we reject the idea that a plaintiff cannot do one without the other. Although we do not agree with Hughes' (P) attempt to apply *Rosenau* to this case, we do agree that the trial court erred in giving an instruction on misuse as a defense in this strict liability action. Misuse is not an affirmative defense, but rather has to do with an element of the plaintiff's case. To treat misuse as an affirmative defense distinct and additional to the plaintiff's burden of proving he used a product in a reasonably foreseeable manner, there would be the possibility of inconsistent jury findings in the same case. There would also be the problem of a shifting burden of proof on the issue. Misuse is to be treated in connection with the plaintiff's burden of proving an unreasonably dangerous condition and legal cause. The plaintiff always has the burden to prove the legal cause of the injury was a product defect that rendered the product unreasonably dangerous in a reasonably foreseeable use. Hughes (P) also asserts that the "misuse" instruction erroneously held him to a "reasonableness" standard in the use of the product. We do not find it necessary to resolve this issue though because the misuse instruction is objectionable on another ground; it gives undue emphasis to what Hughes (P) personally knew or should have known. It stands to reason that if an ordinary user would reasonably be aware that a certain use of a product is dangerous, use of the product in that manner is less foreseeable by the maker than a normal, presumably safe use. But this does not mean that just because the ordinary user knows a certain use is dangerous, such a use is not reasonably foreseeable by the maker. It therefore follows that knowledge that can be reasonably attributed to the ordinary user is to be considered as a factor in deciding if the manner in which the plaintiff used the product was reasonably foreseeable. Here the trial court erred in directing the jury to consider what Hughes (P) knew or ought reasonably to have known about the pilot light. This has little relevance to the issue of whether Magic (D) should reasonably have foreseen the use to which the stove was put. The personal characteristics or knowledge of users becomes relevant only when the characteristics or knowledge are attributable to a substantial group of users. By using Hughes (P) as the reference point, the jury was invited to consider a matter of little relevance to the issue it had to resolve—whether Magic (D) should have reasonably foreseen that users would use the stove without lighting all the pilot lights after an interruption in gas service. We therefore hold that on retrial misuse is not to be treated as an affirmative defense in the instructions. Instead the instructions have to put the burden of proof on Hughes (P) to establish that the use made of the stove was reasonably foreseeable by Magic (D). The instruction may reference knowledge attributable to the ordinary user, but it must make clear that this is but one factor in determining whether the use here was reasonably foreseeable by Magic (D). Reversed.

Analysis:

Just because a product is "misused" does not mean the defendant was not negligent, if the maker could reasonably have foreseen the misuse. For instance, a jury could find that a consumer misused the product—a finding that should bar recovery. But in the same case, the jury could find that even though the plaintiff misused the product, such misuse was reasonably foreseeable by the defendant manufacturer—a finding that would mean the defendant is liable. By holding that misuse is not an affirmative defense, but rather is part of the plaintiff's burden in proving that the use the product was put to was reasonably foreseeable by the defendant, inconsistent jury verdicts are avoided. What it all boils down to is that even if somebody misuses a product, they can still recover for injuries if they can prove the manufacturer could reasonably foresee the misuse. This is akin to saying that manufacturers are required to design products and provide warnings with the realities of use in mind. Their products, therefore, must be safe for reasonably foreseeable misuses.

Doomes v. Best Transit Corp.

(Bus Passenger) v. (Bus Company)

958 N.E.2d 1183 (N.Y. 2011)

WHEN FEDERAL LAW IS SILENT ON A PARTICULAR SUBJECT, A STATE LAW CLAIM ADDRESSING THAT SUBJECT IS NOT PREEMPTED

■ **INSTANT FACTS** Injured bus passengers sued the bus manufacturer under state law for the lack of passenger seatbelts, and the bus manufacturer countered that the applicable federal regulation did not require passenger seatbelts.

■ **BLACK LETTER RULE** Under the Supremacy Clause of the United States Constitution, enforcement of a state law is preempted only if (1) the plain language of the federal statute on the subject expressly states that it preempts state law, (2) the federal legislation is so comprehensive that it is inferable the Congress wished to fully occupy the subject matter ("field preemption"), or (3) the state law conflicts with the federal law.

■ PROCEDURAL BASIS

State's highest court review of an intermediate appellate court decision holding that the plaintiffs' claims were preempted by federal law.

■ FACTS

The driver of a passenger bus dozed off and lost control of the bus, which rolled over several times. Many passengers, including Doomes (P), were injured. They sued various defendants, including the bus manufacturer, alleging among other things that the lack of passenger seatbelts was the cause of their injuries. The manufacturer moved to preclude any evidence that the bus was defective for lack of seatbelts on the grounds that the applicable federal regulation did not require them, and that the federal law preempted the plaintiffs' state law claims. The trial court declined to rule on the motion and the jury found the manufacturer liable. The appellate division reversed, holding that the seatbelt claims were preempted because they conflicted with the federal goal of establishing a uniform regulatory scheme for transit safety. The plaintiffs appealed.

■ ISSUE

Did the appellate court properly hold that the plaintiffs' claims were preempted?

■ DECISION AND RATIONALE

(Jones, J.) No. Under the Supremacy Clause of the United States Constitution, enforcement of a state law is preempted only if (1) the plain language of the federal statute on the subject expressly states that it preempts state law, (2) the federal legislation is so comprehensive that it is inferable the Congress wished to fully occupy the subject matter ("field preemption"), or (3) the state law conflicts with the federal law. There is no express preemption in this case. In fact, the National Traffic and Motor Vehicle Safety Act includes a savings clause stating that compliance with a motor vehicle safety standard does not exempt a person from liability at common law. The plaintiffs also contend that there is neither "field preemption" nor a conflict. We agree. With regard to field preemption, it does not appear that the federal statutes were intended to so greatly envelop the field of motor vehicle safety standards as to leave little room for state participation. The existence of the savings clause supports this conclusion as well. In fact, the existence of a savings clause evinces a congressional determination that occasional non-uniformity is a small price to pay for a system in which juries not only create, but also enforce, safety standards. The savings clause thus represents a purposeful intent to allow meaningful state participation. Consequently, there is no implied field preemption.

The main point of contention between the parties is whether the seatbelt claims are barred under implied conflict preemption. We conclude that they are not. Implied conflict preemption can arise (1) when it is impossible for a private party to comply with both state and federal requirements, or (2) where state law stands as an obstacle to the accomplishment and execution of the objectives of Congress. The latter situation arises only when enforcement of the state law would frustrate a *significant* objective of the federal regulation. A plain reading of the federal regulations at issue here shows that they mandate the inclusion of protective devices at the driver's seat of a bus, but they are silent regarding the installation of passenger seatbelts. This does not make it impossible to comply with both the federal standards and the gravamen of the plaintiff's claims, which seek to impose liability for failure to install such protective devices. The manufacturer could have installed passenger seatbelts without running afoul of the federal regulation. Hence, the plaintiffs' claims are not impliedly preempted based on a conflict with federal law. In sum, we find neither express nor implied preemption of the plaintiffs' seatbelt claims. Reversed.

Analysis:

As noted in this opinion, preemption can be either express or implied. If the federal statute does not expressly indicate that it preempts state law, the court looks beyond the statute's language to determine whether Congress chose to occupy the entire field of law at issue, whether the state law directly conflicts with the federal law, or whether enforcement of the state law would frustrate a significant Congressional purpose. Here, the court found none of these grounds for preemption, and thus concluded that the claim based on the lack of passenger seatbelts did not conflict with federal law, which required a seatbelt only for the bus driver.

■ CASE VOCABULARY

PREEMPTION DOCTRINE: The doctrine based on the Supremacy Clause of the Constitution that holds that certain matters are of such a national, as opposed to local, character that federal laws take precedence over state laws.

Newmark v. Gimbel's Inc.

(Customer) v. (Store Owning Beauty Shop)

54 N.J. 585, 258 A.2d 697 (1969)

PRODUCTS USED BY COMMERCIAL ENTITIES IN THE PROVISION OF RETAIL SERVICES CARRY AN IMPLIED WARRANTY OF FITNESS WITH RESPECT TO THE CUSTOMER

■ **INSTANT FACTS** Mrs. Newmark (P) was given a permanent at one of Gimbel's (D) beauty shops. The solution used in giving the permanent caused Newmark's (P) scalp to blister and her hair to fall out.

■ **BLACK LETTER RULE** There is an implied warranty of fitness of the products a retail service provider uses in providing those services the same as if the customer had purchased the product themselves.

■ PROCEDURAL BASIS

Appeal to the State's highest court after the appeals court reversed the dismissal of Plaintiff's warranty claim by the trial court.

■ FACTS

Mrs. Newmark (P) went to a beauty shop owned by Gimbel's, Inc. (Gimbel's)(D) where she had a standing appointment. Her regular operator, Valante, recommended she get a permanent and Newmark (P) accepted. During the treatment Newmark (P) repeatedly felt a "burning" and Valante took steps to diminish it. However, her forehead later blistered and her hair fell out. A dermatologist diagnosed her with contact dermatitis resulting from the application of the permanent solution. Valante stated that the solution could damage a scalp that had scratches on it or could cause a sting if the solution were rubbed into the scalp. He applied the solution as it came from the original package and his experience had shown that a tingling or burning sensation was fairly common. The label on the package contained a caveat for the beauty operator that cautioned the operator in using the solution, including an instruction to ask the patron if she has ever had a sensitivity to such waving lotion. Newmark (P) did not see the label and there is no indication that Valante asked her about any previous experience with such solutions. It does appear, however, that Newmark (P) had four permanent waves without any ill effects after this incident. Newmark's (P) warranty claim against Gimbel's (D) was dismissed by the trial court, holding that Gimbel's (D) was rendering a service, not making a sale. The Appellate Division reversed, holding that there might be an implied warranty as to the solution applied.

■ ISSUE

Are commercial entities that sell services that include the use of outside products exempt from warranty claims when those products are defective?

■ DECISION AND RATIONALE

(Francis, J.) No. If Gimbel's (D) had simply sold Newmark (P) the permanent solution, there would have unquestionably been an implied warranty of fitness of the product. What Gimbel's'(D) argument boils down to is that if, in addition to recommending the use of the solution and supplying it for use, they also applied it, such fact that they applied it would have the effect of lessening their liability to the patron by eliminating warranty and by limiting their responsibility to the issue of negligence. We disagree. On the contrary, by also administering the product, they might increase the scope of their liability. The transaction here has two parts: the rendering of service, and the supplying of goods for a consideration. We therefore agree with the Appellate division that an implied warranty of fitness of the products used in giving the permanent wave exists with no less force than it would have in the case of a simple sale. The fact that the customer did not specifically pay for the product, but instead had the price included in the flat rate for the permanent, is of no relevance. Common sense demands that such patron be deemed a consumer as to both manufacturer and beauty parlor operator. When a patron responds to the parlor's solicitation she does so confident that any product used in the shop has come from a reliable origin and can be trusted not to injure her. The ministrations and the products used on her are under the control and selection of the operator; the patron is a mere passive recipient. It seems to us that the policy considerations for imposing warranty liability in the case of ordinary sales are equally applicable to a commercial transaction such as that existing in this case between a beauty parlor operator and a patron. Gimbel's (D) claims that to hold them to strict liability would be contrary to *Magrine v. Krasnica.* We cannot agree. *Magrine* was injured during a visit to the dentist when a hypodermic needle, concededly being used with due care, broke off in his gum. The parties agreed the needle broke as the result of a defect. It was held that the strict liability in tort doctrine did not apply to the professional, such as a dentist or doctor, because the essence of the relationship with the patient was the furnishing of professional skill and services. We accepted the view that a dentist's bill for services should be considered as representing pay for that alone. The use of instruments or the administration of medicines or the providing of medicines for use at home cannot give the ministrations the cast of a commercial transaction. Accordingly, the liability of the dentist in ordinary cases must be tested by the principles of negligence. Gimbel's (D) suggests that there is no doctrinal basis for distinguishing the beauty parlor from the dentist or doctor, and therefore the liability for all should be tested by the same rules. But there is a vast difference in the relationships. The beautician is engaged in a commercial enterprise; the dentist and doctor in a profession. The former fulfills not a need, but a form of aesthetic convenience or luxury, involving the rendition of non-professional services. The demand for the doctor stems from need. Doctors and dentist exercise their best judgment in making a diagnosis and then making a recommendation for treatment. Each patient requires individual treatment, not some mechanically identical procedure. Doctors and dentists provide no implied warranty of relief or cure. Thus their paramount function ought to be regarded as the furnishing of opinions and services, which bears such a necessary and intimate relationship to public health and welfare that their obligation ought to be grounded in a duty of competence and care toward patients. The function of these professionals is so important as to outweigh on the policy scale any need for the imposition upon them the rules of strict liability in tort. Affirmed and remanded for a new trial.

Analysis:

What possible rationale could support holding the hairdresser strictly liable for the defective products she purchases from the distributor and uses in her business, but not holding a physician liable for the defective products the doctor purchases from medical supply and engineering companies and uses on and in patients? It can certainly be argued that neither the hairdresser nor the doctor has done anything wrong or is at fault (provided there is no negligence, of course). The proper remedy, it seems reasonable to say, is to sue the manufacturer under strict tort liability. Instead, the court in *Newmark* chose to draw a distinction between doctors, dentists, and presumably other "professionals" and those who minister to the desires or wishes of regular consumers by providing non-essential services. The court says that, as a matter of public policy, the function of doctors and dentists is so essential that it would be unwise to impose strict liability in tort upon them, especially for the defects in products they use in their practice.

CHAPTER TWENTY-FIVE

Settlement and Apportionment

Gleason v. Guzman

Instant Facts: A concussed tort victim signs a release, but later sues the tortfeasor when the injury unexpectedly causes epilepsy.

Black Letter Rule: Tort victims who signed general releases while mistaken about their injury may rescind the release later if they mistook the injury's present nature, but not if they mistook the injury's future prognosis.

Safeway Stores, Inc. v. Nest-Kart

Instant Facts: When a defective supermarket cart injures a shopper, the court finds the supermarket 80% responsible in negligence and the manufacturer 20% responsible in strict product liability. The supermarket claims apportionment proportional to comparative fault is inapplicable between negligent and strictly liable defendants.

Black Letter Rule: In "comparative fault" jurisdictions, if one co-tortfeasor is negligent and another co-tortfeasor is strictly liable, damages should be apportioned proportional to each defendant's degree of fault.

Board of County Commissioners of Teton County v. Bassett

Instant Facts: Bassett (P) and Coziah (P) were injured when a suspect who evaded law enforcement officers' high-speed-chase and roadblock attempts crashed into their vehicle, and the defendant officers contended that the fleeing suspect's willful and wanton or intentional conduct should have been considered by the jury when allocating fault among the defendants.

Black Letter Rule: Each defendant in a case is liable only to the extent of that defendant's proportion of the total fault.

D'Amario v. Ford Motor Co.

Instant Facts: After the plaintiff's minor son was injured in a one-car accident, his injuries were enhanced when the car burst into flames.

Black Letter Rule: In a crashworthiness case against a product manufacturer, evidence of the driver's initial negligence is irrelevant and inadmissible.

Hymowitz v. Eli Lilly & Co.

Instant Facts: DES daughters were unable to identify which drug manufacturer sold the DES that their mothers took decades earlier so they sued various potentially liable drug makers, and the defendants moved for summary judgment based on the plaintiffs' inability to identify the responsible party.

Black Letter Rule: Under the market share liability theory, liability will be apportioned to each defendant according to its share of the market for the product giving rise to the plaintiff's injuries.

Gleason v. Guzman

(Tortfeasor) v. (Tort Victim)

623 P.2d 378 (Colo.1981)

TORT VICTIMS MAY RESCIND RELEASES SIGNED IF MISTAKEN ABOUT INJURY'S NATURE

■ **INSTANT FACTS** A concussed tort victim signs a release, but later sues the tortfeasor when the injury unexpectedly causes epilepsy.

■ **BLACK LETTER RULE** Tort victims who signed general releases while mistaken about their injury may rescind the release later if they mistook the injury's present nature, but not if they mistook the injury's future prognosis.

■ PROCEDURAL BASIS

Appeal from appellate court's denial of summary judgment for defendants in tort action seeking rescission of release, and damages.

■ FACTS

Gleason (D), a truck driver employed by Coin Fresh (D), dropped a vending machine from his truck, striking Ms. Guzman (P), a minor, in the head. Guzman (P) was diagnosed with temporal lobe contusion [meaning, she was struck on the head], and complained of headaches, vomiting, and disorientation, but was treated and believed cured. Since Guzman (P) was a minor, her family sued on her behalf, and received a settlement of $6,114 in exchange for a general release, signed by her guardian (father). [It is possible the father, who was uneducated and spoke little English, did not understand what he was signing.] Later, almost 4 years after the accident, Guzman (P) experienced epileptic seizures. Guzman (P) sued Gleason (D) and Coin Fresh (D) for negligent personal injury. The defendants raised as an affirmative defense the release Guzman (P) signed, and moved for summary judgment. Guzman (P) countered, moving to set aside the release on the ground it was executed under a mistake as to the injury's nature. At trial, the judge granted defendants summary judgment. Guzman (P) appealed. On appeal, the appellate court reversed the summary judgment entry. Gleason (D) and Coin Fresh (D) appeal, contending (i) Guzman (P) made no mistake about the injury actually suffered, but only about future complications, and (ii) the release was a general release encompassing injuries both known and unknown.

■ ISSUE

May a tort victim who signed a general release while mistaken about the injury later rescind the release?

■ DECISION AND RATIONALE

(Quinn) Yes. Tort victims who signed general releases while mistaken about their injury may rescind the release later if they mistook the injury's present nature, but not if they mistook the injury's future prognosis. [Procedurally, the court holds a lawsuit involving a motion to set aside a release ineligible for jury trial.] Since these arguments are presented in the context of a summary judgement review, the issue is whether the record shows a genuine issue as to any material fact. Cases addressing mistakes in the settlement of personal injury claims reflect a tension stemming from the general need for finality in the contractual settlement of suits, as opposed to the recognized need to alleviate the unintended and unfair effects of human error. These policies lean in different directions. One approach—denying rescission even where the injuries were unknown or unsuspected during settlement—makes the releasor assume the risk that the injuries' known nature and extent might be more severe than believed at settlement. Another approach allows rescission based on any mistake about the injured plaintiff's condition, whether the mistake relates to the injuries' nature or their further consequences. Midway between these approaches is the view that rescission is available for mistakes relating to known injuries' nature, but not for mistakes about the future course and effects of those injuries. The assumption in this last approach is that rescission must be based on mistake, and "mistake," for legal purposes, must relate to a past or present fact rather than an opinion or prophecy about the future. This last approach represents the rule in this jurisdiction, as expressed in *McCarthy v. Eddings* [plaintiff who signed release for broken arm, believing it temporary, may rescind the release when the injury was found to be permanent], *Davis v. Flatiron Materials Co.* [plaintiff, correctly diagnosed and aware of nature of condition, cannot rescind release because she was mistaken about course of recovery], and *Scotton v. Landers* [plaintiff who signed release for fractured rib may rescind general release on learning spleen was ruptured]. However, as these cases demonstrate, the analytic distinction between unknown injuries and unknown consequences does not yield a litmus-type resolution to these problems. Here, this is a marginal case, because, when the injury is post-traumatic epilepsy, it is difficult to differentiate a mistaken diagnosis from a mistaken prognosis. Knowledge of an injury's nature requires an awareness and appreciation of its extent, severity, and likely duration. These basic components of knowledge involve comprehending the injury's basic character, as distinct from a prediction or opinion about the future course of recovery. Here, the record provides adequate basis to infer the existence of a mistake in the guardian's execution of the release, because the guardian had little education, was not adept at English, and apparently believed the injury was only a "concussion." Since Guzman (P) experienced only minor symptoms after the accident, it may reasonably be inferred that, when the release was executed, the guardian believed the injury was minor, temporary, and posed no risk of complication, and there is no evidence that the guardian was informed otherwise by doctors or his lawyer. In fact, Guzman's (P) lawyer was unaware the injury posed risk of brain dysfunction, much less post-traumatic epilepsy, as is discernable from his correspondence and in-court statements. On the record, there is a genuine factual issue on whether the guardian was mistaken about the nature of Guzman's (P) injury when he executed the release. Thus, summary judgement was inappropriate. The defendants argue the release bars all Guzman's (P) claims, as a matter of law, because its terms encompass unknown injuries that may develop later. Although some jurisdictions give effect to a release which precludes recovery even for unknown injuries, the tendency of the law is to the contrary. Most courts allow for avoidance (i.e., voiding the release) in appropriate circumstances (e.g., mistake, lack of intent, etc.). Resolving the intent issue necessarily means going behind the release's language. The release will be set aside if the parties did not contemplate unknown injuries. Summary judgement for defendants reversed.

Analysis:

The majority rule is that a release is voidable if signed under mistake, but only if the plaintiff mistook the injury's "nature," and not if he merely miscalculated the duration or difficulty of recovering from a known injury. As the case notes, it is often difficult to differentiate whether a victim was mistaken about the injury's "diagnosis" or its "prognosis." Here, for instance, it could be argued that Guzman (P) was mistaken about her injury's nature (believing it to be a concussion when in fact it was brain damage), and that she understood her injury but miscalculated the recovery (knew she had a head injury and concussion, but did not believe it would develop into epilepsy). Policy suggests that a release should be voidable in any case where the injury turns out to be more complicated than foreseen at signing. The aim of tort is (or should be) to compensate the victim fully for injury inflicted by another. But the purpose of a release is to settle the matter of liability and damages once and for all so that both parties can move on, so there are conflicting priorities here.

■ CASE VOCABULARY

(GENERAL) RELEASE: Plaintiff's signed document releasing defendant from further liability, usually in exchange for a settlement payment.

Safeway Stores, Inc. v. Nest-Kart

(Negligent Co-Tortfeasor) v. (Strictly-Liable Co-Tortfeasor)

21 Cal.3d 322, 146 Cal.Rptr. 550, 579 P.2d 441 (1978)

COMPARATIVE NEGLIGENCE ALLOWS COMPARATIVE APPORTIONMENT BETWEEN NEGLIGENT AND STRICTLY-LIABLE DEFENDANTS

■ **INSTANT FACTS** When a defective supermarket cart injures a shopper, the court finds the supermarket 80% responsible in negligence and the manufacturer 20% responsible in strict product liability. The supermarket claims apportionment proportional to comparative fault is inapplicable between negligent and strictly liable defendants.

■ **BLACK LETTER RULE** In "comparative fault" jurisdictions, if one co-tortfeasor is negligent and another co-tortfeasor is strictly liable, damages should be apportioned proportional to each defendant's degree of fault.

■ PROCEDURAL BASIS

In negligence and strict liability tort action seeking damages, appeal from post-verdict motion seeking reallocation of damages between defendants.

■ FACTS

Elliot (P), a shopper at [the unfortunately-named] Safeway Stores (D), was injured when a shopping cart, owned by Safeway (D), broke and fell on her foot. Elliot (P) sued the cart's owner Safeway (D), its manufacturer Nest-Kart Corp. (D) for personal injury in strict liability and negligence. At trial, the jury returned a verdict of $25,000 against both Safeway (D) and Nest-Kart (D) and made "special findings" that Safeway (D) was 80% liable (in negligence and strict liability) while Nest-Kart (D) was 20% liable (in strict liability only). Safeway (D) moved to require Nest-Kart (D) to pay 50%, contending *American Motorcycle* held that, under California's "contribution" [comparative fault] statutes, multiple tortfeasors' liability may not be apportioned according to comparative fault when one is negligent and another is non-negligent but strictly liable. The trial court granted Safeway's (D) motion and ordered Nest-Kart (D) to pay 50%. Nest-Kart (D) appeals.

■ ISSUE

In "comparative fault" jurisdictions, if one co-tortfeasor is negligent and another co-tortfeasor is strictly liable, can damages be apportioned proportional to each defendant's degree of fault?

■ DECISION AND RATIONALE

(Tobriner) Yes. In "comparative fault" jurisdictions, if one co-tortfeasor is negligent and another co-tortfeasor is strictly liable, damages should be apportioned proportional to each defendant's degree of fault. *American Motorcycle* explicitly held that California's current "contribution" [comparative fault] statutes do not necessarily prohibit apportioning liability among multiple tortfeasors on a comparative fault basis, so the trial court erred in holding otherwise. However, the question remains whether *American Motorcycle's* "comparative indemnity" [comparative fault] doctrine may be applied when some defendants are liable based only on strict liability, to apportion liability based on their degree of fault. We believe it may, based on the same basic equitable considerations. Such a holding would apportion liability between strictly liable defendants and other co-tortfeasors, which does not conflict with the rationale of strict liability. Although one of the social policies served by product liability doctrine is to assign liability to a party who possesses the ability to distribute losses over an appropriate segment of society, this policy is not so absolute that it must allow negligent tortfeasors who contribute to the injury to escape all liability. It is sometimes suggested that apportionment is impossible between defendants who are negligent and those who are strictly liable, since no logical basis can be found for comparing the relative "fault" of a negligent defendant with that of a defendant whose liability rests on "no fault" strict liability. However, these suggested difficulties are more theoretical than practical, and other jurisdictions' experience demonstrates juries are fully competent to apply comparative fault principles between such defendants. We note that holding otherwise—i.e., confining the comparative indemnity [comparative negligence] doctrine to cases involving only negligent defendants—would lead to bizarre and irrational consequences, because, e.g., a manufacturer who negligently produced a product would frequently be in a better position than a non-negligent one sued for strict liability, since the negligent manufacturer could shift liability to negligent co-tortfeasors, but the non-negligent one could not. Thus, to avoid such unjustified results, we hold the comparative indemnity doctrine applies to allocate liability between negligent defendants and strictly-liable ones.

Analysis:

As the court notes, it is difficult to make a rational apportionment of "fault" for a strict liability defendant, because, by definition, the strictly-liable defendant need not be at fault. Some courts skirt the analytic contradiction by referring to fault apportioned to strictly liable defendants as "comparative causation." The alternative is merely to demand each co-defendant pay a pro rata (equal) share of damages, which has no rational basis. The holding in *Safeway* is a compromise between fairness and practicality. In the past, at common law, before comparative negligence was accepted, some courts held that a "passive" defendant (such as a strictly liable but non-negligent products manufacturer) was entitled to (full) indemnity from the "active" negligent co-tortfeasor, which meant the strictly liable defendant would not have to pay anything as long as his negligent co-defendants were solvent. However, this system was even more arbitrary, since it in effect assigns 100% of fault to a negligent defendant and 0% to a strictly liable one, even if the "passive" defendant was actually partly at fault.

■ CASE VOCABULARY

COMPARATIVE FAULT/COMPARATIVE INDEMNITY: Same as comparative negligence, a tort system under which tortfeasors must pay the percentage of total damages which corresponds to their degree of fault.

Board of County Commissioners of Teton County v. Bassett

(County Board) v. (Crash Victim)

8 P.3d 1079 (Wyo. 2000)

JOINT AND SEVERAL LIABILITY IS NOT THE LAW IN WYOMING

■ **INSTANT FACTS** Bassett (P) and Coziah (P) were injured when a suspect who evaded law enforcement officers' high-speed-chase and roadblock attempts crashed into their vehicle, and the defendant officers contended that the fleeing suspect's willful and wanton or intentional conduct should have been considered by the jury when allocating fault among the defendants.

■ **BLACK LETTER RULE** Each defendant in a case is liable only to the extent of that defendant's proportion of the total fault.

■ PROCEDURAL BASIS

State appellate court review of a trial court decision in the plaintiffs' favor.

■ FACTS

The Highway Patrol pursued Ortega in a high-speed chase. He managed to evade the officers, so sheriff's deputies set up a roadblock. They placed improvised road spikes on the roadway in the hope that Ortega would turn off the highway and onto the road, and then stop when the spikes disabled his vehicle. Ortega did not turn off the highway, but instead continued straight ahead. At the same time, and at the same place, Bassett (P) and Coziah (P) were on their way home from fishing when they passed several law enforcement officers on the side of the road. None of the officers made any effort to warn the men about the hazardous situation that was developing. When the officers realized what was happening, they created an opening in the roadblock and frantically gestured the men through. Ortega went through the same opening at 100 miles per hour, smashing into Cozia's (P) car, which was going about thirty miles per hour. Coziah (P) and Bassett (p) were injured, and Ortega was arrested. Coziah (P) and Bassett (P) sued. The jury awarded them damages, allocating fault among the Highway Patrol, the sheriff's officers, and the park service officers. The issue before the court was whether Ortega, whose conduct was willful and wanton or intentional, should have been included among the actors whose fault would be determined and compared to that of the other actors by the jury in apportioning fault. The plaintiffs contended that it should not, and the district court agreed. The defendants appealed.

■ ISSUE

Should the jury have considered Ortega's willful and wanton or intentional conduct when apportioning fault?

■ DECISION AND RATIONALE

(Grant, J.) Yes. Each defendant in a case is liable only to the extent of that defendant's proportion of the total fault. The Wyoming statute on apportioning damages now uses the word "fault," a more inclusive term than the previously used "negligence." Including Ortega in damages apportionment would be consistent with the changes in the statute. Moreover, the inclusion of Ortega would also be consistent with another purpose of the revised statute, the elimination of joint and several liability. To leave an actor such as Ortega out of the apportionment calculation exposes the remaining appellants to the possibility that they will be held to answer for his misconduct. Some states have held that persons who negligently fail to protect against the specific risk of an intentional tort should bear the risk that the intentional tortfeasor is insolvent. But the statutory elimination of joint and several liability in Wyoming forecloses our consideration of the merits of such a policy. The exclusion of Ortega from the verdict form frustrates the legislature's expressed intent. Reversed and remanded for a new trial.

Analysis:

The court references the fact that joint and several liability was eliminated in Wyoming. When two or more parties are *jointly and severally liable,* each party is independently liable for the full extent of the injuries. Thus, if the plaintiff wins a money judgment against the defendants collectively, he or she may collect the full value of the judgment from any one of them, who may then seek contribution from the other defendants. The plaintiff is not shortchanged by the insolvency of a particular defendant. But that is not the law in Wyoming. The court also makes note of the fact that in other states, certain circumstances will justify apportionment of fault among defendants who have failed to protect against the risk of an intentional tort—such as law enforcement officers who fail to protect the public during a high-speed chase.

■ CASE VOCABULARY

JOINT AND SEVERAL: Status where rights and liabilities are shared collectively and also individually among a group of persons.

D'Amario v. Ford Motor Co.

(Injured Minor's Mother) v. (Automobile Manufacturer)

806 So.2d 424 (Fla.2001)

LIABILITY EXTENDS TO ENHANCED INJURIES

■ **INSTANT FACTS** After the plaintiff's minor son was injured in a one-car accident, his injuries were enhanced when the car burst into flames.

■ **BLACK LETTER RULE** In a crashworthiness case against a product manufacturer, evidence of the driver's initial negligence is irrelevant and inadmissible.

■ PROCEDURAL BASIS

On appeal to review a jury verdict for the defendant.

■ FACTS

Clifford Harris, a minor, was severely injured when a car driven by an intoxicated friend crashed into a tree and burst into flames. After striking the tree, a fire started in the engine area and spread throughout the vehicle, causing an explosion. Harris lost three limbs and suffered burns on most of his body. D'Amario (P), Harris's mother, sued Ford Motor Co. (D), alleging that Harris's injuries were caused by a defective relay switch in the vehicle, which resulted in the explosion after the initial impact. Ford (D) denied liability and contended that the injuries were caused by a negligent third party, without identifying the driver as a non-party tortfeasor. At trial, the plaintiff offered expert testimony that a defect in the relay switch prevented the switch from interrupting the flow of fuel to the fuel pump, causing the explosion. Ford's (D) experts testified that the explosion was caused by an oil pan that ruptured on impact. Ford (D) then amended its affirmative defense to include evidence of the driver's intoxication and excessive speed. The parties thereafter stipulated to the driver's intoxication and that the driver's negligence caused the initial impact. After deliberation, the jury found that Ford (D) was not the legal cause of the injuries and returned a defense verdict. After the court of appeals reversed the trial court's order for a new trial and reinstated the verdict, D'Amario (P) appealed.

■ ISSUE

Is evidence of a driver's initial negligence relevant to an automobile manufacturer's liability for product defects that enhance the initial injuries?

■ DECISION AND RATIONALE

(Per curiam.) No. Under the majority view, "the fault of the person causing the accident that created the circumstances in which the second accident occurred should be compared with the role of the automobile manufacturer's negligence in designing a defective product in asserting total responsibility for the claimant's injuries." Under the minority view, on the other hand, a manufacturer "is liable only for the increased injury caused by its own conduct, not for the injury resulting from the crash itself." This view recognizes the initial negligence as remote from the enhanced injury caused by a defective part designed to protect against injury in the event of a collision. Accordingly, evidence of a driver's negligence is irrelevant to the manufacturer's liability for injuries resulting from the defective product.

Unlike cases in which a plaintiff's injuries are caused by multiple defendants' joint and concurrent negligence, crashworthiness cases involve joint and successive negligence. The injuries caused from an initial collision are separate and distinct from those caused by a defective product following the collision. In this respect, crashworthiness cases are analogous to medical malpractice cases, in which evidence of a patient's initial negligence causing his injuries is inadmissible when considering a physician's successive breach of care. Therefore, the minority view is adopted and evidence of the driver's initial negligence is irrelevant and inadmissible when determining the manufacturer's successive liability. By limiting the manufacturer's liability to injuries caused by the defective product, and not by the driver's initial negligence, this view appropriately acknowledges comparative fault principles and avoids unduly confusing the jury. Reversed.

Analysis:

If evidence of the driver's negligence could be introduced as an affirmative defense or to mitigate damages, car manufacturers would nearly always avoid liability in a crashworthiness case. Because most car accidents are caused by someone's negligence, the car manufacturer need only point to that negligence as the cause of the injuries and avoid liability for its design defects. But the driver's negligence is a reasonably foreseeable occurrence, so the manufacturer should be held accountable for the injuries from the crash.

■ CASE VOCABULARY

CONCURRENT NEGLIGENCE: The negligence of two or more parties acting independently but causing the same damage.

SUBSEQUENT NEGLIGENCE: The negligence of the defendant when, after the defendant's initial negligence and the plaintiff's contributory negligence, the defendant discovers—or should have discovered—that the plaintiff was in a position of danger and fails to exercise due care in preventing the plaintiff's injuries.

Hymowitz v. Eli Lilly & Co.

(DES Daughter) v. (DES Manufacturer)

539 N.E.2d 1069 (N.Y. 1989)

THE COURT ADOPTS THE MARKET SHARE LIABILITY APPROACH IN DES CASES

■ **INSTANT FACTS** DES daughters were unable to identify which drug manufacturer sold the DES that their mothers took decades earlier so they sued various potentially liable drug makers, and the defendants moved for summary judgment based on the plaintiffs' inability to identify the responsible party.

■ **BLACK LETTER RULE** Under the market share liability theory, liability will be apportioned to each defendant according to its share of the market for the product giving rise to the plaintiff's injuries.

■ PROCEDURAL BASIS

State appellate court review of the lower court decision denying summary judgment.

■ FACTS

In 1941, the FDA approved the drug known as DES, or diethylstilbestrol, which was prescribed to prevent miscarriages. Ultimately, some 300 companies sold the drug. Although DES first appeared to be safe, over time it became known that the daughters of mothers who took the drug while they were pregnant had an increased risk of developing cancer in adulthood. Many lawsuits ensued in which DES daughters sued the DES manufacturers. In this case, the defendants moved for summary judgment on the ground that the manufacturer that had produced the particular drug ingested by the plaintiffs' mothers could not be identified. It was often impossible for a mother to recall which manufacturer had produced the drug she took some twenty years earlier. The trial court denied the defendants' motions and the defendants appealed.

■ ISSUE

Could the defendant drug manufacturers be held liable even though the plaintiffs were unable to prove which of them manufactured the drug taken by their mothers?

■ DECISION AND RATIONALE

(Wachtler, J.) Yes. Under the market share liability theory, liability will be apportioned to each defendant according to its share of the market for the product giving rise to the plaintiff's injuries. This is the theory of liability that leads to the fairest result. Oftentimes in alternative liability cases, the defendants are in a better position than the plaintiff(s) to identify the actual wrongdoer. That is not the case here, where neither side can actually determine who the manufacturer of the drug taken by the mother was. Nor does the theory of concerted action supply a basis for recovery. There was no agreement to market DES for use in pregnancy without taking steps to ensure the drug's safety. Parallel activity, without more, does not establish an agreement. In short, these common law doctrines provide no relief for the DES plaintiffs unable to identify the manufacturer of the drug taken by their mothers. The present circumstances require recognition of a reasonable avenue of relief.

We believe that a market share theory based on a national market provides the best solution. We choose to apportion liability among all defendants in proportion to the amount of risk of injury each defendant created to the public at large based on the share of the market they held at the time of the mother's ingestion. A defendant will not be held liable if the DES producer satisfies its burden of proof to show that it was not a member of the DES market for use during pregnancy. However, there is no exculpation for a defendant who appears not to have caused a particular plaintiff's injury. It is merely a windfall for a producer to escape liability solely because it manufactured a more identifiable pill, or sold only to certain drugstores. These fortuities in no way diminish the culpability of a defendant for marketing the product, which is the basis of liability here. Finally, we hold that the liability of DES producers is several only, and should not be inflated when all participants in the market are not before the court. This may prevent some plaintiffs from recovering 100% of their damages, but we decline to increase a defendant's liability beyond its fair share of responsibility.

■ CONCURRENCE IN PART, DISSENT IN PART

(Mollen, J.) I believe that there should be exculpation for those defendants who can prove that they did not produce or market the particular pill ingested by the plaintiff's mother. I would also retain the principle of imposing joint and several liability upon the defendants who cannot exculpate themselves.

Analysis:

The court considered the earlier decisions in the *Sindell v. Abbott Labs* case and in *Brown v. Superior Court*. It adopted parts of the reasoning in those cases, but rejected other parts of the decisions. It rejected the holding in *Sindell* that a defendant who could prove it did not actually injure the plaintiff would not be held liable (the dissent's viewpoint here). But it adopted the reasoning in *Brown* that the defendants' liability was several only. The court also referenced the decision in *Collins v. Eli Lilly & Co.*, wherein the court held that each defendant would be liable in proportion to the amount of risk it created that the plaintiff would be injured. Risk in that context was a question of fact, with market share being relevant to the determination. Defendants were allowed under the *Collins* approach to show that their product could not have caused the plaintiff's injury.

■ CASE VOCABULARY

JOINT AND SEVERAL LIABILITY: A form of liability imposed in civil cases where two or more people are found liable. The plaintiff may collect the entire judgment from any one of the parties, or from any and all of the parties in various amounts, until the judgment is paid in full.

CHAPTER TWENTY-SIX

Damages

Martin v. United States

Instant Facts: When 2 schoolboys were burned and permanently disfigured by contact with negligently-maintained power lines, the judge considers damages.

Black Letter Rule: [Omitted. This case is included to demonstrate how judges evaluate personal injury claims, and the court's other findings were omitted.]

Averyt v. Wal-Mart Stores, Inc.

Instant Facts: Averyt (P) slipped and fell while making a delivery to Wal-Mart (D) and was seriously injured; she sued Wal-Mart (D) and the jury awarded her significant damages, but Wal-Mart (D) argued that the damages were excessive and was granted a new trial.

Black Letter Rule: Where the jury's damages award is supported by the evidence, a reviewing court will not reverse it.

McDougald v. Garber

Instant Facts: When medical malpractice renders a patient comatose, the malpractitioners argue the patient cannot recover separately for "lost enjoyment of life."

Black Letter Rule: Tort victims can recover for "pain and suffering" and "loss of enjoyment of life" only as part of a single award, and they cannot recover for "loss of enjoyment" if they are unaware of the loss.

State Farm Mut. Auto. Ins. Co. v. Campbell

Instant Facts: After State Farm (D) failed to settle claims against Campbell (P) for its policy limits and altered information to lessen his culpability, a jury awarded Campbell (P) $1 million in compensatory damages and $145 million in punitive damages.

Black Letter Rule: In evaluating the appropriateness of a punitive damages award, a court must weigh the reprehensibility of the defendant's conduct, the disparity between the actual harm caused and the amount of the punitive damages awarded, and the difference between the punitive damages awarded and the civil penalties imposed under state law.

Mathias v. Accor Economy Lodging, Inc.

Instant Facts: Motel guests sued the motel after being bitten by bedbugs that had apparently infested the motel for years, and the jury awarded them punitive damages that greatly exceeded the compensatory damages award; the defendant argued that the damages award was excessive.

Black Letter Rule: There are no definitive rules establishing a precise methodology for computing punitive damages.

Martin v. United States

(Electrocuted Boys) v. (U.S. Government, as Maintainer of Power Lines)

471 F.Supp. 6 (D.Ariz.1979)

COMPENSATORY DAMAGES INCLUDE COMPENSATION FOR LOST EARNINGS POTENTIAL AND PAIN

■ **INSTANT FACTS** When 2 schoolboys were burned and permanently disfigured by contact with negligently-maintained power lines, the judge considers damages.

■ **BLACK LETTER RULE** [Omitted. This case is included to demonstrate how judges evaluate personal injury claims, and the court's other findings were omitted.]

■ PROCEDURAL BASIS

Inquest in Federal negligent personal injury action seeking damages.

■ FACTS

Schoolboys Burrows (P) and Martin (P), riding a motorcycle, struck a power line maintained negligently by the U.S. government (D), and were severely burned. Burrows (P) and Martin (P) sued the U.S. government (D) for negligent tort under the Federal Tort Claims Act. At trial, the judge found the U.S. government (D) liable, and now considers damages.

■ ISSUE

In this case, how much compensation should plaintiff receive for crippling and disfiguring burns?

■ DECISION AND RATIONALE

(Burns) [Unfortunate.] Plaintiff Melvin Burrows (P) sustained severe burns to his face, head, back, butt, arms, and legs. His current medical expenses were $48,130.97, and future medical expenses will be about $49,000. Finally, we award $5,000 for psychological treatment. We now consider Burrows's (P) lost earnings capacity. As for plaintiff Martin (P), we have heard testimony from Burrows's (P) principal [who is also Burrows's father's employer, and uncle to Martin (D) (!)] that Burrows (P) is of average intelligence or higher, and probably would have become a skilled worker, perhaps a mechanic or carpenter. [Remember, this is 1979.] Another witness, a finance professor and investment counselor, opined that Burrows (P) and Martin (P) would likely gravitate into the construction trades like most of their classmates, and forecast that demand for such trades would be strong. Defendant's witness, a clinical psychologist, testified that intelligence and aptitude tests administered to Burrows (P) show he could not pursue a skilled craft, but instead would probably have become a laborer. Defendant's other witness, an economics professor, opined that neither Burrows (P) nor Martin (P) would enter the skilled trades, and that they would both have earned average wages. Based on my evaluation of the expert witnesses' testimony, experience, and credibility, I conclude Burrows (P) would have become a skilled worker. Expert testimony reveals that a skilled worker in 1978 would earn $9,450 annually for a four-year apprenticeship and $18,900 in wages and $3,900 in benefits annually during a 42-year career. One expert testified Burrows (P) may be employable as a night watchman or night mechanic not involved with the public [Again, this *is* 1979.] Based on this testimony and my observation, I conclude Burrows

(P) will probably be able to work at an entry-level position for at least half his working life, which would generate income of $3,120 in 1978 dollars. Thus, in total, Burrows (P) is entitled to recover (in 1978 dollars) $6,330 annually for the four-year apprenticeship period, then $19, 680 annually for the next 42 years. I find the award can be invested at little risk and return compounded interest of 7.5%. I also find Burrows's (P) annual wage inflation rate can be estimated at 5.5%. Thus, the award for Burrows's (P) lost earning capacity is $548,029. Now we consider Burrows's (P) pain and suffering. The power line burned most of Burrows's (P) head, face, back, and buttocks, and left 6 holes in his skin. When Burrows (P) was treated for 4 months, doctors performed 4 skin grafts and attempted to fashion a functioning eyelid, which still cannot be closed. Burrows (P) lost one ear entirely and part of the other. Scalp rotations were necessary to restore hair growth and build up skin where it was burned down to the skull. These operations left Burrows's (P) face severely scarred, his mouth permanently contorted, and his facial nerves unable to smile. Burrows (P) will also require 11 additional skin grafts, which are unpleasant and risky. In addition to his physical suffering, Burrows (P) has suffered psychologically. Burrows (P) is often ridiculed by classmates and strangers, became reclusive, and may develop schizophrenic tendencies. Nor is it likely Burrows (P) will have a normal social or sexual life. I award Burrows (P) $1,000,000 in compensation for pain and suffering, based upon testimony and my observation. In sum, I award Burrows (P) $1,649,788.97 [and about the same to Martin (P)].

Analysis:

To recap, the court awarded compensation for (1) actual medical expenses; (2) probable future medical expenses, including psychological counseling; (3) projected lost earnings over a working lifetime (i.e., potential earnings but for the accident, minus the projected earnings that might be possible after the accident), including increases due to wage inflation; (4) interest on the above damages, from the accident to the trial, at a rate approximating the return on a low/no risk investment; (5) actual physical pain from the injury, recuperation, and reconstructive surgery; (6) the humiliation of being disfigured; (7) psychological damages already endured; (8) projected future psychological harms; and (9) compensation for an impaired social and sexual life. These items are generally recoverable where applicable, though awards may differ widely depending on how provable the intangible and future injuries are, and how sympathetic the jury is.

Averyt v. Wal-Mart Stores, Inc.

(Commercial Truck Driver) v. (Discount Store)

265 P.3d 456 (Colo. 2011)

NO NEW TRIAL IS WARRANTED WHEN THE JURY'S DAMAGES AWARD IS NOT EXCESSIVE

■ **INSTANT FACTS** Averyt (P) slipped and fell while making a delivery to Wal-Mart (D) and was seriously injured; she sued Wal-Mart (D) and the jury awarded her significant damages, but Wal-Mart (D) argued that the damages were excessive and was granted a new trial.

■ **BLACK LETTER RULE** Where the jury's damages award is supported by the evidence, a reviewing court will not reverse it.

■ PROCEDURAL BASIS

On direct appeal to the state supreme court to review the trial court decision granting a new trial.

■ FACTS

Averyt (P) slipped and fell in grease while making a delivery at Wal-Mart (D). The grease had accumulated in the grocery receiving area. Averyt (P) ruptured a disc in her spine and injured her shoulder and neck as a result of the fall. The injuries ended her career as a truck driver and left her unable to perform many daily functions. Averyt (P) sued Wal-Mart (D), alleging that its negligence in failing to clean up the grease spill caused her injuries. The jury reached a $15 million verdict in her favor, but Wal-Mart moved for a new trial, arguing that the evidence did not support the damages award. The jury verdict included $4.5 million in economic damages, $5.5 million in non-economic damages (which the trial court reduced to $366,250 pursuant to a statutory cap), and $5 million for physical impairment. The trial court found the award excessive and granted Wal-Mart's (D) motion. Averyt (P) appealed pursuant to a statute allowing a direct appeal to the state supreme court under these circumstances.

■ ISSUE

Was Wal-Mart entitled to a new trial?

■ DECISION AND RATIONALE

(Rice, J.) No. Where the jury's damages award is supported by the evidence, a reviewing court will not reverse it. The trial court therefore erred in granting a new trial. The trial court found that the non-economic damages awarded exceeded even the amount asked for by the plaintiff. The trial court described non-economic damages as past and future physical and mental pain and suffering, inconvenience, emotional stress, and impairment of the quality of life. Regardless of the amount requested by the plaintiff, evidence in the record suggests that Averyt (P) has and will suffer significant non-economic losses. She suffers from chronic pain, which induces depression, insomnia, and difficulty concentrating. She can no longer drive her truck, which leaves her feeling that she can no longer be a productive member of society. She misses the independence that she had. This evidence supports the jury's award of non-economic damages, and we will not reverse that award. The jury's award for physical impairment is also supported by the evidence. Averyt (P) has difficulty walking, falls often, is incontinent, cannot work in any kind of job, and has trouble with everyday tasks like cooking and grooming. The jury's award of $6.2 million for physical impairment is supported by this evidence and is not the result of prejudice. We refuse to reverse the jury's award and grant a new trial.

Analysis:

The trial court had specifically instructed the jury in this case that, in determining damages for physical impairment, it should not include the economic or non-economic damages already considered. Wal-Mart (D) most likely asserted that there was an overlap or "doubling up" in the jury's damages award, or confusion on the jury's part. But, particularly where the evidence supports the jury's verdict, the court must assume that the jury understood and followed the court's instructions.

■ CASE VOCABULARY

ECONOMIC DAMAGES: Monetary losses, such as lost wages or lost profits.

McDougald v. Garber

(Comatose Patient and Husband) v. (Negligent Doctors)

73 N.Y.2d 246, 538 N.Y.S.2d 937, 536 N.E.2d 372 (Ct.App.1989)

BRAIN DAMAGED TORT VICTIMS CANNOT RECOVER FOR "LOST ENJOYMENT OF LIFE" IF THEY CANNOT UNDERSTAND THE LOSS

■ **INSTANT FACTS** When medical malpractice renders a patient comatose, the malpractitioners argue the patient cannot recover separately for "lost enjoyment of life."

■ **BLACK LETTER RULE** Tort victims can recover for "pain and suffering" and "loss of enjoyment of life" only as part of a single award, and they cannot recover for "loss of enjoyment" if they are unaware of the loss.

■ PROCEDURAL BASIS

In negligent personal injury action seeking damages, appeal from appellate court's affirmation of post-verdict order reducing nonpecuniary damages.

■ FACTS

Mrs. McDougald (P) underwent a C-section performed by Dr. Garber (D), assisted by anesthesiologists Armengol (D) and Kulkarni (D). During surgery, Mrs. McDougald (P) suffered oxygen deprivation, causing severe brain damage and permanent coma. Mr. McDougald (P) sued, derivatively and on behalf of Mrs. McDougald (P), alleging the injuries were caused by defendants' negligent malpractice, and sought compensation for (i) pain and suffering and (ii) loss of the pleasures and pursuits of life. At trial, the judge charged the jury that, if McDougald (P) was so neurologically impaired she was incapable of experiencing pain or emotional reactions to it, she could not recover for pain and suffering. The judge also charged the jury that McDougald (P) could recover for loss of pleasures and pursuits, even if she was unaware of the loss. The jury found all defendants liable, and awarded Mr. McDougald (P) $1.5M for loss of his wife's services, and Mrs. McDougald (P) $9,650,102, including $1M for conscious pain and suffering, a separate award of $3.5M for lost pleasures and pursuits, and compensation for lost earnings and nursing care. After trial, the defendants moved to reduce the total award. The judge granted the motion, reducing the total award to Mrs. McDougald (P) by striking the award for future nursing ($2,353,374) and reducing the separate awards for suffering and lost pleasures to a single award of $2M. McDougald (P) appealed. The Appellate Division affirmed. McDougald (P) appeals again.

■ ISSUE

Can tort victims recover separate awards for "pain and suffering" and "loss of enjoyment of life" if their injuries leave them unaware of pain and lost enjoyment?

■ DECISION AND RATIONALE

(Wachtler) No. Tort victims can recover for "pain and suffering" and "loss of enjoyment of life" only as part of a single award, and they cannot recover for "loss of enjoyment" if they are unaware of the loss. In negligent personal injury cases, damages are meant to compensate the victim, not punish the wrongdoer. The goal is to restore the injured to the position they would have occupied had the wrong not occurred. Of course, damages for nonpecuniary losses are among those which may be awarded as compensation. While such recovery rests on the legal fiction that money can compensate for injury, we accept this fiction, because money is the best this court can award. However, when awards for nonpecuniary losses overcompensate the plaintiff, they become improperly punitive. We conclude that an award for loss of enjoyment of life, given to a person whose injuries preclude awareness of the loss, does not serve to compensate the victim, and is improper. In such circumstances, monetary damages have no meaning or utility *to the victim,* who cannot derive compensating enjoyment from spending the money. We recognize this holding will sometimes create the paradox that, the greater the brain damage inflicted negligently by the defendant, the smaller the award will be. However, the force of this argument is that a greater award would punish the negligent tortfeasor, but this has nothing to do with compensating the victim meaningfully. Accordingly, we conclude that, to recover for loss of enjoyment of life, the tort victim must retain "some level of [cognitive] awareness" of the loss. However, we will not require the fact finder to determine what level of cognitive function is necessary. As long as there is "some level of awareness," the plaintiff may recover for nonpecuniary losses, which is the standard used by the trial court. Next, we consider whether loss of enjoyment of life should be considered a category of damages separate from pain and suffering, and we conclude it should not. It is undisputed that the fact finder, in assessing nonpecuniary damages, may consider the injury's effect on the plaintiff's ability to lead a normal life. Traditionally, in New York and elsewhere, this aspect of suffering is not treated as a separate category of damages, but is factored into a general award for nonpecuniary damages, commonly known as pain and suffering. Recently, there has been an attempt to segregate the suffering associated with physical pain from that associated with the mental anguish of being unable to engage in certain activities. Some courts have resisted the effort, concluding it would create duplicative and excessive awards. Other courts have allowed separate awards, noting the types of suffering involved are analytically distinguishable. If we are to depart from this traditional approach and approve a separate award for loss of enjoyment, it must be on the basis that such an approach will yield a more accurate valuation of the compensation due to the plaintiff. We have no doubt that separate awards will increase the total award, but this does not necessarily mean the goal of compensation is better served. While we do not dispute that distinctions can be found between physical/emotional suffering and mental frustration, we believe the already-imprecise estimation of nonpecuniary damages will be further distorted by trying to divide a broad award along unclear lines. We conclude the court erred, both in instructing the jury that McDougald's (P) awareness was irrelevant to her damages for lost enjoyment, and in directing the jury to consider lost enjoyment separately from pain and suffering. Reversed and remanded to recalculate nonpecuniary damages.

■ DISSENT

(Titone) The majority's holding is an illogical compromise which neither comports with fundamental principles of tort compensation nor furnishes a logically consistent framework for compensating nonpecuniary loss. I find no fault with granting an award for loss of enjoyment, separate from conscious pain and suffering, because I conclude that loss of enjoyment is objective and conceptually distinct from conscious pain. The capacity to enjoy life is unquestionably an attribute of an ordinary healthy individual, and a victim deprived of this capacity is entitled to compensation. This right exists independently of the victim's ability to apprehend the impairment.

Analysis:

Regardless of the analytical propriety of separating "conscious pain and suffering" from "mental anguish for lost enjoyment of life," the fact remains that allowing separate awards for each type of injury tends to increase the total award, so it is inevitable that personal injury lawyers will invent many logical reasons to adopt separate awards, and insurers'/defendants' lobbyists will argue strenuously against it. Conceptually, it is difficult to know which approach best ensures compensation. The majority states that a separate award for lost enjoyment tends to increase the total award, but suggests this increase is superfluous. However, this argument assumes that, with dual awards, juries will first compute pain and suffering (and include lost enjoyment in that computation), then compute a separate and duplicate award for lost enjoyment. If this is true, the bifurcated award overcompensates. But it is equally likely that, but for the separate award, juries might not include in the "pain and suffering" award compensation for lost enjoyment, which would under compensate the plaintiff.

■ CASE VOCABULARY

NONPECUNIARY DAMAGES: [a.k.a. "pain and suffering."] Non-monetary/non-economic losses, which generally include pain, mental/emotional distress, humiliation from injury or defamation, loss of enjoyment from life, and (sometimes) inconvenience.

State Farm Mut. Auto. Ins. Co. v. Campbell

(Insurance Company) v. (Insured)

538 U.S. 408, 123 S.Ct. 1513, 155 L.Ed.2d 585 (2003)

A $1 MILLION COMPENSATORY DAMAGES AWARD CAN'T SUPPORT $145 MILLION IN PUNITIVE DAMAGES

■ **INSTANT FACTS** After State Farm (D) failed to settle claims against Campbell (P) for its policy limits and altered information to lessen his culpability, a jury awarded Campbell (P) $1 million in compensatory damages and $145 million in punitive damages.

■ **BLACK LETTER RULE** In evaluating the appropriateness of a punitive damages award, a court must weigh the reprehensibility of the defendant's conduct, the disparity between the actual harm caused and the amount of the punitive damages awarded, and the difference between the punitive damages awarded and the civil penalties imposed under state law.

■ **PROCEDURAL BASIS**

Certiorari to review the excessiveness of a punitive damages verdict.

■ **FACTS**

Campbell (P) held an automobile insurance policy with State Farm Mutual Automobile Insurance Co. (D). While driving in Utah, Campbell (P) decided to pass six vans traveling slowly in front of him. As Campbell (P) was attempting to pass, Ospital, who approached from the opposite direction, was forced onto the shoulder to avoid a head-on collision. In the process, Ospital lost control of his vehicle, collided with a vehicle driven by Slusher, and died. Slusher was permanently disabled as a result of the accident. An investigation determined that Campbell's (P) unsafe pass caused Ospital's death and Slusher's injuries. Nonetheless, State Farm (D) decided to contest liability and declined offers from Ospital's estate and Slusher to settle both claims for its total policy limit of $50,000. At trial, a jury found Campbell (P) liable for the accident and returned a verdict for $185,849. State Farm (D) refused to pay the verdict in excess of its $50,000 policy limits and refused to post the supersedeas bond required for Campbell's (P) appeal. Campbell (P) subsequently obtained independent counsel and appealed the verdict. During the appeal, Campbell (P) agreed to pursue a bad faith action against State Farm (D) in exchange for an agreement by Ospital's estate and Slusher not to seek satisfaction of the judgment against Campbell (P). Ospital's estate and Slusher agreed to accept ninety percent of any proceeds received from State Farm (D) in the bad faith suit.

The Utah Supreme Court denied Campbell's (P) appeal from the wrongful death judgment, and State Farm (D) subsequently agreed to pay the full amount of the judgment against him. Campbell (P) then commenced his bad faith suit, alleging State Farm's (D) refusal to accept the settlement offer was a product of a national scheme to control the amount of claims paid. Campbell (D) offered evidence of State Farm's (D) business practices throughout the country over a twenty-year period, although little pertained to payment of third-party automobile claims similar to that asserted by Campbell (D). A jury awarded Campbell $2.6 million in compensatory damages and $145 million in punitive damages. After the compensatory damages award was reduced to $1 million and the punitive damages were reduced to $25 million, both parties appealed to the Utah Supreme Court, which reinstated the punitive damages award.

■ ISSUE

When compensatory damages are $1 million, is an award of $145 million in punitive damages against a defendant excessive and in violation of the Due Process Clause of the Fourteenth Amendment?

■ DECISION AND RATIONALE

(Kennedy, J.) Yes. Unlike compensatory damages, which serve to compensate an injured person for the wrongful conduct of another, punitive damages are aimed at deterrence and retribution against the wrongdoer. Because punitive damages serve a purpose similar to criminal sanctions, but without the procedural protections accompanying criminal punishment, a court must weigh the reprehensibility of the defendant's conduct, the disparity between the actual harm caused and the amount of the punitive damages awarded, and the difference between the punitive damages awarded and the civil penalties imposed under state law. Weighing these factors, the jury's $145 million punitive damages award was excessive.

First, State Farm's (D) conduct cannot be considered so reprehensible as to justify the award. In gauging a defendant's conduct, a court should consider whether the harm caused was physical rather than economic, whether the defendant acted with reckless disregard for the health and safety of others, whether the plaintiff was financially vulnerable, whether the conduct involved a repetitive pattern or an isolated incident, and whether the conduct was intentional. Here, while State Farm's (D) handling of Campbell's (P) insurance claims is not laudable, its conduct does not justify such an excessive punitive damages award. Rather than focusing on the particular conduct at issue in the case, the award focuses on State Farm's (D) nationwide handling of claims. A state court, however, has no authority to punish a defendant for conduct that occurred outside its territorial limits and involving parties who were directly affected by the out-of-state conduct. A defendant's dissimilar conduct, bearing no relation to the harm involved in a particular lawsuit, may not be taken into account when determining punitive damages. Due process does not permit a court to award a party punitive damages merely because the defendant may have caused some harm to others who were not proper parties to the litigation.

Second, although there is no bright-line ratio between the amount of punitive damages and the harm caused to a plaintiff, an award 145 times the actual harm suffered is excessive. Generally, anything over a single-digit ratio calls for close judicial scrutiny. Likewise, as the compensatory damages award increases, the appropriate proportion to the punitive damages award decreases, since a larger ratio is unnecessary to serve the purposes of deterrence and retribution. Here, the 145:1 ratio between the punitive award and the compensatory award is unreasonable given the $1 million compensatory damages award for plaintiff's emotional distress.

Finally, the $145 million punitive damages award is grossly in excess of the maximum $10,000 civil penalty imposed for fraud under Utah law. Applying this factor, too, the punitive damages award is excessive. Because a punitive award more closely approximating the compensatory award would be an adequate and rational punishment for the defendant's conduct, the award is excessive. Reversed and remanded.

■ DISSENT

(Ginsburg, J.) The Utah Supreme Court's reasoned decision on the appropriateness of the size of the punitive damages award and State Farm's (D) reprehensibility should not be superceded by the majority's views. The evidence at trial could reasonably permit the jury to conclude that

State Farm (D) had engaged in a nationwide practice of denying deserving policyholders of insurance benefits, preying on those consumers unlikely to defend themselves, and destroying internal documents likely to reveal its practices. The evidence further supports that State Farm (D) had issued handbooks to insurance adjusters and State Farm (D) representatives in Utah for many years to be followed when dealing with Utah policyholders. This evidence is sufficient to give Utah a strong state interest in the litigation and to establish State Farm's (D) reprehensible conduct in the handling of Campbell's (P) claim. Because the issue of punitive damages is a matter of state law, the Court should not disturb state decisions merely because the ratio between punitive damages and compensatory damages is high.

Analysis:

The Court's fascination with the appropriate ratio between the compensatory damages and punitive damages is interesting. If punitive damages serve a separate and distinct purpose from compensatory damages, why should the amount of compensatory damages affect the amount of punitive damages? If a defendant commits intentional conduct worthy of punishment, should it matter whether the compensatory damages were substantial?

■ CASE VOCABULARY

BAD FAITH: Dishonesty of belief or purpose.

COMPENSATORY DAMAGES: Damages sufficient in amount to indemnify the injured person for the loss suffered.

PUNITIVE DAMAGES: Damages awarded in addition to actual damages when the defendant acted with recklessness, malice, or deceit.

SUPERSEDEAS BOND: A bond that suspends a judgment creditor's power to levy execution, usually pending appeal.

Mathias v. Accor Economy Lodging, Inc.

(Motel Guest) v. (Motel 6)

347 F.3d 672 (7th Cir. 2003)

MOTEL 6 LEFT MORE THAN THE LIGHT ON FOR ITS GUESTS, AND WAS SUBJECTED TO PUNITIVE DAMAGES AS A RESULT

■ **INSTANT FACTS** Motel guests sued the motel after being bitten by bedbugs that had apparently infested the motel for years, and the jury awarded them punitive damages that greatly exceeded the compensatory damages award; the defendant argued that the damages award was excessive.

■ **BLACK LETTER RULE** There are no definitive rules establishing a precise methodology for computing punitive damages.

■ PROCEDURAL BASIS

Federal circuit court review of a jury verdict awarding each plaintiff $186,000 in punitive damages.

■ FACTS

The Mathiases (P), a brother and sister, were guests at a Motel 6 when they were bitten by bedbugs. Evidence showed that the bedbugs had been discovered by an exterminating service years earlier. The service offered to eliminate the bugs for $500 but the motel refused, and each year the infestation grew worse. In fact, one guest was moved from room to room after he complained about being repeatedly bitten, but each new room he moved to was equally infested. Even rooms that were placed on "Do not rent, bugs in room" status were rented out. Desk clerks were instructed to call the bedbugs "ticks," apparently to cause less concern in the guests, but ticks are actually more dangerous and carry disease. The Mathiases (P) sued Motel 6, and the jury awarded them $5,000 in compensatory damages and $186,000 in punitive damages. The defendant appealed, arguing that the punitive damages award was excessive.

■ ISSUE

Was the punitive damages award excessive?

■ DECISION AND RATIONALE

(Posner, J.) No. There are no definitive rules establishing a precise methodology for computing punitive damages. Motel 6 could not have rented any rooms at the price it charged if had informed guests about the bedbugs. There is thus sufficient evidence of willful and wanton conduct to permit an award of punitive damages in this case. But in what amount? The defendant argues that Supreme Court precedent requires a single-digit ratio between punitive and compensatory damages in order to satisfy due process. But the Court actually said that there is a presumption against an award that has a 145-to-1 ratio—a far different statement. That being said, "punitive damages" implies punishment, and a standard principle of penal theory is that the punishment should fit the crime in the sense of being proportional to the wrongfulness of the defendant's action. An award of punitive damages in cases like this also serves the purpose of limiting the defendant's ability to profit from its fraud. When, however, the compensatory damages award is huge, there may be a lesser need for a sizable punitive damages award.

Here, the defendant's behavior was outrageous, but the compensable harm to the plaintiffs was slight and difficult to quantify. We cannot say that the award of punitive damages in this case was excessive. It is probably not a coincidence that $5,000 + $186,000 = $191,000, and there were 191 rooms in the motel (thus the award was $1,000 per room). But as there are no punitive damages guidelines, it is inevitable that the particular amount will be somewhat arbitrary. It would have been helpful if the plaintiffs had presented evidence on the penalties to which the defendant exposed itself by subjecting its customers to a substantial risk of being bitten by bedbugs, but the lack of that evidence does not invalidate the award. We note that a Chicago hotel that permits unsanitary conditions to exist is subject to revocation of its license, without which it cannot operate. We are sure that the defendant would prefer to pay the punitive damages rather than lose its license. Affirmed.

Analysis:

Punitive damages are assessed as a way to penalize the wrongdoer and deter others from acting in the same manner. The Supreme Court has held that three factors should be considered to help determine whether a punitive damages award violates due process: (1) the reprehensibility of the conduct being punished; (2) the reasonableness of the relationship between the harm and the award; and (3) the difference between the award and the civil penalties authorized in comparable cases.

■ CASE VOCABULARY

COMPENSATORY DAMAGES: Damages sufficient in amount to compensate the injured party for the loss suffered.

PUNITIVE DAMAGES: Damages awarded in addition to actual damages when the defendant acted with recklessness, malice, or deceit.

CHAPTER TWENTY-EIGHT

Workers' Compensation

Wait v. Traveler's Indemnity Co. of Illinois

Instant Facts: A telecommuting employee of the American Cancer Society opened the door of her home, during the work day, to a neighbor, and he brutally attacked her; her claim for workers' compensation was denied and she appealed.

Black Letter Rule: In order to recover under the Tennessee Workers' Compensation Act, an injury must both arise out of and occur in the course of an employee's employment.

Carvalho v. Decorative Fabrics Co.

Instant Facts: An employee sought recovery under workers' compensation after he suffered a rectal perforation when a coworker jokingly placed an air hose in the vicinity of his rectum.

Black Letter Rule: For purposes of the workers' compensation statute, where horseplay is customary, it should be regarded as part of the course of employment.

Harris v. Board of Educ. of Howard County

Instant Facts: Harris (P) injured her back when dragging a heavy box of laundry detergent as part of her duties for her employer.

Black Letter Rule: An employee who suffers an accidental injury that arises out of and in the course of employment qualifies for workers' compensation benefits.

Martin v. Lancaster Battery Co., Inc.

Instant Facts: An employee who suffered from several ailments as a result of his exposure to lead in a battery manufacturing plant sought to sue his employer who had intentionally altered and withheld blood test results.

Black Letter Rule: Worker's compensation is not the exclusive remedy for the aggravation of an employee's work-related injury where the employer's fraudulent misrepresentation has been alleged.

Kerans v. Porter Paint Co.

Instant Facts: Suit by an employee against her employer for injuries resulting from sexual harassment and molestation by the store manager.

Black Letter Rule: The exclusive remedy provisions of a workers' compensation statute do not bar a suit against an employer for sexual harassment and molestation inflicted by a coworker.

Wait v. Traveler's Indemnity Co. of Illinois

(Injured Employee) v. (Employer's Insurer)

240 S.W.3d 220 (Tenn. 2007)

RANDOM ASSAULTS ON TELECOMMUTING EMPLOYEES MAY NOT BE COVERED BY WORKERS' COMPENSATION

Working from home is awesome--
unless your neighbor is a violent psychopath.

■ **INSTANT FACTS** A telecommuting employee of the American Cancer Society opened the door of her home, during the work day, to a neighbor, and he brutally attacked her; her claim for workers' compensation was denied and she appealed.

■ **BLACK LETTER RULE** In order to recover under the Tennessee Workers' Compensation Act, an injury must both arise out of and occur in the course of an employee's employment.

■ PROCEDURAL BASIS

State supreme court review of a lower court decision denying the plaintiff's workers' compensation claim.

■ FACTS

Due to a shortage of space at her employer's offices, Wait (P) worked from her home as an executive for the American Cancer Society (ACS). The ACS furnished Wait's (P) office equipment and a budget to purchase office supplies. Wait's (P) supervisor and co-workers attended work meetings in Wait's (P) home. One work day, as she was preparing her lunch, Wait (P) responded to a knock on her door; her neighbor entered, and for no apparent reason he brutally beat her. Wait (P) sought workers' compensation benefits from her employer's workers' compensation insurer, but the court granted summary judgment for the ACS on the ground that Wait's (P) injuries did not arise out of or in the course of her employment. Wait (P) appealed.

■ ISSUE

Do injuries that a telecommuter sustains as a result of a random assault in her home arise out of and occur in the course of her employment?

■ DECISION AND RATIONALE

(Barker, C.J.) No. In order to recover under the Tennessee Workers' Compensation Act, an injury must both arise out of and occur in the course of an employee's employment. "Arise out of" refers to the cause or origin, whereas "in the course of" denotes the time, place, and circumstances of the injury. Turning to the second element first, we note that an injury occurs in the course of employment when it takes place within the period of the employment, at a place where the employee reasonably may be, and while the employee is fulfilling work duties or is engaged in doing something incidental thereto. Generally, injuries sustained during personal breaks are compensable. It is reasonable to conclude that the ACS knew the plaintiff would be taking her personal breaks in her home, and unless instructed otherwise, an employee working from home who answers a knock at her door and briefly admits an acquaintance does not necessarily depart so far from her work duties so as to remove her from the course of her employment. This is not to say that prolonged socializing might well remove the employee from the course of her employment, but that was not the case here. Thus, the injuries in this case occurred in the course of Wait's (P) employment.

We hold, however, that Wait's (P) injuries did not arise out of her employment. "Arising out of" requires a causal connection between the employment conditions and the resulting injury. We have previously delineated three general classifications for determining whether assaults arise out of employment: (1) assaults with an inherent connection to employment, such as disputes over performance, pay, or termination; (2) assaults stemming from inherently private disputes that are imported into the work setting from the claimant's private life, and that are not exacerbated by the employment; and (3) assaults resulting from a neutral force, such as random assaults by individuals outside the employment relationship. Those assaults falling into the first category are compensable by workers' compensation, those in the second category are not, and those in the third group turn on the facts of the particular case. The assault in this case falls into the third category. It was not inherently connected with Wait's (P) employment nor with a personal dispute she had with the assailant. Thus, we look at the particular facts here. For an injury to arise out of employment, it must generally emanate from a peculiar danger or risk inherent in the nature of the employment. An injury that is purely coincidental with or collateral to the employment, like the one at issue here, does not arise out of the employment. Nor does the "street risk" doctrine apply in this case. That doctrine applies when the employee's indiscriminate exposure to the public is one of the conditions under which her work must be performed, and the actions of those persons on the premises are reasonably considered hazards of the employment. The street risk doctrine does not supply the required causal connection between injuries from a neutral assault and the employment unless either the attacker singled out the employee because of his or her association with the employer, or the employment indiscriminately exposed the employee to dangers from the public. The facts of this case suggest neither scenario. Because we hold that the plaintiff's injuries did not arise out of her employment, the decision denying her workers' compensation coverage is affirmed.

Analysis:

Because neutral assaults require a fact-specific analysis, there could be other conceivable scenarios that would be similar to the present case but support workers' compensation coverage. Say, for instance, the neighbor's wife had just died from cancer, and he believed that the American Cancer Society did not do enough to find a cure, so he specifically struck out at Wait (P). In that case, the attacker would have singled her out because of her association with ACS, and her injuries would likely have been compensable. Or consider whether the outcome would have been different if Wait (P) had informed her employer that her neighbor was known to be a violent criminal, and that he knew she worked at home, alone.

■ CASE VOCABULARY

WORKERS' COMPENSATION: A system of providing benefits to an employee for injuries occurring in the scope of employment. Most workers' compensation statutes both hold the employer strictly liable and bar the employee from suing the employer in tort. Workers' compensation laws were designed to provide employees with expansive protection against the consequences of employment-related injuries. Injured workers no longer have to establish negligence attributable to their employer in order to obtain legal redress. They merely have to demonstrate that their conditions arose out of and during the course of their employment.

Carvalho v. Decorative Fabrics, Co.

(Injured Employee) v. (Employer)

117 R.I. 231, 366 A.2d 157 (1976)

WORKERS' COMPENSATION COVERS INJURIES ARISING FROM INNOCENT HORSEPLAY

■ **INSTANT FACTS** An employee sought recovery under workers' compensation after he suffered a rectal perforation when a coworker jokingly placed an air hose in the vicinity of his rectum.

■ **BLACK LETTER RULE** For purposes of the workers' compensation statute, where horseplay is customary, it should be regarded as part of the course of employment.

■ PROCEDURAL BASIS

Appeal to the Rhode Island Supreme Court, challenging the decision of the commission to deny the employee's petition on the ground that horseplay does not arise out of employment.

■ FACTS

Lucindo Carvalho (P) was injured when a coworker jokingly placed an air hose customarily used by employees to brush lint off their clothes near Carvalho's (P) rectum, knocking him to the floor and perforating his rectum. The commission denied compensation on the ground that Carvalho's (P) injury was the result of horseplay, an activity that did not arise out of his employment.

■ ISSUE

May an employee recover under the workmen's compensation statute for injuries resulting from on-the-job horseplay?

■ DECISION AND RATIONALE

(Bevilacqua, C.J.) Yes. For purposes of the workmen's compensation statute, where horseplay is customary, it should be regarded as part of the course of employment. Although early decisions held that injuries resulting from horseplay were not compensable on the ground that employees were not paid to play, we find these decisions contrary to the scope and intent of the statute. These decisions have, essentially, reinstituted the defenses of negligence and fault, which workers' compensation was designed to eliminate. When people are placed together in close proximity there is a natural instinct to fool around and play pranks. These activities are an incident of the employment. The claimant need only establish that the injury arose out of and in the course of employment; a causal connection must be shown. For injuries incurred during horseplay, the claimant must show that the horseplay was customary. Where the use of an air hose to clean off clothes is a daily practice, play with the hose is a risk of the employment. Such activity should be regarded as part of the course of employment, particularly where, as here, the employer places in the hands of the employee the instrumentality which was used in the horseplay and caused the injury. Reversed.

Analysis:

In line with the view of most courts, the Rhode Island Supreme Court holds that horseplay is an accepted part of the job for purposes of workers' compensation. The rule is justified on the basis that horseplay is just a part of life; employees are not robots and should not be expected to attend to their duties every second of every minute they are "on the clock." But courts have also recognized that horseplay can go too far, and that compensation should not be available when horseplay substantially deviates from the employment. For example, courts have permitted an office worker injured in a rubber band fight with a nearby colleague to recover compensation, but have denied recovery to a video store employee injured in a staple gun fight on the basis that the employment did not involve staple guns.

Harris v. Board of Educ. of Howard County

(Injured Employee) v. (Employer)

375 Md. 21, 825 A.2d 365 (2003)

A WORKERS' COMPENSATION INJURY NEED NOT ARISE OUT OF UNUSUAL ACTIVITY

■ **INSTANT FACTS** Harris (P) injured her back when dragging a heavy box of laundry detergent as part of her duties for her employer.

■ **BLACK LETTER RULE** An employee who suffers an accidental injury that arises out of and in the course of employment qualifies for workers' compensation benefits.

■ PROCEDURAL BASIS

On appeal to review a decision of the Maryland Court of Special Appeals affirming a jury verdict for the defendant.

■ FACTS

Harris (P) was an employee of the Board of Education of Howard County (D). After dragging a heavy box of laundry detergent as part of her laundry duties, Harris (P) injured her back while bending down to scoop the detergent into a washer. Harris (P) completed an incident report and consulted a physician. The physician testified that Harris's (P) dragging of the laundry detergent caused her back injury. The Workers' Compensation Commission granted Harris's (P) job-related injury claim, but on review the court requested that the jury consider whether the injury arose out of "unusual activity" to qualify for benefits. The jury returned a verdict for the defendant. After the court of appeals affirmed, Harris (P) appealed.

■ ISSUE

Must a workplace injury arise out of unusual activity in order for the injured employee to be eligible for workers' compensation benefits?

■ DECISION AND RATIONALE

(Eldridge, J.) No. By statute, an employee must suffer an accidental injury that arises out of and in the course of employment to qualify for workers' compensation benefits. Nowhere in the statute is an injury excluded if it does not arise out of "unusual activity." Instead, the language of the statute is clear that any injury that is accidental and that arises out of and in the course of employment qualifies for benefits.

Although Maryland courts have previously required that the injury arise from unusual activity, those cases cannot be reconciled with the plain language of the statute, and courts may not add requirements to a statutory claim that the legislature did not intend. Other cases have included the unusual activity standard within the requirement that the injury arise out of and in the course of employment. Because those cases requiring unusual activity are relatively limited in number and directly conflict with the plain language of the statute, they are overruled. A workplace injury need not arise out of unusual activity to qualify the injured employee for benefits under the workers' compensation statute. Reversed.

Analysis:

While the unusual activity requirement would have helped the employer defend against the employee's workers' compensation claims in this case, it often could expose employers to civil liability *exceeding* the limits of workers' compensation benefits. Workers' compensation laws are designed to protect employers from large civil damages awards for work-related injuries, in exchange for a predictable but limited statutory scheme for workers' compensation benefits. A standard based on the argument that the employee's injuries arose out of "unusual activity" would potentially conflict with the "arising out of and in the course of employment" requirement and could arguably expose the employer to greater liability.

■ CASE VOCABULARY

COURSE OF EMPLOYMENT: Events that occur or circumstances that exist as a part of one's employment; especially, the time during which an employee furthers an employer's goals through employer-mandated directives.

Martin v. Lancaster Battery Co., Inc.

(Injured Employee) v. (Employer)

530 Pa. 11, 606 A.2d 444 (1992)

THE EXCLUSIVE REMEDY PROVISIONS OF WORKERS' COMPENSATION STATUTES DO NOT BAR ACTIONS AGAINST EMPLOYERS FOR THEIR FRAUD THAT AGGRAVATES A WORK-RELATED INJURY

■ **INSTANT FACTS** An employee who suffered from several ailments as a result of his exposure to lead in a battery manufacturing plant sought to sue his employer who had intentionally altered and withheld blood test results.

■ **BLACK LETTER RULE WORKER'S** compensation is not the exclusive remedy for the aggravation of an employee's work-related injury where the employer's fraudulent misrepresentation has been alleged.

■ PROCEDURAL BASIS

Appeal to the Pennsylvania Supreme Court, challenging the appellate court holding allowing a tort claim for fraudulent misrepresentation in spite of the exclusive remedy provision of the workmen's compensation statute.

■ FACTS

Joseph Martin (P) was an employee of Lancaster Battery Co., Inc. (LBC) (D), which was partly owned and managed by Stuart Manix (D). LBC was in the business of manufacturing wet storage batteries, a process involving extensive exposure to lead dust and fumes. Federal regulations required that employees be regularly tested for lead content in their blood. Manix (D), who oversaw the testing at LBC (D), intentionally and willfully withheld from Martin (P) the latter's test results, with Manix (D) also altering the same. Martin (P) was subsequently diagnosed with a variety of lead related ailments, the severity of which would have been substantially diminished if the test results had been accurately reported. Martin (P) sued for fraudulent misrepresentation. The trial court dismissed the action. The appellate court reversed.

■ ISSUE

The workers' compensation exclusive remedy provision notwithstanding, may an employee sue his employer for fraudulent misrepresentation, which exacerbated the employee's work-related injury?

■ DECISION AND RATIONALE

(Larsen, J.) Yes. Workers' compensation is not the exclusive remedy for the aggravation of an employee's work-related injury where the employer's fraudulent misrepresentation has been alleged. Courts so holding have reasoned that: (1) a hazard of employment does not include the risk that the employer will deprive an employee of worker's compensation rights; (2) the state has an interest in deterring this type of conduct; and (3) an employer's fraudulent concealment of diseases already developed is not a risk the employee should have to assume. Those courts that have refused to permit these type of actions have expressed a concern with employee's receiving duplicate money awards. This latter rationale is unconvincing. Martin (P) does not seek compensation for his work related injury; rather, he has alleged that his employer's fraud has aggravated his work-related injury. The legislature could not have intended to shield employers from this type of conduct. There is a difference between an employer who tolerates unsafe working conditions that result in a certain number of accidents and one who actively misleads employees already suffering as victims of workplace hazards. Aggravation of the injury relates to the fraudulent concealment; therefore, Martin's (P) action is not barred by the exclusive remedy provisions. Affirmed.

Analysis:

Workers' compensation is exclusive of all other remedies by the employee against the employer or his insurer. In fact, the basic bargain embodied by workers' compensation statutes is that an employee gives up his right to other remedies in exchange for an "assured" and "prompt" recovery. But there are exceptions to the exclusive remedy provisions. In some circumstances, courts have allowed employees to sue their employers for certain intentional torts. In the context of fraudulent misrepresentation of an employee's medical condition, some courts have held that worker's compensation is the only remedy when the fraud only aggravates a compensable injury. The Pennsylvania Court bases its holding on a "dual-injury" theory. In the court's view, the first injury was the exposure to lead that caused Martin's (P) ailments. The exclusive remedy for this injury is workers' compensation. But the court holds that the second injury—the misrepresentation that aggravated the ailments—was not covered by the workers' compensation statute.

Kerans v. Porter Paint Co.

(Sexually Harassed/Molested Employee) v. (Employer)

61 Ohio St.3d 486, 575 N.E.2d 428 (1991)

AN ACTION FOR A NON-PHYSICAL-INJURY TORT INFLICTED BY AN EMPLOYER OR HIS SERVANT IS NOT BARRED BY THE WORKERS' COMPENSATION EXCLUSIVITY WHEN NO WORKERS' COMPENSATION REMEDY IS AVAILABLE FOR THE PARTICULAR INJURY

■ **INSTANT FACTS** Suit by an employee against her employer for injuries resulting from sexual harassment and molestation by the store manager.

■ **BLACK LETTER RULE** The exclusive remedy provisions of a workers' compensation statute do not bar a suit against an employer for sexual harassment and molestation inflicted by a coworker.

■ PROCEDURAL BASIS

Appeal to the Ohio State Supreme Court, challenging the decision of the appellate court affirming the trial court's grant of summary judgment for the defendants.

■ FACTS

Lewis Kerans (P) and Sally Kerans (P), a decorator for Porter Paint Company (Porter) (D), filed suit against Porter (D) for injuries resulting from her sexual harassment and molestation by Al Levine, a co-worker and store manager for Porter (D). The Kerans' (P) complaint against Porter (D) contained five separate counts: (1) intentionally or negligently maintaining a policy of encouraging, permitting, or condoning sexual harassment; (2) assault and battery; (3) negligent or intentional infliction of emotional distress; (4) negligent or intentional failure to provide a safe working environment; and (5) loss of consortium. The lower courts held the claim was barred by the exclusive remedy provisions of the workers' compensation statute.

■ ISSUE

May an employee sue her employer for injuries resulting from the sexual harassment and molestation inflicted by a coworker?

■ DECISION AND RATIONALE

(Resnick, J.) Yes. The exclusive remedy provisions of a workers' compensation statute do not bar a suit against an employer for sexual harassment and molestation inflicted by a coworker. While workplace injuries rob a person of resources, sexual harassment robs the person of dignity and self-esteem. Workers' compensation addresses purely economic injury; sexual harassment laws are concerned with a much more intangible injury to personal rights. For the following reasons, we reject Porter's (D) position that they are not liable for Levine's actions since they occurred outside the scope of his employment. First, federal courts have held that where an employee is able to harass another by virtue of his apparent or actual authority, the harasser's actions have taken place within the scope of employment. There remains an issue of fact as to whether Levine had such apparent or actual authority. Second, even if the activities occurred outside the scope of Levine's employment, the Restatement imposes upon employers the duty to exercise reasonable care to control an employee from injuring others outside the scope of his employment. Based on this principal, Porter (D) had a duty to provide

Mrs. Kerans (P) with a safe working environment. Here, there is an abundance of evidence that Porter (D) knew or should have known of Levine's perverse sexual proclivities, that the company was unconcerned with the threat posed by Levine, and that they took no action to remedy the problem. The grant of summary judgment was in error. Reversed.

Analysis:

The court holds that a sexual harassment suit is not barred by the exclusivity of workers' compensation because workers' compensation is meant to remedy an economic injury, whereas sexual harassment involves an injury to personal rights such as dignity. But this case should not be taken for the proposition that workers' compensation exclusivity provisions do not bar any sexual harassment claims. Instead, the general rule is if the harassment does not involve an accident or injury and is not the kind of tort workers' compensation was intended to remedy, then tort recovery against the employer is allowed. This rule still leaves open the possibility that an employee's sexual harassment suit will be barred if the employee is physically harmed in a manner compensable under the statute. The court's opinion deals with a secondary issue that often arises in the context of sexual harassment suits—whether the employer is liable for the actions of its employees. The court here holds that an employer is liable if the harassing employee is acting within the scope of his employment. The Ohio court then goes one step further and holds that the employer is liable in tort if he has negligently failed to prevent his employee from harming others while acting outside the scope of his employment.

CHAPTER TWENTY-NINE

Public Compensation Systems, Including Social Security

Heckler v. Campbell

Instant Facts: A disability benefits claimant appealed the decision of an administrative law judge to deny her disability benefits for a back problem.

Black Letter Rule: Even where an agency's enabling statute expressly requires it to hold a hearing, the agency may rely on its rule-making authority to determine issues that do not require case-by-case consideration.

Heckler v. Campbell

(Secretary of Health and Human Services) v. (Disability Applicant)

461 U.S. 458, 103 S.Ct. 1952, 76 L.Ed.2d 66 (1983)

DISABILITY BENEFITS ARE ONLY AVAILABLE TO PERSONS WHO ARE UNABLE TO ENGAGE IN ANY SUBSTANTIAL GAINFUL ACTIVITY BY REASON OF A MEDICALLY DETERMINABLE PHYSICAL OR MENTAL IMPAIRMENT

■ **INSTANT FACTS** A disability benefits claimant appealed the decision of an administrative law judge to deny her disability benefits for a back problem.

■ **BLACK LETTER RULE** Even where an agency's enabling statute expressly requires it to hold a hearing, the agency may rely on its rule-making authority to determine issues that do not require case-by-case consideration.

■ PROCEDURAL BASIS

Certification to the United States Supreme Court of an appellate court decision denying a court's use of medical-vocational guidelines promulgated by the Secretary of Health and Human Services to determine whether a disabled person can perform an alternative job (and therefore avoid being classified as disabled).

■ FACTS

In 1979, Carmen Campbell (P) applied for disability benefits because a back condition and hypertension prevented her from continuing work as a hotel maid. Following the denial, she requested a *de novo* hearing before an Administrative Law Judge. The judge determined that her problem was not severe enough to find her disabled without further inquiry, and thus considered whether she retained the ability to perform a less strenuous job. Relying on the medical vocational guidelines promulgated by the Secretary of Health and Human Services (D), the ALJ concluded that there were a significant number of jobs that Campbell (P) and others in her position could perform. Thus, he concluded that she was not disabled. The Court of Appeals, questioning the validity of the guidelines, rejected the proposition that they provide adequate evidence of a claimant's ability to perform a specific alternative occupation. The Court of Appeals then remanded the case for the Secretary to put into evidence "particular types of jobs suitable to the capabilities of Ms. Campbell" (P).

■ ISSUE

Can the Secretary of Health and Human Services rely on published medical-vocational guidelines to determine a claimant's right to Social Security disability benefits?

■ DECISION AND RATIONALE

(Powell, J.) Yes. The Social Security Act defines "disability" in terms of the effect that a physical or mental impairment has on a person's ability to function in the workplace. It only provides disability benefits to those who are unable "to engage in any substantial gainful activity by reason of any medically determinable physical or mental impairment." Further, it specifies that a person must "not only [be] unable to do his previous work but [must also be unable] to engage in any other kind of substantial gainful work which exists in the national economy." Whether a job that the claimant can do exists in his or her area of the country is irrelevant; it must simply exist somewhere in the national economy. Prior to 1978, the Secretary (D) relied on vocational experts to establish the existence of suitable jobs in the national economy. This practice, however, produced some inconsistent results, so to improve both the uniformity and efficiency of this determination, the Secretary (D) promulgated some medical-vocational guidelines as a part of the 1978 regulations. The guidelines consist of a matrix of four factors—physical ability, age, education, and work experience—and set forth rules that identify whether jobs requiring specific combinations of these factors exist in significant numbers in the national economy. In practice, where a claimant's qualifications correspond to the job requirements identified by a rule in the matrix, the guidelines direct a conclusion as to whether work exists that the claimant can perform. If such work exists, the claimant is not considered disabled. The Court of Appeals discredited use of the guidelines, holding that, in addition, the Secretary (D) must bring forth individualized evidence of an ability of a particular claimant to perform an alternative job. It is this decision that we address today. The Social Security Act directs the Secretary to "adopt reasonable and proper rules and regulations to regulate and provide for the nature and extent of the proofs and evidence and the method of taking and furnishing the same" in disability cases. We do not think that reliance on the guidelines is inconsistent with the Social Security Act. It is true that the Act requires hearings and individualized determinations of disability. But this does not bar the Secretary (D) from relying on rule-making to resolve certain classes of issues. Even where an agency's enabling statute expressly requires it to hold a hearing, the agency may rely on its rule-making authority to determine issues that do not require case-by-case consideration (such as whether a particular type of job exists in the national economy). A contrary holding would require the agency to continually relitigate issues that may be established fairly and efficiently in a single rule-making proceeding. As noted, in determining whether a claimant can perform less strenuous work, the Secretary (D) must make two determinations. First, she must assess each claimant's individual abilities and then determine whether jobs exist that a person having those qualifications could perform. This involves individualized evidence. The second inquiry requires the Secretary (D) to determine an issue that is not unique to each claimant—the types and numbers of jobs that exist in the national economy. This type of general factual issue may be resolved as fairly through rule-making as by introducing the testimony of vocational experts. Finally, we consider Campbell's (P) argument that the Court of Appeals properly required the Secretary (D) to specify alternative available jobs. There is a principle of administrative law that states when an agency takes official or administrative notice of facts, a litigant must be given an adequate opportunity to respond. This principle is inapplicable, however, when the agency has promulgated valid regulations. This is because, in the rule-making proceeding, the accuracy of those facts taken notice of are fairly tested. As such, reliance on the guidelines is proper. Reversed.

Analysis:

The "medical-vocational guidelines" help courts determine the existence of a disability. A court will first look to whether the claimant has a severe impairment that limits his or her ability to work. If so, the court then turns to the listings that provide automatic awards for certain disabilities. If a person's disability is on the list, then the court's job is done and benefits will be awarded according to the regulations. If the listings do not provide an automatic award, the court will then turn to the medical-vocational guidelines to determine the types and numbers of jobs that exist in the national economy. The regulations that make up the medical-vocational guidelines consist of a matrix of four factors—physical ability, age, education, and work experience—and set forth rules that identify whether jobs requiring specific combinations of these factors exist in significant numbers in the national economy. Then, as *Heckler* points out, "where a claimant's qualifications correspond to the job requirements identified by a rule, the guidelines direct a conclusion as to whether work exists that the claimant can perform." If such work exists, the claimant is not considered disabled.

■ CASE VOCABULARY

HEARING *DE NOVO*: A hearing in which a previous decision of some body (such as the Department of Health and Human Services) is reviewed independent of and without deference to the decision below; the party holding the hearing examines the issue anew.

MEDICAL-VOCATIONAL GUIDELINES: A set of guidelines contained in 20 C.F.R. Pt. 404, Subpt. P, App. 2, which helps the government and Administrative Law Judges to determine whether a particular individual with particular characteristics and skills is "disabled" under the Social Security Act.

CHAPTER THIRTY

Private Insurance Solutions

Licari v. Elliot

Instant Facts: A taxicab driver who was injured in a car accident sought to have his injuries held to be "serious injuries" so as to increase his recovery under New York's no-fault law.

Black Letter Rule: Under New York's no-fault law, there is no right of recovery for non-economic loss except in the case of a serious injury; moreover, it is the trial court's responsibility (not that of a jury) to determine whether a prima facie case of serious injury has been made.

Licari v. Elliot

(Injured Party) v. (Not Stated)

57 N.Y.2d 230, 455 N.Y.S.2d 570, 441 N.E.2d 1088 (1982)

WHEN A LEGISLATURE ENACTS A NO-FAULT LAW IT MODIFIES THE COMMON LAW RIGHTS OF PERSONS IN CAR ACCIDENTS TO THE EXTENT THAT PLAINTIFFS IN SUCH ACCIDENT CASES NO LONGER HAVE AN UNFETTERED RIGHT TO SUE FOR INJURIES SUSTAINED

■ **INSTANT FACTS** A taxicab driver who was injured in a car accident sought to have his injuries held to be "serious injuries" so as to increase his recovery under New York's no-fault law.

■ **BLACK LETTER RULE** Under New York's no-fault law, there is no right of recovery for non-economic loss except in the case of a serious injury; moreover, it is the trial court's responsibility (not that of a jury) to determine whether a prima facie case of serious injury has been made.

■ PROCEDURAL BASIS

Certification to the Court of Appeals of New York of an appellate court decision that, as a matter of law, a tort claimant failed to prove a serious injury under the state's no-fault insurance law.

■ FACTS

On February 13, 1979, Licari (P), a taxi driver, was injured in a car accident, suffering a concussion, acute cervical sprain, acute dorsal lumbar sprain, and a contusion of the chest. He was released from the hospital after just a few hours, but two days later returned because he was coughing up red phlegm. The examining physician later testified that Licari (P) suffered nothing but a "very mild limitation" of movement in the back and neck areas. On March 9, 1979, just twenty-four days after his injury, Licari (P) returned to work. The only affect that the injury had on his work performance was his inability to help some customers with their luggage. He was also unable to help his wife around the house as much as he could before, and suffered from "occasional transitory headaches and dizzy spells which were relieved by aspirin." Following the close of evidence, Elliot (D) moved to dismiss Licari's (P) complaint on the ground that he had failed to establish that his injuries were "serious injuries" within the meaning of New York's insurance law. The court submitted the case to the jury, reserving decision on the motion. The jury found that such an injury had been proven. Elliot (D) filed a motion to set aside the verdict, which was denied, and an appeal followed. On appeal, the appellate division reversed the trial court's holding and Licari (P) appealed.

■ ISSUE

May a jury be permitted to decide whether a prima facie case of serious injury has been proved in a no-fault insurance case?

■ DECISION AND RATIONALE

(Jasen, J.) No. The Legislature provided that "there shall be no right of recovery for non-economic loss except in the case of a serious injury, or for basic economic loss." Although the statute sets up eight specific categories which constitute serious injury, we are only concerned with two of them. These are whether the plaintiff suffered a serious injury which resulted in either a "significant limitation of use of a body function or system," or "a medically determined injury or impairment of a nonpermanent nature" which endured for 90 days or more and substantially limited the performance of his daily activities. While it is clear that the Legislature intended to allow plaintiffs to recover for noneconomic injuries in appropriate cases, it had also intended that the court (and not a jury) first determine whether or not a prima facie case of serious injury has been established which would permit a plaintiff to maintain a common-law tort cause of action. It is incumbent upon the court to decide in the first instance whether the plaintiff has a cause of action to assert within the meaning of the statute. By enacting the No-Fault Law, the Legislature modified the common-law rights of persons injured in automobile accidents, to the extent that plaintiffs in auto accident cases no longer have an unfettered right to sue for injures sustained. To allow a jury to make the initial decision would subvert the Legislature's intent and destroy the effectiveness of the statute. The result of requiring a jury trial where the injury is clearly a minor one would perpetuate a system of unnecessary litigation. Thus, we believe the Legislature intended that the court should decide the threshold question of whether the evidence would warrant a jury finding that the injury falls within the class of injuries that, under no-fault, should be excluded from judicial remedy. In this case, Licari (P) was able to maintain his daily routine for most of each day after returning to work. As such, it should be abundantly clear that he was not prevented from performing substantially all of his daily activities during anything close to 90 days following the occurrence of the injury. Thus, the appellate court correctly held, as a matter of law, that Licari (P) did not meet the statutory standard of serious injury. Further, it requires little discussion that Licari's (P) subjective complaints of occasional headaches hardly fulfills the definition of serious injury. He has offered no proof that his headaches in any way incapacitated him or interfered with his ability to work or engage in activities at home. To hold that this type of ailment constitutes a serious injury would render the statute meaning less and frustrate the legislative intent in enacting no-fault legislation. Finally, as to Licari's (P) contention that he suffered a "significant limitation of use of a body function or system," the evidence established only that he suffered a painful sprain which limited the movement of his neck and back. Affirmed.

Analysis:

Licari addresses the application of a no-fault insurance system to the traditional motor vehicle accident. First proposed by Professors Robert Keeton and Jeffrey O'Connell in 1965, a no-fault insurance plan provides a two-tier system for dealing with automobile accident injuries. Under the first tier of the no-fault system, claims under a certain value are wholly covered by insurance similar to medical and disability insurance. Under the second tier of the no-fault system, a claim above a certain value would be adjudicated in the traditional tort system. The Keeton-O'Connell plan includes some other ideas as well. First, no-fault insurance must be compulsory and it must cover not only the car and driver, but also all passengers and pedestrians involved. Second, the tort claims of all those who collect under the no-fault system are abolished, meaning persons with the option must choose either the settlement offered under their own system or give it up and take their chances in court. This is what *Licari* meant when it stated that, "[b]y enacting the No-Fault Law, the Legislature modified the common-law rights of persons injured in automobile accidents, to the extent that plaintiffs in automobile accident cases no longer have an unfettered right to sue for injuries sustained."

■ CASE VOCABULARY

ACUTE CERVICAL SPRAIN: A serious sprain to the cervix, or the back part of the neck (higher up on the body than the dorsal lumbar).

ACUTE DORSAL LUMBAR SPRAIN: A serious sprain to the dorsal lumbar, which is a part of the human vertebrae between the thoracic vertebrae and the sacrum (which is where the vertebrae connects with the pelvis).

CONTUSION: A non-lacerated injury (such as a severe bruise).

NO-FAULT INSURANCE: An insurance system that will, among other things, pay for a policy-holder's injuries without an adjudication of who is at fault, or who is faulted with causing the party's injuries.

NON-ECONOMIC LOSS: A loss that is not of an economic nature, such as pain and suffering (as opposed to lost wages).

SERIOUS INJURY: As defined by the court, a serious injury is "either a medically determined injury of a nonpermanent nature which prevented [a party] from performing substantially all his daily activities for not less than 90 days during the 180 days immediately following the accident," or "a significant limitation of use of a body function or system."

CHAPTER THIRTY-TWO

Communication of Personally Harmful Impressions to Others

New York Times Co. v. Sullivan

Instant Facts: A city commissioner sought to sue a newspaper for defamation based on a published advertisement alleging that the police department, which the commissioner headed, engaged in a course of conduct in opposition to the civil rights movement.

Black Letter Rule: The First Amendment prohibits a public official from recovering damages for a defamatory falsehood relating to his official conduct unless he proves that the statement was made with "actual malice"—that is, with knowledge that it was false or with reckless disregard for the truth.

Gertz v. Robert Welch, Inc.

Instant Facts: An attorney filed a defamation suit against the publisher of an organ that identified him as a Communist and the architect of a frame-up against a police officer.

Black Letter Rule: So long as they do not impose liability without fault, the States may define for themselves the appropriate standard of liability for a publisher or broadcaster of defamatory falsehood injurious to a private individual.

Solano v. Playgirl, Inc.

Instant Facts: Playgirl (D) published an issue with Solano's (D) photograph on the cover, proclaiming that the issue exposed young actors.

Black Letter Rule: To prevail on a false light claim, a plaintiff must prove (1) that the defendant disclosed to one or more persons information about or concerning the plaintiff that was presented as factual, but was actually false or created a false impression about him; (2) that the information was understood by one or more persons to whom it was disclosed as stating or implying something highly offensive and tending to damage the plaintiff's reputation; (3) that the defendant acted with constitutional malice; and (4) that the plaintiff was damaged by the disclosure.

New York Times Co. v. Sullivan

(Newspaper) v. (Commissioner of the City of Montgomery, Alabama)

376 U.S. 254, 84 S.Ct. 710, 11 L.Ed.2d 686 (1964)

THE FIRST AMENDMENT PROVIDES A CONSTITUTIONAL PRIVILEGE FOR DEFENDANTS IN AN ACTION FOR DEFAMATION OF PUBLIC OFFICIALS

■ **INSTANT FACTS** A city commissioner sought to sue a newspaper for defamation based on a published advertisement alleging that the police department, which the commissioner headed, engaged in a course of conduct in opposition to the civil rights movement.

■ **BLACK LETTER RULE** The First Amendment prohibits a public official from recovering damages for a defamatory falsehood relating to his official conduct unless he proves that the statement was made with "actual malice"—that is, with knowledge that it was false or with reckless disregard for the truth.

■ FACTS

The New York Times (D) published an advertisement asking for donations to help defend Dr. Martin Luther King, Jr in a perjury indictment against him. The advertisement alleged that the City of Montgomery police department arrested Dr. King seven times and ringed the campus at Alabama State College, padlocking the campus dining hall in an effort to starve students. Although not expressly named in the advertisement, L.B. Sullivan (P), Commissioner of the City of Montgomery, alleged in a suit for defamation that the advertisement's reference to the police was to be read as implicating him, and that the references to arrests were to be read as accusing him of violence and intimidation. The judge instructed the jury that the statements were libelous per se, which meant that malice, falsity and damage were presumed. The jury returned a verdict in favor of Sullivan (P), awarding him $500,000. The Supreme Court of Alabama affirmed.

■ ISSUE

In a suit for defamation of a public official, may the court instruct the jury that malice is presumed?

■ DECISION AND RATIONALE

(Brennan, J.) No. The First Amendment prohibits a public official from recovering damages for a defamatory falsehood relating to his official conduct unless he proves that the statement was made with "actual malice"—that is, with knowledge that it was false or with reckless disregard for the truth. This Court has stated that the First Amendment's safeguard was fashioned to assure unfettered interchange of ideas for the bringing about of political and social changes desired by the people. Naturally, this commitment to uninhibited and robust debate on public issues may well include attacks on government and its officials. The advertisement at issue, which dealt with a major political issue, clearly qualifies for the constitutional protection. The question here is whether it forfeits that protection because some of its factual statements are erroneous and defamatory. Erroneous statements are inevitable in free debate and must be protected so that public debate is given sufficient breathing space. We believe that neither the factual error nor the defamatory content, either alone or in conjunction with each other, suffice to remove the constitutional protections. Furthermore, the state law providing for a defense based on truth is an insufficient safeguard under the First Amendment. If truth were the only defense to an action in libel per se, as it is under Alabama law, critics of public officials would have to assure themselves of the truth of their assertions. The natural consequence of saddling the defendant with the burden on proving truth is self-censorship; critics will be deterred from voicing their views because of doubt as to whether their truth could be proved in court. Applying these principles to the present case, we find the evidence does not make a clear showing of actual malice. Reversed.

Analysis:

This case established a constitutional privilege for defendants in actions for defamation of public officials. Unlike with common law privileges, the defendant need not affirmatively prove that the statements were privileged. In contrast to the view under the common law that libel *per se* was any statement that was defamatory on its face, Alabama law provided that statements were libel *per se* if they slandered a person's trade or profession. At issue here was the rule allowing for the presumption of damages when a finding of libel *per se* had been made. The Court held that these presumptions ran afoul of the First Amendment when applied in an action for libel by a public official for statements relating to public conduct. The Court held that the First Amendment requires both damages and malice to be proved in such a cause of action. But take note that the Court adopts a different definition of "actual malice" for First Amendment purposes. Under the common law view, the issue of malice focused on the publisher's reason for making the statement; the question was whether the defamatory statements were made for an improper purpose, in which case the defendant lost the protection of any privilege he may have had. In contrast, the Court's definition of malice focuses on the publisher's state of mind regarding the truth or falsity of the statements. But the First Amendment's protection does not extend to every statement made about every government employee. Instead, the First Amendment privilege applies only to those officials who appear to have substantial control over public affairs.

Gertz v. Robert Welch, Inc.

(Defamed Attorney) v. (Publisher)

418 U.S. 323, 94 S.Ct. 2997, 41 L.Ed.2d 789 (1974)

THE FIRST AMENDMENT AFFORDS NO PRIVILEGE TO THOSE WHO NEGLIGENTLY PUBLISH DEFAMATORY STATEMENTS CONCERNING PRIVATE INDIVIDUALS

■ **INSTANT FACTS** An attorney filed a defamation suit against the publisher of an organ that identified him as a Communist and the architect of a frame-up against a police officer.

■ **BLACK LETTER RULE** So long as they do not impose liability without fault, the States may define for themselves the appropriate standard of liability for a publisher or broadcaster of defamatory falsehood injurious to a private individual.

■ PROCEDURAL BASIS

Appeal to the United States Supreme Court, challenging the holding of the Court of Appeals which affirmed a judgment for the defendant on the ground that no "actual malice" was shown.

■ FACTS

Elmer Gertz (P) was an attorney who represented the family of a youth murdered by a police officer in the family's civil claim against the officer. Robert Welch, Inc. (Welch) (D) was the publisher of an organ known as the *American Opinion*, which portrayed Gertz (P) as an architect of the "frame-up" of the police officer, and as a Leninist and Communist-fronter. There was no basis for either of these conclusions. Consequently, Gertz (P) sued for defamation. Although the trial court found that Gertz (P) was not a public official or public figure, it required Gertz (P) to prove actual malice. Accordingly, it entered a judgment for Welch (D). The Court of Appeals affirmed, concluding that "actual malice" was not proved by clear and convincing evidence.

■ ISSUE

May a newspaper or broadcaster that publishes defamatory falsehoods about an individual who is neither a public official nor a public figure claim a constitutional privilege against liability for the injury inflicted by those statements?

■ DECISION AND RATIONALE

(Powell, J.) No. So long as they do not impose liability without fault, the States may define for themselves the appropriate standard of liability for a publisher or broadcaster of defamatory falsehood injurious to a private individual. In *New York Times Co. v. Sullivan* [Supreme Court holds that a newspaper was not liable for defamatory falsehoods it published about a city commissioner] we delineated the constitutional protections appropriate to the context of defamation of a public person. Under that standard, "public figures"—those who have achieved fame by reason of the notoriety of their achievements or the vigor and success with which they seek the public's attention—and those who hold public office may recover in an action for defamation only upon a clear and convincing showing that the defamatory falsehood was made with knowledge of its falsity or reckless disregard for the truth. But the reasons which justify the application of this rule to public persons are not present in an action by a private individual. First, a private individual is more vulnerable to injury because he has limited access to public channels to counteract the false statements. Furthermore, unlike public officials who accept the consequences of their involvement in government and public figures who thrust themselves into the public eye, a private individual has not voluntarily exposed himself to the increased risk of injury from defamation. We, however, find that Gertz (P) is not a public figure. Such a characterization can be met if the individual achieves such notoriety that he becomes a public figure for all purposes, or if an individual purposefully injects himself or is drawn into a particular public controversy. Gertz (D) meets neither standard. Notwithstanding, we do issue one caveat. Damages may not be presumed in an action for defamation where actual malice has not been proved. The State has no legitimate interest in compensating any plaintiff, whether he be a private individual or public person, for an injury that has not been sustained. Reversed.

Analysis:

This case sets the constitutional default standard for liability for the publication of false defamatory statements or materials. The Court rejects the application of the *New York Times* standard to a suit by a private individual. It holds that standard applicable only in suits by public officials and public figures. In place of the *New York Times* standard the Court adopts a standard of liability under which every element of a suit for defamation—publication, "of and concerning the plaintiff," and defamatory meaning—must be judged under at least a negligence standard. In other words, a private plaintiff must prove that the defendant negligently, recklessly, or intentionally defamed him. The exact level of intent is to be determined under state law. But strict liability, which was the common law rule, is flatly prohibited by the First Amendment. The states, however, remain free to adopt the *New York Times* standard for all defamation suits. One issue that has arisen in lower courts is whether negligence is to be judged by the standards of the journalism profession or against the reasonable person standard.

Solano v. Playgirl, Inc.

(Actor) v. (Publisher)

292 F.3d 1078 (9th Cir.2002)

THE PUBLICATION OF AN UNAUTHORIZED SUGGESTIVE PHOTOGRAPH MAY PLACE THE SUBJECT IN A FALSE LIGHT

■ **INSTANT FACTS** Playgirl (D) published an issue with Solano's (D) photograph on the cover, proclaiming that the issue exposed young actors.

■ **BLACK LETTER RULE** To prevail on a false light claim, a plaintiff must prove (1) that the defendant disclosed to one or more persons information about or concerning the plaintiff that was presented as factual, but was actually false or created a false impression about him; (2) that the information was understood by one or more persons to whom it was disclosed as stating or implying something highly offensive and tending to damage the plaintiff's reputation; (3) that the defendant acted with constitutional malice; and (4) that the plaintiff was damaged by the disclosure.

■ PROCEDURAL BASIS

On appeal to review a district court order granting summary judgment to the defendant.

■ FACTS

Playgirl (D) magazine published an issue that included on the cover a photograph of Solano (P), an actor, in red swimming trunks from his role on the television show, "Baywatch." The cover also stated that the issue contained "Primetime's Sexy Young Stars Exposed." Although the only reference to Solano (P) inside the issue was a head-and-shoulders photograph showing him fully dressed, Solano (P) sued the magazine, alleging it deliberately created a false impression that he appeared nude. After the district court granted summary judgment to Playgirl (D), Solano (P) appealed.

■ ISSUE

Did Solano (P) establish a genuine issue of material fact as to whether Playgirl presented him in a false light to withstand summary judgment?

■ DECISION AND RATIONALE

(Fisher, J.) Yes. To prevail on a false light claim, a plaintiff must prove (1) that the defendant disclosed to one or more persons information about or concerning the plaintiff that was presented as factual, but was actually false or created a false impression about him; (2) that the information was understood by one or more persons to whom it was disclosed as stating or implying something highly offensive and tending to damage the plaintiff's reputation; (3) that the defendant acted with constitutional malice; and (4) that the plaintiff was damaged by the disclosure. Here, Solano (P) offered evidence that could permit a jury to conclude that the cover represented him as a "washed-up" actor willing to sell provocative photos of himself to earn a living, that some editors were concerned that the photographs possibly created a false impression, and that he was damaged by personal embarrassment. Solano (P) established a genuine issue of material fact to withstand summary judgment on his false light claims. Reversed.

Analysis:

False light claims often invoke a number of constitutional principles. The subject, often a celebrity, maintains some constitutional right of privacy, although his expectation of privacy is tempered somewhat by his public persona. On the other hand, the media has a First Amendment right to free speech. In a world of media sensationalism and the profitability to be gained by the public's fascination with celebrities, these two rights often collide in false light actions.

■ CASE VOCABULARY

FALSE LIGHT: In an invasion-of-privacy action, a plaintiff's allegation that the defendant attributed to the plaintiff views that he or she does not hold and placed the plaintiff before the public in a highly offensive and untrue manner.

MALICE: The intent, without justification or excuse, to commit a wrongful act.

CHAPTER THIRTY-THREE

Communication of Commercially Harmful Impressions to Others

Brunson Communications, Inc. v. Arbitron, Inc.

Instant Facts: Arbitron (D) published false information concerning the number of viewers tuning into a television station owned by Brunson Communications (P).

Black Letter Rule: One who publishes a false statement harmful to the interests of another is subject to liability for pecuniary loss resulting to the other if he intends for publication of the statement to result in harm to interests of the other having a pecuniary value, or either recognizes or should recognize that it is likely to do so, and he knows that the statement is false or acts in reckless disregard of its truth or falsity.

Alyeska Pipeline Service v. Aurora Air Service

Instant Facts: Alyeska (D) induced RCA to breach its contract with Aurora (P) thereby intentionally interfering with Aurora's (P) economic benefits under the RCA contract.

Black Letter Rule: The privilege to procure a breach of another's contract, because the interest advanced is superior to the social importance to the interest invaded, is forfeited when the act is motivated by a desire to injure the contract party.

Qualitex Co. v. Jacobson Products Co.

Instant Facts: Qualitex (P) sued Jacobson Products (D) for trademark infringement under the federal Lanham Act.

Black Letter Rule: Trademark protection applies to those product characteristics that assist consumers in identifying the source of the product, including any word, name, symbol, device, or combination thereof.

Sears, Roebuck & Co. v. Stiffel Co.

Instant Facts: Stiffel (P) sued Sears (D) for making and selling a substantially similar pole lamp to the one created by Stieffel (P).

Black Letter Rule: A State's unfair competition law cannot encroach upon, or give protection of a kind that clashes with, the objectives of the federal patent laws.

Brunson Communications, Inc. v. Arbitron, Inc.

(Television Station Owner) v. (Viewership Surveyor)

266 F.Supp.2d 377 (E.D.Pa.2003)

PECUNIARY DAMAGES MUST BE ASSERTED WITH SPECIFICITY

■ **INSTANT FACTS** Arbitron (D) published false information concerning the number of viewers tuning into a television station owned by Brunson Communications (P).

■ **BLACK LETTER RULE** One who publishes a false statement harmful to the interests of another is subject to liability for pecuniary loss resulting to the other if he intends for publication of the statement to result in harm to interests of the other having a pecuniary value, or either recognizes or should recognize that it is likely to do so, and he knows that the statement is false or acts in reckless disregard of its truth or falsity.

■ PROCEDURAL BASIS

Trial court consideration of the defendant's motion to dismiss.

■ FACTS

Brunson Communications (P) owned an independent television station. Arbitron, Inc. (D) purported to measure the number of viewers watching each television station in the market, but did not actually do so. Instead, Arbitron (D) published erroneous viewership information to advertisers, television stations, and others, representing the information as accurate. Brunson Communications (P) sued Arbitron (D) for commercial disparagement, alleging that Arbitron's (D) false statements caused the plaintiff to lose advertising revenue. Arbitron (D) moved to dismiss the complaint.

■ ISSUE

Did the plaintiff sufficiently plead a claim of commercial disparagement to withstand a motion to dismiss, when it failed to specifically identify its pecuniary loss?

■ DECISION AND RATIONALE

(Baylson, J.) No. Under the Restatement (Second) of Torts § 623A, "[o]ne who publishes a false statement harmful to the interests of another is subject to liability for pecuniary loss resulting to the other if (a) he intends for publication of the statement to result in harm to interests of the other having a pecuniary value, or either recognizes or should recognize that it is likely to do so, and (b) he knows that the statement is false or acts in reckless disregard of its truth or falsity." Here, although the plaintiff did not specifically reference the particular television station at issue, the allegations of the complaint sufficiently allege that the defendant made a false statement that it should have recognized would harm the plaintiff and that the defendant knew was false. However, the plaintiff has not specifically identified any pecuniary loss. To sufficiently plead disparagement damages, the plaintiff must allege "facts showing an established business, the amount of sales for a substantial period preceding publication, and amount of sales subsequent to the publication, facts showing that such loss in sale were the natural and probable result of such publication, and the facts showing the plaintiff could not allege the name of particular customers who withdrew or withheld their custom." The plaintiff here does not allege its damages with sufficient specificity. The claim for commercial disparagement is dismissed without prejudice to allow the plaintiff to amend its claim. Motion granted.

Analysis:

Unlike in many cases, the court here establishes a reasonable means to calculate a party's damages in a commercial disparagement case. By comparing business revenue before the alleged act with revenue after the alleged act, a plaintiff at a minimum can establish its damages to proceed with its claim. Often times, lost revenue and lost business opportunity are not so easily proven.

■ CASE VOCABULARY

DISPARAGEMENT: A false and injurious statement that discredits or detracts from the reputation of another's property, product, or business. To recover in tort for disparagement, the plaintiff must prove that the statement caused a third party to take some action resulting in specific pecuniary loss to the plaintiff.

Alyeska Pipeline Service v. Aurora Air Service

(Interfering Party) v. (Victim of Breached Contract)

604 P.2d 1090 (Alaska 1979)

INDUCING A BREACH OF ANOTHER'S CONTRACT FOR OBJECTIVELY PROPER REASONS MAY STILL RESULT IN LIABILITY IF DONE IN BAD FAITH

■ **INSTANT FACTS** Alyeska (D) induced RCA to breach its contract with Aurora (P) thereby intentionally interfering with Aurora's (P) economic benefits under the RCA contract.

■ **BLACK LETTER RULE** The privilege to procure a breach of another's contract, because the interest advanced is superior to the social importance to the interest invaded, is forfeited when the act is motivated by a desire to injure the contract party.

■ PROCEDURAL BASIS

Appeal after jury trial, challenging denial of motion for summary judgment in action for damages for inducing breach of contract.

■ FACTS

Alyeska Pipeline Service (Alyeska) (D) entered into a contract with RCA to provide communication systems along the Alaska oil pipeline, and giving Alyeska (D) the option to terminate the contract. RCA in turn contracted with Aurora Air Service (Aurora) (P) to provide a plane, pilot, parts and service along the pipeline, and giving RCA the option to terminate Aurora's (P) services. After services under both contracts commenced, Alyeska (D) and Aurora (P) had a dispute about an earlier arrangement and Alyeska (D) exercised its option under its contract with RCA to take over the flight services itself. [Notice that by so doing, RCA no longer needs Aurora's (P) services.] As a result, RCA terminated its contract with Aurora (P). Thereafter, Aurora (P) [believing that Alyeska (D) was motivated to cause it harm] sued Alyeska (D) alleging that it induced RCA to breach its contract with Aurora (P). The trial court denied Alyeska's (D) motion for summary judgment. The court held that although Alyeska (D) was entitled to terminate RCA under the contract with it (and hence, indirectly terminate Aurora's (P) services), if it did so in bad faith, then it, Alyeska (D), could be liable to Aurora (P). The matter was submitted to the jury and it found in favor of Aurora (P). Alyeska (D) appealed.

■ ISSUE

Is the privilege to procure a breach of another's contract, because the interest advanced is superior to the social importance to the interest invaded, forfeited when the act is motivated by a desire to injure the contract party?

■ DECISION AND RATIONALE

(Connor, J.) Yes. We hold that when bad faith motive is the basis for inducing a breach of another's contract, any privilege that may exist for procuring such breach is forfeited. Alyeska (D) makes three contentions on appeal. The first is that the right to modify the contract (in this case the right to terminate RCA), is absolute and may be exercised regardless of motive. We reject this contention. One party to a contract may sue a third party who intentionally procures the breach of that contract by the other party without justification or privilege. Recent authority even holds that a claim of unjustifiable interference can be made when the contract is terminable at will. Alyeska (D) next contends that it was permitted to terminate its contract with RCA due to overriding economic and safety interests. A privilege does exist that allows one to invade a contractual interest if the interest advanced by him is superior to the social importance to the interest invaded. The immunity afforded by this privilege may be forfeited however if one does not act in a good faith attempt to protect his own interest or that of another but, rather, is motivated by a desire to injure the contract party. Whether the justification for invading the interest was made in good faith or bad faith is a question normally reserved for the trier of fact. In this case, there was a conflicting factual issue whether Alyeska (D) was furthering its own economic and safety interests or was using them as a façade for inflicting injury on Aurora (P). This issue was correctly submitted to the jury. [The jury obviously thought Alyeska (D) intended to cause harm to Aurora (P) by going through RCA.] Alyeska (D) also claims error in not giving its proposed jury instruction that Aurora (P) had the burden of proving by a preponderance of the evidence that Alyeska's (D) actions were malicious and committed with the sole intent of injuring Aurora (P). We reject this contention and hold that the issue of whether Alyeska (D) acted in good faith or in bad faith goes to the question of justification, and that Aurora (P) did not have the burden of proof on this issue. The matter is affirmed, with the exception of an error in computing damages, which is reversed as to permit a correction.

Analysis:

Inducing a breach of contract requires that the interference be improper or unjustified and that it cause at least partial breach of the contract. One of the issues in this case was whether Alyeska (D) was *justified* in terminating its own contract with RCA so that it could provide the flying services itself out of concern for economics and safety. It is a valid defense if one induces a breach to protect his own existing financial interests; however, interference cannot be justified on the ground that the interferer is competing. Alyeska's (D) motion for summary judgment was denied by the trial court because there was an issue of whether it terminated its contract with RCA in bad faith. Remember that the contract between Alyeska (D) and RCA provided that Alyeska (D) had the option of terminating the contract. Alyeska (D) claimed that it did so because of economics and safety concerns. So how can Alyeska (D) be sued? Because of an improper motive. If it terminated the RCA contract in bad faith so that Aurora (P) would lose its contract with RCA, Alyeska (D) can be held liable to Aurora (P) for inducing RCA to breach the contract. If the reason for interfering were superior in social importance to the contractual interest invaded, there would be no liability.

■ CASE VOCABULARY

CONTRACT TERMINABLE AT WILL: A contract that can be terminated with or without cause.

Qualitex Co. v. Jacobson Products Co.

(Trademark Holder) v. (Infringer)

514 U.S. 159, 115 S.Ct. 1300, 131 L.Ed.2d 248 (1995)

A PRODUCT'S PARTICULAR COLOR QUALIFIES FOR FEDERAL TRADEMARK PROTECTION

■ **INSTANT FACTS** Qualitex (P) sued Jacobson Products (D) for trademark infringement under the federal Lanham Act.

■ **BLACK LETTER RULE** Trademark protection applies to those product characteristics that assist consumers in identifying the source of the product, including any word, name, symbol, device, or combination thereof.

■ PROCEDURAL BASIS

Certiorari to review a decision of the Ninth Circuit Court of Appeals in the defendant's favor.

■ FACTS

Qualitex (P) sold distinct green and gold pressing machine pads to dry cleaners. Jacobson Products (D) started selling pads of the same colors. After Qualitex (P) registered its pad colors with the Patent and Trademark Office, it sued the defendant under the federal Lanham Act. The Ninth Circuit Court of Appeals barred Qualitex's (P) use of color as a trademark.

■ ISSUE

Can a seller or producer of a product register a trademark for the product's color?

■ DECISION AND RATIONALE

(Breyer, J.) Yes. Under the Lanham Act, a seller or producer has the exclusive right to register a trademark and prevent its competitors from using that trademark. Among the broad characteristics that qualify for trademark protection, the Lanham Act includes "any word, name, symbol, or device, or combination thereof." This language has been applied to afford trademark protection to a particular shape, a particular sound, and a particular scent. Similar to these characteristics, a particular color identifies and distinguishes one's goods and may indicate the source of the goods. Although the color of a good itself is not a characteristic that automatically tells a customer the source of the product, over time the color of a product or its packaging gains special significance in associating the product with its source by secondary meaning. This secondary meaning easily assures consumers of the product's quality and allows producers to reap the financial rewards its reputation generates. Therefore, once a product's color effectively distinguishes it from similar products, it is entitled to trademark protection.

The functionality doctrine, which precludes protection of those product features essential to the function of the product, does not apply to colors. Although a particular color may enhance the demand for a product, color does not always have such an effect. Because color is not always essential to the proper functioning of a product, the functionality doctrine does not preclude trademark protection. Reversed.

Analysis:

While color may be a permissible characteristic for a trademark, special considerations must be made before a color can obtain that protection. For instance, a charcoal manufacturer will not likely obtain a trademark on the color black. Only when the color develops a secondary meaning that identifies the product with its specific manufacturer is color eligible for trademark protection. Trademark law attempts to strike a balance between protecting the producers' financial investment in their products and the avoidance of a monopoly over the manufacture of certain products.

■ CASE VOCABULARY

INFRINGEMENT: An act that interferes with one of the exclusive rights of a patent, copyright, or trademark owner.

TRADEMARK: A word, phrase, logo, or other graphic symbol used by a manufacturer or seller to distinguish its product or products from those of others.

Sears, Roebuck & Co. v. Stiffel Co.

(Copy Cat) v. (Pole Lamp Inventor)

376 U.S. 225, 84 S.Ct. 784, 11 L.Ed.2d 661

THE RIGHT TO COPY AND SELL AN UNPATENTED ITEM MAY NOT BE CURTAILED BY THE STATES

■ **INSTANT FACTS** Stiffel (P) sued Sears (D) for making and selling a substantially similar pole lamp to the one created by Stieffel (P).

■ **BLACK LETTER RULE** A State's unfair competition law cannot encroach upon, or give protection of a kind that clashes with, the objectives of the federal patent laws.

■ PROCEDURAL BASIS

Supreme Court granted certiorari in action where injunctive relief and damages were ordered pursuant to State's unfair competition statute.

■ FACTS

Stiffel Company (Stiffel) (P) secured design and mechanical patents on a "pole lamp", which is a vertical tube standing between the floor and the ceiling with lamp fixtures along the outside. The pole lamps were a commercial success. Soon after Stiffel (P) brought them onto the market, Sears, Roebuck & Co. (Sears) (D) put a substantially identical lamp on the market for a retail price about the same as Stiffel's (P) wholesale price. Stiffel (P) sued Sears (D) claiming that the copying of the lamp design infringed Stiffel's (P) patents, and that by selling copies, Sears (D) had violated Illinois' unfair competition law by causing confusion among the public as to the source of the lamp. The District Court first held that Stiffel's (P) patents were invalid for want of invention. It then found that because of the confusion caused by the substantially exact lamps, Sears (D) was liable for unfair competition. It enjoined Sears (D) from selling the lamp and ordered an accounting to fix the profits and damages resulting from Sears' (D) unfair competition. Sears (D) appealed and the court of appeals affirmed, holding that Sears (D) was liable under Illinois law for copying and marketing an unpatented article. Sears (D) appealed to the United States Supreme Court.

■ ISSUE

Is a State's unfair competition law inconsistent with federal patent laws where it imposes liability for, or prohibits the copying of, an article which is protected by neither a federal patent or copyright?

■ DECISION AND RATIONALE

(Black, J.) Yes. We hold that a State's unfair competition law cannot encroach upon, or give protection of a kind that clashes with, the objectives of the federal patent laws. We conclude that the use of the State's unfair competition law in this case is not compatible with the federal patent law. When a patent is issued under federal law, others may not make, use, or sell the patented product without authority for the term of years fixed by the patent. However, once the patent expires the monopoly created by it expires too and the right to make the article passes to the public. Because of the Supremacy Clause of the Constitution [federal law is the supreme law of the land and is controlling over any conflicting state law], a State may not extend the life of a patent beyond its expiration date or give a patent on an article that lacks the level of invention required for federal patents. Nor can a State encroach upon the federal patent laws directly, or give protection of a kind that clashes with its objectives. In this case, the lower court held that Stiffel is not entitled to a patent. Accordingly, like an article on which the patent has expired, the public may make and sell an unpatented article. Sears (D) thus had every right to copy the lamp design and sell almost identical lamps to those sold by Stiffel (P). However, to allow a State by use of its unfair competition law to prevent the copying of an article which represents too slight an advance to be patented would permit the State to block off from the public something which federal law has said belongs to the public. If this were permitted, the States could allow perpetual protection to unpatented articles. [This means that the patents would never expire.] This would be too great an encroachment on the federal patent system to be tolerated. Because of the federal patent laws, a State may not prohibit the copying of the article or award damages therefore when the article is unpatented and un-copyrighted. Reversed.

Analysis:

The State's unfair competition law improperly encroached upon the federal patent laws and, pursuant to the Supremacy Clause of the United States Constitution, the federal patent laws were controlling and displaced the State law. Note that Stiffel (P) had obtained design and mechanical patents on the pole lamp, but the district court held that they were invalid. The basis for the decision was that it was for want of invention. Without a valid patent, Stiffel (P) could not sue under the federal patent laws. As a result, it attempted to seek relief under the State's unfair competition law. The Supreme Court rejected the conclusion of the court of appeals that Stiffel (P) only had to prove that there was a likelihood of confusion as to the source of the products to make a case of unfair competition. It held that the State could not give protection to an article where doing so would conflict with the objectives of federal laws. Because the district court had declared the patents invalid, the use of state law to obtain rights that, in effect, clashed with federal patent laws, was held to be in violation of the Supremacy Clause.

■ CASE VOCABULARY

COPYRIGHT: Registering rights to the author or originator of literary or artistic works.

PALMING OFF: Selling goods as the goods of another or doing business as the business of another so as to mislead the public into believing it is dealing with someone other than the actual seller.

UNFAIR COMPETITION: Misappropriating for commercial advantage the goods of another for one's own goods.

CHAPTER THIRTY-FOUR

Misrepresentation and Other Misdealings

Ultramares Corp. v. Touche, Niven & Co.

Instant Facts: After preparing an independent audit of a business to be used by potential lenders, public accountants were sued for fraudulent and negligent misrepresentation after the business collapsed.

Black Letter Rule: Traditionally, negligence could not form a basis of liability for misrepresentation under tort law.

Gauerke v. Rozga

Instant Facts: A real estate company is sued by its client and found liable under a theory of strict liability, after misrepresenting the acreage of hotel property, despite believing the representation to be true.

Black Letter Rule: A speaker may be held strictly liable for innocent misrepresentations relied upon, if the speaker professes personal knowledge.

Pinnacle Peak Developers v. TRW Investment Corp.

Instant Facts: An investment corporation is unable to recover damages under a theory of misrepresentation, despite relying on an oral representation contemporaneous to a formal written contract.

Black Letter Rule: Justified reliance is a prerequisite for the claim of misrepresentation.

Ollerman v. O'Rourke Co., Inc.

Instant Facts: A seller of property is found to have a duty to close "material facts," and is held liable for his "silent" misrepresentation.

Black Letter Rule: A seller has a duty to disclose "material facts" that are known to the vendor and not readily discernable by the purchaser.

Ultramares Corp. v. Touche, Niven & Co.

(Investors) v. (Lazy Accountants)

255 N.Y. 170, 174 N.E. 441 (1931)

NEGLIGENCE DID NOT TRADITIONALLY FORM A BASIS FOR LIABILITY UNDER TORT LAW

■ **INSTANT FACTS** After preparing an independent audit of a business to be used by potential lenders, public accountants were sued for fraudulent and negligent misrepresentation after the business collapsed.

■ **BLACK LETTER RULE** Traditionally, negligence could not form a basis of liability for misrepresentation under tort law.

■ PROCEDURAL BASIS

Appeal to the Court of Appeals of New York for a dismissal of an action for scienter fraud and negligent misrepresentation.

■ FACTS

Touche, Niven & Co. (Touche) (D) were public accountants who, pursuant to a contract with Stern, prepared an independent audit of the business showing a net worth of over a million dollars. Touche (D) certified the audit as accurate and prepared 32 originals. The audit was to be used by potential lenders, who, depending on Stern's financial situation, would lend money to Stem. Relying on the defendant's audit, Ultramares Corp. (P) loaned $165,000 to Stern. When Stern Collapsed, the plaintiff was unable to obtain repayment of the loan. Ultramares (P) brought this action against Touche (D) for the damages suffered, claiming both scienter fraud and negligent misrepresentation. There was evidence that Touche (D) did not examine Stern's books with appropriate care and that if they had done so, discrepancies would have been revealed which would have led to a more accurate audit. The trial judge set aside the jury's verdict for Ultramares (P). The Appellate Court dismissed the fraud action but not the negligence claim.

■ ISSUE

Can negligence form a basis of liability for misrepresentation under tort law?

■ DECISION AND RATIONALE

(Cardozo, J.) No. Negligence cannot form a basis of liability for misrepresentation under tort law. Touche (D) owed a legal duty to their employer, to make their certificate without fraud, and a duty from their contract to make it with care and caution proper to their calling. Fraud, includes the pretense of knowledge when there is none. Accordingly, because there was notice that the employer did not intend to keep it to himself, Touche (D) owed a duty to make the certificate without fraud. However, a different issue arises when we ask whether Touche (D) owed a duty to make the certificate without negligence. If liability for negligence exists, a thoughtless slip or blunder, the failure to detect a theft or forgery beneath the cover of deceptive entries, may expose accountants to a liability for an indeterminate amount, for an indeterminate time, to an indeterminate class. In the field of contract law, the beneficiary of a promise, clearly designated as such, is seldom left without a remedy. However, the remedy is narrower where the beneficiaries of the promise are indeterminate or general. The promise must be such as to "bespeak the assumption of a duty to make reparation directly to the individual members of the public if the benefit is lost." In the field of tort law, a manufacturer who is negligent in the manufacture of a chattel, in circumstances pointing to an unreasonable risk of serious bodily harm to those using it thereafter, may be liable for negligence though privity is lacking between the manufacturer and user. If liability for negligence is imposed in this case, it will extend to many callings other than an auditor's. Lawyers who certify their opinions as to the validity of municipal or corporate bonds, with knowledge that the opinion will be brought to the notice of the public, will become liable to the investors if they have overlooked a statute or a decision, to the same extent as if the controversy were one between client and adviser. A person making a promise having the quality of a contract will have a duty apart from the contract to an indefinite number of potential beneficiaries when performance has begun. Thus, the assumption of one relation will mean the involuntary assumption of a series of new relations. Our holding does not emancipate accountants from the consequences of fraud. It does not relieve them if their audit has been so negligent as to justify a finding that they had no genuine belief in its adequacy, for this again is fraud. It does no more than say that if less than this is proved, if there has been neither been a reckless misstatement nor insincere profession of an opinion, but only honest blunder, the ensuing liability for negligence is one that is bounded by the contract, and is to be enforced between the parties by whom the contract has been made. Remanded as to the fraud action and dismissed as to the negligence action.

Analysis:

Fraudulent misrepresentation, fraud or deceit, and negligent misrepresentation are torts that cause only financial harm, without causing physical harm either to persons or property. As illustrated in the case, scienter is required in order to be held liable on the basis of fraud or deceit. In other words, it is required that the accused party make a knowingly false statement, or at least make the statement with a conscious ignorance or reckless disregard of whether it was true or false. More importantly, however, this court follows the traditional rule that negligence may not form a basis of liability for misrepresentations under tort law. In cases of honest blunder, ensuing liability for negligence is bounded by the law of contracts, not torts. Put another way, negligent misrepresentation may form a basis of liability when there is a duty to perform with reasonable care. However, this duty is limited to contracting parties.

■ CASE VOCABULARY

FRAUDULENT MISREPRESENTATION: A false representation made with scienter, intended to induce reliance upon the representation.

SCIENTER: Knowledge that a representation is either false or made with a reckless disregard as to whether it is true or false.

Gauerke v. Rozga

(Land Seller) v. (Property Buyer)

112 Wis.2d 271, 332 N.W.2d 804 (1983)

STRICT LIABILITY MAY BE IMPOSED FOR INNOCENT MISREPRESENTATION

■ **INSTANT FACTS** A real estate company is sued by its client and found liable under a theory of strict liability, after misrepresenting the acreage of hotel property, despite believing the representation to be true.

■ **BLACK LETTER RULE** A speaker may be held strictly liable for innocent misrepresentations relied upon, if the speaker professes personal knowledge.

■ PROCEDURAL BASIS

Certification to the Supreme Court of Wisconsin of a decision by the trial court finding strict liability for innocent representation.

■ FACTS

Rozga (D1) owned hotel property which was listed for sale with Gudim Realty (Gudim). Rozga (D1) told Gudim that according to former owners, the property was five and one-half acres, and Gudim put this information on a specification sheet. Gauerke (P) in search of a hotel property, asked Robert Frost Realty, Inc. (Frost) (D2) to act as their agent. Frost contacted Gudim, obtained the specification sheet, submitted it to the Gauerkes (P), and Gauerkes (P) eventually bought the property. However, two years later, Gauerkes (P) discovered that the property contained less than three acres. They brought this action against Rozga (D1), Frost (D2), and Gudim. Gudim settled, and Frost (D2) was held liable on a theory of strict liability for misrepresentation. Frost (D2) appeals.

■ ISSUE

May strict liability be imposed for an innocent misrepresentation?

■ DECISION AND RATIONALE

(Ceci, J.) Yes. A speaker may be held strictly liable for innocent misrepresentations relied upon, if the speaker professes personal knowledge. Frost (D2) argues that the strict responsibility theory is only applicable where the defendant could normally be expected to know the facts represented to be true without investigation. The court of appeals held that in strict liability, the innocent defendant, and not the innocent plaintiff, should bear the loss. Wisconsin law requires: 1) a representation made as of defendant's own knowledge, concerning a matter about which he purports to have knowledge, so that he may be taken to have assumed responsibility as in the case of warranty, and 2) a defendant with an expectation to gain some economic benefit from the transaction into which the plaintiff enters. In other words strict responsibility applies when a speaker indicates that he either had particular means of ascertaining the pertinent facts, or his position made possible complete knowledge, and the statement fairly implied that he had it. We agree with the court of appeals that the application of strict liability requires only that the speaker profess or imply personal knowledge. The other key element is the buyer's reliance on the statement. A factor in determining a buyer's justifiable reliance, might include taking into consideration whether the fact represented is something that one would not expect the speaker to know without an investigation. Affirmed.

Analysis:

Traditionally, scienter was required in order to be held liable for misrepresentation. Today, it is generally accepted that negligent misrepresentations are actionable under special conditions. Some courts may hold a defendant strictly liable for negligent misrepresentations that cause stand-alone economic harm, when the defendant undertakes to guarantee the truth of the matter represented. Accordingly, under the Wisconsin statute, two elements are required for the imposition of strict liability. The first element requires that the defendant make a statement that implies that the defendant has personal knowledge. The second element requires that a buyer justifiably rely on the misrepresentation. Factors to consider in determining a buyer's "justifiable reliance" include whether the buyer chose his or her conduct because of the misrepresentation, or, as the court notes, whether the fact represented is something that one would not expect the speaker to know without an investigation. This case is distinguishable from cases of fraud where a speaker purports to have knowledge, but in fact has none. In the instant case, Frost (D2) did believe that it had appropriate knowledge as to the acreage of the property, based on a specification sheet. However, because its "knowledge" was incorrect, and because it gave a "guarantee" of its accuracy, Frost (D2) could still be liable for its innocent misrepresentation.

■ CASE VOCABULARY

NEGLIGENT MISREPRESENTATION: A false representation which, although believed to be true, was made with the failure to exercise reasonable care in ascertaining the true facts.

Pinnacle Peak Developers v. TRW Investment Corp.

(Land Developers) v. (Investment Firm)

129 Ariz. 385, 631 P.2d 540 (1980)

NO ACTION FOR MISREPRESENTATION WILL LIE FOR UNJUSTIFIED RELIANCE

■ **INSTANT FACTS** An investment corporation is unable to recover damages under a theory of misrepresentation, despite relying on an oral representation contemporaneous to a formal written contract.

■ **BLACK LETTER RULE** Justified reliance is a prerequisite for the claim of misrepresentation.

■ PROCEDURAL BASIS

On appeal from grant of summary judgment in favor of Pinnacle (D).

■ FACTS

TRW Investment Corporation (TRW) (P) entered into a purchase with Pinnacle Peak Developers (Pinnacle) (D) for 40 acres, which required TRW (P) to make certain off-site improvements, such as roads and electrical systems. TRW (P) was given the option to purchase additional acreage, but only if a certain portion of the off-site improvements had not been completed by the option deadline. When the option deadline was reached, the improvements had been made, and Pinnacle (D) took the position that the option for additional acreage had expired. TRW (P) took the position that Pinnacle (D) fraudulently induced TRW (P) to forego the improvements. TRW (P) claimed that it was induced to enter into the purchase and option agreement by reliance on Pinnacle's (D) misrepresentation that the off-site improvements would be no obstacle to the exercise of the option so long as there was reasonable progress on those improvements. The trial court granted summary judgment for Pinnacle (D). TRW (P) appeals.

■ ISSUE

Is a party with some expertise and business experience, justified in relying on an oral representation contemporaneous to a formal written agreement?

■ DECISION AND RATIONALE

(O'Connor, J.) No. A promise is a misrepresentation which can give rise to an action for fraud, if it is made with a present intention not to perform it. The representation must be of matters of fact which exist in the present, and not merely an agreement or promise to do something in the future. Nor can the representation which may give rise to an action for fraud, be an expression of opinion or judgment as to something which has happened or is expected to happen. The only exception to this is when a promise to perform a future act is made with the present intention on the part of the promisor, that he will not perform it. Such a representation will give rise to an action of fraud. According to the parol evidence rule, any evidence of prior or contemporaneous oral or written understandings, which would contradict, vary, or add to a written contract which was intended as the final and complete statement or integration of the parties agreement, is inadmissible. The problem raised in this case arises when the well recognized notion of promissory fraud, collides with the policies underlying certain prophylactic legal rules like the Statute of Frauds and the parol evidence rule. Both these rules are designed to prevent fraudulent claims or defenses, by excluding evidence that is easily fabricated and too hard to meet. While not meant to shield fraud, these rules may have the effect of preventing a party from showing that he or she has been deceived by an oral promise, made to induce reliance and action but without the slightest intention of keeping it. Courts are split on whether to permit parol evidence which contradicts a writing when fraud in the inducement is alleged. In practice, courts generally apply the parol evidence rule to exclude allegations of prior or contemporaneous oral promises which contradict the written agreement in cases involving formal contracts which were the result of negotiation between parties with some expertise and business sophistication. On the other hand, courts show a greater tendency to allow such evidence, in cases dealing with "informal contract" between people who lack sophistication in business. In cases involving abuse of the bargaining process, such as unconscionable contracts or contracts involving duress, courts almost always disregard the parol evidence rule. In the instant case, both parties had experience in business transactions and the written option agreement was prepared as the result of negotiations between the parties who were represented by counsel. It involved a relatively substantial and sophisticated real estate transaction. Furthermore, the written option agreement was a "formal contract". The contradiction of the written agreement and the oral representation is clear. Therefore, TRW (D) was not justified in relying on the oral representation. The facts are such that courts in most jurisdictions would exclude the evidence of the prior oral statement on the basis of a strict application of the parol evidence rule. The trial court correctly granted summary judgment to appellee on Count II quieting title to the property covered by the option agreement in appellee.

Analysis:

In an action for misrepresentation, the plaintiff must not only rely on the misrepresentation, the plaintiff's reliance must be justified under the circumstances. In the instant case, the court recognized that when a promise is made to perform a future act with a present intention not to perform, an action for fraud will rise. However, with present state of mind, proof may be too much of an obstacle. Non-performance may result for other reasons, such as a change of heart. Therefore, mere proof that the statement was made and then not performed would not be sufficient proof of fraudulent misrepresentation. This obstacle is further heightened by legal rules such as the Statute of Frauds and the parol evidence rule, which may have the effect of preventing a party from showing that he or she has been deceived by an oral promise. Despite the parol evidence rule, courts may generally allow evidence of an oral misrepresentation in cases dealing with "informal contract" between parties that lack sophistication in business.

■ CASE VOCABULARY

JUSTIFIED RELIANCE: Reliance is justified if it was reasonable for a party to rely on a representation, in consideration of the party's subjective view.

RELIANCE: Reliance on a representation occurs when a party either acts or refrains from acting because of the representation.

Ollerman v. O'Rourke Co., Inc.

(Seller) v. (Buyer)

94 Wis.2d 17, 288 N.W.2d 95 (1980)

SILENCE MAY BE ACTIONABLE AS A MISREPRESENTATION WHEN THERE IS A DUTY TO DISCLOSE

■ **INSTANT FACTS** A seller of property is found to have a duty to close "material facts," and is held liable for his "silent" misrepresentation.

■ **BLACK LETTER RULE** A seller has a duty to disclose "material facts" that are known to the vendor and not readily discernable by the purchaser.

■ PROCEDURAL BASIS

Certification to the Supreme Court of Wisconsin of trial court decision to overrule a motion to dismiss an action for "silent misrepresentation".

■ FACTS

Ollerman (P) after purchasing a lot from O'Rourke (D) and excavating to build a house, discovered an underground well which was uncovered and uncapped, and water was subsequently released. Ollerman (P) alleged he had spent over $2700 to cap the well and that building changes costing over $10,500 were necessitated by its presence. He alleged that O'Rourke (D) knew of the underground well but did not disclose it. The trial court overruled O'Rourke's (D) motion to dismiss. O'Rourke (D) appeals.

■ ISSUE

Does a seller have a duty to disclose known "material facts" of a transaction?

■ DECISION AND RATIONALE

(Abrahamson, J.) Yes. A seller has a duty to disclose "material facts" that are known to the vendor and not readily discernable by a purchaser. When there is a duty to disclose, silence is equivalent to a misrepresentation of fact, and a seller could be held liable for an "intentional" representation. The traditional rule for Wisconsin is that of caveat emptor. That is, a seller of real estate, dealing at arm's length with the buyer, has no duty to disclose information to the buyer, for in a free market, the diligent should not be deprived of the fruits of superior skill and knowledge lawfully acquired. Therefore the seller has no liability in an action for intentional misrepresentation for failure to disclose. Over the years society's attitudes toward good faith and fair dealing in business transactions have undergone significant change, and this change has been reflected in the law, by carved out exceptions to the traditional rule. Thus courts have held that this rule does not apply where the seller actively conceals a defect, prevents investigation, has told half-truths, has made an ambiguous statement with the intent to create a false impression, where there is a fiduciary relationship, or where the facts are peculiarly and exclusively within the knowledge of one party to the transaction, and the other party is not in a position to discover the facts for himself. The case at bar does not appear to fall into one of these well-recognized exceptions to the "no duty to disclose rule." However, there is a tendency in most courts toward a finding of a duty of disclosure in cases where the defendant has special knowledge and is aware that the plaintiff is acting under a misapprehension as to facts which could be of importance to him. The attitude of courts toward nondisclosure is undergoing a change and it would seem that the object of the law in these cases should be to impose on parties to a transaction, a duty to speak whenever justice, equity, and fair dealings demand it. In an effort to formulate a rule embodying this trend to a more frequent recognition of a duty to disclose, the Restatement of Torts Second sets forth conditions under which a duty to disclose exists. It states that a party to a transaction is under a duty to exercise reasonable care to disclose to the other facts basic to the transaction, if he knows that the other is about to enter into it under a mistake as to the facts, and that the other would reasonably expect a disclosure of those facts. These conditions are limited to the disclosure of those facts basic to the transaction. A basic fact is defined as a fact that is assumed by the parties as a basis for the transaction itself. O'Rourke (D) contends that if this court affirms the trial court, this court would be adopting a strict policy of "let the seller beware." We do not find O'Rourke's (D) argument persuasive. Where a vendor is in the real estate business and is skilled and knowledgeable and the purchaser is not, the purchaser is in a poor position to discover a condition which is not readily discernible, and the purchaser may justifiably rely on the knowledge and skill of the vendor. Therefore, in this case, a strong argument for imposing a duty on the seller to disclose could be made on this "reliance factor." We hold that a subdivider-vendor of a residential lot has a duty to a "non-commercial" purchaser to disclose facts which are known to the vendor, which are material to the transaction, and which are not readily discernible to the purchaser. A fact is "known," if the vendor has actual knowledge of the fact or if the vendor acted in reckless disregard as to the existence of the fact. The use of the word "know" is the same as in an action for intentional misrepresentation based on a false statement. A fact is material if a reasonable purchaser would attach importance to its existence or nonexistence in determining the choice of action in the transaction in question, or if the vendor knows or has reason to know that the purchaser regards or is likely to regard the matter as important in determining the choice of action, although a reasonable purchaser would not so regard it.

Analysis:

Traditionally, the bargainer was not obliged to make affirmative revelations of known material facts. This case illustrates the modern trend away from the harsh rule of caveat emptor. As the court notes, due to the change in society's attitudes toward good faith and fair dealing, courts readily except many situations from the traditional rule whenever justice, equity, and fair dealing demand it. Accordingly, this court held that a seller has a duty to disclose material facts that are known to the vendor, and that silence, when there is a duty to disclose, is equivalent to a misrepresentation of fact. The facts must be material or basic to the transaction. In other words, this duty to disclose only pertains to facts that the seller knows or has reason to know that the purchaser regards, or is likely to regard, as important in determining his or her choice of action. Furthermore, courts agree that a buyer is not justified in relying upon representations that are not material to the transaction. "Materiality" is an extension of the element of justified reliance, required for misrepresentation liability.

■ CASE VOCABULARY

MATERIAL FACTS: Facts that a reasonable person would want to consider in determining a course of action.